The British Atlantic World, 1500–1800

Other books by the editors

David Armitage, *The Ideological Origins of the British Empire* (Cambridge, 2000)

Michael J. Braddick, *State Formation in Early Modern England, c. 1550–1700* (Cambridge, 2000)

The British Atlantic World, 1500–1800

Edited by

DAVID ARMITAGE

and

MICHAEL J. BRADDICK

First published 2002 by
PALGRAVE MACMILLAN
Houndmills, Basingstoke, Hampshire RG21 6XS and
175 Fifth Avenue, New York, N. Y. 10010
Companies and representatives throughout the world

PALGRAVE MACMILLAN is the global academic imprint of the Palgrave
Macmillan division of St. Martin's Press, LLC and of Palgrave Macmillan Ltd.
Macmillan® is a registered trademark in the United States, United Kingdom
and other countries. Palgrave is a registered trademark in the European
Union and other countries.

ISBN 0–333–96340–7 hardback
ISBN 0–333–96341–5 paperback

This book is printed on paper suitable for recycling and
made from fully managed and sustained forest sources.

A catalogue record for this book is available from the British Library.

Library of Congress Cataloging-in-Publication Data
The British Atlantic world, 1500–1800 / edited by David Armitage and
Michael J. Braddick.
   p. cm.
Includes bibliographical references and index.
ISBN 0–333–96340–7 – ISBN 0–333–96341–5 (pbk.)
   1. America–History–To 1810. 2. Great Britain–Colonies–America–
History. 3. United States–History–Colonial period, ca. 1600–1775.
   4. Caribbean Area–History–To 1810. 5. West Indies, British–History.
   I. Armitage, David, 1965–   II. Braddick, M. J. (Michael J.), 1962–

E18.82 .B75 2002
970–dc21   2002025837

   9   8   7   6   5   4   3   2   1
   10   09   08   07   06   05   04   03   02

Printed and bound in China

Contents

     Joyce E. Chaplin

Part IV: Politics

  9 Empire and State   175
     Elizabeth Mancke

 10 Revolution and Counter-Revolution   196
     Eliga H. Gould

 11 The Politics of Slavery   214
     Christopher L. Brown

     Afterword: Atlantic History: A Circumnavigation   233
     J. H. Elliott

     Notes   250

     Further Reading   295

     Index   311

List of Maps

List of Tables

Acknowledgements

This volume has its origins in discussions held during the International Seminar on the History of the Atlantic World at Harvard University in 1997. Drafts of all the papers were presented at a workshop held at Harvard in September 2001 under the auspices of the seminar and of the Charles Warren Center for American History. Bernard Bailyn's essay derives from the plenary lecture which opened the workshop and J. H. Elliott's is a revised version of his closing comments. We are grateful to Professor Bailyn and Professor Elliott for framing the event so effectively and for allowing us to include their papers in the volume. We are also grateful to Bernard Bailyn and Laurel Thatcher Ulrich for putting the material resources of the seminar and the center at our disposal and for their moral support of our project from its inception to its completion. The participation of graduate students in the conference was made possible by the Center for the Humanities at the University of New Hampshire and the Department of History at Columbia University, for which we thank Bert Feintuch and Alan Brinkley. The audience at the conference made a more than usually important contribution to the revision of the essays and to the shaping of the volume as a whole; our thanks to them for their vigorous and focused engagement. No part of the long passage from the initial discussion to the finished manuscript would have been achieved so quickly or so smoothly without the indispensable help and crucial counsel of Pat Denault.

The support of our editors at Palgrave Macmillan has exceeded all expectations. From Britain, Terka Acton has encouraged and expedited the editorial process at every stage; the enthusiasm of Michael Flamini and Debbie Gershenowitz has been an inspiration on the other side of the Atlantic. Their co-sponsorship of the Harvard workshop was an unusual (and very welcome) sign of their faith in the volume.

Finally, the editors are grateful to the contributors for producing their essays to a tight agenda under strict deadlines. All undertook revisions – some very substantial – in light of the workshop but did so with remarkable efficiency and seriousness. Their outstandingly cooperative commitment to this project not only made it possible but genuinely pleasurable and gave proof of the excitement and originality Atlantic history can generate.

Notes on Contributors

David Armitage (Ph.D., Cambridge) is James R. Baker Chair of Contemporary Civilization and Associate Professor of History at Columbia University. He is the author of *The Ideological Origins of the British Empire* (2000), editor of *Bolingbroke: Political Writings* (1997) and *Theories of Empire, 1450–1800* (1998), and co-editor of *Milton and Republicanism* (1995). He is working on a study of the foundation of modern international thought (1688–1848), a global history of the American Declaration of Independence, and an edition of John Locke's colonial writings.

Bernard Bailyn (Ph.D., Harvard) is Adams University Professor Emeritus at Harvard University and the director of the International Seminar on the History of the Atlantic World. He is the author of many books and essays on the history of the colonies, the American Revolution, and the Anglo-American world in the pre-industrial era, including *The Ideological Origins of the American Revolution* (1967), *The Origins of American Politics* (1968), *The Ordeal of Thomas Hutchinson* (1974), *The Peopling of British North America: An Introduction* (1986), and *Voyagers to the West* (1986).

Michael J. Braddick (Ph.D., Cambridge) is Professor of History at the University of Sheffield. He is the author of *Parliamentary Taxation in Seventeenth-Century England* (1994), *The Nerves of State: Taxation and the Financing of the English State, 1558–1714* (1996), and *State Formation in Early Modern England, c. 1550–1700* (2000), and co-editor of *Negotiating Power in Early Modern Society: Order, Hierarchy and Subordination in Britain and Ireland* (2001). He is currently working on a social history of England during the 1640s.

Christopher L. Brown (D.Phil., Oxford) is Assistant Professor of History at Rutgers University. He is the author of 'Empire Without Slaves: British Concepts of Emancipation in the Era of the American Revolution', *William and Mary Quarterly* (1999), and of *Foundations of British Abolitionism* (forthcoming).

Joyce Chaplin (Ph.D., Johns Hopkins) is Professor of History at Harvard University. She is the author of *An Anxious Pursuit: Agricultural Innovation and Modernity in the Lower South, 1730–1815* (1993) and *Subject Matter: Technology, the Body, and Science on the Anglo-American Frontier, 1500–1676* (2001). She is working on studies of science and colonization in the eighteenth century and Benjamin Franklin's science.

Sir John Elliott (Ph.D., Cambridge) is Regius Professor Emeritus of Modern History at Oxford University. Among his many publications are *The Revolt of the Catalans* (1963), *Imperial Spain, 1469–1716* (1963), *The Old World and the New, 1492–1650* (1970), and *The Count-Duke of Olivares: The Statesman in an Age of Decline* (1986). He is working on a comparative study of Spanish and British colonization in the New World.

Alison Games (Ph.D., University of Pennsylvania) is Associate Professor of History at Georgetown University. She is the author of *Migration and the Origins of the English Atlantic World* (1999). She is working on a study of 'Agents of Empire: English Cosmopolitans in an Age of Expansion, 1558–1660'.

Eliga H. Gould (Ph.D., Johns Hopkins) is Class of 1940 Associate Professor of History at the University of New Hampshire. He is the author of *The Persistence of Empire: British Political Culture in the Age of the American Revolution* (2000) and co-editor of *Empire and Nation: The American Revolution in the Atlantic World* (2002). He is working on a study of America and the Atlantic world in the seventeenth and eighteenth centuries.

Elizabeth Mancke (Ph.D., Johns Hopkins) is Associate Professor of History at the University of Akron. Her publications include 'Negotiating an Empire: Britain and Its Overseas Peripheries, c. 1550–1780', in Christine Daniels and Michael Kennedy, eds., *Negotiated Empires: Centers and Peripheries in the New World, 1500–1820* (2002), and 'Another British America: A Canadian Model for the Early Modern British Empire', *Journal of Imperial and Commonwealth History* (1997).

Sarah M. S. Pearsall (Ph.D., Harvard) is Lecturer in History at the University of St Andrews. Her publications include 'The State of the

Union: Sexuality in American History', *Gender and History* (2001). She is working on a study of transatlantic family letters from the Age of Revolution.

Carla Gardina Pestana (Ph.D., University of California, Los Angeles) is Associate Professor of History at the Ohio State University. She is the author of *Quakers and Baptists in Colonial Massachusetts* (1991) and *Liberty of Conscience and the Growth of Religious Diversity in Early America, 1636–1786* (1986), and co-editor of *Inequality in Early America* (1999). She is completing a study of *The English Atlantic in an Era of Revolution, 1640–1661*.

Keith Wrightson (Ph.D., Cambridge) is Professor of History at Yale University. He is the author of *English Society, 1580–1680* (1982) and *Earthly Necessities: Economic Lives in Early Modern Britain* (2000), co-author (with David Levine) of *Poverty and Piety in an English Village: Terling, 1525–1700* (1979) and *The Making of an Industrial Society: Whickham, 1560–1765* (1991), and co-editor of *The World We Have Gained: Essays in the History of Population and Social Structure* (1986).

Nuala Zahedieh (Ph.D., London School of Economics) is Lecturer in Economic and Social History at the University of Edinburgh. She is the author of *The Capital and Commerce: London and the Atlantic Economy in the Late Seventeenth Century* (forthcoming) and articles in the *Journal of Imperial and Commonwealth History* (1990), the *Economic History Review* (1986 and 1994) and Nicholas Canny, ed., *The Oxford History of the British Empire*, vol. 1, *The Origins of Empire: British Overseas Enterprise to the Close of the Seventeenth Century* (1998).

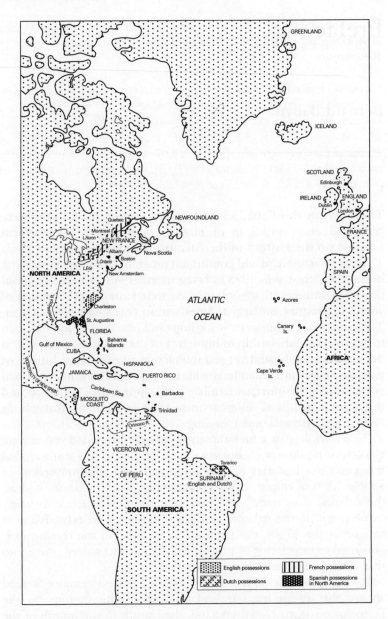

Map 1 The British Atlantic world in the seventeeth century, adapted from Alison Games, *Migration and the Origins of the English Atlantic World* (Cambridge, Mass., 1999), p. 2, and D. W. Meinig, *The Shaping of America*, vol. 1, *Atlantic America, 1492–1800* (New Haven, Conn., 1986), p. 56.

Preface

Bernard Bailyn

I

The essays in this book, which was initiated by the editors, were presented at a workshop of Harvard University's International Seminar on the History of the Atlantic World in September 2001. That seminar, a broad and continuing program of studies in Atlantic history, was created in 1995 to bring together young historians from the four continents that border the Atlantic basin for presentation of works in progress on large themes within that vast historical area. The aim of the seminar, its workshops and other activities, has been to advance the scholarship of historians of many nations interested in the common, comparative, and interactive aspects of the history of the peoples of the Atlantic world; to help create an international community of historians familiar with approaches, archives, and intellectual traditions different from their own; and ultimately to further international understanding.

The workshop at which these papers were presented was unique in concentrating not on broad themes, typical of the seminar, that transcend the histories of individual nations – the movement of people, ideas of empire, cultural encounters, the circulation of ideas, the Atlantic slave trade – but on one nation's experience. Britain's involvement in the Atlantic world was, however, so extensive at its apogee in the 1760s, the range of its interests in the territories it governed so broad, that its proper study is in effect a deep probe into that entire inter-hemispheric civilization.

By the mid-eighteenth century Britain's Atlantic empire formed an arc that swept from Ireland west to fishing stations on the Labrador coast, to Newfoundland, then south to the mouth of the St Lawrence River and Nova Scotia, then south again to New England, which stretched west to the Great Lakes, then farther south to the mid-Atlantic colonies extending out beyond the

Appalachians, and to the southern plantation world, then still farther
south to the Caribbean islands – the Bahamas, Jamaica, Bermuda,
Barbados, the Leewards – and finally to a scattering of minuscule
settlements, some mere encampments on the coasts of Central
America, transitory communities of loggers and fishermen. And
there were valuable British outposts on the African coast. To all of
this was added, as a result of victories in the Seven Years War, four
more Caribbean islands and the enormous, still largely unexplored
realm of Canada.

This vast swath of territory was no singular cultural entity, nor did
it constitute a systematically organized legal or governmental unit. It
was a congeries of entities – cultural, political, economic – distinctive
in themselves, each with peculiar, anomalous features. Wherever one
turns in Britain's Atlantic empire there is a diversity of lifeways
constantly forming and changing.

These discrete, regional sub-cultures and constitutional entities – in
Ireland, New England, the mid-Atlantic colonies, the mainland south,
the West Indian islands, Canada, and lesser dependencies in the
western hemisphere – made up Britain's Atlantic empire. But not
Britain's Atlantic world – and that distinction, between Britain's empire
and Britain's Atlantic world, is as important as the multiplicity and
variety of the vernacular differences within Britain's formal possessions.

Britain's economic involvement in the Atlantic world far transcended the constraints of its nationalist, mercantilist regulations; it
radiated through the entire inter-hemispheric system. In some places
the constraining navigation laws were so weakly enforced, the
customs officials so inefficient, that restrictions were effective only
when it was more profitable to obey the law than to violate it –
which in some places was not often. The waters at Monte Cristi on
the northern coast of Hispaniola and Portobello on the Panama
isthmus were crowded with British traders engaged in all sorts of
illegal operations, chiefly with the Spanish; and the *Asiento* contrac-
tors turned their legal advantage in the slave trade into a huge illegal
trading operation with tentacles that spread throughout the Spanish-
American commercial economy. The wars made possible a range of
quasi-legal operations for privateers and flag-of-truce manipulators,
licensed to exchange prisoners, that made possible a flood of British
goods into French ports, with profits said to reach 5,000 percent.

Such bonanza profits were not always ephemeral. Often they laid
the basis for substantial enterprises. The financing of Jamaica's
immensely rich plantation system was created by the island's illegal

trade with the Spanish. Its main commercial center, Port Royal, was at first a base for a fleet of highly profitable privateers, then the center of a huge contraband trade, and ultimately, a market for slaves imported in great numbers by the Royal African Company for re-export to the Spanish islands and mainland plantations.

But Jamaica was only one among many British distribution points in the slave trade. The full dimensions of that trade – its vast, trans-national reach and basic importance to Britain's commercial primacy in the eighteenth century – can best be seen in the elaborate inter-continental transaction cycles in that fiercely competitive and immensely lucrative business. Britain's slave trade flourished because its merchants were able to coordinate the timing of shipments of trading commodities drawn from all over the British Isles first with caravans of captives moving west from the African hinterland to coastal shipping areas and then with the cycles of labor needs not only in British terri-tories but throughout the western hemisphere. A multitude of contin-gencies in these vast Atlantic trading cycles had to be considered. Success was measured by the degree of transnational, intercontinental integration that a merchant could achieve.

The ultimate dynamic in much of this commercial boundary-crossing was the magnetism of the European markets reached through the re-export trade. In the course of the seventeenth century England switched from being an importer of American products, especially tobacco and sugar, to being an exporter; a large segment of the nation's ships, capital, and labor supply was directly or indirectly involved in the trans-shipment of colonial goods. As a result the entire economy of the North American upper south depended on the success of British merchants in continental markets, working through hubs in the Netherlands and France. In the 1770s 85 percent of the 100 million pounds of tobacco shipped annually to Britain ended in Europe. Without the continental markets one cannot imagine how the south would have developed – the labor force, race relations, ecology, and community life would have been profoundly different. Similarly New England depended on Iberian markets for its fish exports – mules carried shiploads of dried fish south from Bilbao to markets in inland Spain – and much of the lower south's rice production ended in southern Europe.

But it was not commerce alone that linked Britain to the broader reaches of the Atlantic world. It was the movement of people as well. England's population moved about the Atlantic world as the people of no other European nation. In the seventeenth century approximately 400,000 English men, women, and children, of a nation of some 5 million, emigrated, largely to the west; 300,000 (now more British than English) followed in the eighteenth century. Britons spread out across the Atlantic world from the Wine Islands to Honduras and from Nova Scotia to the Amazon delta. The Irish, Catholics as well as Protestants, could be found in Spanish America as well as the 13 mainland colonies, and, like the Scots who were also scattered throughout Britain's Atlantic possessions, they enlisted in the armies of the European powers. And beyond all that, Britain proved to be the transit through which and by means of which at least 100,000 Germans, from as far south as the Swiss border and as far east as Pomerania, moved into North America.

As to Britain's profound involvement in the intellectual currents that flowed through the Atlantic world – from the anthropology of the Spanish intellectuals of the sixteenth century to the economics, ethics, and political thought of the *philosophes* – it is enough to refer to Professor Chaplin's essay below, and perhaps also to think of Gibbon. English but crucially educated in Lausanne, his first works were written in French; his intellectual sources flowed as much from Amsterdam and Paris as from Edinburgh and London; and his masterpiece became an Atlantic phenomenon.

Britain was part, and an increasingly important part, of the entire Atlantic system that involved the interaction of the peoples of the four continents that frame the Atlantic basin, and we will understand it best within that large inter-hemispheric, transnational perspective.

II

The enlargement of scale and broadening of perspective involved in the study of the Atlantic world has been in motion for half a century, though only recently has Atlantic history been given conceptual form, or has seemed to require it. As I have elsewhere explained, the idea of Atlantic history, the sense that this is a useful unit for understanding a significant phase of early modern history, entered into the thinking of many historians in many parts of the Western world after World War II – in part because of the pressure of events in the 'outer', public world of international relations in the early Cold War years, but in greater part – essentially, in my view – because of the force of 'inner' developments within scholarship itself: the propulsion of expanding knowledge and the perception of hitherto unremarked filiations.[1]

But there is, I believe, another force at work in this broadening of perspective.

From the time historical study became a profession, and even before, it has been an international enterprise in the sense that scholars of one nation have not only mastered another country's or people's history but contributed substantially to it, even dominated it. Besides the small army of scholars from so many countries who followed Burckhardt in the study of the Italian renaissance, there were (to speak only of an earlier generation) American historians like Clarence Haring and Earl Hamilton on Spain and Herbert Bolton on Latin America; French historians like Élie Halévy on nineteenth-century Britain; Russians like Boris Porshnev on seventeenth-century France; Italians like Franco Venturi on Russian populism; and Englishmen like G. M. Trevelyan on Italy and R. W. Seton-Watson on the Balkans and eastern Europe.

But their careers involved migrations of the mind, not physical relocations. Few of these historians transferred physically to the land of their studies, though there were always a few, especially those from the north, who chose to live in Italy or France or the Middle East.

In recent years, however, there has been a different kind of migration, one that *is* physical – and the movement is in one direction.

After World War II and increasingly in recent years an academic migration has taken place, largely from east to west, though also from south to north, that has had important consequences in historical study. That migration is entirely voluntary, concentrates in the United States, and involves young people with promising careers ahead of them. Most are scientists, but a significant number are historians. Some figures supplied by the American Historical Association are suggestive.

Of the 13,000 historians who teach in American colleges and universities, about 4 percent have higher degrees from universities in other countries, almost all of them from universities in their native lands. But if one isolates the Ph.D.-granting universities, the proportion of foreign degree-holders rises sharply, to 7 percent of all faculty members in history. And if one further isolates a group of 11 major research universities, the percentage of foreign degree-holders in the history departments almost doubles, to 13 percent. And if, beyond that, one isolates an even more restricted group of research universities, one gets the following figures: Princeton, 25 percent; Yale, 23 percent; Chicago, 24 percent; Columbia, 15 percent; Berkeley, 14 percent.

Finally, of all those with foreign degrees who teach in Ph.D.-granting institutions, 26 percent come from the United Kingdom, most of whom teach some version of English, British, or European history relevant to the Atlantic world.

This migration of historians to the United States is part of a degree of internationalism in scholarship and teaching, a mingling of scholars and themes from Europe and the Americas, that has not existed before – and the question is, with what effect?

I am not certain – but it is clear that the foreign educated, mostly foreign born, historians in the United States are located disproportionately in the major research universities, and that there, their influence is considerable since they shape the views and subjects of the historians of the next generation. For some – perhaps a small number, but scholars of peculiar influence – there is a natural drift toward the local interests of the host institution and nation, and I believe that drift moves in the direction of linking European history with the history of the western hemisphere. The result is that there is a group of scholars for whom, by career orientation, a pan-Atlantic perspective is peculiarly attractive, and for some of them, some version of Atlantic history, whether they call it that or not, seems natural.

III

History is a story, but it is also a study, a questioning, probing and analyzing of what we know about what happened; and for this, conceptual terms are always needed. The concepts we use, in periodization and classification, reflect the state of our knowledge, our public concerns, and our ways of thinking; and they change from time to time as circumstances shift, as knowledge grows, and as new terms of analysis become available which we use in the search for greater understanding.

The idea of Atlantic history is an emerging formulation which reveals more clearly than we have seen before a transnational, multicultural reality that came into existence over a certain passage of years and has persisted. It helps one explain relationships that had not been observed before; it allows one to identify commonalities of experience in diverse circumstances; it isolates unique characteristics that become visible only in comparisons and contrasts; and it provides the outlines of a vast culture area distinctive in world history.

This broad perspective is no doubt only one of several ways of viewing comprehensively the development of the peoples of the

Western world in the early modern period, and no doubt it will in time be superseded by or absorbed into other formulations. But at this stage it seems to organize freshly and coherently material that is otherwise scattered; the interactions and contrasts it reveals are illuminating; and for all its complexity, the world it comprehends has a unity that distinguishes it in the course of recorded history. All of this is exemplified in the essays that follow.

Introduction

David Armitage and Michael J. Braddick

> Contributors will understand that we are established, not under the Meridian of Greenwich, but in Long. 30° W.
>
> Lord Acton, Letter to the contributors to the
> *Cambridge Modern History* (1898)

I

The British Atlantic world was created by kaleidoscopic movements of people, goods, and ideas. Networks of kinship and exchange bound together expanding communities of settlement and trade, their geography patterned by the circulation of the winds and currents of the north Atlantic. Settlers, traders, and migrants encountered foreign and exotic societies and were forced to come to terms with challenging physical and social environments. In doing so they reinvented themselves, and contributed to the reinvention both of the societies they encountered and of their home cultures.

This world of traders, settlers, and migrants is clearly an historical phenomenon of considerable significance but its boundaries are extremely difficult to draw. Within its limits an empire took shape and that empire itself became the means to shape the development of a specifically British Atlantic world. But although the essays collected here touch on the history of Britain's Atlantic empire they are concerned with a phenomenon both larger and less easy to delimit: what J. H. Elliott terms below the 'creation, destruction and re-creation of communities as a result of the movement, across and around the Atlantic basin, of people, commodities, cultural practices, and ideas.' This includes, but also takes us beyond, institutional and political histories, drawing us towards studies of connection, identity, and solidarity in their broadest senses. To the west, British people moved into a middle ground of negotiation with an Indian world; to the south and west they entered onto the margins of the Hispanic

1

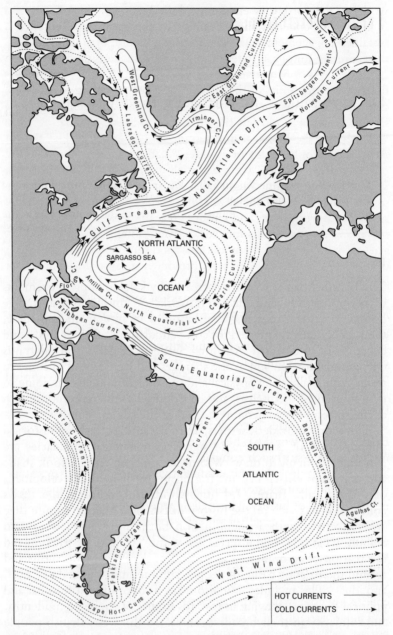

Map 2 The major Atlantic currents, adapted from Ian K. Steele, *The English Atlantic, 1675–1740* (New York, 1986), p. 8.

world; to the north they encountered the Francophone Atlantic; and in the south and east their dealings in the slave trade entailed a sustained engagement with African polities. And, of course, competition among European states made the Atlantic an issue of European significance too. Moreover, the influence of these movements was felt beyond the limits of the British presence, reaching towards the centre of the African and North American continents; and the British Atlantic world felt the effects of pressures emanating from well beyond the limits of direct trade and settlement. The British Atlantic was only a part of a wider Atlantic, and since all seas are one, the larger Atlantic world was itself not a bounded social system.

The British Atlantic might be an imprecise geographical expression but it was a real social phenomenon. Over time, identifiable networks of trust, trade, and kinship grew up between British people moving in this larger Atlantic world. Even though the spatial boundaries of these networks were indistinct and shifting these connections can still be traced. They in turn provide a meaningful context for comparative history: it is not an arbitrary creation of historical scholarship but corresponds to real networks of social, political, and economic connection in the past. Many of the chapters of this book pursue this kind of Atlantic history: learning both what was general and what was particular by placing differing local historical experiences in a larger, comparative, context. Most of the comparisons are internal to the English-speaking Atlantic; however, they should inspire further comparisons with other Atlantic histories – Spanish, Portuguese, Dutch, or French – which can only be undertaken when those histories have all been mapped as the history of the British Atlantic world has been here. Although not all topics would merit (or even suit) such comparative treatment all of the time, we hope that it is clear that this comparative approach (what Armitage terms trans-Atlantic history) can be enlightening for practitioners of many varieties of history. This will depend on further histories conducted at the local level which set particular places in their more general Atlantic contexts (what Armitage terms cis-Atlantic history). In pursuing these agendas the essays also contribute to the accumulation of material from which we might, eventually, write another kind of Atlantic history: a synoptic treatment of the Atlantic experience as a whole (what Armitage terms circum-Atlantic history).

The subject of this synoptic Atlantic history would be a social system, with permeable boundaries, created by the interactions of migrants, settlers, traders, and a great variety of political systems. These connections were vectors for the transmission of ideas and became the means by which identities were constructed and reconstructed. These exchanges were both complex and interdependent: to try to capture them simultaneously with a sensitivity to change over time is a daunting task. Finding routes into this complexity is easier, however, since there are many individual connections which can be followed. The essays in this book pursue some important connections, covering central topics such as the history of the movements of people and goods, of understandings of social difference, or of forms of political and religious connection and debate. Clearly, however, other avenues into the study of these complex exchanges could also be revealing: studies of disease, exotic encounters, or of particular groups or institutions, for example. The essays here cover some, but not all, of the most important ways of approaching an Atlantic history.

What is offered here, then, is not comprehensive or exhaustive; it is intended instead to demonstrate the potential of an Atlantic approach to elements of the shared history of societies normally considered separately. In our view, the time is not ripe for a comprehensive treatment of Atlantic history in its fullest sense: this book is not a textbook but a collection of individual views of how to approach a new, expanding, and very exciting field of study. The essays here introduce students to what Elliott has called 'one of the most important new historiographical developments of recent years.'

II

For historians of early, or colonial, America the shift to an Atlantic perspective is a familiar historiographical maneuver. It has already borne considerable fruit, and there is a growing appetite for this kind of work among both faculty and students. Elsewhere the potential of these approaches has been less fully realized. A number of English political historians have placed the seventeenth-century civil wars in a British context, turning their attention to the political and religious connections between the three kingdoms of Britain and Ireland. But this political history of the British Atlantic archipelago is episodic and has not been accompanied by an attempt to establish a wider social and cultural history of the kind Atlantic approaches would encourage.

For English social historians in particular it has been presumed that the turn to the 'New British History' has little to offer. The concentration on village studies, and more recently micro-histories, has emphasized the relatively narrow geographical bounds of the lives of ordinary people, and this has militated against a widening of the focus of social histories. But this is not an inescapable framework of analysis. Recent studies of industrial villages – not least the study of Whickham in County Durham co-authored by Levine and Wrightson – point to the integration of English villagers into larger webs of exchange. Those webs embraced the Atlantic, and the inventories of the middling sort of the later seventeenth century bear witness to the social and geographical spread of the fruits of empire. Moreover, along with these goods went subsistence, or betterment migration: long-distance migration within England (as also in Scotland) fed larger westward movements.

The economic history of the seventeenth century is only now taking a cultural turn, but an obvious direction for that turn is towards an examination of the implications of the diversifying patterns of consumption made possible by international exchange through the Atlantic basin. This was taken for granted in older histories of the 'commercial revolution', but more recently economic histories of this period have concentrated on the domestic economy, and particularly demographic and agrarian history. Eighteenth-century economic history, however, is now concerned much more with consumers and the goods that they sought, a concern which is necessarily alert to the importance of wider networks of exchange. The seventeenth-century origins of the world are widely acknowledged, but generally little studied, at least in England. A history at once British and Atlantic can do a great deal to elucidate these linkages, both forwards and backwards in time.

There are also signs that the traditional concerns of Irish, Welsh, and Scottish historiography may be proving too constraining for the current generation of historians. These national historiographies have been shaped by a concern with the relationship with England. This was, perhaps, a product of the predominance of political and constitutional history at the times when these agendas were set. More recent social, economic, and cultural history has, as in all national historiographies, been less concerned with the grand narratives of constitutional history. The result is a body of work which sets the religious history of the Irish peasantry, or the transformation of Highland culture, in a comparative perspective, offering the possibility of an integration of these histories into the mainstream of European historiography. This has, by the same token, made these historiographies more alert to the potentialities of an Atlantic approach. Merchants and migrants from all three kingdoms, and from Wales, helped to make the empire, and those societies were in themselves made and remade by the empire over the course of the sixteenth, seventeenth and eighteenth centuries. In short, although there is a growing body of work from an Atlantic perspective, there is much more potential to be realized.

III

The book is not organized in order to give a canonical account of Atlantic history or of how to approach it. Instead, by approaching the subject from a variety of angles, each chapter offers a complementary perspective on an extremely complex historical phenomenon. Nor do all the essays conform to the same chronology. Each covers a period of time most significant for its specific topic. None covers less than two centuries, and taken together they encompass every dimension of the British experience in the Atlantic world from the immediate after-math of Columbus's voyages to the age of abolition. The essays in Part II explore some of the connections that helped to create the British Atlantic world. That world was bound together primarily by the movement of goods and people, the connections explored in the essays by Games and Zahedieh. These essays are the most circum-Atlantic in their approach. Ideas, tastes, and fashions circulated along with these movements, of course. Pestana's essay explores how religious identities helped to forge solidarities within the broader Atlantic world and how the attempt to extend religious communities across and around the anglophone Atlantic created novel religious configurations, especially in the eighteenth century.

The Atlantic world was bound together in part by shared identities, then. Issues relating to collective identities are the subject of the essays in Part III. Braddick explores the relationship between authority and notions of civility in a comparative context. Perceptions of civility, refinement, and distinction provided the basis for the creation of a political community based on a common elite identity. But the very complexity of these processes also fostered the possibility of social divergence and conflicts of political interest. These problematic issues of identity are also the subject of the essays by Pearsall, Wrightson, and Chaplin. The larger exchanges of populations, ideas, and commodities problematized many forms of identity in the early modern period. New forms of employment, and new ways of getting and spending, affected social hierarchies and gender roles, for example. They did so, moreover, in a context that brought previously quite separate ethnic worlds into closer contact; social relations, particularly those associated with forms of hierarchy and subordination, ethnic identities, and gender roles were all reconceived or solidified in the light of contrasting views of these roles. In short, the ways in which social hierarchies were experienced and imagined were affected by the diversity of experience available in the Atlantic world. Pearsall, Wrightson, and Chaplin trace these issues thematically, by exploring changes in both perceptions and the realities of gender, class, and racial difference. In each case they confront the impact of an Atlantic perspective on well-developed but often nationally based historiographies.

These essays seek in differing ways to evoke a sense of an Atlantic world, bound by the movement of people, goods, and ideas. The final three essays (Part IV) explore the political life of that world. Mancke examines elements of the institutional relationship between early modern British state formation and empire-building by focusing on the international context within which empire-building took place. Gould examines the reverberation of political crises through the British Atlantic world from the English revolution and British civil wars of the mid-seventeenth century through to the era of the Napoleonic wars. Brown looks at the political ramifications of an issue that was wholly a product of the Atlantic world: slavery. In each case they bring a fresh, comparative, perspective to well-established fields of study and contribute to the development of an Atlantic approach to political history.

Each essay therefore offers new perspectives on issues familiar in other historiographical contexts and contributes to a development of a genuinely inclusive Atlantic history. Each also offers a perspective from which to observe the processes that created the British Atlantic world. The relationship between these more limited exercises and the overall project is the subject of Armitage's introductory essay which, in one sense, offers an overview of how these various studies might be seen to be components of a larger Atlantic history. In his afterword, Elliott places these essays in the history of the British Atlantic in the context of a fuller Atlantic history, and brings to the collection insights arising from similar historiographical developments in Hispanic studies. Clearly there is more to be done and the difficulties confronting this approach to the study of the past are considerable. But it is equally clear that the potential dividend is formidable.

Part I
Frameworks

1

Three Concepts of Atlantic History

David Armitage

We are all Atlanticists now – or so it would seem from the explosion of interest in the Atlantic and the Atlantic world as subjects of study among historians of North and South America, the Caribbean, Africa and western Europe. The Atlantic is even beginning to shape the study of literature, economics, and sociology on topics as diverse as theatrical performance, the early history of globalization, and the sociology of race. However, no field seems to have taken an Atlantic perspective with more seriousness and enthusiasm than history. Indeed, Atlantic history has been called 'one of the most important new historiographical developments of recent years.'[1] It is affecting the teaching of history at all levels, especially in the United States; it now has its own conferences, seminars and graduate programs; prizes are being awarded for the best books on it; even the first textbooks are being planned. Like the national histories it is designed to supplement and even replace, Atlantic history is becoming institutionalized. This might therefore be a good moment to ask just what Atlantic history is and where it is going, before it becomes entrenched and inflexible.

The attraction of Atlantic history lies, in part, in nature: after all, is not an ocean a natural fact? The Atlantic might seem to be one of the few historical categories that has an inbuilt geography, unlike the histories of nation-states with their shifting borders and imperfect overlaps between political allegiances and geographical boundaries. Atlantic history also seems to have a reasonably clear chronology, beginning with its first crossing by Columbus in 1492 (though of course he went to his death largely in ignorance of the implications of his discovery) and ending, conventionally, with the age of revolutions in the late eighteenth and early nineteenth centuries. There is thus a distinguished pedigree for identifying Atlantic history with 'early' modernity, before the onset of industrialization, mass democracy, the nation-state, and all the other classic defining features of full-fledged modernity, a condition whose origins both Adam Smith and Karl Marx associated with the European voyages of discovery and especially with 1492.[2]

The Atlantic's geography should be considered flexible, for 'oceans' are no less mythical than continents.[3] The Atlantic was a European invention. It was the product of successive waves of navigation, exploration, settlement, administration, and imagination. It did not spring fully formed into European consciousness any more than 'America' did, though it could certainly be found on maps – and hence in minds – two centuries before the full extent and outline of the Americas would be. It was a European invention not because Europeans were its only denizens, but because Europeans were the first to connect its four sides into a single entity, both as a system and as the representation of a discrete natural feature. The precise limits of the ocean were, of course, fluid: exactly where it ended was less clear than what it touched and what it connected as long as 'the Ocean' was thought of as a single body of circulating water rather than as seven distinct seas.[4] The chronology of Atlantic history should also be considered fluid. An Atlantic approach has already made inroads into nineteenth- and twentieth-century history, at least since Daniel Walker Howe urged an expansive agenda for placing American history in Atlantic context in his Oxford inaugural lecture of 1993, for example in Daniel Rodgers's connective history of early twentieth-century social policy in Europe and the US, *Atlantic Crossings: Social Politics in a Progressive Age* (1998), or Kevin O'Rourke and Jeffrey Williamson's study of globalization in the nineteenth-century Atlantic world.[5]

That such fundamental questions about the geography and chronology of Atlantic history can be raised at all is one sign of the healthy self-consciousness of the subject at present. Until quite recently, however, Atlantic history had been both intermittent and underexamined as an object of study. There have been Atlantic historians since at least the late nineteenth century; there have also been avowedly Atlantic histories. But only in the last decade or so has Atlantic history emerged as a distinct subfield, or even subdiscipline, within the historical profession. Only now does a broad range of historians, and other academics, seem to have made a fetish of their Atlanticism.

E. P. Thompson once remarked that whenever he saw a new god he felt the urge to blaspheme. Many have felt the same way about Atlantic history and its recent rise to prominence. Their skepticism has generated pertinent questions. Does Atlantic history reveal new problems or help historians to ask better questions than more traditional areas of inquiry, such as those centered on particular nation-states like the United Kingdom or the United States? Can any historian hope to be able to say anything substantial about a history that, at its most expansive, links four continents over five centuries? And is it not just a more acceptable way to study the history of the Spanish, Portuguese, French, British, and Dutch seaborne empires? In short, what makes Atlantic history a novel approach to genuine problems rather than just a license for superficiality or an apology for imperialism?

If blasphemy is one response to the rise of Atlantic history, it is unlikely to provide good answers to these important questions. More profitable approaches can be found in genealogy – in the history of Atlantic history – and in anatomy – in the forms Atlantic history has taken and might yet take. In the first mode, Bernard Bailyn has recently proposed a genealogy of Atlantic history which traces its origins back to anti-isolationist currents in the history of the twentieth-century United States.[6] The particular strain of international engagement that would give birth to Atlantic history had its roots in World War I but flourished most vigorously during and after World War II. Anti-isolationist journalists like Walter Lippmann and Forrest Davis found common cause with historians, many of them Catholic converts, first in the fight against Fascism in Europe and then in the early Cold War struggle against Communism. In order to rally their ideological allies, they proposed the idea that there had existed, at least since the Enlightenment, a common 'civilization' in the North Atlantic world that linked North American societies (especially, of course, the United States) with Europe by means of a common set of pluralist, democratic, liberal values. That set of values had its own deeper genealogy in a common religious heritage which came to be called, for the first time and in the same circles in the United States in the 1940s, 'Judeo-Christian'.[7] So, for example, when the historian Carlton J. H. Hayes delivered his address as President of the American Historical Association in 1945 as the question 'The American Frontier – Frontier of What?', the answer

he gave was simple and very much of its time: 'of the Greco-Roman
and Judeo-Christian tradition.'[8] Within this context, the Atlantic
became 'the inland ocean of western civilization' as well as the
Mediterranean of the postwar American empire. Atlantic histories
produced in the immediate aftermath of the war – for example,
those by Jacques Godechot (*Histoire de l'Atlantique* [1947]), Michael
Kraus (*The Atlantic Civilization: Eighteenth-Century Origins* [1949]),
and R. R. Palmer (*The Age of the Democratic Revolution* [1959–63]) –
took for granted the centrality of the Atlantic to this conception of
civilization.[9] This idea of Western civilization thus owed more to
NATO than it did to Plato.

The history of the slave trade and slavery, and of Africa, Africans,
and of race more generally, played little or no part in this strain of
Atlantic history. This 'western civ.' version was the history of the
north Atlantic rather than the south Atlantic, of Anglo-America
rather than Latin America, and of the connections between America
and Europe rather than of those between the Americas and Africa. It
was racially, if not necessarily ethnically, homogeneous. The revolution in Saint-Domingue – the largest and most successful slave revolt
in the western hemisphere and a culminating event in the cycle of
revolution that had shaken the Atlantic world since 1776 – was not an
event within this version of Atlantic history and so did not appear in
Palmer's *Age of the Democratic Revolution*. Nor were practitioners of the
history of the black Atlantic recognized as participants in a common
historiographical enterprise. W. E. B. Du Bois, C. L. R. James, and
Eric Williams, to take just the three most prominent examples, had
been pursuing subjects that were obviously and consciously Atlantic
in scope – the dynamics of the slave trade and abolition, the relationship between slavery and industrialism, the Haitian Revolution itself –
for more than 60 years before the fortunes of Atlantic history were
linked to the rise of NATO.[10] Their decades-long contribution to the
field provides a genealogy both longer, more multi-ethnic, and more
genuinely international than that espoused by most proponents of the
white Atlantic who, like many another genealogist, had overlooked
these inconvenient or uncongenial ancestors.

Atlantic history has recently become much more multicolored.
The white Atlantic has itself become a self-conscious field of study
rather than the defining model for all other Atlantic histories.[11] The
black Atlantic of the African diaspora has been joined by the green
Atlantic of the Irish political and demographic dispersal.[12] There is
even now a red Atlantic history, written in Marxian mode, which

describes the formation of a multinational, multi-ethnic, multi-cultural working class in the English Atlantic world, making up a 'many-headed hydra', in the eyes of their masters.[13] This has little in common with the traditional political histories of the white Atlantic and more with cultural studies of the black Atlantic, especially Paul Gilroy's account in *The Black Atlantic* (1993) of the Atlantic as the crucible of a modernity defined by upheaval and dispersal, mass mobility, and cultural hybridity.[14] No longer is Atlantic history available in any color, so long as it is white.

The genealogical approach to Atlantic history exposes a white Atlantic with Cold War roots, a black Atlantic with post-Civil War origins in the United States, and a red Atlantic reaching back to the cosmopolitanism of Marx. Their radically different ancestries may, in themselves, have prevented any reconciliations between these different strains of Atlantic history until the advent of a supposedly post-ideological – that is, both post-Cold War and post-imperial – age. The emergence of multicolored Atlantic histories, and of histories of the Atlantic world that encompass more than just the anglophone north Atlantic, testifies to the success of cross-fertilization. Building on that success, I should like to turn to the anatomy of Atlantic history in order to propose a threefold typology of Atlantic history. Like all good trichotomies, this one is meant to be exhaustive but not exclusive: it should cover all conceivable forms of Atlantic history but does not preclude their combination. With that caveat in mind, then, let me offer these three concepts of Atlantic history:

1. *Circum*-Atlantic history – the transnational history of the Atlantic world.
2. *Trans*-Atlantic history – the international history of the Atlantic world.
3. *Cis*-Atlantic history – national or regional history within an Atlantic context.

My aim in what follows is to describe each approach, to account for its utility, and to suggest its relationship with the other two forms. I will pay particular attention to the third concept – cis-Atlantic history – both because it needs the most elucidation, and because it may prove to be the most useful as a means of integrating national, regional, or local histories into the broader perspectives afforded by Atlantic history. I will also ask in conclusion what are the limitations of Atlantic history, both as an example of oceanic history and as a fashionable mode of historical inquiry in the English-speaking world.

1. Circum-Atlantic history

Circum-Atlantic history is the history of the Atlantic as a particular
zone of exchange and interchange, circulation and transmission. It is
therefore the history of the ocean as an arena distinct from any of
the particular, narrower, oceanic zones that comprise it. It certainly
encompasses the shores of the Atlantic but does so only insofar as
those shores form part of a larger oceanic history rather than a set of
specific national or regional histories abutting onto the Atlantic. It is
the history of the people who crossed the Atlantic, who lived on its
shores and who participated in the communities it made possible, of
their commerce and their ideas, as well as the diseases they carried,
the flora they transplanted and the fauna they transported.

Circum-Atlantic history may be the most self-evident way to
approach Atlantic history. However, of the three possible concepts of
Atlantic history it is the one that has been least investigated. It is
only in the last decade that this concept of Atlantic history has found
a name, in a brilliant work of performance studies by the theatre historian Joseph Roach entitled *Cities of the Dead: Circum-Atlantic
Performance* (1996). '[T]he circum-Atlantic world as it emerged from
the revolutionized economies of the late seventeenth century,'
Roach writes, '... resembled a vortex in which commodities and
cultural practices changed hands many times.' Accordingly, '[t]he
concept of a circum-Atlantic world (as opposed to a transatlantic
one) insists on the centrality of the diasporic and genocidal histories
of Africa and the Americas, North and South, in the creation of the
culture of modernity.'[15]

This is circum-Atlantic history in two senses: it incorporates
everything *around* the Atlantic basin, and it is mobile and connective,
tracing circulations *about* the Atlantic world. There were, of course,
many smaller zones of interchange around the fringes of the Atlantic
basin, whether in West Africa, in western Europe, or around the
Caribbean, which had possessed similar characteristics. Such lesser
systems existed within more limited seafaring cultures which had
developed their own identities and interdependence thousands of
years before Columbus's voyages. The European achievement was to
link these subzones together into a single Atlantic system. Within
that system there was continuing interaction between the societies
migrants had left and those they created together across the Atlantic:
it is this achievement that allows us to say that the Atlantic was a
European invention, while also acknowledging the contribution of

non-European peoples to this development. In contrast, the Indian Ocean's subzones had been integrated long before the arrival of the Portuguese or other Europeans.[16] Some commentators have seen the history of the early modern Atlantic as 'a sort of precursor of globalisation at the turn of the twenty-first century.'[17] However, this overlooks the precocious integration of the Indian Ocean, not to mention that of the Mediterranean.

Most circum-Atlantic histories have followed the 'white Atlantic' model and have emphasized integration at the expense of circulation. Alternative circum-Atlantic histories that have taken their inspiration from the history of the black Atlantic have stressed mobility rather than stability and have been less whiggish as a result. In the words of Paul Gilroy, the Atlantic was a crucible of 'creolisation, métissage, mestizaje and hybridity'; out of that crucible of identities emerged what Roach has called an 'interculture ... along the Atlantic rim.'[18] This interest in culture and identity, rather than commerce or politics, has directed attention to the fluidity of the process of exchange rather than any fixity in the results of that process. Accordingly, it has become increasingly less persuasive to write Atlantic history within linear narratives, whether of modernization or of globalization.

Circum-Atlantic history is transnational history. Its conventional chronology begins in just the period usually associated with the rise of the state, that is, in the late fifteenth and early sixteenth centuries, but it ends just before the epoch of the nation-state, in the mid-nineteenth century. Empires and composite monarchies, not states, were the characteristic political units of this era.[19] The history of the Atlantic world has often been told as the sum of the histories of those empires, but such a history could necessarily encompass only European perspectives on the Atlantic system. A truly circum-Atlantic history eludes the history of nation-states chronologically; it also overflows the boundaries of empires geographically, like the silver bullion that was drawn from the Spanish American empire into China, creating a link between the Atlantic world and the Asian trade that has been identified as the starting point for a truly global economy in the sixteenth century.[20]

As the history of a zone, its products, and its inhabitants, circum-Atlantic history is therefore a classic example of a transnational oceanic history: classic, but not defining, because, unlike the Mediterranean of Fernand Braudel's account, it does not make up a single identifiable climatic and geological unit. As Braudel himself

noted, '[t]he Atlantic, stretching from pole to pole, reflects the
colours of all the earth's climates'.[21] It is thus too diverse in the range
of climatic zones it straddles – from the Arctic to the Capes, and
from the coastal regions of western Europe to the archipelago of the
Caribbean – for geographical determinism to have any useful
explanatory force.[22] It resembles the Indian Ocean in that variety, as
well as in the cultural and economic links gradually forged within it,
but not insofar as those links long preceded the intervention of
Europeans. And if the Indian Ocean was precocious, the Pacific was
belated when judged by the standards of the Atlantic world. The
Pacific also had expansive subzones which had been created by
Polynesian seafaring cultures thousands of years before the entry of
Europeans, but it, too, was ultimately a European creation, in the
sense that it was Europeans who first saw it whole; it was also they
who first distinguished it from its neighbor and tributary, the
Atlantic. Yet, for all these significant differences, the oceanic histories of the Mediterranean, the Indian Ocean, the Atlantic, and the
Pacific share one important defining characteristic: that as
specifically *oceanic* histories (rather than maritime or imperial histories, for example) they join the land and the sea in a relationship
which is 'symbiotic, but asymmetric': that is, the two are interdependent, but the history of the ocean predominates and is not the
only object of study, as it would be in a strictly maritime history.[23]
The national histories of territorial states or empires are only part of
this history when an ocean creates long-distance connections
between them. Like all such oceanic histories, then, circum–Atlantic
history is *trans*national but not *inter*national. That is instead the
province of what can be termed '*trans*-Atlantic' history.

2. Trans-Atlantic history

Trans-Atlantic history is the history of the Atlantic world told
through comparisons. Circum-Atlantic history makes trans-Atlantic
history possible. The circulatory system of the Atlantic created links
between regions and peoples formerly kept distinct. This allows
trans-Atlantic historians to draw meaningful – rather than merely
arbitrary – comparisons between otherwise distinct histories. Unlike
the 'symbiotic, but asymmetric' relations of land and sea traced by
Atlantic history as an oceanic history, trans-Atlantic history concen-
trates on the shores of the ocean, and assumes the existence of
nations and states, as well as societies and economic formations (like

plantations or cities), around the Atlantic rim. It can bring those different units into meaningful comparison because they already share some common features by virtue of being enmeshed within circum-Atlantic relationships. Their common Atlantic history defines, but does not determine, the nature of the connection between diverse entities; it may be excluded from comparison, as a common variable, but might itself become the object of study within a specifically circum-Atlantic history.

Trans-Atlantic history can be called international history for two reasons. The first is etymological and contextual; the second, comparative and conceptual. Both terms – 'trans-Atlantic' and 'international' – first made their way into the English language during the American War of Independence. The earliest usages of 'trans-Atlantic' can be found in England during the war in 1779–81. The Englishmen who first used it, like Richard Watson (bishop of Llandaff) and the historian Charles Henry Arnold, generally employed the term in a more precise sense than the one I intend or, indeed, than its conventional meaning today to mean 'across and on the other side of the Atlantic', like Britons' 'Trans-atlantic Brethren' in North America or the 'present trans-atlantic war' being fought in, as well as for, British America; only John Wilkes used it in its modern sense, when he referred to a 'trans-atlantic voyage'.[24]

The term 'international' emerged at exactly the same moment, but in a slightly different context, in the legal writings of Jeremy Bentham. In his *Introduction to the Principles of Morals and Legislation* (1780/89), Bentham sought to define a particular segment of the law that, as yet, had no clear definition in English. This was the law between states as sovereign agents, as distinct from what had traditionally been called the law of nations or a law which applied to all people as members of larger ethnic or political societies. 'The word *international* ... is a new one,' wrote Bentham. 'It is calculated to express, in a more significant way, the branch of law which goes commonly under the name of the *law of nations*.'[25] The context was only different to the extent that Bentham addressed his neologism to fellow-lawyers, in a work written in 1780 but not finally published until 1789. However, it was similar in that Bentham had been a keen, indeed deeply implicated, observer of the American war, and was the co-author of the only formal response to the American Declaration of Independence sponsored by the British government in 1776.[26]

Yet more than this common origin in the context in the American war identifies trans-Atlantic history with international history. Just as international history may be said to be the history of the relations between nations (or, in fact, states) within a larger political and economic system, so trans-Atlantic history joins states, nations, and regions within an oceanic system. Trans-Atlantic history is especially suited to the seventeenth- and eighteenth-century histories of the Atlantic world, when state-formation went hand-in-hand with empire-building to create a convergent process we might call 'empire-state-building'.[27] And it is particularly useful as an approach to the histories of those Atlantic states most prone to exceptionalism in their history – for example, the United Kingdom and the United States – but whose common features can be excavated and displayed more readily within a transatlantic frame of comparison.

Trans-Atlantic history as comparative history has most often been conducted along a north–south axis within the Atlantic world. It has therefore been performed more often as an exercise in inter-*imperial* history than as one in international history. The earliest studies in this vein, notably Frank Tannenbaum's 1946 essay on slavery in Spanish and British America and Herbert Klein's later comparison of British and Iberian slavery, like J. H. Elliott's much more comprehensive ongoing history of the British and Spanish empires in the Americas, compare the Iberian and British empires according to their differing systems of law, economic regulation, religious belief, or institutional structure.[28] However, the potential for comparative trans-Atlantic histories along an east–west axis remains largely unexplored. When it has been undertaken – for example, in Bernard Bailyn and John Clive's examination of Scotland and America as 'cultural provinces' of the English metropolis – it has usually been within an imperial framework, often explicitly divided between centers and peripheries.[29]

Yet the units of analysis could be larger and the framework more generous. To take an example from the anglophone Atlantic: no systematic comparison has ever been made of the United Kingdom and the United States as enduring political unions from the eighteenth century. The United Kingdom was created by the Treaty of Union of 1707; the United States, announced initially in the Declaration of Independence, was united by the Articles of Confederation and then supplied with a more lasting union in the Constitution of 1788. Both can be seen in retrospect to have conjoined statehood with a fictive nationalism: the British forged through antagonism with Catholic France (in the course of the eighteenth century and into the nineteenth century),[30] the American as a result of, rather than precondition for, independence and victory in war.[31] Both defined citizenship politically rather than ethnically, so that neither conformed to the classic primordialist vision of the nation-state as the political realization of an immemorial identity.[32] Each remains defined by its eighteenth-century origins, and those definitions can be traced back to their trans-Atlantic relations: the American, in part due to the long-standing links with Britain and the effort to assert independence of Britain; the British, in part due to the impact of defeat in the American war and the re-creation of the nation in its aftermath.[33] To these two political products of the war we might also add British North America, later Canada, to make three states forged in the last quarter of the eighteenth century, joined in a common trans-Atlantic history. They might usefully be compared with regard to their origins, their divergent paths since the late eighteenth century, and their common history within the anglophone Atlantic world.

Comparison as an historical tool may most usefully reveal difference, but it depends for its viability on some initial similarity. A history within the context of empire, and a history of resistance to empire, provides an obvious point of comparison between the United States and the Latin American republics, though their divergent institutional origins and distinctive traditions of religion, governance, and inter-ethnic relations also reveal intractable differences.[34] Such comparisons can help to define more precisely the historical features of segments of the Atlantic world but only within the context of that larger trans-Atlantic perspective. Such precision of definition, taken one stage further, and out of the context of comparison, is the aim of the third and final concept of Atlantic history, '*cis*-Atlantic history'.

3. Cis-Atlantic history

'Cis-Atlantic' history studies particular places as unique locations within an Atlantic world and seeks to define that uniqueness as the result of the interaction between local particularity and a wider web of connections (and comparisons). The term 'cis-Atlantic' may seem like a barbarous neologism but, like 'trans-Atlantic' and 'international', it was also a child of the late eighteenth century. The parentage belongs to Thomas Jefferson, and the barbarism, not to the coinage itself, but to the very condition against which Jefferson defined the term. That barbarism – along with feebleness and shrinkage – had been imputed to the fauna of the New World by European naturalists like the comte de Buffon. Jefferson, in his *Notes on the State of Virginia* (1785), had replied by adducing a wealth of information to rebut charges based (as he thought them) on mere ignorance and prejudice:

> I do not mean to deny that there are varieties in the race of man, distin-guished by their powers both of body and mind. I believe there are, as I see to be the case in the races of other animals. I only mean to suggest a doubt, whether the bulk and faculties of animals depend on the side of the Atlantic on which their food happens to grow, or which furnishes the ele-ments of which they are compounded? Whether nature has enlisted herself as a Cis or Trans-Atlantic partisan?[35]

Jefferson thus used the term to mean 'on this side of the Atlantic', to distinguish it from the trans-Atlantic world of Europe, a meaning he amplified politically when he told James Monroe in 1823 that it was the interest of the United States 'never to suffer Europe to inter-meddle with cis-Atlantic affairs.'[36] The term was thus both a badge of difference and a marker of a novel American perspective just as it was defined in relation to the Atlantic Ocean.

Cis-Atlantic history, in the more expansive sense proposed here, is the history of any particular place – a nation, a state, a region, even a specific institution – in relation to the wider Atlantic world. Its greatest monument is likely to remain Huguette and Pierre Chaunu's eight-volume *Seville et l'Atlantique* (1955–9), which expanded outward from a single city to encompass the entire Atlantic world.[37] Working almost in reverse, large-scale cis-Atlantic history has been undertaken, albeit not under this precise rubric, by historical geographers like D. W. Meinig and E. Estyn Evans or, most recently, by the archaeologist Barry Cunliffe, in their studies of 'Atlantic America' (Meinig), 'Atlantic Europe' (Evans), or the broad Atlantic cultural zone 'facing the ocean' (Cunliffe) from Greenland to the Canaries.[38] Their work integrates seemingly disparate regions within a common Atlantic context, geophysically, culturally, and politically. The Atlantic Ocean, and the regions' common relation-ship with it, provides the link but is not itself the object of analysis. This approach comes close to circum-Atlantic history but concen-trates not on the ocean itself but rather on the way specific regions were defined by their relationship to that ocean. That relationship over time enables scholars like Meinig, Evans, and Cunliffe to describe larger patterns and then to descend from those broad linkages to the particular impact of Atlantic relations on specific regions. For example, Cunliffe begins with pre-history and ends just before the onset of early modernity; similarly, Meinig encompasses the history of a whole continent right up to the twentieth century. Their approaches suggest what might be achieved by cis-Atlantic histories of the early modern period (and beyond) if they concentrate on smaller units of analysis and less extensive swaths of time.

Cis-Atlantic history may overcome artificial, but nonetheless enduring, divisions between histories usually distinguished from each other as internal and external, domestic and foreign, or national and imperial. The rise of nationalist history in the nineteenth century coincided with the invention of extra-national histories, whether of diplomacy or of imperial expansion. The boundaries between such histories have, until recently, remained mostly impermeable until the rise of postwar multilateralism, decolonization, and the creation of transnational federations, along with separatist sentiment at the sub-national level, together helped to dissolve some of those boundaries. Larger narratives of historical development may be harder to dislodge. For example, the processes implied by the labels 'early modern' in European history and 'colonial' in the histories of British or Spanish America are distinct from one another: 'early modern' implied a movement toward modernity, while 'colonial' denoted subordination within an empire that would precede independence and the acquisition of nationhood and statehood. Latin American history rarely, if ever, has the label 'early modern' applied to it, and attempts to encourage the replacement of 'colonial' with 'early modern' in North American history have not been entirely successful. The incompatibility of such master-narratives has been especially debilitating in studies of the period called, variously, 'early modern' and 'colonial', not least because it has obscured the continuities between processes usually kept apart, such as state-formation within Europe and empire-building beyond it.[39] Like the comparisons made possible by trans-Atlantic history, so cis-Atlantic history confronts such separations by insisting on commonalities and by studying the local effects of oceanic movements.

Cis-Atlantic history, at this local level, can be most fruitfully applied to the very places most obviously transformed by their Atlantic connections: port towns and cities. For example, Bristol's economy moved from a fifteenth-century dependence on the wine trade to its seventeenth-century concentration on Atlantic staples. This involved not only a radical re-orientation from east to west, and from Europe to the Americas, but also upheavals in the social order, in the disposition of cultural space, and in the distribution of power.[40] Similar transformations can be traced in other settlements around the Atlantic basin, whether on the Atlantic coasts of Europe and Africa, in the cities of the Caribbean, or along the eastern seaboard of North America. For example, crossing points within the Atlantic world gained new significance when imperial rivalries increased and local polities took advantage of the competition for their allegiance, as among the Kuna Indians of the isthmus of Darién.[41] Wherever local populations encountered or collided with outsiders (not always Europeans), 'middle grounds' of negotiation and contest arose like this which would not have existed were it not for the circulation and competition created by the thickening of the connections within the Atlantic system.[42] Likewise, new economies arose to meet novel demands, whether by the wholesale export of the plantation system from the Mediterranean to the Americas in the sixteenth and seventeenth centuries or, arising more organically, by gradual specialization like that among the wine-producers of Madeira in the eighteenth century who created their eponymous wines in direct response to various consumers' tastes.[43]

The greatest potential for cis-Atlantic history may lie in the histories of places larger even than cities, isthmuses or islands, that is, in the histories of the nations and states that faced the Atlantic Ocean. The histories of the three kingdoms of Britain and Ireland in the early modern period provide a useful set of interlocking comparisons. Such a cis-Atlantic approach (though not called this) has characterized the writing of Irish history since the 1930s, when historians like G. A. Hayes McCoy and David Beers Quinn first began to put the history of Ireland into the context of westward expansion.[44] A more recent strain of Irish historiography has stressed instead the similarities between Ireland's place within a British composite monarchy and the situation of other provinces, such as Bohemia, within contemporary European empires and compound states. Ireland was certainly part of pan-European patterns of confessionalism, militarization and state-building, but equally it shared experiences with other British Atlantic colonies that together defined it as 'a mid-Atlantic polity having some of the features of both the Old World and the New.'[45] Similarly, Scotland now appears less as a 'cultural province' of England than as an Atlantic nation, albeit one that weighed the alternatives of migration and commerce with northern Europe against the novel opportunities afforded by the westward enterprise.[46] From the early seventeenth century its inhabitants intermittently sought new Scotlands in the Americas, even as some English presbyterians were said to have sought a more religiously tolerant 'America in Scotland' in 1638 during the Bishops' Wars.[47] By the end of the eighteenth century, even the Scottish Highlands were deeply enmeshed within the political economy of the Atlantic world, as the export of soldiers for Britain's imperial armies became 'simply one of the specialised economies that emerged from the region's inclusion within empire – Gaeldom's equivalent of the Glasgow tobacco trade.'[48]

The English were comparatively early and enthusiastic Atlanticists compared to the Irish and the Scots, but a cis-Atlantic history of early modern England remains the least developed of all those that might apply to the three kingdoms. This is all the more curious because so many of the defining features of early modernity in England joined processes within England itself and those in the Atlantic world. For example, we now have a much clearer picture than ever before of the continuities between internal and external migration, so that we can see migration into the Atlantic world (and then often within it) as the extension of mobility within England itself, especially as it was chan- neled through key ports like London and Bristol in the seventeenth century.[49] Politics is susceptible to a similar analysis. As Michael Braddick has recently argued, the English state in this period colo- nized two kinds of space simultaneously, by the intensification of its authority over England itself and by the extension of that authority over territories well beyond England. The needs to co-opt local elites and to assert authority symbolically proved to be common problems in both arenas.[50] Similarly, the creation of an Atlantic economy was not simply a matter of finding new markets abroad but also involved the increasing implication of the domestic economy in Atlantic exchange, even before the commercial revolution of the eighteenth century. The dimensions of that involvement in Atlantic trade still need to be investigated at the most intimate levels of town, village, and even household. Cis-Atlantic history will thus have to encompass both the widest extent of the English state and the most intimate focus on the domestic sphere. By treating each inquiry as part of a common and developing Atlantic experience, it should be possible to provide more complex and persuasive accounts of the relationships between the state, the market, and the family than has hitherto been the case.

***

Braudel warned that 'the historical Mediterranean seems to be a concept of infinite expansion' and wondered aloud: 'But how far in space are we justified in extending it?'[51] One might wonder the same about the Atlantic, and about Atlantic history. Circum-Atlantic history would seem to extend no further than the ocean's shores; as soon as we leave the circulatory system of the Atlantic itself, we enter a series of cis-Atlantic histories. Trans-Atlantic history combines such cis-Atlantic histories into units of comparison; the possibilities for combination are various, but not infinite, because adjacency to the Atlantic determines the possibility of comparison. Cis-Atlantic histories, though superficially the most precisely bounded, may in fact be those of greatest extension: such histories protrude deep into the continents of the circum-Atlantic rim, indeed as far as the goods, ideas, and people circulated within the Atlantic system penetrated. Cis-Atlantic histories of entirely land-locked regions would then be possible.

The three concepts of Atlantic history outlined here are not exclusive but rather reinforcing. Taken together, they offer the possibility of a three-dimensional history of the Atlantic world. A circum-Atlantic history would draw upon the fruits of various cis-Atlantic histories and generate comparisons between them. Trans-Atlantic history can link those cis-Atlantic histories because of the existence of a circum-Atlantic system. Cis-Atlantic history in turn feeds trans-Atlantic comparisons. Such a set of cross-fertilized histories might show that the Atlantic's is the only oceanic history to possess these three conceptual dimensions, because it may be the only one that can be construed as at once transnational, international, and national in scope. Global comparisons among different oceanic histories have barely been imagined yet, but they should be central to any future oceanic history.

Atlantic history has not yet suffered the death by a thousand textbooks that has befallen other fields. It has no agreed canon of problems, events, or processes. It follows no common method or practice. It has even begun productively to escape the early modern boundaries of *c.*1492–1815 within which it has most usually been confined. Like the Atlantic itself, the field is fluid, in motion, and potentially boundless, depending on how it is defined; that is part of its appeal, but also one of its drawbacks. It is unlikely to replace traditional national histories and it will compete with other forms of transnational and international history. However, as a field that links national histories, facilitates comparisons between them, and opens up new areas of study or gives greater focus to better-established modes of inquiry, it surely presents more opportunities than disadvantages. Atlantic history – whether circum-Atlantic, trans-Atlantic, or cis-Atlantic – pushes historians towards methodological pluralism and expanded horizons. That is surely the most one can ask of any emergent field of study.

Part II

Connections

2

Migration

Alison Games

The year 1500 saw a world as fully in motion as did the year 1800, yet by 1800 the degree, pace, character, and impact of that migration were fundamentally different. During this period, migration within the British Isles made parts of Ireland and England British, it eroded local cultures, and it produced urban societies, of which one, London, was comprised of migrants from all over Britain and became the largest city in Europe. Patterns of migration from Britain and Ireland similarly shaped migration across the Atlantic. Like Ireland, parts of America became British long before Britain itself, measured not in colonial public and legal cultures, which were initiated and codified in official charters and patents and thus highly derivative of English (and later British) legal and institutional practices, but in the composition of the migrant and settler populations. The British Atlantic world was made by migration, on both sides of the ocean, and for all members of society.

One advantage of a British Atlantic perspective on migration in this period, rooted as it is initially in Britain itself, is that migration emerges as an entirely normal activity, a regular part of the life cycle, a common response to personal ambition, economic hardship, or perceived opportunities elsewhere. A migrant is someone who moves, if not permanently then for a significant period of time. The issue of permanence is problematic: it is difficult to tell whether people intended migrations to be permanent; the habit of migration often prodded people to move again; and in any case premature death in the adverse disease environments of cities and colonies frequently dictated an alternative ending to the one a long-distance migrant might have envisioned. A migrant might be a woman who moved at marriage, a company official sent to govern a colony, an African transported to toil in the cane fields of Jamaica, or a person seeking sanctuary – whether a religious refugee or a runaway slave. Migration thus includes both those who took part in chain migrations and those who migrated in chains.

Common as it was, migration did not necessarily herald a new worldview, although at times and especially for particular populations, migration was a deliberately political response to adverse circumstances. An appreciation of its very mundane quality helps to sever it from the teleological questions about migration and national identity which particularly plague discussions of migration to British North America and the subsequent United States. Migration, in fact, may have had a greater impact creating a *British* identity because of the ways in which migration patterns in this period eroded regional cultures and brought people from remote parts of Britain into contact with each other in both the British Isles and America. Although the act of migration was deeply rooted in European cultural norms, and thus an endemic and characteristic feature of life in the British Atlantic world, it nevertheless altered societies all around the Atlantic. Migration gained a momentum of its own as a catalyst for cultural elaboration not because of any innovative aspirations of migrants themselves but simply by virtue of their proximity to unfamiliar people, in unfamiliar lands, in societies profoundly shaped by the demographic peculiarities of migrant populations.

The period 1500–1800 embraced both continuity and dramatic change. While enduring features – local migration and long-distance internal migration – were found in the British Isles throughout, it is possible to identify periods of change which originated in Britain but which had important implications for the Americas. Migration is intimately connected to population growth and to times of economic hardship and dislocation (two generally related phenomena). From roughly 1580 to the middle of the seventeenth century, population growth in England, Wales, and Lowland Scotland generated enhanced rates of long-distance migration which linked Lowland Scotland more intimately to Ireland and to Europe, fed the growth of London, and, crucially, produced hundreds of thousands of able-bodied English men to labor in colonial and commercial ventures overseas. These patterns both ensured the success of early imperial aspirations and made those ventures distinctly English in character. From the 1650s to roughly 1720, the English population declined.

Transatlantic migration consequently became more heavily African, as planters sought laborers for export crops, it became more heavily British, as Irish and Scots were drawn into overseas enterprises, and, finally, it became more distinctly European, as promoters recruited Protestant migrants from the continent. While the British population grew from the 1720s on, the rate of growth accelerated in the second half of the century (and both Scotland and Ireland grew more quickly than did England) and coincided with other local economic pressures, thereby fueling a huge outburst of migration from the British Isles to America, increasing suddenly the rate of urbanization in the British Isles, and shaping revolutionary activity. Patterns of population growth and migration within the British Isles, then, were intimately, critically, transformingly connected to overseas migration and to the commensurate shape of societies in the Americas.

The exception to the general chronology outlined above was Gaelic Ireland: while Lowland Scotland and England experienced population growth and underemployment in the late sixteenth and early seventeenth centuries, the Irish population remained low, with resulting labor shortages. Just when the English population began to decline in the mid-seventeenth century, however, the Irish population took off, primarily through high fertility and migration from England and Scotland. Moreover, despite its low population, Ireland shared trends toward long-distance migration. The very factors that depressed the size of the population, particularly war and the dispossession of native land, prompted migration by Irish Catholics, while population pressures and economic circumstances prompted Ulster Protestants to emigrate in large numbers in the eighteenth century. Thus Ireland's population history reflects its awkward position as both kingdom and colony. While the population history of Highland Scotland remains incomplete, it is likely that the Highlands followed the Irish pattern, with a steady growth from the 1650s on.[1]

Internal migration, I: the British Isles, 1500–1800

Migration was a fundamental feature of English life before this starting point. Local migration patterns found in England, Lowland Scotland, and Wales resemble patterns observed elsewhere in western Europe. Migration occurred regularly over the course of the life cycle, for both women and men. It was not aimless, but purposeful, and regularly occurred within a narrow geographic field of 10–15 miles, thus in the first part of the sixteenth century reinforcing, not undermining, regional cultures. Yet local migration, while found in all elements of society, was especially common among one particular group, young men. Thus a community with high rates of migration might in fact have a stable core ('stayers') and a highly mobile population of young laborers ('movers'). These high rates of rural migration were dictated largely by labor requirements, and here both population dearth and abundance played a role. During outbreaks of plague, for example, laborers moved to fill labor needs, while in times of population growth (and accompanying rent increases and scarcity of food and employment), men (and a few women) migrated in search of employment.[2]

Paralleling endemic patterns of local migration were trends in long-distance migration. Some long-distance migration (characterized by Peter Clark as 'betterment' migration), such as the movement of a child for an apprenticeship, was endemic regardless of other economic pressures, and indeed better-off members of English society were more likely to engage in long-distance migration than were the more impoverished. But in times of population growth and enhanced economic hardship (between 1580 and 1650 for England and Wales, until the end of the seventeenth century for Lowland Scotland because of harvest failures, and after 1750 for all regions), long-distance subsistence migration increased dramatically, as migrants desperate for ways to keep body and soul together trekked long distances from town to town, 'overshadowed by the tramping curse of necessity.'[3]

During such periods, migrants traveled longer distances in search of employment, and they especially moved toward provincial towns and to London. Large towns acted as magnets for young men looking for work, with the larger towns drawing people from hundreds of miles away. Urbanization is a crucial theme of this period in the British Isles, and is directly connected to migration. In 1500, 3.1 percent of the population of England and Wales lived in towns with over 10,000 inhabitants, and 1.6 percent of the population of Scotland did. By 1800, that figure had soared to 20.3 percent for England and Wales and 17.3 percent for Scotland. Ireland urbanized more slowly, with no towns over 10,000 before 1600, but the percentage of urban dwellers jumped from zero percent in 1600 to 7 percent in 1800.[4]

Cities (especially London) had their own demographic regimes. In London, a city whose population was fed steadily by streams of young male apprentices, the sex ratio before 1650 favored men, but seems to have shifted after that period to emulate a larger European urban pattern as a place characterized by a shortage of men. Cities also possessed their own unique disease environments, thus causing newcomers the same high mortality rates found in colonies. Migrants, predominantly young men and boys between the ages of 10 and 30, were the most likely to die in times of plague or other epidemic diseases, and thus this population was forced constantly to replenish itself. In 1625, for example, 35,000 people died from a plague outbreak in London, but within two years, the loss in population had been replaced by rural migration. Childhood mortality was a constant. And overall, deaths outnumbered births, at their worst by 65 percent, although better off urban dwellers enjoyed natural increase. For migrants, children, and the poor, cities were death traps.[5]

These challenges to natural increase meant that migration to cities enabled them to sustain their size and especially to grow. The huge growth of British cities in this period directly reflects patterns of long-distance migration. London's growth was the most significant: the city grew from 40,000 people in 1500 to 900,000 in 1801. Edinburgh shared London's early and rapid rise, doubling in size between 1540 and 1640, primarily because of migration from the countryside.[6] No other city compared with London, although other cities experienced similarly rapid growth, especially Dublin (5000 in 1550 to 168,000 in 1800): indeed, most of the major cities in Britain and Ireland *became* cities in this period, particularly during the years between 1750 and 1800, when Glasgow, Liverpool, and Manchester more than tripled in size.[7] While some towns attracted people from nearby regions, many others became places of considerable geographic and regional heterogeneity, with London, as always, the most vivid example of this cultural elaboration. Dublin in particular was a creation of migration, central as it was to English rule of Ireland. And Scottish migration in the eighteenth century brought Lowland and Highland Scots together in Edinburgh and Glasgow.

Long-distance migration did not take migrants only to cities, nor did it engage only young men. Approximately 20,000–30,000 Scots migrated to Ireland, where they joined the approximately 170,000 English and Welsh who migrated to Ireland before 1672.[8] The English migrated to Ireland to settle and to secure the Munster plantation, while the Scots migrated primarily to Ulster. Many of these English migrants to Munster were people with considerable financial resources, and they traveled in family groups, thus illuminating two simultaneous and enduring processes of long-distance migration, one family oriented, the other characterized by labor migration.[9] The infusion of British settlers in Ireland, accompanied as it was by repeated wars and the steady encroachment on native lands and privileges, prompted migration from Ireland at the same time as the kingdom seemed such a promising destination to invaders. Approximately 349,000 Irish left Ireland between 1600 and 1775 for destinations in America, the Caribbean, England, the continent, and further afield.[10]

This infusion of English, Welsh, and Scots settlers in Ireland made Ireland 'British' in a way that other parts of Britain were not. In no other place – except later in America – did people from such different parts of the three kingdoms find themselves in such proximity. It is important not to overstate this proximity: English and Scottish migrants tended to settle different parts of Ireland, and proximity to the Irish was often regarded with apprehension, yet Ulster was described by contemporaries as 'British' because of the proximity of Scots and English there.[11]

British overseas migration, 1600–1800

If Ireland became British in the early seventeenth century, however, other sites of British activity did not. It was a surplus *English* population that traveled disproportionately overseas in this period.[12] It was not merely fortuitous that English enterprises overseas (in the Mediterranean, in India, in the Americas) coincided with population growth. All overseas ventures required personnel, especially young, able-bodied laborers, and the rising population that dislodged so many young men from their home parishes and launched them on the road to port towns was not coincidental, but causal, in the success of English overseas ventures. In times of declining opportunities in home parishes, men did not necessarily venture to cities with the plan of traveling overseas. (The exception here seems to have been the Irish and Scots in the eighteenth century, who viewed imperial destinations as alternatives to, not second choices after, urban employment.[13]) Many urban migrants, indeed, found a quick grave in the city. Those who survived sought their fortune in the metropolis, but for many, other opportunities ultimately beckoned, often after a long delay while migrants sought work.[14]

Travels to the continent highlight an important but understudied element of English migration east, not only to Europe but to Asia and the Mediterranean. Comparing the different options migrants faced is not easy, but a rare passenger list for London in 1635 suggests the extent of the migration. In that year, 1595 men left London to serve as soldiers on the continent, and another 1000 people (men, women, and children) left for the continent. Hundreds of other men, factors and merchants for England's overseas companies and mariners on England's commercial ships, would have sailed that year as well for India, Indonesia, West Africa, Turkey, Moscow, Lisbon, and any number of other places where men pursued profit. They were joined, moreover, by recreational travelers, young men undertaking a tour of Europe, an experience later ritualized in the eighteenth century as the Grand Tour. These destinations never rivaled American or Irish destinations in this or later periods: in 1635, almost 5000 people left London for American destinations. Thousands more sailed in the same year from other English ports, while hundreds of merchants, mariners, and seasonal fishermen were regular denizens of the Atlantic, although they tend to be neglected in discussions of migration. Even in the eighteenth century, the British presence (excluding soldiers and officers) in India was small, with a mere 232 male heads of households, not all of whom were British, listed in Calcutta in 1766, and only a few hundred East India Company employees in Bengal.[15] Thus measured in numbers of travelers, English interests lay more to the west. In their Atlantic orientation the English were distinct from the Scots, who were precociously European in orientation. Between 1600 and 1650, somewhere between 30,000 and 40,000 Scots migrated to Poland, with another large contingent bound to Scandinavia (between 25,000 and 30,000). The burden of migration fell disproportionately on young men, with one estimate that in this period almost 20 percent of the population of young men left Scotland.[16]

While the growth in population provided English manpower for military and maritime ventures around the globe, it was American endeavors that benefited in particular from this population growth. Many early colonial ventures were debacles – Roanoke, countless efforts to settle along the Amazon, Sagadahoc, Newfoundland, Providence Island. And some that were not debacles deserved to be, particularly Jamestown. Yet enough colonies endured to give the English a permanent foothold in North America and the Caribbean. More particularly, enough migrants to the colonies endured and replenished populations depleted by attacks by Native Americans and European rivals (the Spanish and French especially), and especially by endemic and epidemic diseases. A steady stream of men was crucial to the viability of these enterprises, particularly in the 1630s and 1640s, and thus government concerns about vagrants in England coincided with investors' hopes for men to populate their holdings. Transatlantic

migration, fueled by changing patterns in internal migration, generated that mobile population and secured colonial viability at a crucial
time. In the seventeenth century approximately 300,000 English
migrated to the Americas, along with 20,000–40,000 Irish, 7000
Scots, and a smattering of people from the continent, primarily to the
West Indies and the Chesapeake.[17] This seventeenth-century migration was predominantly a migration of servants, and particularly of
young men. Their destinations signaled their purpose: to produce
export crops to bring profit to planters and investors. As one plantation agent reminded his employer from Barbados, 'a plantation in
this place is worth nothing unless they be good store of hands upon it.'
Without able hands, 'there is no way to live.'[18]

People from all different parts of England itself were flung
together in America. Although the impact of particular regions is
well known in New England, for example, every county of England
was represented in the region, bringing strangers and regional
cultures together with immediacy and proximity. The pattern was
replicated everywhere. Moreover, although the period through 1660
was characterized by largely English migration, the presence of
people from other parts of Britain contributed to the emerging
heterogeneity of American life. On Providence Island, that most
precarious English colony off the Central American coast, the
governor recorded that he went to another part of the island for a
feast given by all the Welshmen of the island. Montserrat, with its
Irish majority, was similarly heterogeneous. Thus one element of
cultural elaboration was the introduction to new rituals, new ways of
speech, and new material cultures.[19]

After 1660, new British elements joined and dominated European
transatlantic migration. By around 1660, in the wake of the slow-
down in population growth, and the upheaval of civil war, revolution, and commonwealth, it was clear that British overseas endeavors
could no longer rely on a steady emigration of English men. The
eighteenth century was characterized by two distinct shifts, first from
English to British migration, and, second, toward European migration. From 1700 to 1780, 70 percent of the approximately 270,000
British migrants were Irish or Scots. A big exodus from the
Highlands began in the eighteenth century, when population growth
prompted many to leave the region permanently, to destinations
both elsewhere in Britain and overseas. They were joined by
approximately 100,000 German-speaking migrants from the
Rhinelands. Not all groups settled in the same places, of course:

New England retained its English character, and eighteenth-century migrants bound for North America went disproportionately to the Middle Colonies. But most colonial regions were inhabited by people from a variety of groups, and patterns of geographic dispersal did not negate the importance of cultural contact and exchange. Thus in terms of the white population, America became first English, then British, while a few places became European, well ahead of much of Britain itself.[20]

Like the Scots who went to northern Europe, or the English who went to Ireland or India, all those who made the transatlantic voyage came from worlds embedded in much larger patterns of migration. The different options available might have been equally dangerous or fatal, but the choices were real. A transatlantic voyage was hardly foreordained for a long-distance migrant. German-speaking people from the Rhinelands comprised the largest continental contingent of migrants to North America in the eighteenth century. Yet this number, large as it was in terms of the total European transatlantic migration, was only a small percentage of all German-speaking migrants, the vast majority of whom voyaged not west but rather east, into central Europe and Russia.[21] Of 200,000 Huguenots to leave France before 1705, only a few thousand went to North America and the Caribbean. Some 60,000 went to England and Wales, despite their large numbers a poorly studied group, while the remainder stayed on the continent.[22]

For European migrants, it is clear that a large labor market existed that transcended the Atlantic, embracing options closer to home and in central and eastern Europe. Refugees, exiles, and laborers alike could make decisions about where to go. To speak of options for enslaved Africans is obviously rebarbative, yet the Atlantic slave trade, too, functioned as part of a larger labor market. In fact, we can understand the demographic composition of slave populations exported from Africa only by understanding this larger market, both within Africa and to the Mediterranean. The trans-Saharan trade, supplying markets that preferred women and children, included roughly 1,425,000 slaves between 1600 and 1800. An important internal market for slaves in West and Central Africa meant that certain kinds of slaves, again especially women, were kept at home. Most fundamentally, when British slave traders sought to purchase primarily male slaves in Africa, African merchants sold women. Those who were transported across the Atlantic went to a variety of destinations – the British Atlantic absorbed roughly 27 percent of the total.[23]

For any single migrant stream in the transatlantic migration to British America, British holdings were only one of many possible destinations. What brought particular migrants to particular places is difficult to recover, yet there were clear dynamics at work. First, investors in colonial and commercial ventures sought men to populate them, and thus engaged in formal and informal recruitment, from publishing broadsides boasting the salubrious conditions of places as diverse as Virginia or Newfoundland, or searching out likely prospects in the cities that attracted vagrants. By the middle of the seventeenth century, as the population declined and able-bodied men could find options closer to home, recruitment became more formalized, embodied particularly in the efforts of proprietors to recruit European settlers from the continent, as was the case both for the founders of Pennsylvania and the Carolinas, and later for the Trustees of Georgia, who sought Highland Scots and Salzburgers to secure their turbulent borders. Regularized commercial networks and trade routes are also clear in the case of the Atlantic slave trade, with particular African regions feeding particular colonial destinations. Thus slaves bound for Jamaica sailed disproportionately from the Bight of Biafra, with other large contingents from the Gold Coast and the Bight of Benin.[24]

Informal networks played a role as well. People followed the routes of friends, kin, and neighbors. And religious and commercial networks were clearly important. The most common information available is the least recoverable – gossip and news from freshly arrived ships and sailors. Clearly, potential migrants were not totally uninformed, as the shift away from the Chesapeake in the 1660s suggests. But at the same time, it is clear that no one could be fully informed nor prepared to act on the logic of the information available. For the great majority of European migrants, bound to the charnel houses of the Chesapeake, the Lower South, or the Caribbean, migration was a disaster, especially in the seventeenth century during the peak period of European migration to the Caribbean. Life expectancy dropped, and the age of marriage rose. The typical migrant would likely live to lament his choice, as did Touchstone when he found himself in Arden and reflected, 'the more fool I. When I was at home I was in a better place, but travellers must be content.'[25]

While British migrants dominated European transatlantic migration as a whole, they were dwarfed by the presence of Africans. Table 2.1 delineates the scale of transatlantic migration for the whole period. The figures are conservative estimates, and particularly for

Table 2.1 *European and African migration to British America, 1600–1800* (000s)

	Mainland		Caribbean		Total	
	Europeans	Africans	Europeans	Africans	Europeans	Africans
1601–25	6.0		0.1		6.1	
1626–50	34.3	1.4	80.9	2.00	115.2	3.40
1651–75	69.8	0.9	64.6	53.30	134.4	54.20
1676–1700	67.0	9.8	32.9	182.40	99.9	192.20
1701–25	42.0	37.4	27.1	266.90	69.1	304.30
1726–50	108.8	96.8	28.7	342.10	137.5	438.90
1751–75	194.3	116.9	33.3	634.95	227.6	751.85
1776–1800	230.0	24.4	22.3	563.90	252.3	588.30
1600–1800	752.2	287.6	289.9	2045.55	1042.1	2333.15

Sources: Europeans: James Horn and Philip D. Morgan, 'Settlers and Slaves: European and African Migrations to Early Modern British America', Table 2, in Carole Shammas and Elizabeth Mancke, eds., *The Creation of the British Atlantic World* (Baltimore, forthcoming); Africans: David Eltis, 'Volume and Structure of the Transatlantic Slave Trade: A Reassessment', *WMQ*, 3rd ser., 58 (2001), 45, Table III.

some regions based on problematic sources. But these figures make it possible to compare the destinations and the chronology of different migrant streams.

Table 2.1 makes some important features of migration in the British Atlantic world emphatically clear. Transatlantic migration, for the population considered in its entirety, was centered around the dismal themes of enslavement, violence, and mortality. First of all, transatlantic migration was predominantly an African experience: African captives comprised 69 percent of the total migrants between 1600 and 1800. The African majority reminds us that transatlantic migration was largely experienced through force. The violence in the African case is obvious, not only in their capture in Africa and shipment across the Atlantic, but also in the violence that anchored slavery in America, embodied in grotesquely imaginative punishments inflicted by planters and overseers. And of European migrants, as many as 75 percent overall traveled as indentured servants, redemptioners, and convicts (of whom there were as many as 54,000). Although tales of kidnapping or 'spiriting' out of Britain were overstated, the treatment of servants in America was similarly shaped by violence. Thus migration was bolstered by force, and in turn it sustained the violent regimes which subjugated bound laborers, European and African alike.

The second important feature of transatlantic migration is the dominance of the Caribbean, the destination for 68 percent of all travelers across the Atlantic. Despite the clear centrality of the Caribbean compared to other colonial regions, the West Indies are poorly represented in the historiography, and the experiences of both European and African migrants to the region remain opaque. Indeed, even the numbers of European migrants are suggestive. One historian has estimated European migration to Jamaica alone between 1655 and 1780 as 500,000, a figure which is not improbable given the catastrophic mortality of the island for Europeans in particular.[26] Clearly much research remains to be done on the West Indies in general.

Further breakdown of these different migrant streams reveals important demographic features that shaped life for migrants in fundamental ways. For Europeans, transatlantic migration was an overwhelmingly male affair. For example, the percentage of migrants to the Caribbean who were men was staggering: 94 percent in 1635. Of indentured servants to British America more broadly over time, the percentages were still high: 75 percent for those from England between 1640 and 1699, and 90 percent for the years 1700–75. While we might expect indentured servant migrations to be predominantly male, it is still impossible to dismiss the centrality of these statistics. Indentured servants were the majority of European migrants, and those Europeans who did migrate in family groups were the anomaly. The sex ratio for enslaved Africans was slightly more even, and a significant percentage of African migrants were children, both features which distinguished this flow from European migration patterns: David Eltis's assertion that 'at least four-fifths of the females and over 90 percent of the children sailing to the Americas were not European' is arresting indeed.[27]

These demographic features had lingering repercussions in the Atlantic world, for both Europeans and Africans. Colonies peopled by unfree men had peculiar demographic regimes. Indentured men married late, after their terms of service concluded. More crucially for population growth, indentured women married late. Infant mortality in most regions (the Chesapeake, the Low Country, and the West Indies) was high for Africans and Europeans alike born in the New World. But far more fundamental were the disease environments and labor regimes that greeted the vast majority of travelers – the 2.3 million who went to the Caribbean, the hundreds of thousands bound for the Chesapeake and the Carolinas. There, life expectancies declined, highlighting an important commonality shared by all first-generation migrants, whether free or enslaved, whether

European or African. Moreover, migrant populations, slave or free, were unable to reproduce themselves in these regions, leading to the net decline of the population – and to the importance of continued migration to ensure a steady labor supply. If long-distance migration within Britain brought many young men to an early grave in cities, migration across the Atlantic (the voyage itself saw high mortality rates) made premature death even more likely.[28]

Persistent high rates of mortality shaped colonial societies. Any discussion about migration's impact on British America must include an appreciation of the constraints imposed by peculiar demographic regimes. The Atlantic destinations of the overwhelming majority of migrants were places characterized by high mortality, low fertility, male majorities, and stunted family formation throughout the colonial period. These features circumscribed the ability of newcomers to transfer Old World cultures. Migrant streams comprised in overwhelming numbers of young men who could not reproduce themselves could hardly be expected to reproduce their home cultures intact. The ethnic cultural expressions we might expect to find in the British Atlantic, then, should be deeply gendered – articulated in traditionally male habits of recreation, labor, or warfare. Thus, for example, we find young English migrants bowling in the streets in Jamestown in the face of starvation, or enslaved Africans in South Carolina drawing on the martial culture of Kongo in the Stono Rebellion.[29] The characteristics of migrating populations defined colonial societies in fundamental ways, and understanding the timing, character, and pace of transatlantic migration is crucial to assessing the evolution of the British Atlantic.

Internal and repeat migration, II: America and the West Indies

Once migrants reached colonial destinations – if they managed to survive – those able to exercise options demonstrated a willingness to move on again at least once. The centrality of migration within British America has been oddly obscured. Beginning in the 1960s, historians of Britain sketched the centrality of internal migration, the growth of the population, and the dynamics of long-distance migration. Historians of early America neglected two important lessons of this demographic literature: first, they failed to appreciate the consequences of the population upheaval of the late sixteenth and early seventeenth centuries for local regional cultures; second, they did not take to heart the centrality of migration within Britain.

So when historians of early America looked at colonial societies, they emphasized both the ways in which migrants transmitted small regional cultures in the New World and the geographic stability of the population, a trend particularly exacerbated by the tendency of colonial historians to focus on single geographic and political units (the town or the county). While historians of British parishes and towns used local records to identify mobility, historians of America used town and church records to privilege stability. Thus European voyagers to the New World registered not as *migrants*, but rather as *settlers*. Native Americans comprised in many respects the consummate migrants: as indigenous communities weathered the ravages of European contact, as tribes moved to escape European invasions or to take advantage of new trade opportunities, they formed and reformed communities composed of remnants of old bands. With some notable exceptions, however, North American Indians have rarely been conceptualized as migrants. This approach stands in contrast to the thrust of the historiography in Latin America, particularly for the Andes, in which indigenous people, especially laborers, have long been considered as migrants by historians of the region.[30] Yet it is obvious that migration characterized the experience of native North Americans as well, however much that experience has been overshadowed in the historiography by other consequences of contact, most particularly death by disease and violence.

For European migrants, the pattern of a second dispersal in America is clear. Virginia DeJohn Anderson has memorably referred to this process as the 'great reshuffling.' Indeed, a comparison of some first-generation places of settlement reveals rates of persistence and mobility that compare closely with those of London, reinforcing the unlikely but legitimate comparison of isolated colonial outposts and the great metropolis. The reshuffling occurred among all free migrant groups, including the English in New England and the Chesapeake and among the Germans in the Middle Colonies, although Aaron Fogleman argues that German-speaking migrants were 'stable ethnics,' willing to move once but then settling down permanently. The great arc of inland settlement in the late eighteenth century, as new arrivals spread out into frontier regions of North America, demonstrates this process clearly.[31]

Some regions, particularly those that enjoyed natural increase and those that attracted large numbers of migrants, were great exporters of people. Sometimes migrants brought other colonial cultures with them: a contingent of Barbados planters participated in the settlement of Carolina and transplanted the Barbados slave code; likewise, migrating South Carolina planters shaped the character of slavery in eighteenth-century Georgia. Elsewhere, circumstances might hinder the ability to transfer intact colonial cultures. In Nova Scotia, for example, the 7000–8000 New Englanders who migrated there between 1758 and 1762 found their efforts to implement their own inclusive style of local government thwarted by the government in Halifax.[32]

European migrants who traveled on cemented ties around the Atlantic, not just with Europe but also with new colonies. Migration did not necessarily separate but rather could thicken attachments in a new way, creating new vectors of familiarity and communication. The process of connection was clearly easier for the literate.[33] Thus slaves who were forced to move from a plantation in eastern Virginia west, across the Shenandoah river, could communicate with those left behind through the men who went back for supplies or through plantation managers. For Virginian slaves, James Sidbury has argued, these wrenching separations played a crucial role in the eighteenth century in creating an expansive African-American identity that transcended individual or neighboring plantations.[34]

Europeans were not the only active migrants in British America: Native Americans were launched into new patterns of migration by the European presence. For thousands of native people, migration was forced: Indians were enslaved in many colonies, particularly in the Carolinas, but also in the wake of various English–Indian wars, when defeated rivals were transformed into slaves. For the majority, migration was a considered response to the challenges of European invasions. In fact, migration was a fundamental strategy of Native Americans. It promised both passive and active resistance to new circumstances. The Catawba of southern North America, for example, were a people comprised of refugees from other tribes. Other tribes in the same region undertook longer and more complex migrations to evade English settlers: the Saponis of Virginia moved first within their region several times, joined the Catawba, returned to Virginia, and then ultimately made a longer migration north to join the Iroquois of northern New York, Canada, and the Great Lakes.[35] The Iroquois similarly lived among a region of refugee communities and absorbed supplicant tribes, while communities of Indians in the Ohio valley were composed of many who were two-time refugees from European expansion.[36] For many native tribes in British America, the proximity of rival European powers offered other forms of sanctuary to those who migrated across imperial borders, a strategy similarly employed by runaway slaves, most notably those of the southernmost British colonies in North America, who fled south to Spanish Florida where privileges were extended them.[37] Thus whether or not they have been regarded as migrants, migration was clearly a central, fundamental strategy Indians employed in their response to European invasions, and their migrations created new, conglomerate, polyglot communities.

The frequency of repeat migration for all inhabitants of the Atlantic world shaped the emergence of new cultures, in cities, in towns, and in colonies. It has been a central argument of this chapter that migration was an ordinary activity, embedded in a cultural context in the British Isles, similarly fundamental as a response to economic, political, or religious adversity in those parts of Europe which sent migrants to British America, and similarly pervasive within the West Indies and North America. And yet clearly the fact of such frequent and abundant migration altered the world in which people lived. For migrants to colonies, as for those to cities, the new overpowered the old in the emergence of new cultures. Indeed, for Europeans, Native Americans, and Africans alike, the creation of both new identities and new hybrid cultural expressions was simultaneous with the process of erosion and redefinition of old cultures, either those transported from Europe and Africa or those of Native American societies. Cultural knowledge was incomplete, its transmission muted and hindered by demographic anomalies. Rituals subsequently lost their meaning, as one settler in South Carolina reported of Indian traditions in 1710: 'they keep their Festivals and can tell but little of the reasons: their Old Men are dead.'[38] Adaptation to new circumstances became the order of the day, essential for the spiritual and physical survival of mill ons of displaced people living in unfamiliar circumstances throughout the Atlantic.

War, migration, and the imperial schism, 1754–1808: the British Atlantic world redefined

As this chapter has intimated, war and migration were intertwined in a variety of ways. Demographic expansion and commensurate economic strains in England and Scotland produced able-bodied men in abundance, who served not only in English colonial and commercial schemes but as soldiers and mercenaries in Europe. In Ireland, waves of rebellion against English rule and the punitive treatment of Irish Catholics generated thousands of soldiers for service in British and other armies. Wars, similarly, created migrants. Each conquest produced captives and refugees, European, African, and Indian, of whom the Acadians or the Highland Scots after 1745 are perhaps the best-known. Some wars, notably the English Civil War, even attracted those who had previously migrated, drawing exuberant puritans back to England and to Ireland to realize God's vision there. In the final half-century covered by this volume, however, migration and warfare took on a more complex relationship, with enduring political ramifications.

An important context was the increased rate of growth in the British population beginning roughly around 1760, growth which contributed to another explosion of interest in emigration that rivaled the busy decades of the 1630s and 1640s. Rates were so high in this period that troubled landowners in Britain, vexed to see their tenants abandon their holdings, lobbied Parliament for restrictions on emigration. Yet migrants poured into colonial territories, as many as 221,500 to North America alone from 1760 to 1775 (125,000 from the British Isles, 11,000 German speaking, 84,000 Africans), plus 668,000 people to the Caribbean between 1751 and 1775.[39] The pace of this migration had unexpected consequences: those colonies which received migrants at the highest rate were those least likely to join the revolutionary colonies. This pattern stands in contrast to the radical political activity of eighteenth-century cities, the other important sites of migration, in Britain or in the colonies. Such colonies include East and West Florida, new colonies composed entirely of migrants (especially since few Spanish colonists had elected to remain under British rule, but instead evacuated to Cuba), or Nova Scotia, who   those colonies most committed   New England colonies and Virginia – were least likely to welcome newcomers, but were characterized by intense internal migration and out-migration. Between 1773 and 1776, for example, 9.1 percent of British emigrants went to New England and Virginia. Colonies with more entrenched Loyalist populations received much higher percentages: New York (20.9), Pennsylvania (15.1), and Maryland (24.9). The Carolinas and Georgia accounted for only 16.2 percent of British migrants, but ensnared almost 69,000 Africans between 1751 and 1775.[41]

If there was a correlation between migration and revolutionary fervor, there was another correlation between the peace of 1783 and migration. The end of the American War of Independence, and the war itself, initiated new patterns of migration which altered the shape of North America after 1783, now officially British only in its northern and western portions. The exodus of the Loyalists, anywhere between 60,000 and 100,000 altogether, transformed Canada and the Bahamas. With as many as 15,000 Loyalists in New Brunswick, 40,000 in the Maritimes, 7000 in Quebec, and 6000 in the future Upper Canada, Canada acquired in one fell swoop an Anglo-American population that created new regions of British settlement and which with the postwar migration rivaled the larger French-speaking population of Lower Canada (although by 1800 francophones remained 60 percent of the population). The result was the enhanced viability of Canadian regions and the ultimate organization of the new provinces. Moreover, the Loyalists added new cultural complexity and, ultimately, hybridity, particularly in regions like the Maritimes, which had possessed a cultural homogeneity derived from earlier migrations from New England, but which acquired Loyalists disproportionately from the Middle Colonies.[42] The Bahamas attracted 1600 white Loyalists and their 5700 slaves, a number that had an enormous impact on the islands, changing the ratio of slave to free and bringing new islands under settlement.[43] This migration of the Loyalists was overshadowed by a much larger burst of transatlantic migration in the postwar years: between 1776 and 1800, 252,300 Europeans crossed the Atlantic for the new United States and British America.

Former slaves were a part of the exodus and upheaval of the war and postwar years. Estimates for the 'loss' of slaves in the American colonies are imprecise, but Allan Kulikoff has suggested that perhaps as much as 5 percent of all southern blacks became fugitives during the revolution. For the Lower South the statistics are even more compelling, with estimates that the slave population dropped in Georgia by two-thirds and in South Carolina by one-quarter, with a total possible loss of 35,000 for the two colonies.[44] Some former slaves settled in Canada, of whom some ultimately found their way to Sierra Leone, while others seized the upheaval of the revolution to make a permanent migration out of slavery.[45] Indian allies of the British also migrated to British territory. Even Indian allies of the American revolutionaries found migration an expedient response to new circumstances, as the Stockbridge Indians (already a composite tribe) demonstrated when they migrated from western Massachusetts to upstate New York to join the Oneidas in the 1780s.[46]

Migration became a feature so central to the new American republic that it was embedded in the US Constitution, which provided for the admission of new states. The land ordinances preceding the Constitution made the connection clear: 60,000 people was sufficient to become a state. Migration made states, and state policy supported migration. By 1820, 2 million people inhabited the new states. Slaveholders brought their human property with them. As many as 250,000 slaves were forced migrants to new territories, where they were joined by at least 100,000 Africans. European migration, on the other hand, was simultaneously characterized by a shift away from bound labor. The Constitution, together with the land ordinances, then, reiterated a commitment to the violence of forced migration by simultaneously encouraging migration and supporting slavery. Every movement west by white Americans, moreover, necessitated the forced migration of Native Americans.[47]

Finally, perhaps the most dramatic shift in the age of revolution was the cessation of the largest transatlantic migration, the slave trade. Here Britons and Americans agreed. In the United States, the decision to end the slave trade was codified in the new Constitution of 1789. In Britain, white and black abolitionists (the latter part of a vibrant migrant community in London) together joined to prod Parliament to end the trade in 1807. The consequence in the British Atlantic was a decline in the size of the slave population. Low birth rates and high rates of mortality had always retarded the natural increase of slaves in the sugar islands, and planters' schemes for amelioration were too hesitant to alter patterns of brutality and hardship embedded in two centuries of exploitation. In the United States, where the enslaved population was able to reproduce itself, the end of the legal slave trade produced new patterns of coerced migration: a large internal trade developed to transfer slaves to regions where labor was in highest demand.

* * *

Thus the British Atlantic of 1800 looked very different from that of 1500. Still characterized by migration, it had been transformed by this process. What remained of British America contained a small minority of British subjects: Canada had a francophone majority, while enslaved Africans and people of African descent vastly out-numbered creoles and Europeans in the West Indies. The most British parts of North America in terms of population – the 13 mainland colonies – had severed themselves from Britain to strike their own course. Thus British America, once a precocious model of

British settlement, in population more British than Britain, was demographically British no more, and only continued high rates of European migration to Canada would ensure that the region would in fact become British. The West Indies followed a different trajectory in the decades to come, replacing ex-slaves with migrant labor from Asia and India. In the British Isles, migration had transformed Ireland, had undermined the integrity of regional subcultures, and had created new urban areas that were themselves migrant societies with distinctive urban cultures. Demographic changes were often invisible and often poorly understood by contemporaries. Yet both incremental shifts in domestic populations and migration within the British Isles and the British Atlantic world shaped that world. If demography did not always dictate destiny, it altered the landscape as surely as any other source of historical change.

3

Economy

Nuala Zahedieh

In 1584, Richard Hakluyt the younger presented Queen Elizabeth with a program for England's westward expansion. Conquest, tribute, and the rich mines that had been prominent in the successful Iberian empires played little part in Hakluyt's vision. English settlers would harness American soils and climate to produce goods to satisfy all England's imported wants, at once relieving the country of surplus population and rendering it independent of foreign suppliers. Furthermore, the settlers would require a vast array of manufactured goods from the mother country, compensating for flagging demand in European markets and creating employment for England's idle poor. A sealed, self-contained commercial system would coordinate the getting and spending of producers and consumers throughout the Atlantic world and, through increases in trade and shipping, would raise England to unprecedented heights of wealth, health, and strength.[1] Hakluyt's scheme was too ambitious to be realized in simple and straightforward form. He did not capture the full complexity and compromise that marked the English Atlantic system as it developed in the seventeenth and eighteenth centuries, but his program did encapsulate the overarching and lasting ambitions of England's, and later Britain's, imperial expansion and did anticipate the main lines of development in the British Atlantic economy.

Around 300,000 Englishmen swarmed across the Atlantic in the seventeenth century, with more than half of them making for the Caribbean and the rest for North America.[2] Some were drawn by promise of spiritual gain. Most expected material betterment, seeking escape from the rising landlessness, unemployment, and

51

falling real wages which accompanied population growth and structural shifts in an increasingly commercialized English economy.[3]
Most of the migrants were single young men and their departure
helped to halt English population growth after 1650, easing the pressure on resources until well into the eighteenth century.[4]

The lands successfully colonized by the English did not possess rich
mines or organized, settled societies which would provide labor and
tribute. Nor, before the capture of Jamaica in 1655, did they acquire a
permanent base for securing a share of Spanish American wealth by
contraband trading or plunder, although both activities had drawn
Englishmen to the Indies since the early sixteenth century.[5] Fish and
furs offered early English settlers immediate financial rewards but these
extractive industries soon ran into diminishing returns. A prosperous
future rested on clearing land and cultivating cash crops that could be
sold in Europe at a price that would support high transport costs. A
handful of bulky commercial crops came to dominate individual
regions, securing investment in transport and distribution networks
that could be used by a range of other minor staples, including all 54 of
the commodities listed as possible by Hakluyt. These exports provided
Americans with the credits needed to purchase European goods and
create employment for those left at home.[6]

The successful staple trades, which grew fast at a time when most
branches of England's commerce with Europe were flagging, raised the
stakes in the English Atlantic empire and determined its institutional
structure.[7] Once the benefits of expansion were apparent the state
(which had played no direct role in promoting early settlement) moved
to reserve them for the mother country. The Commonwealth passed
the first Navigation Act in 1651, and the legislation was re-enacted and
refined at the Restoration in 1660. The acts aimed to reserve the valuable colonial trade for the citizens of the empire (who had provided the
men and money necessary for settlement) and exclude foreigners,
above all the Dutch, who had taken advantage of both England's dis-
tractions during the Civil War years, and their own strength in shipping and commerce, to obtain a strong foothold in England's infant
colonies. Charles Davenant summarized English aspirations:

> To make these colonies a lasting benefit to this nation ... the principal
> care will be to keep them dependent upon their mother country and not
> suffer those laws upon any account to be loosened whereby they are tied
> to it, for otherwise they will become more profitable to our neighbours
> than to us.[8]

By the act of 1660, all trade to and from the colonies was to be carried in English or colonial ships, and the captain, and at least three-quarters of the crew, were to be English or colonial men, encouraging the expansion of the empire's merchant marine which, at a time when England could afford only a small standing navy, was vital for national security. Scotland was treated as a foreign nation and, as the country recovered from the bitter conflicts of the mid-seventeenth century, Scots began to think of settling their own territories, with some success in New Jersey, and bitter disappointment in the Darién isthmus.[9]

In addition to confining trade to English carriers, the most valuable colonial commodities, almost all from the West Indies, were listed, and these 'enumerated' goods were required to be carried direct to an English or colonial port, even if intended for another final market. This provision was partly intended to facilitate taxation, a major income stream for the state, but a more important ambition was to promote England as a European entrepôt to rival Amsterdam, which had shown what prosperity such middle-man business could bring. The aim was highlighted by a clause which allowed English merchants to draw back almost all tax when goods were re-exported. Trade in the less valuable staples was not constrained in the same way as that of the enumerated products. Fish, which were perishable, and wheat, which competed with British cereals, could be carried direct to markets in Europe or foreign colonies. These unregulated trades provided gateways into other empires, providing cover for smugglers: ships from New England or the Middle Colonies were notorious for their regular carriage to Spain, or to foreign colonies, of sugar or tobacco hidden by a thin layer of fish or flour.

Another act of 1663 required that foreign goods (with strategic exceptions such as slaves, Madeira wine, and salt for the fisheries) were to be shipped to colonial markets via England. This further promoted England's role as entrepôt and raised the costs of foreign manufactures in colonial markets in favor of English products. The various acts were consolidated in 1696 and, although there were some adjustments to the list of enumerated products and minor improvements in the enforcement machinery, the only major changes in the legislation, until its repeal in 1849, were the inclusion of Scotland within the free trade area after the Union with England in 1707, and the exclusion of the 13 mainland colonies after the American Revolution.[10]

Needless to say there was evasion of the legislation, especially in its early years. The colonies were remote from the gaze of central government and subjected to lax enforcement machinery. In the Caribbean, nearby foreign islands provided convenient transhipment points for illicit commerce. Direct trade with Europe was a strong temptation, especially in periods of commercial difficulty, above all war. Illegal trade between the North American colonies and the foreign West Indies was highly lucrative and was always substantial. However, as the English became increasingly able (with the help of North American shipping resources) to provide convenient carriage at competitive rates, and as growing French competition in the European market for colonial staples made the highly protected British home market more attractive, there seems to have been more general compliance, as reflected in the growth of the English Atlantic fleet from around 70,000 tons in 1660 to over 500,000 tons in 1770, and a more than fivefold increase in the value of colonial trade between the end of the seventeenth century and the American Revolution.[11] Adherence to the legislation was certainly sufficiently strong to impose a shape and pattern on the lines of commerce and communication within Britain's Atlantic empire until 1849. Furthermore, it is clear that the impact of the acts, reinforced by the three Anglo-Dutch wars (in 1653–5, 1665–7, and 1672–4) that they helped provoke, was an important factor in the decline of Dutch commercial supremacy in Europe, and the rise of London as Europe's leading entrepôt to replace Amsterdam in the early eighteenth century.[12] By the accession of William III in 1689, the English perceived France as their main competitor in the Atlantic, and the rivalry between the two imperial systems, both with an eye on access to the rich pickings in Spanish America, was a repeated cause of expensive conflict in the eighteenth century. Between 1688 and 1815 tax revenues increased much more rapidly than the economy at large: by a factor of 18 in real terms besides a threefold increase in national income. The British ruling classes had no doubt of the importance of their Atlantic empire in providing national prosperity and, as Patrick O'Brien has demonstrated, were convinced that 'national success depended on the sustained use of force, backed up by a skilful deployment of diplomacy in order to make and retain economic gains at the expense of their major rivals.'[13]

A native American staple, tobacco, ensured the success of England's first permanent settlement in the New World. After some years of experimentation, the colonists in Virginia had established commercial production of the crop after 1612 and it remained British North America's most valuable commodity export until the end of the colonial period.[14] The 'vicious weed' did not conform to mercantilist ideals. Tobacco could as easily be grown in northern Europe as in America (although, for fiscal reasons, cultivation was outlawed in England in favor of colonial producers).[15] It had no valuable industrial applications and, although it was claimed to have medicinal benefits in certain circumstances, its consumption was neither essential nor desirable, being generally regarded as damaging to health and family well-being.[16] But the crop was easy to grow and required a small capital investment. The high prices prevailing in the early years ensured good returns and encouraged further migration to America, and a rapid extension of cultivation in the Chesapeake and other regions, although by the 1640s prices had fallen to levels where planters complained it was difficult to make a profit. Recorded imports into England reached 10 million pounds by the 1660s and 36 million by the 1680s. After 20 years of stagnation, which encouraged some rationalization in the industry, legal imports rose to 50 million pounds by the 1730s and 100 million pounds by 1770, with an increasing proportion being re-exported.[17]

The growing consumption of tobacco, a quintessential luxury, rested on a large reduction in price. Income distribution in early modern England was highly skewed. In 1688 Gregory King reckoned that 3 million out of a population of 5 million were 'reducing the wealth of the country'.[18] Few had much money to spend on anything other than necessities. In 1600 tobacco retailed at around 30 shillings per pound and use was largely confined to metropolitan gentlemen but, by the 1680s, as the price fell to 0.5 shillings per pound, and as tobacco could be consumed in tiny quantities, with a group of friends sharing a pipe, the addictive habit had spread out from London to the remotest corners of the realm. Taking tobacco had become 'a custom, the fashion, all the mode ... so that every plowman has his pipe.'[19] Retained legal imports were sufficient to allow annual per capita consumption of 2.21 pounds in the 1690s. After this peak there was a small decline but, in conditions of very high taxation on tobacco after 1685, there was also large-scale illegal import for home consumption.[20]

The falling price of tobacco is explained by improvements in both production and distribution. The costs and risks of planting fell, especially in the early experimental years when the secrets of the 'mystery' were acquired, the supply of white indentured servants (on which expansion depended) was more efficiently organized, and labor productivity improved.[21] Russell Menard has shown an impressive decline in freight charges, with the real cost of shipping one pound of tobacco from the Chesapeake to England reduced from 3 pence in the 1620s to less than a penny in 1770, with most of the savings captured in the seventeenth century.[22] The most important efficiency gains came from better packing which allowed more of the crop to be fitted into a standard-sized container. Small improvements in ship design increased stowage capacity and safety, reducing risk, as did more accurate charts and ships' instruments. Although piracy and privateering remained prevalent in the Atlantic, especially in wartime, colonial governors and the navy became increasingly successful in protecting British traders from depredations at sea, reducing defence costs.[23] With greater volumes of trade, and more experience, there were lower risks of underlading and reduced turn-around times in colonial ports. Harbor and warehousing facilities were improved in London (which dominated colonial trade in the seventeenth century) and the major west coast ports (Bristol, Liverpool, and Glasgow), which handled an increasing proportion of the trade in the eighteenth century, as the Thames became more congested. Better road, river, and canal networks reduced the costs of distributing tobacco throughout British and European markets.

Tobacco figured prominently in the first permanent English settlements in the Caribbean, established in the 1620s on the eastern side, where the wind system provided some protection from Spanish harassment. As the price of tobacco fell the colonists experimented with other crops, notably cotton, allowing them to accumulate capital and labor.[24] By the 1640s, circumstances combined to promote trials with sugar which was already well established in Brazil but which, combining agricultural and industrial operations, required considerable expertise and a large capital investment. War had disrupted Brazilian supplies and European prices soared. The Dutch were turned out of Brazil and their slave traders were looking for new customers. Barbadian planters took the opportunity to introduce sugar into their island and, although the first experiments produced very poor crops, the returns were spectacular. Even in the 1650s, when prices had fallen to lower levels, a planter was able to make a net return of £37 10s. per acre.[25] This was four times the return on high value industrial crops in England, such as rape seed or woad, and six times the return on wheat, the most remunerative grain crop.[26] By the 1680s it was reported that every acre of land in

Barbados was cleared and planted. Meanwhile, as the planters accumulated sufficient capital, sugar cultivation spread to the other
English islands in the Caribbean, and with the capture of Jamaica (in
the heart of the Spanish Indies) in 1655, the land available to the
English for cane production increased tenfold. The islands ceded by
the French at the end of the Seven Years War in 1763 provided a
further large extension of the sugar frontier.[27]

The high returns to labor in sugar cultivation stimulated massive
demand for hands. As population stabilized in England after 1650 and
real wages rose, the supply of white servants dwindled and the price
of their labor increased. Meanwhile, black slaves, sold for life, were
becoming more readily available as English traders became better
organized, with the establishment of an African company after the
Restoration, and settlement of forts and trading posts in Africa.[28]
Although the initial outlay remained two or three times as high as
that for a servant, when slaves survived the seasoning period the
investment was rapidly recouped.[29] In 1645 Downing reported to
Winthrop that the Barbadians had purchased 1000 slaves 'and the
more they buy the more they are able to buy, for in a year and a half
they will earn as much as they cost.' By 1700 Barbados had almost
70,000 slaves and black labor dominated sugar production.
Meanwhile, the white population fell, from around 30,000 in 1650
to around 15,000 in 1700, where it remained until the late
eighteenth century. White migrants continued to be attracted to
professional and managerial positions in the Caribbean but the white
population never mastered the disease environment to become self-
sustaining.[30] As sugar production extended in the British West Indies
and the slave labor force increased, the ratio between blacks and
whites rose, and it is estimated that in 1780 489,000 blacks lived
under the control of 48,000 whites.[31]

Unlike tobacco, sugar could be grown only in tropical climates,
and its production in English territory exactly fitted Hakluyt's ideal
of empire, the colony complementing, rather than competing with,
the mother country. Englishmen felt satisfaction as recorded colonial
exports of sugar rose from around 8000 tons in 1663 to 25,000 tons
in 1700, matching those of Portuguese Brazil. Around two-thirds
was retained for home consumption. Preferential tax rates ensured
that the bulk of the imports were semi-processed muscovado and
much was refined in Britain, stimulating the emergence of an
important new industry concentrated in London, Glasgow, Bristol,
and other ports. By 1770 the British Caribbean's recorded sugar

exports reached around 97,000 tons, of which 90 percent was retained in Britain, leaving the French, who became major producers in the eighteenth century, to supply the European market.[32] Between 1768 and 1772, Britain's sugar imports from the West Indies were worth over twice as much as total commodity imports from North America, and four times as much as tobacco which was North America's leading commodity. Sugar, 'the king of sweets', overtook linens to become Britain's most valuable import in the 1750s (see Table 3.1).

As with tobacco, increased consumption of sugar rested on a large price reduction reflecting improved efficiency in both production and distribution. The retail price of white sugar fell from 14 pence per pound in the 1640s to around 6 pence at the end of the century, where it stayed until the outbreak of the Seven Years War in 1756, after which it rose slightly. Sugar was, like tobacco, addictive and had the added advantage of multiple uses as medicine, preservative, spice, elaborate decorative material, sweetener, alcoholic beverage, and ingredient in a range of industrial processes. In the 1690s, Dalby Thomas remarked that sugar was most heavily used by 'the rich and opulent people of the nation' but it was becoming increasingly useful to 'all degrees of men'.[33] By 1700, retained imports of sugar allowed for annual per capita consumption of 4 pounds which, according to Gregory King's estimates, would have accounted for around 4 percent of the annual food budget.[34] By the 1770s, annual per capita consumption had more than doubled to around 10 pounds, a long way

Table 3.1 *Average annual value of commodity exports from British America, 1768–72* (£ sterling)

	Britain	%	All	%
Sugar	3,384,386	63	3,929,366	53
Other West Indian	597,161	11	690,106	9
Tobacco	756,128	14	756,128	10
Grain	26,387	–	628,851	9
Rice	198,590	4	305,533	4
Fish	6,730	–	286,087	4
Indigo	111,864	2	111,864	2
Whale products	52,626	1	77,840	1
Other North American	248,687	5	562,955	9
Total	5,382,559	100	7,348,730	100

Source: John J. McCusker and Russell R. Menard, *The Economy of British America, 1607–1789* (Chapel Hill, NC, 1985), pp. 108, 115, 130, 160, 174, 199.

short of the 120 pounds a head consumed in the 1970s, but none-theless a significant presence.[35]

Although sugar never accounted for more than a small part of the nation's food budget, it had strategic significance in that it helped to relieve pressure on domestic resources in important ways. Sugar promoted the consumption of inferior grains (such as oats and rice) to supplement wheat by making them palatable. Early modern Englishmen ate and drank grain. In 1700, the leading cereal crop was barley and most went to make beer. In the eighteenth century the barley acreage declined, output was fairly constant, as was beer production, and per capita beer consumption almost halved.[36] The increasing British population was substituting hot beverages, es-pecially tea sweetened with sugar, which required simple equipment, was easy to prepare, and provided a quick burst of energy. As Sidney Mintz has indicated, sugar made possible new forms of consumption ideally suited to an increasing pace of work, the rise of urban living, and a growing separation between home and workplace.[37]

The English settlers in the Carolinas, which were colonized in the 1660s, took some time to find a profitable export staple, but, after much experiment, rice production was placed on a firm footing by the 1690s and became North America's third most valu-able export crop, after tobacco and grain. In the 1740s, with official encouragement, indigo became important as a second staple when war interrupted French sales of the important dyestuff and high-lighted the value of an imperial supply. Georgia, settled in the 1730s, was planned as a colony for independent yeomen farmers, but by the 1750s it was clear that it would follow the Carolina model. As with sugar, the returns to labor in rice and indigo production were high and justified investment in slave labor. The organization of production, labor systems, unequal distribution of income, and limited diversification away from the staple in the Lower South resembled the Caribbean colonies more than any other North American region.[38]

The commercial success of the major export commodities pro-duced in the American South and the Caribbean stimulated the pro-vision of transport and distribution networks across the Atlantic which could be used to ship a wide range of minor, but important, staples: dyestuffs for England's infant textile finishing industries; raw cotton for the expanding Lancashire industry; ginger, pimento, and various drugs and spices. The substantial overplus of American prod-ucts not consumed in Britain was re-exported and used to pay for a

wide range of imported needs or desires, such as naval stores from
the Baltic or luxuries from the Levant.

The success of the plantation colonies also created a market for the
farming and fishing colonies in the north that failed to produce commodities that could be sold in any quantity in Britain. Fish remained
New England's most valuable commodity export throughout the
colonial period and, in the period between 1768 and 1772, around
60 percent of the supply was sent to the West Indies, as were large
quantities of the northern region's salt meat, and lumber used for
making barrels, buildings, and fuel.[39] Over half the grain exported
from the middle colonies in the period between 1768 and 1772 was
shipped to the West Indies, as were most of their wood, and livestock
products.[40] Although England's islands in the West Indies failed as
white settler colonies, they did assist in securing the prosperity of
those in the north, by providing them with opportunities to earn
export credits and enabling them to purchase manufactured goods in
Britain. The three-way division of labor within Britain's Atlantic
system was not entirely as Hakluyt had envisaged but, on the whole,
it was viewed as beneficial. The white farm colonies provisioned the
plantations, allowing the mother country to focus on manufacturing,
and Davenant reasoned that 'the southward and northward colonies
having such a mutual dependence upon each other, all circumstances
considered are almost equally important.'[41]

The northern colonies were also major providers of ships, shipping,
and other commercial services throughout the English Atlantic world.

Table 3.2 *Sources of imports to Britain, 1772–3*

	(£000s)	%
NW Europe (Flanders, France, Germany, Holland)	1220	9
The North (Baltic, East Country, Poland, Prussia, Russia)	1629	12
The South (Mediterranean, Canaries, Madeira)	1793	13
British Islands (Ireland, Isle of Man, Channel Islands)	1437	11
N America	1977	15
West Indies	3222	24
East Indies	2203	16
Africa	80	1
Fisheries (Greenland, Iceland, Northern and Southern Fisheries)	27	–
Total	13,595	101

Source: Adapted from a table entitled 'Geographical distribution of eighteenth-century foreign
trade', in Phyllis Deane and William A. Cole, *British Economic Growth, 1688–1959* (Cambridge,
1967), p. 87.

In the mid-eighteenth century half England's merchant fleet was American built, and, without the resources of the American frontier, Britain would have found it difficult to supply sufficient shipping at a reasonable price to comply with the demands of the Navigation Acts.[42]

A large proportion of export earnings in the south was used to purchase additional labor, especially in the West Indies where the black population, like the white, was not self-sustaining until the nineteenth century. With the help of their own protected colonial markets the English supplanted the Dutch as the leading slave traders in the Atlantic in the 1670s, and continued to dominate the trade until abolition in 1807.[43] In this period, around 3 million slaves were purchased with manufactured goods and carried in British ships from Africa to America where a large proportion were sold to other nations, above all the Spaniards, who never became involved in the trade themselves. After obtaining labor another large proportion of colonial export earnings was used to buy food, lumber, and horses from Ireland, and other colonies. Large quantities of wine were purchased from Madeira and the Canaries. Most of the remaining export income was used to buy manufactured goods from Europe, stimulating industrial employment as envisaged in Hakluyt's optimistic projections:

> And if it be high policy to maintain the poor people of this nation in work I dare affirme that if the poor people of England were five times as many as they be, yet all might be set on work in and by working linen, and such other things of merchandise as the trade into our Indies doth require.[44]

Extensive growth in America did, indeed, allow a growing population to be 'set to work', converting it from a burden, pressing on Britain's limited land resources, to an asset used to produce manufactured goods.[45]

The American market became increasingly important to Britain in the eighteenth century as colonial population grew almost sevenfold between 1700 and 1770, far outpacing anything experienced in Europe (see Table 3.3). Colonial export income, or buying power, seems to have kept pace with population growth, even outstripping it from the 1740s, when demand for American staples increased with an upturn in European population growth, and the terms of trade moved in favour of raw materials.[46] Whereas exports to Africa and British America accounted for around 15 to 20 percent of the English export total in 1700, they accounted for around 40 percent by the 1770s (see Table 3.4). Furthermore, there was a new diversity

Table 3.3   *Estimated population of Britain and British American colonies, 1650–1770* (000s)

	England	Scotland	West Indies	North America
1650	5228	n/a	59	108
1700	5058	n/a	148	265
1750	5772	1265	330	1206
1770	6448	n/a	479	2283

Source: England: Edward A. Wrigley and Roger S. Schofield, *The Population History of England, 1541–1871* (Cambridge, 1981), pp. 208–9; Scotland: B. R. Mitchell and Phyllis Deane, *Abstract of British Historical Statistics* (Cambridge, 1962), p. 5; America: McCusker and Menard, *The Economy of British America*, p. 54.

Table 3.4   *Exports from England, 1700–1 and 1750–1, and Britain, 1772–3* (£000s)

	North America	West Indies	All British America	Total
1700–1	256 (6%)	205 (5%)	461 (11%)	4461
1750–1	971 (11%)	449 (5%)	1420 (16%)	9125
1772–3	2649 (26%)	1226 (12%)	3875 (38%)	10,196

Source: Adapted from a table entitled 'Geographical distribution of eighteenth-century foreign trade', in Deane and Cole, *British Economic Growth, 1688–1959*, p. 87.

in the product range. In 1600, England exported wool and woollen cloth (much unfinished), and little else. By the late eighteenth century, British exports included a wide range of textiles and other miscellaneous manufactures, including metalwares, clothing accessories, earthenware, glass, paper, and furnishings. O'Brien and Engerman suggest that 95 percent of the addition to the volume of commodity exports in this period, when foreign trade was growing faster than national income, was sold on imperial markets.[47] Export markets were especially important to the cotton, woollen, and iron industries, which were the most dynamic and innovative sectors in the period. Adam Smith echoed others in remarking on the value of this 'new and inexhaustible market' in America in encouraging new efficiency in industry. Organizational improvements allowed producers to reap economies of scale and reduce the unit costs of manufacturing, before the great technological breakthroughs of the late eighteenth century, by increasing division of labor and specialization.[48] Furthermore, the growth of the larger export industries such as Lancashire cottons, Yorkshire woollens, and Birmingham metalwares generated external economies connected with specialization within regions which contributed to increases in national efficiency.

Despite the smaller total population (and very small white population) in the British West Indies, their demand for manufactures more
or less equalled that of British North America until the 1730s, and
continued to match it in many years until the 1770s. This was partly
because not all the Caribbean imports were consumed by British
colonists. The islands were gateways to the Spaniards' rich American
markets which had aroused covetous ambitions, and bitter rivalries,
among other Europeans since the first discoveries. The 'El Dorado',
as it was perceived, remained officially closed to foreign manufactures, with only occasional licenses to trade outside the monopoly
fleet system, such as that granted in 1713 to the South Sea Company
with the *Asiento* (contract to supply slaves) after the War of the
Spanish Succession.[49] But a well-organized contraband trade, valued
at £200,000 per year in a Board of Trade report of 1786, flourished
from the mid-seventeenth century, with official approval, if not sanc-
tion, for fear of offending Spanish mercantilist sentiments.[50] Slaves
and manufactured goods were shipped from strategic bases and the
rich returns were dominated by bullion, earning Jamaica, the most
important British entrepôt, its reputation as a 'silver mine'.[51] In 1683,
a visitor reported that there was 'more plenty of running cash [in
Jamaica] proportionately to the number of its inhabitants than is in
London,' and the island served as the main supplier of coin throughout the British colonies until the end of the colonial period.[52]

Apart from the entrepôt trade, which may have typically accounted
for around a quarter of the manufactures despatched to the British
Caribbean, the high levels of imports reflected the islands' own
affluence. The manufactured goods retained in the islands served to
supply slaves with simple clothing, plantations with tools and mill
machinery, and the whites with a level of comfort and display unthink-
able in other parts of the British Atlantic. Visitors remarked that whites
of all levels dressed, and ate, in a more extravagant style than their
equivalents in Britain. A Loyalist North American, Ann Storrow, who
had spent time in London and was living in Jamaica in the 1790s, was
astounded by the luxury she saw: 'indeed they dress here prodigiously,
the muslins exceed everything of the kind I ever saw for fineness and
variety ... everybody here wears handsome shoes ... all sandals or
painted leather. Silk stockings are almost as common as legs.'[53] As
already noted by Josiah Child a century earlier, 'In our West Indian
plantations ... one Englishman with the ten blacks that work for him
accounting what they eat, use and wear would make employment for
10 men in England ... whereas peradventure of 10 men that issue from

us in New England what we send to or receive from them does not employ one man in England.'[54]

Hakluyt, and later mercantilist writers, were anxious to promote a division of labor between mother country and colony, in which the former specialized in manufacturing and the latter produced raw materials. The looked-for dependence was greatest in the early years of settlement when all tools and other necessities needed to be imported. However, given America's abundant supplies of wood, iron, leather, and other raw materials which could, with simple skills, be turned into useful commodities, the dependence was not long-lasting.[55] Even in the plantation colonies in the West Indies, with the greatest incentive to concentrate on cash crop production, the settlers could build and repair boats, make fine furniture and silverware, tortoiseshell novelties, cotton hammocks, bricks, sugar pots, and a range of everyday essentials. Import substitution proceeded much more rapidly in the poorer and more populous mainland, especially in those regions with less valuable export commodities, and especially in wartime when British supplies were interrupted. In 1695 Sir Thomas Lawrence reported from Virginia, 'If store of shipping and clothing come in the people will mind nothing but planting tobacco; but if otherwise, necessity will enforce them to go upon manufactures and handicrafts, the want of which in the present war makes them go much upon cotton.'[56]

In the eighteenth century Americans became increasingly able to supply themselves with everyday needs, and the northern colonies also began to add simple manufactures to the cargoes of food and timber they shipped to the West Indies. British craftsmen complained about the unwelcome competition, but there was little that the authorities, divided from the colonies by a long ocean crossing, were able to do to help. Occasional legislative intervention, such as the Hat Act of 1732, which forbade inter-colonial trade in American manufactured hats, had little impact because the home government did not have the power to enforce such measures.[57]

American consumption of British goods was increasingly a consumption of 'mere conveniences' and 'superfluities', above all better quality textiles, fashion items, and novelties.[58] American consumers displayed some autonomy in taste and preferences, especially the more marginal groups. In the 1690s William Byrd, who traded with Native Americans, gave careful directions about the colors his customers preferred, and Caribbean plantation owners relayed information about slave preferences for brightly colored, gaudy handkerchiefs and ribbons.[59] But Europe remained the prime source of taste and fashion especially among those with aspirations to gentility. Mrs Brodbelt, a doctor's wife living in Jamaica in the 1790s, pleaded for regular information on fashion from her daughter in England, for although she claimed that she 'did not attend to [it] much myself' she admitted that ignorance of these British defined standards would make her 'appear ridiculous'.[60]

Early modern economic commentators had long made the connection between fashion, conspicuous consumption, and economic growth. Foreign trade was needed to support national extravagance but as American planters and merchants became increasingly interested in cutting the ties of empire after 1763 they condemned vain fashion and promoted the virtues of frugality and self-sufficiency. The non-importation movements of 1765–6, 1768–70, and 1774–6, in which British goods were boycotted, demonstrated America's capacity to support itself, and homespun cloth was worn by fine ladies as a badge of patriotism.[61] After the Revolution, Alexander Hamilton moved quickly to build protective barriers around American markets, drawing heavily on the mercantilist ideals that had shaped the British Atlantic world from the early years of settlement.

Within the walls of the national monopoly provided by the Navigation Acts there was staunch resistance to any sort of regulation or exclusive privileges in British Atlantic trade. The reasons were both practical and ideological. British colonial projects were initiated by individuals, partnerships, or joint stock companies who obtained charters and privileges from the crown. The success of the ventures depended on large numbers of individuals being transplanted to the New World and undertaking the labour of clearing and planting land. Absentee landowners seldom flourished and colonial proprietors were no exception. Long distance made it difficult to impose the close, careful supervision that was imperative for success, and land abundance made it impossible to restrain individual enterprise. Settlers soon obtained proprietary rights, even when they were not granted in the initial stages of colonization, and England's Atlantic world was peopled with hundreds of independent producers, all able to sell to competing merchants and ships' captains. The system was not amenable to regulation and restricted entry.

Apart from the practical difficulties inherent in enforcing distant monopolies and charter privileges, they were distributed by the king, and groups prominent in early colonization were also active in opposition to the crown and disputed the legitimacy of this royal bounty.[62] By the Restoration, the exceptional success of colonial (and other unregulated) trades appeared to demonstrate the superiority of 'free trade' and was used to argue in favour of limiting crown, and other, encroachments on commerce. So-called 'free trade' was elevated to an article of faith. 'Trade is by its nature free, finds its own channels, and best directeth its own course,' exclaimed Davenant, 'and all laws to give it rules and direction ... may serve the ends of private men but are seldom advantageous to our public.'[63] Charles II did grant monopolies of the slave and fur trades but they were strongly attacked, and widely abused, from the start and were largely abandoned in the 1690s, after the Glorious Revolution put government on a new footing.

The resistance to regulation and monopoly presented colonial traders with novel challenges. Long-distance trade had not only high transport costs but very high information and monitoring costs. Overseas traders had usually resorted to regulation and company organization to reduce risks by restricting entry, inflating prices, and in essence passing the costs of inadequate market information and cheating on to the consumer. As colonial trade was open to all citizens of the empire, entry costs were low and, especially in the early years, large numbers took part. As Price and Clemens have shown for the Chesapeake trade, all colonial commerce became heavily concentrated by 1700, but a long chain of small participants limited the scope for price fixing and other restrictive practices.[64] As intense competition prevailed, profit margins were squeezed and participants tried to reduce risks in various important ways.

Success in colonial trade depended above all on developing effective trust networks able to provide reasonably fast and accurate information about business conditions, coordinate multiple far-flung transactions, and secure good behaviour from distant, difficult-to-monitor agents.[65] Kin networks were important tools, especially in the early stages of empire, but they often proved disappointing. The pool of talented family members was usually small and the capacity to check or punish delinquency was often limited: even disinheritance counted little to many younger sons who received nothing from their parents beyond their education and apprenticeship premium. Religious networks were more robust. Groups such as the Quakers and Jews had extensive, well-organized communication links throughout the Atlantic world (even beyond imperial boundaries), disseminating up-to-date and accurate information about business conditions and individual reputations. They provided members with strong support in times of need and could obtain good behavior, largely because the threat of exclusion as punishment for delinquency really counted in a community which provided the entire economic and social framework of members' lives.[66] The advantages held by such groups were reflected in their conspicuous success in colonial commerce, and other associations, such as freemasonry and various business and social clubs, developed networks emulating their tools for ensuring trust and mutual cooperation. The importance in Atlantic trade of well-established networks of trustworthy agents raised the costs of casual, opportunistic trade, which was inevitably the nature of many illicit operations, and, no doubt, played an important role in obtaining adherence to the Navigation Acts. The skill in managing business risk through the creation, and maintenance, of effective trust networks was also an important element in the emergence of London as the financial centre of Europe, and this lead in commercial services (including banking, insurance, shipping, and commodity brokerage) was retained far longer than Britain's celebrated lead in manufacturing, secured in the late eighteenth century and lost by the end of the nineteenth.[67]

In the seventeenth and eighteenth centuries the British set about constructing a maritime Atlantic empire which, within the framework of the Navigation Acts, served them well and substantially realized the clear-cut aims presented by Hakluyt in the late Elizabethan age dubbed by Williamson as 'narrow and needy'. Surplus population was transplanted out of a 'tight place' to new lands in America and set to work producing valuable cash commodities.[68] The colonies provided Britain with substitutes for a wide range of imports and an overplus for sale in European markets. As American production increased and real prices fell, luxuries such as sugar and tobacco became available to all, fundamentally changing British consumption patterns in ways which helped to stretch limited resources. The colonies also provided a growing market for British manufactured goods, encouraging product diversification and improved organization in industry to reduce unit costs. Markets for manufactures were available not only in the rich, staple-producing southern regions. In Africa, manufactures were exchanged for slaves. In the poorer north, which also lacked an agricultural staple for sale in Britain, export credits were earned through provisioning the southern plantations and the Iberian peninsula, as well as by providing ships and shipping services. Middlemen throughout the British Atlantic world accumulated capital and the commercial skills necessary to coordinate an

increasingly complex, multilateral system without the traditional protection of monopolies or corporate privileges.

The role of trade and empire in stimulating Britain's industrial
revolution has long been contested.[69] All numbers claiming to show
that 'the periphery was peripheral' to Britain are too small.[70] They
measure the scale of trade without capturing the extent of its
influence and its long-term contribution to the increasing commercialization of the British economy from the early seventeenth
century. Most British historians would agree that overseas trade and
empire should not be 'inflated into one basic process that continuously fuelled the transformation into an industrial market
economy.'[71] Nonetheless, it is acknowledged that overseas trade grew
more rapidly than the British economy as a whole in the eighteenth
century; that the growth was almost entirely concentrated in the
long-distance and, above all, the American sector; and that the most
innovative industries were those dependent on American markets.
Few would argue that the resources employed in manufacture for
export markets (above all labor) could have been put to equally productive use in the domestic economy.[72] Needless to say, not all the
effects of the increasing importance of Atlantic trade were benign.
Above all, defence of imperial interests involved Britain in repeated
wars and major expense of men and money. But it is clear that
empire shaped the economic priorities, institutional framework,
accumulation of capital, and acquisition of knowledge, skills, and
capabilities in important and lasting ways, not only in Britain but in
all regions of its Atlantic empire.

4

Religion

Carla Gardina Pestana

European religion, especially Christianity, invaded the Atlantic world and was dramatically transformed in the process. England's forays were intended to bring Protestant Christianity to the natives and to counter Spanish Catholicism's missionary campaign. English rulers assumed that their subjects in the New World would adhere to the Church of England, transplanting the hierarchy, ritual, and loyal worship that they also sought to inculcate in their kingdoms. Religion would, it was assumed, accompany expansion, tie the natives to the colonizers, and cement loyalty to the crown. All of these expectations were disappointed. Native Americans largely rejected the prospects of Christian conversion. Efforts to coerce conformity in the colonies failed miserably, as did policies intended to command conformity in England and Wales, Scotland and Ireland. Diversity became a fact of life in Britain and its dominions. Beyond these thwarted expectations, unforeseen changes occurred. Christianity in the wider Atlantic world was profoundly influenced by the settler societies' interaction with the African diaspora. Slaves, imported as laborers, their spiritual needs ignored, became Christians fairly late in the history of the British Atlantic world, but when they did so they remade their new faith. The social and political conservatism that religion was supposed to bring also proved illusory: radicals seized upon it repeatedly to criticize the status quo and to encourage popular revolt. In the end, the religious milieu of the British Atlantic was quite unrecognizable to early proponents of colonization. The transfer of institutions from the Old World, the impact of the Atlantic experience on religion, and the relationship of religion and politics all illustrate that the history of religion in the British Atlantic was a story of unintended consequences and unexpected outcomes.

Transfer of institutions

A lasting British presence in the wider Atlantic basin began after 1603, by which time the Protestant Reformation had reconfigured the religious landscape of England, Wales, Scotland, and Ireland. After tortuous decades of religious upheaval England and Wales were firmly within the Protestant camp. Following the widely held assumption that religious uniformity was essential to political stability, the English and Welsh state supported the episcopal Church of England as the legally mandated faith. Scotland took its own path to a Protestant establishment, and its state church was Presbyterian. These two state churches had been yoked together when James VI of Scotland became James I of England, but the working out of a relationship between the two had not been resolved. The English completed the conquest of Ireland in the early seventeenth century and imposed a Protestant state church upon it. Strangely, that church differed yet again from the established faiths in the other kingdoms. Within each of these Protestant establishments, divisions existed. In addition, Ireland's population remained largely Catholic, and Catholics lived as persecuted minorities in the other Stuart kingdoms. Officially, however, all the polities ruled by James I and Charles I were Protestant.[1] As their subjects entered the wider Atlantic world, the early Stuart kings expected that a Protestant state church patterned upon the Church of England would go with them.

Yet the divisions within the religion of the three kingdoms boded ill for the realization of such expectations and indeed for continued peace within those kingdoms themselves. Once James VI of Scotland assumed the throne of England as James I, he ruled three kingdoms, each with its own religious establishment. Charles I's effort to bring all these churches into conformity helped to spark the wars and rebellions that culminated in his own death in 1649. The range of religious options available in the three kingdoms, from Catholicism through Anglicanism and Presbyterianism to more radical Protestantism, was recreated in the wider Atlantic world. The first migrants into the English Atlantic were typically drawn from these groups. Within the colonies, however, these options recombined to create new forms that were unknown in the metropolitan

culture. So Massachusetts Bay produced a radical Protestant establishment in which Presbyterians and Anglicans were defined as dissenters and the presence of Catholics was actively discouraged.
Other permutations prevailed in other locations, and nowhere was
religious homogeneity achieved.

A fundamental assumption guiding the colonization of the Atlantic
was that the king's dominions would recreate metropolitan institutions, including the Church of England. As a result many colonies
had, either from the outset or eventually, an official Anglican establishment. Such was the case in all the Caribbean island colonies, in
New York, New Jersey, and all the colonies south of Pennsylvania as
well as those north of New England. In these circumstances, settlers
supported the building and maintenance of churches financially and
paid the salaries of clergymen to staff them. In theory all colonists
supported the established church, regardless of their personal religious
proclivities, and non-Anglican worship or failure to attend the neigh-
borhood parish church could be punished. In fact, laws mandating
attendance and proscribing other churches were occasionally honored
only in the breach. Colonies – like some parts of Britain – often had
difficulty staffing their pulpits at all, and the men hired were occasionally less orthodox than the authorities desired. Colonists founded
colleges to facilitate the training of ministers locally, beginning with
Harvard in 1636, but the Church of England did not have its own
college until William and Mary was founded (1693). Even then,
prospective ministers had to travel to England for ordination since no
colonial bishop existed to perform this rite.

In order to transfer the Church of England intact to the New
World, extensive resources had to be invested. This necessity guided
the Spanish export of Catholicism from the first, but the Church of
England only gradually learned this lesson. The church did not
succeed in transplanting the entire Anglican hierarchy to the
colonies until bishops were appointed for Nova Scotia in 1787 and
Quebec in 1793. Colonists throughout the colonies, including many
Anglicans, often opposed efforts to appoint a bishop. The church
hierarchy only came to other parts of North America after colonial
Anglicanism had foundered on the rocks of revolution. In 1784,
when Samuel Seabury, Jr was ordained as the first American episcopal bishop, the church was well on its way to being re-made as the
Protestant Episcopal Church of the United States. Transferring the
Church of England *in toto* onto the American strand took nearly two
centuries, and the effort came too late for many erstwhile Anglicans.

In the interim, the church adopted a new approach to non-Anglican subjects of the crown, whether in Europe or elsewhere. No longer able to coerce conformity even in England by the late seventeenth century – a coercion that had not proven especially successful in any event – the clergy took up the challenge of educating and converting the unchurched and those who belonged to other churches. The aim, in Britain and Ireland as well as in the Americas, was to reach out to the European population. By the eighteenth century the church, working through the Society for the Propagation of the Gospel in Foreign Parts (SPG), committed resources to expand its influence. The first sustained effort to evangelize in the British Atlantic was aimed at the settler rather than the native or African population. The SPG's most famous preacher, George Whitefield, made almost no effort to bring those whom he reached with his message into the Anglican fold, but rather endorsed attendance at their own churches.[2] As a tool for expanding the influence of the Church of England, the SPG enjoyed only modest success.

A state-mandated religious establishment that enforced conformity among colonists was most successful in seventeenth-century New England. But, oddly enough, the state church in Massachusetts and Connecticut was Congregationalist, a dissenting faith in England. In these colonies, Anglicans were treated as dissenters, eventually tolerated but always viewed with suspicion. When James II reorganized the northern mainland region into the Dominion of New England and gave the Church of England state endorsement, many New Englanders identified this move as one of the injustices that necessitated James's overthrow in 1689. Religious (and, in New York, related ethnic) divisions shaped the response to the Glorious Revolution in the colonies, but only in Massachusetts did ministers take a prominent role in responding to the crisis.[3] As the New England example amply illustrated, the English or British state was not the sole or even the most effective agency for the creation of a functional state church system in the New World.

Colonial organizers also expected to unseat Catholicism by their own expansion into the Atlantic, a goal that was realized only in the most limited way. The initial impulse for English expansion was Protestant and had a decidedly anti-Catholic edge. While England was embracing Protestantism, Spain and Portugal between them gained control of the most lucrative and populous sections of South and Central America and introduced Catholicism through a well-supported conversion campaign. According to its English critics,

Spain not only spread false religion, it also used the wealth it extracted to support Catholic interests in Europe. Patriotic Englishmen thus supported colonization as part of a campaign to eliminate Catholicism from the Americas and to capture the great wealth available there in support of godly religion. This agenda came to the fore in the Elizabethan period and again during the interregnum of the mid-seventeenth century. The link between Protestantism and an anti-Catholic foreign policy continued as part of the British sense of identity and of its role in the world at least through the eighteenth century.[4] The British never succeeded in unseating Catholic Spain (beyond the conquest of the relatively inconsequential – to the Spanish at least – colony of Jamaica), but their presence may have somewhat limited additional expansion.

The religious practice of the British Atlantic was remarkably diverse. One source of this complex religious environment was the diversity that reigned in and among the Stuarts' three kingdoms. Another source was migration from other locations into the colonies. The Dutch (often either members of the Dutch Reformed Church or Sephardic Jews who had taken refuge in the Netherlands) were a presence in many colonies, particularly New York, which they had originally founded. After the Portuguese recaptured Brazil in 1654, they forced out Jews, who established enclaves in a number of English colonies. As the debate over the readmission of the Jews to England raged, Jews quietly took up residence in numerous colonies.[5] Later in the seventeenth century, Huguenots banished from France migrated, their Protestantism not the problem in the British Atlantic that it had been in their homeland. Eighteenth-century immigration from German-speaking areas of central Europe introduced pietistic and mystical sects, particularly to Pennsylvania and the adjoining colonies.[6] With the exception of the Jews these groups felt welcomed in British colonies because the governments permitted Protestant worship. The potential availability of land for settlers and the general acceptance of all varieties of Protestants made the British Atlantic, and especially North America, attractive. Only Montserrat, settled by Irish Protestant gentry and Irish Catholic laboring people, had a Catholic majority in the seventeenth century, a sort of Ireland writ small. Elsewhere Irish Catholics were a minority, often a tiny minority, and they tended, especially in the West Indies, to be treated with suspicion for their supposed sympathy for the Spanish. European migration enhanced the diversity of both Britain itself after 1690 and the British Atlantic more generally. The

resulting religious mix was unlike anything in either Britain or
Europe, bringing together most of the faiths that prevailed in northern Europe but placing them in closer proximity than in the Old
World. It was a Protestant conglomeration – with almost all the
variants of Protestantism available in Europe represented – as
opposed to offering a monolithic face to the world.

Impact of the Atlantic experience

The Atlantic experience reshaped religion in various ways. The relative dearth of institutional forms tended to favor those faiths that
functioned well in an institutionally simplified environment.
Missionary activity became a central component of the religious
landscape, as proselytizers traveled to spread their faiths and thereby
created religious networks knitting disparate communities together.
Despite much discussion of the need to Christianize the Indians,
British missionary activities among the native peoples of the
Americas was modest and largely unsuccessful. The encounter with
Indian and African alternative belief systems, however, had a pro-
found impact on the religious culture of the European invaders. In
all these areas – religious simplification, missionary activity, and the
encounter with others of African and American origins – the
Atlantic experience transformed religion.

Managing with partial or simplified religious forms was fundamental to the experience of religion in the Atlantic from the first.
Whenever a religion was carried out into the wider Atlantic world,
it initially experienced a process of simplification. The accoutrements associated with religious faith and worship in Europe –
from church architecture to church courts, from church furnishings
to religious art – were unavailable in the colonies, especially at
first. Anglicanism as practiced in Virginia in 1630 shared fundamental features with the English or Welsh version, but the
Virginians did without an uplifting worship space, a variety of
devotional publications and sometimes even a minister. They relied
heavily on the Book of Common Prayer, which had the virtue of
being portable. A layman might read from the prayer book in the
absence of a minister, and instances of this sort of compensating
can be found in many places. Anglicans everywhere cherished the
prayer book, as the reaction to the ban placed upon it in the 1650s
indicated, but colonists were unusual in the extent of their reliance
upon it.[7]

In the face of such institutional poverty, however, believers maintained their religious traditions as best they could. Virtually every person who plied the Atlantic until the later eighteenth century carried religious beliefs and practices that were rooted in family tradition and local community. Anglicans literally took the Book of Common Prayer to Virginia and the Somers Islands; Catholics carried their rosaries to Maryland where their presence on a 1654 battlefield was cited by their opponents to malign the 'popery' of those who cherished such trinkets; and people of many confessional camps carried their Bibles.[8] Faiths that were highly portable adapted best to such circumstances. Congregationalism, the details of which were worked out in early New England, had the advantage of being localized, with powers that would be vested in a church hierarchy in many other Protestant churches instead residing in the congregation. The same could be said of the Quaker faith: the Society of Friends flourished in the New World, especially after the founding of Penn's colony, in part because Quakers relied on decentralized institutional arrangements. The rural Welsh and other isolated households in Britain responded well to John Wesley's creation of Methodist cells that met in private homes, separate from any church. The Shakers' success in the late eighteenth century and beyond arose in part from the way in which Shaker villages functioned as semi-autonomous units, able to carve out their own niche on the American landscape. Such faiths were highly adaptable to the New World environment, in ways that were not true for more centralized and hierarchical religious organizations. Believers in other traditions – including the Muslims among the enslaved population and the scattered Catholics – had to manage with a highly simplified, even attenuated version of their faiths, living without Qur'anic schools or priests to say mass and hear confessions.[9]

Spirituality could flourish even where institutional forms were poorly developed, and this fact was central to the experience of faith in many locations during these centuries. For the individual German pietist, Anglican parishioner, puritan reformer, Quaker colonizer or Methodist cell member (and even more so for the native American or African faithful), personal belief and communal practice mattered more than church architecture or other accoutrements of worship. This 'making do' and relying on personal faith in the absence of institutional supports could be found in many parts of Britain itself. In rural Wales, for instance, isolation promoted household religious practices, often led by women, over the formal observances that took place in a church.[10] A statement reported by Roger Williams in

1652 could have been made with equal conviction in the eighteenth century: 'an eminent Person lately spake (upon occasion of a Debate touching the Conversion of the Indians) [that] we have Indians at home, Indians in Cornewall, Indians in Wales, Indians in Ireland.'[11] The dearth of institutions in colonial environments should be placed on a continuum with the situation in various locations in Britain and Ireland: the differences were often in degree rather than in kind.

Colonists and colonial officials in the metropole worked to enhance the institutional base of religion in the colonies. All colonial era colleges, with the exception of the unaffiliated school in Pennsylvania, had links to a specific church, usually the Church of England, and worked to educate prospective ministers for those pulpits. By the late eighteenth century most mainland colonies boasted such a college. This development reduced reliance on European centers of education. This trend was given a boost during the revivals of the 1730s and after, with the Presbyterian seminaries in New Jersey and the adjoining colonies offering the classic example. Church building increased dramatically in the eighteenth century, providing worship space that had been lacking in an earlier era. Jon Butler described the result as the 'newly sacralized American wilderness.'[12] The diversity of the urban landscape was documented in its skyline, which included the churches of various faith traditions. Wealthy colonists donated communion silver and other church art. Print culture developed in many Atlantic urban centers, and what was produced on the local printing presses met, among other things, community needs for religious news and spiritual edification. The simplified conditions that had initially prevailed in the wider Atlantic world were gradually overcome by the maturation of institutions, although the process was both uneven and slow.

In this fluid religious environment, missionary work increased diversity and transatlantic connections among co-religionists. With only one or two exceptions, missionary efforts were designed to fortify an already extant faith. The Church of England proselytized after about 1690. In the 1760s and 1770s, Baptists, previously a minority with few adherents, began a major evangelical campaign in the southern mainland colonies that eventually bore considerable fruit. The efforts of these missionaries might add to the diversity within a particular locale. For example, Anglican efforts led to the development of an identifiably Church of England faction in Scotland in the eighteenth century. An upsurge in Anglicanism in New England in the same period was most dramatically expressed when a group of Yale tutors and the institution's president left the 'orthodox' congregationalist fold to join the Anglican communion in 1706. However, the most important force making for increased diversity was the attempt of a new faith which set out to win converts. The Quakers, who traveled widely throughout England, Wales, Scotland, Ireland, and all the colonies in the middle decades of the seventeenth century, were the most startling early example. In the eighteenth century Moravians and Methodists were similarly active in all parts of the British world. Moravians made converts among the slaves of Jamaica from the 1750s, while their encounter with John Wesley in Georgia sparked his conversion and led to the founding of the Methodist movement.[13] When representatives of these new faiths succeeded in securing conversions, they increased the varieties of Protestantism available in the Atlantic basin.

The connection among co-religionists that missionaries forged through their travels from place to place within the Atlantic world shaped an expansive sense of religious community. Residents of the British Atlantic lived in locales that were fractured religiously. At the same time that they confronted diversity locally, however, they felt connected to like-minded individuals in far distant places. Whenever an isolated religious community wrote for assistance, whether from Congregationalists in New England or Lutherans in Halle, they acted on this sense of commonality. Missionaries who visited various faith communities and reported what they saw in their travels encouraged this feeling of connection. In this regard the religious revivals of the 1740s tied together believers in North America, Britain, and the Caribbean. Although from Charles Chauncy's study in Boston the revivals appeared divisive, tearing apart the once stable religious community in New England, from an Atlantic perspective the revivals created a sense of community that bound proponents together. Missionary work usually cut both ways, increasing local diversity while also building unity among converts and between enclaves of coverts scattered around the Atlantic basin.[14]

Over time, printed materials played a larger role in fostering these links. Originally a sense of attachment resulted largely from the movement of peoples, either migrants with ties to those left behind or missionaries with links to communities visited and, in some cases, created by their own movement through the Atlantic world. The rising importance of print worked in tandem with traveling missionaries. George Whitefield's serially published journal of his preaching tours or the writings of Quaker 'Public Friends' functioned in this way.

Religious periodicals, beginning with the revivalist organ the *Christian History*, also linked the faithful and provided a sense of shared purpose.[15] Both missionaries and written materials circulated through the Atlantic world in much the way that trade goods did, and they tended to traverse the same pathways, as their movements of necessity followed the shipping routes outlined by Nuala Zahediah in her essay in this volume. This is not to say that commerce was a driving force behind religion, although one scholar has recently made this suggestion.[16] It was significant if not determinative that a Presbyterian in Scotland could read of revival among her co-religionists in Virginia, or a Quaker in Barbados could listen to a description of Ireland from a newly arrived traveling Friend. The medium of print had been important from the first in the dissemination of Protestantism. Elizabethan reformers realized the centrality of vernacular Bibles and other religious works in spreading the new faith to Wales and England in the sixteenth century. That they initially neglected to do the same for Ireland was one more reason why the efforts to convert the Irish to Protestantism made little headway. During the eighteenth century the print medium helped to create an Atlantic community of Protestants.

Although they profoundly shaped the Atlantic world, missionaries fell short of the one expectation that early colonial promoters had for them: they did not undertake a massive campaign to convert the native peoples to Christianity. English expansion from the Elizabethan period on assumed English dominance would spread true religion. The complete conquest of Ireland, concluded just as King James took the English throne (1603), was motivated in part out of the desire to extirpate Catholicism from a neighboring island with ties to Catholic Spain. Conquest, it was assumed, would lead to Protestant conversion of the natives or to their displacement in favor of Protestant settlers. The same assumptions guided the colonization in the wider Atlantic world. At the outset, colonial promoters and royal charters that authorized colonization declared the commitment to Christianize the natives. According to these sources, extending Protestantism was the primary goal of colonization. The Massachusetts Bay seal famously depicted a Native American saying 'Come Over and Help Us.'[17] This fantasy of the heathen eager to be instructed by the Christian invader survived among those who remained at home long after encounters with flesh-and-blood Americans disabused colonists of the idea. Continued impetus for Christianization of the natives came from Britain, where involvement in the wider Atlantic world continued to be equated with advancing true religion.

Ministers who might participate in Christianization faced a number of hurdles, not the least being organizational. Without an overarching religious organization to pay for missionary work, clergymen had to fit catechizing local Indians into their other pastoral duties. Since their salaries came from their congregation or parish, they had a full slate of duties without taking up a missionary project. Theology, too, played a role. Protestant ministers generally expected a fairly sophisticated level of understanding from new converts. They dismissed the far more successful missionary efforts of Catholics in Spanish America and New France, because these conversions were often not accompanied by a complete re-education effort. Protestants scoffed at Catholics who 'sprinkled' natives and considered them Christians. They were also horrified to see the Catholic, especially Jesuit, willingness to reinterpret Native American beliefs in the context of Christianity. Instead of co-opting native religion, Protestants aimed to obliterate and replace it. Despite such attitudes, a few natives resided within colonial communities unobtrusively adhering to their traditional faiths or combining these creatively with the new religion introduced by the Europeans. When colonists thought about native conversion, however, they raised the bar so high that they thwarted missionary impulses.[18]

The only sustained, state-supported effort to convert Native Americans in the British Atlantic demonstrated the problems that arose from Indians' lack of interest as well as the exaggerated expectations and hostility of settler society. By the mid-1640s English settlement had displaced the surviving native population of much of southern New England, and some who remained indicated a willingness to receive Christian instruction. New England minister John Eliot took up the missionary project, combining his duties as pastor to the English church at Roxbury with his efforts to convert Indians. He oversaw the creation of a series of Indian-only villages, organized along English lines in terms of land distribution, household composition, and agricultural practices. He viewed making the Indians English as the first step to making them Christians. The so-called 'Praying Indian Villages' also kept native converts and prospective converts away from colonists, who were hostile or, Eliot thought, set bad examples. Eliot's efforts received financial support and encouragement from English backers. In 1649 Parliament created the Corporation for the Propagation of the Gospel in New England, which raised funds to finance Eliot's missionary campaign. A series of pamphlets published under the auspices of the corporation created public support and preserved invaluable accounts of the missions. In keeping with the Protestant emphasis on vernacular Bibles, Eliot undertook to publish the scriptures and other religious works in Algonquin. The missions were never popular in New England itself. Animosity reached a crescendo in King Philip's War (1675–6), and the missionary program was dealt a crippling blow when the villages were dispersed and most of the inhabitants died.[19] The missions started by Eliot, limited though they were, marked the high point of official efforts to Christianize the natives. Later efforts lacked state support – or those that had it, such as an early Georgia plan, came to naught[20] – and they usually involved missionaries who went to reside in Indian villages, away from the hostile gaze of settler society.

Beyond the failure of Indians to convert in large numbers, the encounter with Native America was unsettling to the colonizers on a number of other counts. From the moment the Americas were discovered their very existence challenged European thinking in various ways, including the veracity of biblical history on the origins of humanity.[21] The religion of the natives existed for European settlers as the ultimate 'other'. A few commentators wondered if North Americans even had a religion, but most recognized that they did have a belief system that governed their relationship to the supernatural. Confronted with a radically different cosmology, Europeans sometimes concluded that Native Americans worshiped the devil. Surprisingly, given this understanding of their spirituality, Native Americans were not usually charged with witchcraft, as some hapless settlers were. Accused Salem witch Tituba offered an exception. Residing as a slave with a prominent settler family, Tituba's close association with white society combined with her strangeness made her vulnerable. The encounter with native spirituality sparked fears among the settlers, despite their supposed confidence about their ability to convert 'the saddest spectacle of degeneracy upon earth, The poore Indian people.'[22] The presence of native religion helped Europeans to appreciate their own commonalities, and in this way the presence of natives as 'other' may have contributed toward toleration within the European settler community.

Colonists were surprised that Native Americans held to their own beliefs and appalled when any of their own number seemed to prefer to become 'heathens'. Colonial leaders and many settlers brought to their initial encounters the conviction that their religion and their God would easily emerge as the victor in any contest with native spirituality. This assurance led them to believe that conversion, or at least a native desire for conversion, would be easily achieved. Because native spirituality was flexible in allowing the incorporation of new concepts and novel spiritual beings, Indians could adapt some of the new religion brought by Christians without rejecting their own traditions. Even natives who converted to Christianity – and they were few over these two centuries – typically maintained aspects of their traditions and worldview. In a shocking turn, some colonists found native life appealing, abandoning their Christian communities altogether to live among Native Americans. These former Christians who crossed into native life were viewed as traitors to English culture and Christianity, and their choice appeared inexplicable to many chauvinistic Christians.[23] The encounter with native spirituality did not unfold at all as colonial promoters had anticipated.

The same could be said of the encounter with African spirituality, although the dynamic between it and Christianity unfolded differently. From our perspective a dramatic source of diversity in the British Atlantic was one that the colonists tended not to perceive: the presence of African beliefs. Huge numbers of Africans were imported into British America between 1607 and 1800, more than twice the number of Europeans. Africans far outnumbered European migrants, as Alison Games's essay in this volume documents, but their comparatively high death rate reduced the effect of that fact on New World demographics. Still, Africans were a majority in some colonies and a sizeable minority in many others. A few were Muslim, but the vast majority were adherents of West African faiths that combined a supreme deity with lesser gods or spirits. Until the late eighteenth century, little sustained effort was made to Christianize these slaves, and enslaved Africans were left to their own devices. Their slave status rendered it difficult for them to recreate the world of African spirituality that they had lost. The limited prospects for remigration to find their fellow countrymen and -women hampered Africans' abilities to recreate their religious communities fully in British America. Moreover, the renewal of African religion was hampered by the linguistic and cultural differences that often separated newly arrived slaves from one another. Still, enough evidence of African belief and practices survives (though difficult to document) to demonstrate the continuation of different worldviews and the rituals that accompanied them.[24]

Of all the unforeseen consequences of the invasion of the Americas, the transformation of Christianity through its encounter with African religion was the most exceptional. Because African religion in the British Atlantic endured a violent uprooting, the European residents of the British Atlantic confronted it out of its original context, removed from the community of believers that sustained faith and participated in shared ritual. The individual Africans they met had been torn from their communities and redefined as commodities and laborers in the Atlantic economy. Under these circumstances it was easy for them to avoid seeing indications of imported belief systems. Slave owners might identify Muslims among their bound labor force, especially if their command of a written language seemed to pose a security threat, but other religious rituals and concepts often went unremarked. For many decades slave masters ignored the spiritual state of their slaves, as Christopher Brown shows in his essay in this volume. They refused the few requests for permission to proselytize among them, initially on the grounds that Christian conversion might necessitate a slave's liberation. Later they worried that Christianity would make slaves restive and give them a rationale for their emancipation. Although there is no evidence that a converted slave was liberated when he was no longer a 'heathen', the slave owners' fears of the radical potential of Christianity were amply borne out in later years.

In the later eighteenth century, once missionaries received permission to preach to slaves – usually by promising to convey a message of Christian meekness and the need to await one's reward in heaven – slaves and free blacks took the Christian faith of their oppressors and reshaped it. African–American converts demonstrated clear preferences for some versions of Christianity over others, helping to catapult particular churches into prominence within the British Atlantic world. The Baptists and later the Methodists converted many more slaves and freed blacks than did Anglicans or Presbyterians. In the new United States and in the Anglo-Caribbean, the former pair of churches eventually claimed more adherents than the latter pair, at a time when Episcopal and Presbyterian churches continued to hold sway in the metropolitan centers of British culture. Confronted with prejudice within the churches that reached out to convert them, African Americans eventually founded the separate African Methodist Episcopal Church (1816). The style of southern and Caribbean Christianity that emerged in the late eighteenth and early nineteenth centuries owed much to African influence.[25] The religion of the new United States as well as that of the British Caribbean was suffused with African spirituality. In an ironic twist the enslaved reshaped the religious culture of the dominant society.

Religion and politics

Religion in the British Atlantic intersected with politics at numerous points. The diversity within Britain and in the Atlantic community sparked efforts to coerce conformity as well as the potential for toleration and even liberty of conscience. Anti-Catholicism, central to the original conception of the English of their role in the Atlantic world, proved a contested political issue up to 1800 and beyond. Political radicalism might have religious causes or consequences, as was the case for various resistance movements and for the American and French revolutions. In all these areas, the hopes of conservatives that religion would provide political stability proved illusory more often than not.

The religious fragmentation in the British Atlantic both led to and was fostered by a commitment to toleration that grew unevenly over time and across space. The early Stuarts did not see diversity as a positive good or even as a necessary evil, and they believed that the religious differences within and among their kingdoms were a problem. The uprisings and civil wars of the mid-seventeenth century that resulted eventually in the execution of Charles I were sparked in part by the religious tensions within the three kingdoms and by Charles's efforts to coerce conformity to the Church of England in both England and Scotland. Over the course of the century, monarchs were forced to relinquish the goal of conformity to the state church, and with the arrival of William and Mary on the throne in 1688, toleration of Protestant dissent became the settled policy.[26] This toleration within a generally Protestant framework attracted European Protestants to Britain and its colonies at a time when Protestantism was in retreat on the continent.

British imperial policy eventually abandoned the Protestant agenda that had given meaning to early expansion, as military successes forced the rethinking of the relationship of Protestant identity to membership in the empire. Hostility toward Catholicism in the seventeenth century threatened the small province of Maryland, with its Catholic proprietor and leadership. Maryland's government was subjected to a series of Protestant coups and, in the aftermath of 1688, was wrested from Catholic hands altogether. On the rare occasion that the English or later the British captured a colony away from a Catholic power, policy makers had to decide what to do with the resident population. In the seventeenth century they banished Catholic settlers. When they drove the Spanish from Jamaica, they self-consciously emulated the treatment meted out to English colonists on Providence Island in 1641.[27] Catholic colonists, clearly inimical to the imperial agenda, were sent away despite the demand for labor in the Atlantic basin. In the eighteenth century, however, British imperial policy was reversed, as policy makers chose to retain settlers despite their confessional identity. When the British conquered Quebec, the authorities permitted Catholic settlers to stay. The British Atlantic, born with an agenda of chauvinistic anti-popery, ended the period incorporating additional Catholic subjects. When the Catholic Relief Act in Britain (1778) granted improved conditions for Catholics there, riots, especially by Lord George Gordon's Protestant Association, demonstrated the continued hostility to Catholics.[28] Some colonists similarly objected to this change in policy. Suspicion of popery continued to motivate some members of the British Atlantic community, just as it had the first English adventurers in the Americas. With the success of the American Revolution, the British empire became proportionately more Catholic, as it lost a substantial proportion of the king's Protestant subjects when 13 colonies left to create the United States.

In spite of the continued force of anti-Catholicism, the colonies tended to be ahead of the metropolis on the issue of religious liberty. State mechanisms for coercing conformity were always weaker on the periphery than at the center, with the exception of 'puritan' New England in the seventeenth century. It was no coincidence that the most vehement anti-Catholicism in late eighteenth-century North America was centered in that very region, since opposition to popery and the impulse to create a godly orthodox society had once been so intimately connected. Generally, though, colonial societies tended to be more diverse religiously than the metropolis, so that the compulsion to accommodate alternative faiths was felt strongly in these areas. Some colonies, like Maryland (1634), Rhode Island (1636), and Pennsylvania (1682), allowed liberty of conscience from the start. Maryland could not institute a Catholic establishment in violation of the laws (and popular prejudices) of England, and liberty for all Christians offered a means to attract settlers to a sparsely settled province. Rhode Island was a sort of squatter colony, founded on Indian lands without authorization from England, by people with a variety of (Protestant) religious views, most of whom had wrangled with the intolerant Massachusetts Bay Colony. William Penn's colony was governed in accordance with Quaker principles of non-violence, which included strictures against the coercion of conscience. Other colonies, though they had Anglican religious establishments, offered toleration if not liberty of conscience earlier than did England itself. Such was the case with the Carolina colony from its inception, and many of the West Indian colonies appear not to have enforced conformity from an early period.

The religious environment on the North American mainland – its diversity within and between colonies and the tradition in some locations of either toleration or even religious liberty – helped to bring about the separation of church and state that would be enshrined in the first amendment to the United States Constitution. Although colonists lived with diversity and toleration, few people theorized these developments. Some radicals, like Roger Williams of Rhode Island, explicitly argued in favor of religious liberty. Others fought for their own freedom without asserting a general right to liberty of conscience. As a result the push toward the policy that granted religious liberty to all in the new United States arose more from the religious environment and the impossibility of coercing conformity than it did from a generalized commitment to rights. By the time of the founding of the United States, many political leaders, including Thomas Jefferson, believed that religion represented a public good because it shaped morals and guided behavior, but that the specific faith was of little consequence. Men like Jefferson could join together with determined advocates of specific faith traditions, like the Virginia Baptists, to fight for religious liberty. The Baptists hoped that they would be able to use the new freedom to increase adherence to their own faith.[29] In any event, virtually all revolutionary Americans were agreed about the impossibility of selecting a specific church to be elevated to national established church status – the religious landscape was too variegated for that. The most likely candidate because it had once had establishment status in many colonies was the Anglican Church, but its association with the British monarchy in the aftermath of the revolution discredited it. The socio-religious environment and the political context thus pointed the way to the separation of church and state in the United States.

Many leaders in the British Atlantic in these centuries, among them slave masters, expected religion to serve as a bulwark against radicalism, but as often as not they were disappointed. The radical potential of religion was repeatedly demonstrated in the wider Atlantic world. The 'Great Migration' of the 1630s disgorged numerous radical critics of Stuart government and its religious settlement into the colonies, where many of them pursued religious alternatives or returned to fight against their king in the 1640s. The radical nature of the 'New England way' is often forgotten because of that region's stability and its association with intolerance, but it represented a decentralized and controversial alternative to the Church of England.[30] Opposition to the government in Scotland after 1688 had a religious component, as did Irish opposition throughout these centuries. Quaker refusal to perform military service and their challenges to the dominant faith and social hierarchy created problems for the authorities everywhere from the 1650s. Baptists in eighteenth-century Virginia were similarly associated with a radical critique of the prevailing social order.[31] Handsome Lake, a Native American prophet of the late eighteenth century, combined traditional and Christian elements to create a revitalization movement among the Iroquois that would become the focal point of resistance to settler encroachments. In 1800 Virginia slave Gabriel Prosser organized a rebellion drawing upon both the political radicalism of the French Revolution and the Christianity of the slave quarters.[32] Religion could be turned to radical purposes as easily as to conservative ones, a fact that the authorities worried about in 1800 just as they had in 1600.

The politics of religion in the British Atlantic world alone cannot explain the coming of the American Revolution, however. J. C. D. Clark famously called that conflict the 'last war of religion,' but religious divisions did not account for the fissures in late colonial society.[33] People of every denomination supported both the royal and the patriot causes, and religious sympathies did not lead inexorably to any particular political position. Anglicans, who owed allegiance to the king both as their monarch and as the head of their church, nonetheless failed to unite in support of the king's cause. Only a disproportionate number of Anglican clerics became Loyalists. Individuals who adhered to a minority faith worried that the local majority would prove intolerant should the revolution succeed in severing ties with Britain, and these people found loyalty to the crown appealing too. But such loyalties arose from calculations about the local political context, and members of a specific denomination might favor loyalism within one colony but patriotism in another. The convergence of religious and political positions was stronger in Britain, where dissenters and deists overwhelmingly supported the revolutionaries' cause. Although religion did not dictate political affiliation in the colonies that were becoming states, popular opinion assumed that it might do so. Patriots, for instance, viewed some religious groups with suspicion. They harassed Ann Lee and her tiny following of Shakers, worried that the newly arrived group might operate as a fifth column for the British army. The pacifism of the Quakers made them seem British sympathizers, and they too were subjected to harassment, especially in Pennsylvania. Methodists, although counseled by Wesley to remain out of politics, were suspected of supporting the crown in part because of Wesley's own political writings.[34] Religion's role was less direct than Clark argued and patriots occasionally feared. It may have encouraged revolution- aries to question authority based on their private convictions about what was right, and the language of millennialism proved highly effective in stirring up revolutionary zeal.[35] However, although re- ligion played a part in the revolutionary struggle, that conflict cannot be understood primarily in terms of it.

As with the American Revolution, the French Revolution was more important for its religious consequences than for its religious causes. British radicals found inspiration in France, which seemed to demonstrate that the old order was being swept away to make room for a better future. Some support was religious in nature, often expressed in millennial terms.[36] Other supporters were more secular in their concerns, such as enlightenment advocate Jefferson. As it brought down monarchy and the state church in France, the revolu- tion raised concerns among conservatives. Deism and outright atheism were on the rise in the 1790s, and this fueled a backlash. Thomas Paine, popular author of the American pamphlet *Common Sense* (1776), became a pariah in some circles after he published his deist *Age of Reason* (1794). Conservatives throughout the British Atlantic community (in both the British empire and the United States) shared fears of rational religion and atheism. Those who believed that religion itself was threatened might become more tol- erant of alternative faiths. The backlash against the French Revolution's excesses even opened the way for Protestants to find common ground with Catholics against the shared foe of atheism.

Conclusions

Taking the long view, both religion and the early modern Atlantic were reshaped by their interactions. The British intrusion into the wider Atlantic world created a major Protestant presence, but that Protestantism was multivalent and decentralized. The British trans- ferred neither the established Church of England nor even some recognizably British form of Protestantism into the Americas.

Rather a wide swath of northern European Protestantism (with a few Jews and a few more Catholics added to the mix) were thrown together in a New World environment where liberty of conscience was more easily achieved than religious conformity. In the United States and in other parts of the British Atlantic world by 1800, it was possible to speak of multiple denominations and even alternative religions coexisting in relative peace, a situation that would have seemed impossible to the first colonizers two centuries before. That religion had been reshaped by its encounter with Africa as well as by confronting European diversity was harder for contemporaries to perceive.

The Atlantic too was transformed by its encounter with the religious milieu that grew up under English and later British control. In 1500, the three major monotheistic religions of Judaism, Christianity, and Islam were centered on the Mediterranean basin and reached only as far west as the Atlantic coasts of Europe and northern Africa. The remainder of the lands touching upon the Atlantic basin, including North and South America as well as most of Africa, held to the non-monotheistic faiths common to most of the world at the time. By 1800 Mediterranean monotheism, especially in its Christian form, dominated the western coast of the Atlantic from Canada to Tierra del Fuego and was making additional inroads into Africa. The traditional beliefs of the Native Americans, although displaced and suppressed in the region under European control, had not been obliterated. But the uncontested dominance of the western shores of the Atlantic by these faiths was a thing of the past. Christianity had spread its dominion widely, but it had been altered by its experience in the Atlantic world.

In surveying this history, we can appreciate the peculiarity of religion in the British Atlantic. Founding an empire out of the three kingdoms of the Stuarts had inherent difficulties, since England and Wales, Ireland and Scotland lacked religious unity from the outset. As the first post-Reformation empire, Britain's Atlantic empire was, almost of necessity, fragmented religiously. Toleration arose less from a forward-looking willingness to embrace 'progress' and more out of despair at achieving a longed-for unity. Religious liberty was similarly the result of lack of better options. The British Atlantic world (distinct from the British empire) fostered a vibrant religious culture. A sense of religious community bound together believers in Britain, Ireland, North America, and the Caribbean. These bonds transcended those of the empire, lasting well beyond the sundering of the political unity of the British Atlantic in 1776. The contest with

Catholicism formed one abiding component of that broader culture, though the urgency of and meaning accorded to that contest changed with time. Encounters with Native America and Africa that occurred in the context of the invasion of the wider Atlantic world had unexpected results. British Christians failed to convert Indians, but they found their own faith transformed by the encounter with African spirituality. To borrow a phrase of Jim Merrell's, it was in this sense a new, and indeed an unanticipated, world for them all.[37]

Part III
Identities

The great dangers for Afro-Americans
was that when the power occured
for them, it was inside the
Spanish vorbes. They thous
aught adament & Affilatur with th
U.S. rather than valevidrer

5

Civility and Authority

Michael J. Braddick

This is essentially the case for Afro-American System then.

The movement of goods and people around the British Atlantic world created a shared material culture which reflected common assumptions about status distinctions. These assumptions about social difference were fundamental to the legitimation of political authority, which was exercised not just between center and locality but between local elites and their social inferiors. In that sense, then, the development of this shared language of social distinction provided the cultural basis for the exercise of political authority. By the eighteenth century these forces had fostered a marked convergence of elite sensibilities across all the territories of the nascent British empire. However, by that point disintegrative forces were also at work, in particular the potentially divisive effects of increased imperial regulation and control of colonial life. It is also clear that the local societies over which elites presided were, by that time, extremely diverse and that local variations on the common culture of the British Atlantic elite were becoming quite marked. In some colonies this combination of factors led to a re-evaluation of local identities in the light of political circumstances and the declaration of a new, independent, political identity. This chapter seeks to outline these processes and in so doing to demonstrate the potential for a social and cultural history of political authority, explored in an Atlantic context.

Local elites and political authority

The power of the state in the early modern period rested on the cooperation of local elites, and that cooperation was secured through the establishment of commonalities of interest. In sixteenth- and seventeenth-century England this partnership was so successful that initiatives in the use of state power often originated in the localities rather than at the center. When they laid claim to this political power, local elites had to negotiate their authority, and their claim to that authority often rested on claims about their social and moral qualities. Submission to political authority entailed acknowledgement of the claim to these credentials.[1]

This was because political and social order in early modern England was conceived of as an organic whole. Political authority flowed from, and reinforced, social position. Social order was described by contemporaries in terms of social roles – particular social positions (landlord, father, wife, laborer) were defined in standardized ways and the behavioral expectations attaching to each of the stations in life were explained. Social order was understood as an 'interaction order' based explicitly on difference and inequality.[2] Order lay in a harmonious interaction of dissimilar elements: for much of this period contemporaries saw inequality as an intrinsic and necessary feature of social order rather than an undesirable outcome of social and economic life.

Political roles were embedded in these wider expectations about social order. For example, officeholders in sixteenth- and seventeenth-century England were frequently described as 'fathers of their country', ruling it in the best interests of their inferiors. This political patriarchalism set limits on how officeholders could be seen to behave: domestic disorder, or the suspicion of it, was disabling for local governors. Accusations that they lacked the necessary personal qualities for rule robbed them of 'natural' authority – the fact that it was supposedly natural authority meant that the conflation of the personal and the official was inevitable. In part this was a reflection of the assumption that only the rich could be sufficiently educated and disinterested to govern. According to Sir Thomas Smith,

> whosoever studieth the lawes of the realme, who studieth in the universities, who professeth liberall sciences, and to be short who can live idly and without manuall labour, and will bear the port, charge and countenance of a gentleman, he shall be called master, for that is the title which men give to esquires and other gentelmen, and shall be taken for a gentleman.

Such people could bear rule, unlike their inferiors, 'the fourth sort of men which doe not rule': 'these have no voice nor authorities in our commonwealth and no account is made of these but onlie to be ruled, not to rule other.'[3]

There was a local elite.

Early modern government was not just a matter of negotiation between center and locality, therefore, but also of the projection of the 'natural' authority of local elites, and this latter dimension of political power has to be understood in cultural terms. In the sixteenth and early seventeenth centuries, for example, gentility was a necessary prerequisite for those seeking to rule and was understood partly in terms of the performance of a more generalized social role. In contemporary advice literature these social roles were distinguished by particular sets of expectations about demeanor and conduct: social order was described in behavioral terms. For example, the fifth earl of Hastings advised his son on a variety of public concerns which would be important to him as a local dignitary. These included details of manner and comportment at table, in the hunt, and towards his neighbors, superiors, and inferiors. It also included advice on his choice of wife and how to treat her. In short, his father outlined a full range of behavior consonant with a particular social role. Manner, comportment, and gesture were crucial here.[4] Public performance – the presentation of the self – was equally important to the legitimation of the rule of their successors, the patricians of eighteenth-century social life.

Political authority was projected and sustained in terms of a language of rule which included the material expression of social distinction: to rule one had to be able to live appropriately, 'to bear the port, charge and countenance of a gentleman.' Of course, such claims to legitimacy were not always, or even usually, made explicitly. Political authority constituted a part of an interaction order, sustained by appropriate demeanor and gesture or disrupted by inappropriate conduct – the dignity of age, or the relationships of the gender order were reflected in, and to a degree constituted by, the actions of individuals in each other's presence.[5] Gesture and material culture served as signifiers of position in these interaction orders. So important was this dimension of political order that in the sixteenth and seventeenth centuries governments across Europe (including those in Britain and the American colonies) passed sumptuary legislation, setting down in law who could wear what. In other words, they sought to regulate forms of dress and consumption precisely in order to maintain clarity about the social and political significance of particular material objects.[6] Needless to say, this was a losing battle, abandoned in England by the seventeenth century, but the aspiration is very revealing of contemporary ideals.

Although not susceptible to governmental control, issues of social distinction were of practical significance in the exercise of political power. Such assumptions lay behind Richard Pickford's question to taxpayers in Cornwall in the 1590s: 'did you not stand in doubt to pay any moneys unto the said John Bonnifant being a man of so small means and credit, and ... have you heretofore known at any time any of so mean estate amongst you to have been appointed collector of [parliamentary taxation]?' His aim was to rob Bonnifant of authority because he was not of 'competent estate and livelihood.'[7] During the 1630s a reluctant ship money contributor complained about the fitness of the sheriff in these terms: 'he is the rarest Justice of peace and shirieff, for his domesticall attendance, that hath bynne known in Shropshire for these many yeeres.'[8] Clearly he was not bearing the office of a gentleman and could not, therefore, claim the authority that went along with that position.

By the later seventeenth century Englishmen were more likely to acknowledge publicly that virtue might also be found among those of humbler rank. Richard Gough, writing a history of his Shropshire village in 1700, lamented the fact that William Watkins had never held a higher office than that of under-sheriff. The pity was that, despite being a husbandman and therefore working for a living, Watkins had many of the attributes that fitted him for higher office. These were that he was well-educated and 'fit', 'a cheerful, merry gentleman' who 'kept a plentiful table for his own family, and strangers.' Significantly he was also commended for his good husbandry – he was evidently an agricultural improver on a small scale.[9] By the time Gough wrote, gentility was becoming an imprecise term, or at least was losing the technical precision that Smith had given it. For Smith it would have been oxymoronic to describe a husbandman as 'merry gentleman' but by 1700 the word had acquired the more general meaning it still retains. That Gough recognized Watkins's virtues is a sign of decreasing emphasis on gentry status as a guide to virtue; that Watkins never held high office perhaps bears testimony to the continuing force of the link between gentility and political authority.

Throughout this period virtue was demonstrated in refinement, comportment, dress, and manner. In the early years of the eighteenth century ideals of politeness gained wide currency, contrasting the restrained virtues of the middling sort with aristocratic excess and plebeian lack of refinement. What remained the same, however, was that widely recognized signifiers of social distinction continued to serve as the often unarticulated legitimation for political power. Although there were modulations in the description of social distinction, such distinctions remained central to the exercise of political authority.

By the same token, and throughout this period, to deny public gestures of respect was in effect to deny a claim to authority. For example, Quakers were notorious for refusing to remove their hats in the presence of 'superiors'. This has to be understood as a symbolic repudiation of this larger interaction order – the basis of authority recognized by the Quakers was quite different from the authority projected by patriarchal justices. In fact this was a gesture of defiance not limited to the Quakers. In 1630 an oatmeal maker appeared before the High Commission

> where, keeping on his hat and being asked, why did he not put it off? He answered, he would never put off his hat to bishops.
> 'But you will to Privy Councillors?', said one of them. 'Then as you are Privy Councillors,' quoth he 'I put off my hat; but as ye are *rags of the Beast*, lo! – I put it on again.'[10]

The later seventeenth-century cleric Edmund Hickeringill made a similar gesture, refusing to remove his hat in the Court of Doctors' Commons until the jurisdiction of the court was proved to him. He later explained that 'it was not pride, insolence, nor any design to affront them, that made him then to be covered, but a sense of his duty.' Indeed he had challenged his prosecutors to see 'if they could argue his Hat off his head.'[11]

These gestures of respect, or the refusal to make them, could be calculated with precision. Clearly, distinctions could be drawn between respecting the office or the person, or particular offices. Thus, Henry Bellasis expressed his lack of respect for Thomas Wentworth, President of the Council of the North during the 1630s, as Wentworth left a meeting of the council with the mace bearer ahead of him and every head in the room uncovered. Bellasis 'stood with his Hat on his head, looking full upon his Lordship without stirring his said Hat, or using any other Reverence or Civility to the said Lord President.' So gross was the affront that Bellasis was called before the Privy Council and imprisoned for a month. At the end of the month he was willing to make a submission acknowledging his fault 'But he hoped the Submission was understood to have relation to the Place, and not the Person of the Lord President.'[12] These small gestures were worth reporting to the Privy Council, or going to prison for: they were part of the reality of political power. Recognition of the signifiers of political power was crucial to its maintenance.

When it worked, the representation of power 'naturalized' it – obedience and submission were unquestioning, or at least there were no respectable means of denying submission. In practice, the presentation of authority and responses to it revolved around the contested construction of standardized social roles that could be recognized as legitimate forms of political power. Appeal to those values was made in standardized ways – strangers could be recognized to be magistrates or constables because they reproduced these standardized roles. These appeals offered both a means to resist the exercise of power as well as a means to justify it.

Social roles and the creation of functional space

Political innovation had implications for the construction of these social roles. Extending the functional capacity of the state, or its territory, entailed a process of legitimation which was, in part, a cultural issue. At the same time, the dissemination of new ideas about social distinction, or the nature of civic virtue, might call forth political innovation: the development of the state and the developments of social and political discourses were reciprocally related. For example, what might loosely be termed a Calvinist vision of the marriage between magistracy and ministry gained wide currency in later sixteenth-century England. It entailed a commitment to the idea that the role of magistrate required its incumbent to participate in moral and social reformation. The terms in which the authority of the magistrate was legitimated were extended by reference to new ideas about standards of moral and social order. Religious reformation, the purging of human corruptions in the church, was associated with a new sense of what godliness entailed in social contexts. The requirements of religious, social, and moral discipline were raised, and the encouragement of conformity to these standards was seen to lie with the magistracy as well as with the ministry. This led not so much to the definition of wholly new areas of governmental concern as to an intensified concern with moral and social discipline. More importantly, this responsibility lay with the magistrate – the regulation of sexual and social conduct was a matter for the godly magistrate rather than, say, the manorial court. Henry Sherfield, for example, fired by a vision of godly magistracy, set in train a number of administrative initiatives in Salisbury, including a communal brewhouse whose profits were to be used to support the poor, a hospital and a grain store. The 'godly' magistrate occupied a larger political space than the magistrate whose authority was not justified in these godly terms.[13]

The claim to godly authority might conflict to some extent with other self-representations, and the godly were sometimes offended by the forms of behavior that constituted the normal gentry claim to natural authority – these things often smacked of worldliness and vanity. On the other hand, standardized forms of manner or dress might communicate a specifically godly form of magistracy. Godly authority, for example, frequently found physical expression in the growth of a suitable beard. For example,

> John More, the apostle of mid-sixteenth-century Norwich, 'was said to have grown the longest and largest beard of his time so that no act of his life would be unworthy of the gravity of his appearance,' while William Gouge, another puritan preacher, had come to resemble 'the Picture which is usually made of Moses.' John Earle characterised the appearance of an ideal-typical alderman in similar terms: 'he is venerable in his Gowne, more in his Beard, wherein he setts not forth his owne so much as the Face of a city.'[14]

The exciseman offers a contrasting case in that it was a new office, not just a redefinition of an old one. The introduction of parliamentary consumption taxes was of enormous financial significance and figures prominently in accounts of modernization – of the state in the form of bureaucracy and in the creation of an empire. Legitimating the excise was difficult in terms of established political and social norms – the tax prompted fears both about executive power over Parliament and about the power of these officers over their civilian victims. Before the Civil War it proved impossible to introduce the tax, so terrible was its reputation. When it was eventually introduced, during the crisis conditions of the 1640s, excisemen were described in print in terms of a biblical plague and this was often associated with accusations of corruption. Calming these fears about individual liberty was achieved by insisting on precision and the impersonal rules guiding the behavior of the exciseman. The individual holding this office was the neutral instrument of larger rules which were applied impersonally and precisely. In practice, of course, these things were negotiated, but the legitimation of the excise was enabled by a new language of precision and political arithmetic quite different from the ideals that legitimated the position of justices of the peace who held authority alongside them. At the same time excisemen had to negotiate the complaints and concerns of taxpayers, avoiding overtaxing them or cheating the state. In the heat of these arguments it was important for excisemen to try to present themselves (or each man his self) in a particular way.[15] The godly magistrate and the exciseman offer, therefore, contrasting examples of how successful legitimation could increase the functional space of the state.

Authority in the wider Tudor and Stuart world

In England, then, the exercise of political power was a cultural as much as a political issue. The territorial expansion of the state can also be viewed in this way. In the first generations of British overseas settlement it was conventionally said that good government rested on the establishment of social order. This required the maintenance or establishment of the full range of social roles, the complete interaction order, of a civil society throughout Britain, Ireland, and across the Atlantic. Such a social order would support and foster the values in terms of which political authority was justified. Much of this comment was expressed in terms of an ill-defined but nonetheless powerful conception of 'civility': 'The multiple uses of the term "civil" served to integrate rather than differentiate what we might term the political and the social, the personal and the public within a common framework of order.' Consequently, 'changing conceptions of social and political order were encoded in everyday rules of behaviour.'[16] The force of these ideas can be seen in the metropolitan core, for campaigns against vice and disorder were clearly informed by these presumptions about the forms of social interaction that characterized a healthy society. In the Tudor and Stuart world at large, the exercise of authority was not simply a question of making the 'king's writ run,' but the more ambitious one of fostering civility. In all these territories there was at least some evidence of an alliance with local elites: there was a shared interest in the maintenance of local social order.[17]

For early modern commentators there was a conceptual relationship between settled, commercial agriculture and the achievement of social and political order. In the Tudor and Stuart period numerous authors celebrated visions of the English countryside and in doing so lauded rural social harmony, linking it to classical values of civility.[18] The countryside was not just a physical space, but a social order and a theater of virtue: the personal qualities of William Watkins, the Shropshire husbandman praised by Richard Gough, were, as we have seen, manifest in his careful husbandry. Samuel Hartlib spoke for many when he argued in 1655

> that when God set Adam in the Garden of Eden to keep it and dresse it, He meant to exercise his industry, as well about the discovery of the fruitfulnesse of perfect nature, which could not be without much delight to his understanding, as about the pleasantness of the place, which he could have by dressing increased, and made completely answerable to his own imagination.

The *Reformed Virginia silk-worm* (1655) made a similar case in arguing for the replacement of tobacco with silk in Virginia. The production of silk, it was argued, encouraged admirable qualities; the production of the tobacco encouraged laziness and vice. Thus, tobacco growers in the winter 'spoile themselves by lying along the fire all that while and foxing themselves worse than beasts.' Silk production would keep them active and industrious year-round. Similarly, they were told that

> when the Indians shall behold and see you begin the business [of silk production], they will with all alacrity set upon it likewise, and imitate you .... And thus by the blessing of Almighty God, there may be good hope of their civilising and conversion; so that they might be great gainers both in body and soul by this thing.

Here was an extension of the domestic program of reform – encouraging the able but unemployed into productive endeavor. Settled agriculture encouraged honest labor and differentiated humans from brute beasts.[19]

This aspiration is revealed in Tudor and Stuart writings about the margins of crown authority, in particular, but not exclusively, in Ireland. The assumption that political instability was a product of the nature of Irish lordship was common to the well-known analyses of the problems of Irish government written by Edmund Spenser, Rowland White, and Edmund Tremayne: the solution, they argued, lay in a restructuring of rural social relations as much as in the reform of political institutions. Incivility was, according to these commentators, a problem both of social and political order. Similar horror was expressed by Lowland English and Scots in relation to their Highland neighbours in the Scottish Highlands or the Anglo-Scottish borders.

Robert Pont, an advocate of closer union between England and Scotland after 1603, referred to the 'wild and savage Irish of the English dominion,' and the 'Hebrediani' of the Scottish Islands 'who for the most part are enemies also to tillage, and wear out their days in hunting and idleness after the manner of beasts.' Similar concerns were expressed in the act of 1536 uniting Wales and England.[20] In Scotland the 'improvement' of the Highlands consisted, in part, of the transformation of settlement pattern. Government in America was more obviously a matter of creating settler societies rather than reforming the local population but the vision that lay behind this aspiration was again similar.[21]

Settled societies were not envisioned, of course, as egalitarian societies. A distinctive genre of writing developed in Elizabethan England, referred to as 'chorography.' In these writings landscape, history, legal liberties, and local genealogies were intertwined. They celebrated not simply material aspects of local life but their history and antiquities, particularly the history of important local families. Distinctive local societies were erected over the land and around local social hierarchy.[22] These local and social distinctions were expressed in display. The chimney, the parlor, the glazed window were all signs of social status – in effect they represented a material expression of the right to rule. As we have seen, keeping up appearances – playing the part of a gentleman – was essential to the maintenance of 'natural' authority. This rested in part on material expressions of taste and distinction on the landscape, in the home, and on the body.

It is easy to see, therefore, why the planting of civility in Ireland was thought to be a matter not just of expropriation, but also (or even preferably) of the spread of English settlement and building patterns, of English dress, language, and manners. Generations of migration and trade between the west of England and Munster, for example, transformed the physical appearance of the province by the mid-seventeenth century. Bridges, roads, fields, vernacular architecture, clothing, and language were transformed by the presence of English and Welsh settlers, making it appear 'a slightly raffish county on the English borders.'[23] In early seventeenth-century Ireland the language of commonwealth was deployed in the creation of a social order which did, to some extent, resemble English life. Local elites, both native Irish and Old English, found its stress on social order helpful. Here, too, gentility was closely associated with the power to govern, with justice: 'Social order could only be maintained by a securely-established social elite.' And that security came from an acceptance of a range of values, rhetorics, and gestures of gentility, albeit interpreted in the light of local traditions of Bardic eulogy and Gaelic lordship.[24]

This was also recognized in reverse: the misgovernment of uncivil societies was diagnosed in terms of a larger package of social roles; and that had implications for relations between men and women, native and newcomer, old and young as well as between rich and poor. Elizabethans and Jacobeans in America, for example, remarked upon the gender division of labor there, which marked out an ethnic (and inferior) identity. Observers of Algonquian Indians thought that the women were in slavery to the men, since the gender division of labor left only the hunting to men. Hunting was, of course, an important source of the protein in the Algonquian diet but Europeans thought it a leisure pursuit indulged in by the men while the women did the real work.[25] Apparently orderly, but alien, societies were interpreted in terms of familiar social roles, and measured against them. Early paintings of Indians in North America, for example, sought to represent differentials of rank in terms that would be familiar to an Old World audience.[26] Claims to legitimacy in the New World were grounded, in part, on these claims to be establishing civility in the wilderness. Within the colonies these social orders provided the means of rendering that world comprehensible and ordered. The promotion of civility, as in the domestic core, served elite interest and was not just a program of the state. In those cases where it was a more or less conscious government policy it was, nonetheless, something which could not simply be imposed by an act of will.

Trade, distinction, and material culture

Trade was crucial to the development of this world. Of course, trade has always been seen as crucial to the history of empire. The commercial revolution of the seventeenth century transformed English overseas trade so that it was global in extent. That revolutionized the range of English strategic interests and made the protection and promotion of trade a central concern of state policy. Commerce increasingly provided the resources which underpinned state finances and created the expertise necessary to administer them. But more was being carried in these exchanges than simple commodities. Exchange rested on assumptions about the self, value, interests, honesty, and fairness. Moreover the commodities being exchanged carried larger meanings – the fruits of empire fed not just material appetites and had more than a merely material impact on their consumers. The material culture of the empire created an environment in which the signifiers of power and distinction familiar at home could be reproduced in new circumstances. Trade was, in this sense, the vector by which a vocabulary of distinction and power was transmitted across great physical distances.

For many contemporary commentators, trade was closely associated with civility, something demonstrated by the history of Greek and Roman civilization – classical republicanism had as its model a society in which expansion came through the establishment of towns with improved agricultural hinterlands. For example, Edward Johnson discerned God's 'wonder-working providence' in the commercial transformation of the Massachusetts Bay by the mid-seventeenth century, which had made Boston the center of a 'well-ordered commonwealth.'[27] Plantation schemes in Ireland and the New World were built around plans for settled agriculture, market towns, and productive exchange, for example, lending weight to the claim that they were intended to bring civility to the wilderness.

Over the coming generations, and particularly from the later seventeenth century onwards, trade created an Atlantic mercantile elite whose members connected the port towns and their hinterlands in Britain and the New World. They dominated government in those places, and operated as effective lobbyists in London. In England they were often skeptical about the possibilities, or value, of pursuing the status of gentlemen in the narrow sense, adhering to their roles in urban life rather than seeking an uncertain acceptance into county society. But these people nonetheless acquired the trappings of refinement that made them, and their counterparts elsewhere, substantial figures in the port towns of the Atlantic world. Their charitable acts, their officeholding, their art collecting marked out their place in local society – these grave civic figures bore rule, not as gentlemen in the strict sense, but as men of refinement. Their refinement was in relation to aristocracy a statement of independence; for their social inferiors it continued to mark out a superior social role. They were not only products of the Atlantic world of course, but were also the means by which it was created and held together – their associational life really was at the heart of the Atlantic world, and it was transnational. Here were the original 'citizens of the world.'[28]

The territorial expansion of the Tudor and Stuart polity was the result of complex economic and social processes operating not just at the behest of the crown; the Atlantic trades carried more than just commodities. The movement of peoples across the Atlantic was an extension of patterns of migration within the British Isles – long-distance subsistence migration might lead to Bristol or London and from there to Virginia. Migration between colonies – between Barbados and South Carolina, for example – meant that the visions of 'English order' being created were no longer directly imported from England.[29] Trade also allowed for the material reproduction of the homeland, and the built environment of colonies of settlement in more distant places drew to a considerable extent on the vernacular architecture of England. This was, in Ian Steele's phrase, an empire of migrants and consumers.[30] And, of course, 'English' populations in the Atlantic world at large were connected in this Atlantic world with non-English populations – American Indians, Africans and other Europeans.[31] Finally, all this was, from the point of view of the metropolis, reciprocal. The goods that came to England in these trades in their turn provided the means by which social distinctions and social boundaries could be given material expression, or, perhaps, expressed in terms of an ever more diverse material culture. The exotic fruits of empire – tobacco, silk, sugar, tea, and coffee, for example – all had, at different times, important functions as markers of social distinction at home.[32] Trade, in addition to increasing the spatial extent of rule in direct ways, was therefore part of a broader process that fostered a common vocabulary of identification and distinction.

Empire, interest, and identity

By the eighteenth century these integrative processes were well established and there was a marked convergence in elite culture across the Atlantic world. This culture was not monolithic or unchanging, however. We have already seen that elite manners varied over time; modes of self-presentation varied according to new tastes and fashions. Moreover, as a result of economic change, new forms of social distinction became important – particularly the assertion of a middling-sort refinement distinct from the virtues claimed by landed society. There was, therefore, a creative tension between differing kinds of claim about social distinction and refinement. It is striking that in the eighteenth century these movements and tensions seem to have occurred in common across the Atlantic world. It has been suggested that in the seventeenth century overseas colonies represented simplified versions of aspects of English local society – lacking the complexity and social differentiation of the homeland they necessarily lacked the full range of social and institutional means by which local societies sustained themselves. As societies developed and diversified, however, they did not necessarily do so in isolation from the homeland. In fact, in many ways they drew on English values and practices in order to cope with growing complexities overseas.[33] These issues of social distinction have a common history across the Atlantic, then: it is not just a matter of how far one society or another managed to reproduce, or escape from, the manners of the metropolis.

In Scotland and Ireland elite manners had long been converging with those in England. In the Scottish Highlands clan society was undermined not only by pressure from the Scottish kings, but also by economic transformation – the realignment of relations between chief and clan along commercial lines. In the sixteenth century the Campbell earls of Argyll successfully bridged two worlds of Gaelic chiefdom and Lowland aristocracy, and the mores of the Lowland aristocracy were increasingly akin to those of their English counterparts. The spread of English manners – which for Scots meant an increasing formality and distance between inferior and superior – attracted hostile comment prior to 1640 but was an accepted feature of the conduct of the aristocracy by the later seventeenth century. Commercialization, and the interest of local elites in its promotion, played a significant role in the transformation of Highland social relations, perhaps more significant than acts of government will.[34] By the later seventeenth century the process of making Ireland British was well advanced; it has been argued that eighteenth-century Ireland resembled many other landed societies around Europe, and its material culture was similar to that of Hanoverian Britain.[35]

By 1700, however, many contemporaries thought that the American settlements had failed to become the improved versions of European societies for which many had hoped. In the course of the eighteenth century, though, rapid population growth, associated both with very rapid natural increase and with immigration, created more complex social orders, and as these societies matured they sought to emulate English (or British or European) standards of dress, behavior, and architecture. The refinement of America sought to restore to these wilderness settlements the standards of civility which had originally been hoped for. For example, from 1690 onwards, in rural Delaware, there was a rapid spread of the material culture and behavioral mores of English gentility, and this reflected an aspiration that we can trace over a longer period in the use of conduct books by puritan elites in the seventeenth century, or the social aspirations of Barbadian planters. Everywhere, social distinction in the British colonies drew on standards of behavior, dress, and building current in the metropolitan core.[36]

But this convergence, driven by the increasingly intimate trading connections between these places, was in tension with forces of divergence, at least to some degree. The social realities of life in Ireland and the American colonies continually forced the reinvention of European ideals: local elites could not simply reproduce the conditions envisaged in conduct books in England but had to actively create a local form of Englishness. This was true in England too, of course, but in the Atlantic world at large the range of these local variations was much greater.

These differences reflected marked variations in social structure. The presentment of civility was affected, of course, by the audience for that presentment: a Virginian gentleman, a Jamaican planter, and a Boston merchant were playing to quite different audiences and their performances therefore acquired distinctive local characteristics.[37] Such differences in manner might, in relation to the larger world of elite culture, mark out particular groups as rustic or lacking in true refinement. In mainland America, for example, manners were often said to be less deferential, reflecting perhaps the less polarized distribution of wealth, and this coarseness of deportment contrasted with the metropolitan emphasis on deference. Planters, by contrast, projected an image of gentility that rested on a brutality which came, eventually, to be repugnant to mainland British sensibilities.[38] Provincial figures who laid an unconvincing claim to metropolitan refinement were stock comic figures in seventeenth- and eighteenth-century drama and it is easy to document anxiety in the colonies about movements of taste and fashion in the metropolis.[39] The claim to gentility was potentially contested – as Smith made clear it rested in part on performance, but the reception of that performance was not guaranteed. And in any case, there was more to gentility than simply performance, as Smith had also pointed out. Irish peers were not really noble; elites elsewhere in the Atlantic world were not routinely granted titles.

Despite these local variations, however, we can identify a single world of elite culture, in which movements of taste were shared. Variety was a feature of English society too, after all. After 1660 perceptions of taste and refinement in England were dominated by London society rather than the royal court, but the manners of

English provincials remained a matter for humorous comment. Changing tastes in dress and architectural or decorative display spread at different rates in the light of local taste and the local availability of building materials. At any given moment, however, the vocabulary of distinction was commonly understood – a gentleman's house in Northumberland might seem old-fashioned, or to owe something to regional taste, but it was recognizable as the house of a gentleman nonetheless. Chorographical writings, although they emphasized local histories and identities, also celebrated an image of England.

Variations between localities were evidently regarded as the equivalent of dialect variations within a single language of Englishness. The much-noted tension in American manners, for instance, between refinement and egalitarianism was not unique to America. England also had a rising middling sort which, although it did not profit from the absence of aristocracy, could at least muster the confidence to be critical of it.[40] And in other colonies, of course, there were even more extreme versions of social hierarchy; nothing in England compared to the racially based social exclusion practiced in plantation societies. In these plantation societies local elites seem to have adopted the manners of British gentility without a qualm. For much of our period the language of social distinction in the New World was much like that of the Old World. Virginian gentlemen were unlike Boston merchants, but the distinction between them was expressed in the vocabulary of what was thought to be the shared culture of the English-speaking world. Buildings, the division of lands, and farming practices all established a social world in which patterns of interaction could be established which were recognizable to the colonists as representing social order.

Shared taste need not support a shared political identity, however. The conduct books and fashions in dress and architecture were not really English, or British, in origin, of course. They drew on French, Italian, and other sources and were invested with local meanings which marked them out as English or British. Taste and fashion, in other words, were not nationally bounded, but particular modulations of these international distinctions might assume national significance. This is particularly important here because these boundaries were redrawn – in the years around 1776 significant numbers of English (or British) people began to think of themselves as American.

The explanation for that is political. As we have seen, authority was a social or cultural as well as an institutional phenomenon. Governments negotiated their authority, taking advantage of (but not themselves creating) the means by which authority might be legitimated. The movements of people, goods, and ideas around the British Atlantic provided the means for the creation of an Atlantic governing elite. But the institutional complexities of the empire that was created within the larger British Atlantic world, and the increasingly complex local variations on the shared culture of the Atlantic elite, destabilized these communities and the institutional relationships that they supported.

As Gould argues elsewhere in this volume, this in a sense reflected the exportation of tensions experienced in seventeenth-century England to the peripheries of the eighteenth-century empire. Fiscal–military mobilization had caused considerable problems in the relationship between center and locality in England prior to the civil wars of the mid-century. In that decade the military and fiscal capacity of the English state was transformed, and the instruments of that authority – the navy, customs and excise services, for example – offered the potential for an increased regulation and control of colonial life. In some areas, and some trades, London's direct control remained very limited, but the navy and the customs system were crucial elements of the emerging 'navigation system.' This capacity, and the potential conflicts associated with it, increased in generations to come.[41] In the English localities there were continuing tensions between 'natural governors' and these agencies, but it was possible in general to reconcile their activities with the national interest. The tensions in the Atlantic world at large were ultimately more destructive. The social and political orders of the colonies took shape within a developing imperial shell made up of specialized agencies. The legitimacy of this imperial administration was asserted with reference to a different set of interests and values than the social orders that they contained, and there is no reason to suppose that patriarchs in Jamestown should find the relationship any more comfortable than did patriarchs in, say, Yorkshire.

These developments acted on differing local economic and institutional conditions, and the resulting tensions varied both in nature and degree of seriousness. There were marked differences in economic and social structures and in legal relationships with the metropolis. As a result, the political geography of the British Atlantic was diverse. The great trading routes to Africa, the Caribbean, and Hudson Bay supported valuable commodity trades but only limited settlement. The growth of the population of those areas depended not on natural increase but on migration, most of it forced, and their ties with the metropolis were very visible. In plantation economies white elites ruled over numerically dominant black populations; in western and northern frontier settlements they traded with Indian populations. In many of the mainland colonies of North America, by further contrast, settlements produced prodigious natural increase in population and economies were more loosely tied to the workings of the navigation system.[42] Although movements of people, goods, and ideas around the Atlantic continued to create bonds with the metropolis, the political relationships developing within the empire were rather looser. In the plantation colonies local elites sought to present themselves as representatives of a common British gentility; elsewhere merchant elites claimed rather different credentials for rule. Elite interests varied according to local social structure and to whether those elites were settlers, traders, or planters.

As in England, therefore, there was a complex relationship between the overarching needs of the crown as defined in London and the social and ideological interests of elites in particular localities upon which government depended. By the later eighteenth century, however, these issues had become much more complex in the Atlantic world at large than they were at home, and in some colonies dominant groups argued successfully that these interests represented the basis for nationhood. In the course of that revolution a pre-existing American consciousness came to be seen by many people as the most important of their potential identities – as British, female, white, or Bostonian, for example. Commonalities with the larger British world were taken for granted and differences given greater emphasis: the financial, commercial, and military interests of the British imperial state were said to be incompatible with the interests of Americans. The Declaration of Independence was a declaration of statehood,[43] and it was through that state that a new national identity could be articulated – Virginians and Bostonians could now see the political force of their American-ness, even if Jamaicans and Nova Scotians could not.

There was in the Atlantic world a shared language of social distinction which supported broadly congruent views of how social order could be constituted. It also supported, to some extent, the power of the empire. But it was not under the control of government – these identifications and divergences were the product of the complex exchanges of the Atlantic world, not the operations of the British empire. The origins of the rupture in the empire in the later eighteenth century were political and were associated with the assertion of a new identity, but it was the political structure of the empire that was ruptured rather than the larger world of cultural exchange. Americans continued to draw on European (including British) modes of behavior in order to define propriety, and that continued to lend legitimacy to the distribution of political and social authority: the repudiation of the functions and legitimacy of the British imperial state did not necessarily entail a repudiation of other forms of legitimate political power which had operated within its protective shell. With the emergence of an American national consciousness, however, many of these things were domesticated as American, or at least ceased to be regarded as signifiers of a larger British identity. This was a political matter arising from the institutional relationships of the British empire, rather than simply from the great diversity produced by the larger economic, social, and cultural exchanges of the British Atlantic world.

★★★

It is clear that power was not simply exercised between centre and locality – the intensification of governance, and its extension across new territories, also allowed for the expression of gender, class, and racial difference and for the establishment of primacy in these hierarchies. To emphasize the local demand for these things is not to plead for a democratic vision of the empire, therefore, but to bring into view a wider range of power relationships. Accounts of 'imperial' history frequently emphasize the role of official policy and the axis of political power between centre and periphery. An Atlantic approach draws attention to a larger set of processes and a wider range of power relationships – hierarchies of gender, age, wealth, and race, for example – and thereby allows for the integration of the agenda of social history into the study of political authority. It is also a helpful perspective from which to understand a process which seems to have owed so little to policy.

This essay has not only sought to draw a distinction between Atlantic and imperial history, however. It has also sought to make a connection between the history of social regulation at home (the history of the state) and the development of social orders under English authority around the globe (the history of the empire). The study of political power in this social and cultural context raises fundamental questions about the formation and reformulation of identities and communities; about the relationship between material culture and identity and community formation; and about the political significance of these processes. By the same token it offers the possibility of a reawakening of interest in the commercial revolution. Overall, it opens up a very wide agenda for economic, social, and cultural historians. At the margins of civil society people were led to express some of their core values – values which could be taken for granted closer to home. The integration of the history of empire with the history of the state enriches our understanding of both and takes us closer to understanding some influential contemporary presumptions.

6

Gender

Sarah M. S. Pearsall

Both the history of gender and the history of the Atlantic world have blossomed as fields of inquiry in the last 30 years, but the relationship between these two subjects remains unclear. Melding them is a profound challenge to historians in both fields. In part there is a need to make Atlantic history more than simply imperial history in a new guise. Rather, for the history of the Atlantic to be as wide-ranging as the Atlantic world itself, it is requisite that Atlantic history meets the challenge of gender. The place of gender – that is, the social and cultural categorization of sexual difference – in this world needs to be understood, as do other questions about cultural values, behaviors, and the organization of power at levels both large and small. Equally, gender historians can benefit from the more expansive, multinational approach offered by Atlantic history, placing broad changes into more precise contexts and replacing outmoded narratives of improvement or decline with more complex models of change and continuity.

Beliefs about gender shaped the nature of English colonization and indeed the British Atlantic world itself. At the moment of England's founding of its permanent Atlantic colonies, gender roles and behaviors were under significant scrutiny. In the 'crisis of order' that occurred in the late sixteenth and early seventeenth centuries, those individuals who challenged traditional gender roles caused concern among authorities. Since the traditional household, 'the little commonwealth', was the basis for the order of society and government, disorder within the household was an indicator that the times were 'out of joint'.[1] Political and social pressures directed at the most intimate functioning of the

113

household, from the cuckolding of a husband to the shrewishness of a wife, generated much more fluid boundaries between what we consider to be the public and the private. To instill order into the household was to lay the basis for a stable and godly society. Debates over the nature of women and their status further manifested the conflicts present in England itself as authorities reached across the Irish Sea and the Atlantic to colonize alien peoples.

To combat disorder, in the guise of those termed scolds, witches, or savages, English and later British authorities directed anxious attention at their gender regimes. In a bid to establish order in places seen by the English authorities as disturbingly disorderly, gender relations continued to be, as they had been in England itself, emblems of larger societal order. As an assertive but nervous metropolitan government reached into geographic areas previously held by other European powers and by native authorities, the gender order worked as an emblem of the way in which the English could settle themselves and govern over new areas. To export traditional English gender roles and household structures to the new colonies was a critical part of achieving colonial success, at least once it became clear that quick routes to gold and spices were not to be found.

At the same time, differing systems of gender organization among alien people provided the English with evidence of their inferiority and ultimately of their 'need' for colonization. Part of the 'improvement' of these different peoples lay in their adoption of English gender norms. Just as magistrates and communities in England patrolled the boundaries of acceptable behavior, so too colonial and metropolitan authorities attempted to regulate the households and sexualities of subject and settler populations alike. The perceived gender and household inadequacies of non-English peoples provided one of the strongest justifications for English colonial expansion and also for slavery. Within England and later Britain itself, the gender order of the other people with whom the British had come into contact became a way of measuring them, and of signifying British superiority. Confident in their avoidance of the tyranny of polygamy or the 'female governments' of African and Native American nations, the English and later the British and British-Americans felt themselves superior to peoples who had revealed themselves to have committed failures of the grossest natures in their gender order.

Finally, the presence and occupations of English women became a vital means of measuring the settled status of the colonies established by the English. As the Lord Deputy of Ireland declared in the 1620s, to 'make a good nation … it is noe great matter of wha[t] nation the men bee soe the women bee Englishe.'[2] The presence of English and later British women allowed for the smooth transmission of property, language, and custom; they also bolstered proper household structures.[3] In metropolitan eyes, colonies did not become civilized when there were only English men there; they only truly did so when English women were there too. Those colonies that mirrored metropolitan gender and household orders became more quickly those colonies that made claims to a settled and in some cases a national status. Those areas with a demographic imbalance in the sex ratio and those areas in which English men turned to native Irish or American or African partners were considered not to have achieved the same level of civility as England itself. Those societies that were unable to replicate traditional structures of marriage and family were never counted as true 'homes' for the English settlers there. In part, liaisons between English men and native women were dangerous not only for their implications for the social and racial order, but also because they too closely approximated those of England's Catholic enemies, Spain and France. In order to distinguish themselves both from their European foes and from 'savage' Irish, Native American, and African peoples, the English sought to maintain traditional household structures. Likewise, those areas where English women were forced to perform 'men's' labor were considered potentially barbarous, as such problematic systems of labor organization threatened to undermine traditional English social order.

In these ways, then, it should be clear that gender was central to the way in which a British Atlantic world was created. At the same time, transatlantic currents shaped gender orders throughout this world. Adopting an Atlantic approach to the history of gender illuminates both the history of gender and the history of the British Atlantic world. It allows for a more concise understanding of points of change, so that causes and effects can be more easily pinpointed. That gender relations changed between 1600 and 1800 is obvious, but how and why they did so is a much more hotly contested question. Taking a multinational perspective allows historians to determine which factors might have been relevant in any given change in gender dynamics. It also helps them to avoid simplistic models of improvement or declension. This brief overview necessarily simplifies and smoothes out the vast and vibrant variety within the British Atlantic world, but in focusing on broad changes and continuities, local patterns should then be clearer.

Starting points

In 1600 Elizabeth I ruled England. She had come to the throne because the system of hereditary monarchy in England, like most monarchies, privileged blood over sex in determining who should rule the nation. However, her presence on the throne did not mean that gender and sexuality were not of considerable importance to her subjects. Indeed, her virginal status was requisite to her rule. After all, had she married, it would have meant that England would have fallen under the sway of a foreign power. During and after her reign there was a heated pamphlet campaign on the nature of women and their authority.[4] Misogynist tracts such as Joseph Swetnam's *The Arraignment of Lewd, Idle, Froward, and Unconstant Women* (1615) met replies in works such as Ester Sowernam's *Ester Hath Hang'd Haman* (1617). The anti-woman pamphlets argued that women had far too much authority, and that they used those powers to seduce, to scold, and to nurse their own vanity. In part, these female powers were thought to be verbal and sexual. Swetnam pronounced flatly that women 'are ungrateful, perjured, full of fraud, flouting and deceit, unconstant ... proud, discourteous and cruel.'[5] The pro-woman pamphlets argued against these claims, declaring to a presumed female audience: 'You are women: in Creation, noble; in Redemption, gracious; in use, most blessed.'[6] These literary debates were inaccessible, most likely, to the majority of English women (and indeed a number of men). Nonetheless, the issues they crystallized – about women's use of authority and their possibly malevolent and simultaneously seductive powers, about men's potential weakness in the face of fearsome women – mirrored and were mirrored in thousands of less well-recorded debates in which individual women and men debated each other's roles, responsibilities, and failings.

In theory it was the male head of household, backed up by communal and legal authority, who was expected to monitor the behavior of his family and also of his servants. Of course, this theoretical model did not always work in practice. Even in theory it was not a rigid system; for instance, there was room for widows to gain economic and social authority and to hold property, especially among the elite.[7] Nonetheless, the household was at the center of the social order, especially since the Reformation had dissolved any alternatives in the form of convents or monasteries.[8] At marriage, a woman became *feme covert*, that is, subsumed under her husband's legal identity. Most people, although by no means all, married. Accordingly, both masculine and feminine identities depended to a large degree on this adult setting up of household. Although a minimum of 10 percent of the population never married, with that number rising to approximately 20 percent in times of economic hardship, those who did marry tended to have relatively large families.[9] In general, men were the providers and women the helpmeets. Sometimes, as in the workshop of the London artisan Nehemiah Wallington, the wife would help in the running of a household workshop or household farm.[10] Many men served as apprentices in order to learn the trade that would allow them some day to set up their own household; independence was a prime goal for men.[11] Many women worked as servants in other households, acquiring useful housewifely skills. Some also served as midwives, tavern keepers, and shopkeepers, especially when widowed.

It is vital to acknowledge that although the system was patriarchal in its orientation, it was not only men who assigned roles to women. From the whispered endearments between a husband and a wife to the shouted insults that might drag embittered individuals into courts on slander charges, men and women constantly defined each other's positions and roles. Indeed, in many slander cases men accused men and women accused women. By and large, men sued over charges relating to their honesty in business dealings or their ability to regulate their households, so that they might go to court after being described as 'knaves' or 'cuckolds'. Women tended to sue for slander relating to their sexual honor. At this time it was considered acceptable and in fact desirable for women to experience sexual pleasure in marriage, in part because conception was thought to depend on both female and male orgasm. Authors of midwifery manuals often acknowledged 'a delightful and mutual Itch in the Parts of Men and Women.'[12] Nonetheless, women's sexuality was to be confined to marriage, and their sexual reputations were carefully monitored. In 1625, when one Ellen Tillsbury shouted to her neighbor, 'hang thee whore thou keepest a bawdy house', the neighbor sued for slander.[13] Such slander cases were common in this period, and they indicate the extent to which communities themselves, as well as legal authorities, defined gender roles and behaviors.[14]

In this same era, from roughly 1560 to 1640, there was a 'crisis of order', in which there was considerable economic dislocation, population increase, land shortages, inflation, and increased poverty and vagrancy. Fewer people could afford to marry and set up households. There thus appears to have been a rise in illegitimacy, and prosecutions for this crime increased in these years as well.[15] This situation led to a more general anxiety about deviance and disorder, some of it based on gender behaviors. Indeed, some historians have gone so far as to identify 'a crisis in gender relations' in the years around 1600.[16] It is certainly true that in these years there were significant prosecutions for sexual crimes such as illegitimacy and for social crimes such as scolding and witchcraft, for which women were disproportionately targeted. Both women and men were accused of behavior that breached the public peace, but for women to be 'disorderly' or 'unruly' was particularly worrisome.[17]

It was in this context of rising economic and social uncertainty that English colonization projects began in earnest. The English had of course been involved in exploration, trade, and colonization in the Atlantic basin for at least a century, but it was in this critical era that permanent outposts became fully fledged colonies in Ireland, Virginia, New England, and Barbados. Therefore concern with the gender order, and with the need for stable married households to underpin the new societies, became a dominant motif in English settlement. Alien groups would be measured by their ability to conform to English gender orders, and settler societies would also be measured by these standards. Changes would come throughout the British Atlantic, but these changes could be characterized neither as improvements nor as declines, or what an earlier historiography identified variously as 'golden ages', 'universal oppression', and 'separate spheres'.[18]

The limited analytical purchase afforded by these historiographical models has more recently led scholars to eschew these narratives, replacing them with a more complex and variegated view of change. In part, taking an Atlantic point of view can help to pinpoint moments of transition. Certain shifts were regional or national, while others were transatlantic. The relative importance of factors can also be weighed with greater precision. Such an approach also allows historians to see how wider patterns interacted with local circumstances and took on new forms. Numerous changes affected the entire British Atlantic, but they did so in different ways, at different times, and among different people. Nonetheless, to be able to appreciate the unique trajectories of individuals, communities, and even nations, it is vital to have a sense of larger transatlantic changes in the realm of gender frontiers, the movement of people and goods, and shifting cultures of refinement, literacy, and Enlightenment.

Gender frontiers

Without the expansion of the English into Ireland and later into the Americas, this British Atlantic world would not have come to be. Conquest and colonization created significant 'gender frontiers', defined by Kathleen Brown as 'the meeting of two or more culturally specific systems of knowledge about gender and nature.'[19] Just as gender and household order had signified social soundness in England itself, so too would they continue as emblems for larger social and colonial stability. In part, English colonial views were hammered out in Ireland, in the realm of gender as elsewhere. English authorities there were eager to prevent the largely male population of settlers from intermingling with native women reckoned by the English to be barbarous and even dangerous. Edmund Spenser even asked his readers 'how can such matching but bring forth an evil race?'[20] In the uncertain settlements the English forged in Ireland there was also a concern that Irish wives would prove treacherous. One English commentator complained that such women 'lye in the bosomes of ore greate men, to maintaine the cutting of ore throats.'[21] The English insistence on their male settlers staying away from native women, a tendency absent in much of the Spanish and French colonial enterprise, almost certainly had its source in the damp and difficult Gaelic experience. Gender regimes came into play in the earliest English colonial ventures.

When the English later encountered Native Americans, they felt that their superiority, and their right to the land held by the indigenous people, was partly tied to the correctness of their system of gender. According to the English, because Indian men did not till their fields and control the sexuality of their women, they were open to colonization. They lacked the 'manliness' the English held so dear, and thus they could be considered weaker, in need of both aid and conquest. In addition, their household organization, at variance with English ideals, if not practices, of matrimony, was another reason for the English to look upon natives with disfavor. In New England, for instance, many Native American nations allowed for easier divorce, at the instigation of either partner, and they did not necessarily condemn multiple partners. The English viewed such configurations with horror, and considered their eradication part of the civilizing and Christianizing process.[22]

The fact that many indigenous cultures were matrilineal augmented the English sense that the natives lacked proper understanding of patriarchal and patrilineal systems of descent and property ownership, and so the English could render their 'superiority' in gendered terms. Barbarism in part depended on unacceptable configurations of gender. Such discussions continued to inform English and later British and American thinking, into the Scottish Enlightenment and beyond. So David Hume, for instance, pronounced that 'Barbarous nations display superiority, by reducing their females to the most abject slavery … But the male sex, among a polite people, discover their authority in a more generous, though not a less evident manner; by civility, by respect, by complaisance, and, in a word, by gallantry.'[23] Such comparisons served Britons and British-Americans with a means of 'discovering their authority' in the face of alien cultures. In Adam Ferguson's stadial theories, in which societies moved from savage to barbarous to polished to corrupt, the matrilineality of Native Americans proved their location at the lowest stage of development: that of the 'savage'.[24] In these views, more advanced nations proved their civility by their organization along patrilineal and indeed patriarchal lines. Relations between men and women were a vital way of measuring the distance between barbarous and civilized. Polygamy, for instance, was universally derided as an inferior system of partnership, associated with cultures lacking the civility of Europe. In his *History of the American Indians* (1775), James Adair detailed a marriage between a French man and an Indian woman that foundered due to the woman's apparent infidelity.[25] Adair used this marital failure as evidence that the matrilineal and matriarchal systems of the natives, 'that wanton female government', were unreliable, and that alliances made with them could not be trusted. In joining with them, Europeans were placing their manhood in a precarious position indeed.

For their part, many native groups equally considered the English lacking in terms of their gender organization. English men worked in the fields, and hence performed what was accounted 'women's work' in many native societies, thus indicating the effeminacy and powerlessness of English men 'for their folly in spoiling good working creatures', according to an early New England commentator. It also demonstrated the laziness and ineptitude of English women. That same New England commentator reported a case in which an Indian sachem reacted with shocked horror to the scolding of an Englishman by his wife, the sachem thus concluding that the Englishman 'was a great fool to give her the audience and no correction for usurping his character and abusing him by her tongue.'[26] The fact that English men did not hunt as frequently as native men also signified their inability to provide properly. An Englishman's seeming preference for a single marriage partner might also be suspect. Native systems of gender organization sometimes lay uneasily submerged under British colonial rule, rising to the surface of written records only occasionally. Despite the imbalance in written sources it is clear that, in these gender frontiers, each side saw disorder where the other side saw order, and this sense of disorder caused problems for each side and for their interactions with each other.

These 'gender frontiers' could also be 'sexual middle grounds'.[27] After all, the colonial world was full of European men and their Native American wives, and there were general concerns about the relations, sexual and otherwise, between Europeans and natives. The English did not join with non-English in the same numbers as French and Spanish settlers and traders did, but there were many partnerships nonetheless. Metropolitan English authorities did not monitor their settlers as much as French and Spanish governments did, nor did they encourage the marriages and conversion of natives with anything like the same fervor. Still there were sexual and indeed marital relations between English and Native Americans, just as there had been relations between English and Irish and as there would be such relations later between English and Africans. British and British-American authorities felt that localities with high numbers of such unions existed in the wilderness, and were therefore not part of the civilized worlds of the colonial project.

In part, early English settlers were uneasily aware of their own failures to replicate metropolitan gender models. In many colonial ventures, especially in their origins, English men outnumbered women significantly, and this configuration worried metropolis and colony alike. Among the more obvious examples are sixteenth-century Ireland, seventeenth-century Virginia, and eighteenth-century Jamaica.[28] In these regimes there were relatively few Englishwomen but an abundance of young men. These configurations were not conducive to a sense of household or, therefore, of social stability. English women allowed for the rightful transmission of property within legitimate marriages; they also passed on language and culture to their children. Areas in which English and later British men had difficulty in finding similar women as partners, or in which they chose other women, could never count as entirely civilized in metropolitan eyes, whatever institutional and legal growth occurred there.

    Despite metropolitan distaste, relationships between colonizing
and native populations continued throughout this era, especially as
the British adopted African chattel slavery as the bedrock of their
first empire. European men's impressions of female African bodies,
viewed as both sexual and monstrous, provided a justification for
slavery, since African women were linked with both productive and
reproductive capacities.[29] For Edward Long, an infamous historian of
Jamaica, the 'hot temperament' of African women provided solid
justification for their enslavement. Similarly, the 'taste for women'
among African men was further proof of their inability to make
progress in civility, thus implying that it was fair to enslave them.[30]
At the same time, gendered systems of labor in various West African
regions meant that women were often exported as slaves in high
numbers, especially from areas such as the Bight of Biafra, where
their labor was considered less critical.[31]
    Even regions with relatively few slaves, such as Britain and New
England, were deeply implicated in the structures created by a
British Atlantic slave trade. In part, shifting cultures of refinement
meant that it became increasingly unacceptable for English women
to perform field work. Indeed, that the English considered field
work unacceptable for Anglo-American women but acceptable for
African-American ones meant that gender beliefs also influenced the
adoption and structure of slavery. African women were imported
along with men into the English colonies, and were put to work in
tobacco, sugar, and rice fields. In part, the willingness of the English
to put African women to work in fields meant that slavery was
adopted more quickly than it might otherwise have been.[32]
    Gender beliefs influenced the adoption and shape of African
chattel slavery, but equally slavery reshaped gender relations in the
British Atlantic. Many British settlers in the West Indies, for
instance, fretted that African mores, especially those involving
unmarried sexuality, would rub off on British settlers (which
indeed they sometimes did). These fears were especially pronounced in the eighteenth century.[33] There were worries that the
British in islands like Jamaica would contaminate themselves by
their proximity, both physical and emotional, to the different
systems of gender and sexual organization of the Africans who
surrounded them. In part, that the British departed from metropolitan norms in adopting local systems of gender organization, in
which non-legal unions replaced legal ones, was one of the reasons
that the British Creole became such a questionable character in

metropolitan eyes. The refusal of British men in Jamaica to marry British women but instead to form attachments with African and African-American women undermined the system of marriage, and its concomitant gender roles, and thus threatened the stability of the entire colonial enterprise. Furthermore, the children of these unions could not be counted on as defenders of Britain, and might instead rise up in rebellion. Such sexual middle grounds within slavery altered gender roles and also meant that again the presence or absence of English or British women remained a key variable in understandings of social stability.

In addition, slavery extended the lines of authority inherent in master–servant relations by giving owners the power of life and death over slaves and their children and the economic benefits of offspring produced by female slaves. This was a horrific combination for slave women and men, in that the power of ownership was inserted into reproduction. The inherited nature of chattel slavery meant that intimate matters of sexuality and reproduction were put into a distinctive socio-economic framework. It also meant that slavery descended through the mother, creating an anomalous and unfortunate matrilineality in the British colonies. Slave women suffered from sexual attention from owners.[34] Slave men lost much of the power to monitor their own households, a serious blow to their masculine identities.

Not all masters, of course, were men. Women too could rule slaves with whips.[35] However, the juxtaposition of the growth of African chattel slavery concurrently with the rise of transatlantic cultures of refinement meant that these mistresses, whatever brutality they might have inflicted, came to define themselves as 'ladies' in contrast to the African-American (and Native) 'wenches' who surrounded them. That 'wenches' could perform field work and were considered by many to be sexually available meant that they were further to be distinguished from 'ladies'. In the British American colonies, race was superimposed on class in unforeseen and pernicious ways.

The movement of goods and ideas

Slavery became critical to a British empire that depended on trade goods and on a triangular trade between Britain, the mainland colonies, and the British West Indies. In fact, the British Atlantic was developed on the basis of the movement of goods and people, and its shape was strongly determined by its trade and labor systems. There were two major shifts in this realm which had effects on gender organization. British and British-American women seem on the whole to have become less involved in the productive work of their husbands. That is, in household workshops earlier in the era the wife was a helpmeet in the business as well as the home, and she might be fully aware of the details of the business. By the end of this period, wives tended to know less about the running of the business, as the business increasingly separated from the household. The labor of these women was thus directed differently. While these changes affected women in all parts of the Atlantic world, they did so in distinct ways. Elite women had greater access to consumer goods, while slave women were caught in an expanding plantation system. Rural women in the British Isles increasingly participated in outwork production, while farm women in British colonies became household manufacturers. Overall, however, there was also an increase in the consumer powers of both women and men and a decline in the numbers of household workshops.[36]

Despite this decline, such venues could retain strength in some areas. Indeed, in the later eighteenth century Benjamin Franklin termed his wife 'a good & faithful Helpmate, [who] assisted me much by attending the Shop.'[37] It has been all too easy for economic historians to focus exclusively on the contributions of men to building an Atlantic world. In part, they have been sustained in this orientation by the records that men have left, created in business but also in sources as diverse as family letters and autobiographies. But the labor of women, as wives, as mothers, as servants, was critical to the creation of citizens of the world like Franklin. To understand the integrative workings that depended on the productive and consumer choices of both men and women is to recapture the complexity of a world that was hardly built or sustained exclusively by men. On the other hand, it is equally critical to recognize the disproportionately gendered nature of the Atlantic economic links, and the strains that its workings placed on men. British Atlantic men's identities were intimately connected with their ability to prosper and to achieve independence, and the uncertainties of a more global economy brought with them attendant anxiety.[38] British and British-American fathers tried to raise boys who could withstand these pressures and be masters of businesses, households, and selves.

In part, the regulation of the self was a central aspect of the rise of cultures of refinement. Correspondingly, the massive growth of trade contributed to the availability of luxury and other goods. The material worlds of the British Atlantic were utterly transformed, and cultures of politeness became increasingly important for middling and elite sorts.[39] 'Ladies' might gain leverage from new discourses of refinement, and they often may have gained tools for negotiating with male family members. These shifts gave new spaces for homosociability, such as coffee houses for men and tea tables for women (although tea tables could often include men too). Middling and elite identities as ladies and gentlemen depended on newer models of refinement and sensibility. Not all elite women characterized these changes in positive ways. For all the women who took up their teacups and embroidery and who wittily discussed the most recent issue of the *London Magazine,* there were some, like Esther Edwards Burr, who in 1756 lamented the loss of the older ways and more traditional housewifely apprenticeships, now that 'our young women are all Ladies, and it is beneath them to go out.'[40]

Men, too, felt the call and the tensions of newer models of behavior and deportment.[41] Refinement in the American colonies bolstered not only gender and class status, but also proved that colonials had not departed too wildly from metropolitan norms. At the same time, the lack of aristocrats in the colonies meant that gentlemanly status could not depend so strongly on lineage. While the ideal of the polite gentleman may have united Britain and its colonies, it took distinct forms in different places. For instance, Jamaican elite men felt less call to adhere to the dictates of polite sociability such as literary salons or coffee houses. Nevertheless, they were determined to provide abundant hospitality to visitors to their plantations, a different and in some ways more archaic vision of politeness.[42] Indeed, metropolitan visitors were often revolted by the displays of food and drink in the warm climates of the Caribbean. Lady Maria Nugent, an English sojourner in Jamaica in the earliest years of the nineteenth century, grumbled to an English friend of one party in which 'there were 36 Dishes ... in broiling hot weather ... Nothing can be more disgusting.'[43] For Nugent, planter politeness was a lower and less pleasant version of the metropolitan refinement she held so dear. Other metropolitan sojourners in Jamaica derided it for its lack of refinement, a situation partially attributed to the relatively low numbers of elite British women.

Despite local and national variations, it is clear that cultures of refinement became increasingly important for an ever-wider swath of the population in the British Atlantic world. At the same time, sensibility, defined here as the ability to possess and display a feeling heart, developed critical impetus by the later eighteenth century.[44] The discourse of sensibility could serve to increase women's authority, in that they might make claims to greater sensibility and might monitor men's ability to display sensibility in such critical periods as courtship. At the same time, if sensibility was associated too much with emotion and the nerves, women might be thought to exist outside the realm of reason and masculine vigor. As with refinement, it could also signal differences in terms of race and class, so that only certain populations were included in a circle of sensibility.

These newer cultures of refinement and sensibility depended, obviously, on vast increases in literacy and the rise of print culture, which had similarly varied effects on gender configurations. Literacy rose dramatically in this era, for men but especially for women, the vast majority of whom were illiterate in the sixteenth century.[45] The rise of literacy was especially dramatic in the eighteenth century. Literacy and greater access to print culture could have liberating aspects for women, and many scholars have focused on the ability of women to shape lives and selves based on printed models.[46] Books, magazines, and newspapers, which became more widely circulated throughout the British Atlantic world, could open up new perspectives. Whereas family and community stories, injunctions, and gossip, with courts and churches adding their voices, had been the central forms of communication for most in the sixteenth century, now there was a multiplicity of voices. Some of these voices, however, often purveyed the same traditional gender roles and stories, and did not serve any especially liberating purposes. Novels, although a new form, often stressed older ideas of female purity, the dangers of seduction, the dangers of foppishness, and the place for submissive women. Moreover, literacy did not affect all worlds equally. Many non-British groups such as Native Americans and Africans were left out of these developments in large degree, as were some of the poorest individuals in Britain and its colonies.

Certainly, however, more people could not only read and thereby gain access to an ever-burgeoning world of print but, increasingly, they could also write. Again, there were considerable variations based on class, race, and age, but by and large more and more individuals gained access to writing, both in the skills and in the tools (such as quills, ink, and paper) needed for it. Diaries, commonplace books, and letters became more widely accessible,

especially to women. These forms of communication, in addition
to the many needed for trade and business, could provide useful
social and personal outlets and means of negotiating selves and relationships. Scholars have tended to see these new abilities as liberating, but they could sometimes serve conservative purposes.[47] The
variation in their dissemination meant that if they provided authority, they provided it disproportionately to those who already possessed it to some degree. Still, they did alter the parameters for
performances of gender and other identities. Increasingly, by the
end of this era, women such as Mary Wollstonecraft and Judith
Sargent Murray were entering the world of print to demand better
education and greater rights for women.[48] No longer was the production of print the province only of men and the occasional
aristocratic woman.

Print culture also gave impetus to the shift in ideas known collectively as the Enlightenment. Although the Enlightenment of course
had many facets and indeed many definitions, it could safely be
stated that an improving and classifying impulse lay at its core. Many
individuals adopted the larger eighteenth-century concerns for
improvement, classification, and control. Even in his older years, one
ambitious, acquisitive and improving Jamaican planter ruefully
noted, 'instead of indulging in bed & nursing my [gout], I must
crawl on Horseback & be doing something.'[49] This restless drive
always to 'be doing something', even at some personal cost, was a
central product of the civilizing process, although it may have had
its roots in what has been termed the Protestant work ethic. It
meant an increase in reform movements and what would come to be
called 'the humanitarian revolution', but it also meant an increase
in repressive control, counting, tabulating, and surveillance.[50] In
addition, those who surveyed and tabulated, usually men, might
wield disproportionate influence. Moreover, many Enlightenment
thinkers drew significant contrasts between the savage and the
civilized, and gender orders became a way of signifying this gulf. To
classify was to lend authority to certain categories of peoples. In
part, this desire to understand 'the science of man' had its roots in
the expansion of Europe and a desire to make sense of alien peoples.
It was at this moment that many intellectuals fixed racial difference
in the body.[51]

A few also fixed sexual differences there too, or at least gave
weight to the biological basis for social differences between men and
women. As theorists sought to explain the mechanism of human

reproduction, there was a decline in the ancient Galenic view that there was, in essence, only one sex, and that women's reproductive organs were merely an inverse, and therefore inferior, version of men's. The eighteenth century witnessed a new emphasis on the notion that women and men were in fact two different sexes. This process occurred concurrently with a diminishing sense that female orgasm was requisite for conception, so that uteruses became passive vessels for vital fluids from the male. These views, while limited in their reach, would ultimately reshape the way in which gender, the social category of difference, would come to depend highly on the physical differences thought to exist between men and women.[52] Such visions would ultimately reinforce older notions of the weak female and give impetus to the idea that a woman's identity was tied to her reproductive capacities. Such is not to say that there had not long been arguments in favor of female inferiority, but these new scientific understandings altered the terms of this debate from purely social theories to theories that combined the physical and the social in ever more particular ways. Indeed, it might be said that the Atlantic moment brought with it new ways of implicating the body in social and cultural difference, in ways that would define the modern Western world.

Change and continuity

It should be clear that these sorts of changes affected all of the British Atlantic world, even if they did so differently depending on timing, location, and population. This Atlantic perspective can help illuminate even those classic issues of religious participation and the republican redefinition of citizenship. Martin Luther's original notion of the 'priesthood of all believers' was taken more literally by some Protestant denominations than others. At the more radical edges, groups such as the Society of Friends, founded in the seventeenth century, took this idea to mean that every believer communicated directly with God, without any priestly intermediaries. The implications of these beliefs obviously altered the possibilities for women and religion, as there were now no male priests to preside over the communion of believers. Most visibly, Quaker women preached throughout the British Atlantic world, often to the consternation of non-Quakers.[53] The great revivals and awakenings of the eighteenth century, which again linked the British Atlantic world, also gave more visibility to the laity. In this sense, women and other groups who held little institutional authority might find a certain kind of authority in religion. The revivals also gave impetus to the development of further Protestant denominations such as the Methodists and the Baptists. While these groups were often founded in a bout of radical religious enthusiasm, this situation did not always translate into radical gender configurations, as in the case of the Quakers. Rather, as these groups became more institutionalized they tended also to grow more traditional in their gender patterns, as exemplified by the Baptists in New England.[54] Religious radicalism thus did not always equate to gender radicalism, even as access to religious authority shifted and opened up in new ways throughout the British Atlantic.[55]

A similar trajectory characterized political changes. Certainly, the settings of war and revolution presented new opportunities for women to organize for patriotic efforts, even if in highly traditional ways, as in the spinning bees of the American Revolution.[56] Equally, while times of revolution in the British Atlantic led to the increase of voices demanding radical changes in all areas, they also inspired conservative backlashes, in the Restoration era and in the early American republic. Indeed, such post-revolutionary moments could lead to even greater emphasis on traditional gender roles. Equally, the contractual models of government that so informed the American Revolution meant that while middling to elite white men gained new powers, they may have done so to the exclusion of women. Many of these ideas had their origins in British political theories, and in fact the early republican obsession with 'virtue' also had British origins.[57] In the new United States, women were excluded from the contract between the state and the individual. That is, whereas the older system had, albeit uneasily, allowed women access to the highest powers in the land as queens, the newer system did not. In this era, except for a brief period in New Jersey, women could neither vote nor obtain political office. Elite white women still retained certain leverage, whether as 'republican mothers', 'republican wives' or indeed as players in the political contests of the capitols.[58] But although they might have been 'Republican Queens' like Dolley Madison, they could never be true queens with the legal and personal authority of a woman like Elizabeth I.[59]

Changes then were rife, but there were at least some continuities. After all, the desire to insist upon and even legislate for order, within the most intimate relations between women and men, had long marked out the parameters of English authority. The Atlantic moment reinforced these long-standing concerns and gave them a variety of new shapes, but the impulse to find in gender relations a model and a mirror for other kinds of social order remained the same. There was a desire to regulate, from the broadest institutional structures to the most minute anatomy of the individual. There were new axes of authority as the English and then the British reached out and created a British Atlantic, but the desire for an orderly gender organization to underpin an orderly society provided a critical impulse throughout this era.

In addition, the household remained a central arena for the definition and enactment of gender roles. During this time, British and British-American men and women defined their adult gender status in terms of their ability to begin and to run an orderly household. There were of course exceptions, but the ideal of the independent household headed by husband and wife was a central one throughout the British Atlantic world. For British and British-American men, to achieve financial independence was a key variable in setting up a household, choosing a partner, and starting a family. For British Atlantic women, marriage would remain '*the* important crisis, upon which our Fate depends.'[60] With limited birth control, most women would then devote themselves to the demands and joys of childbearing and -rearing. Moreover, beliefs in women's inferiority, whether social, theological, legal, or biological, remained constant, even as they took different forms. It was a legacy that would haunt later generations.

Integrating gender into the history of the British Atlantic thus reveals the complex formulation of authority for scales both large and small. Ideas about gender and its practices were vital to the ways in which individuals and societies defined themselves and others. A scolding English wife in New England in the early seventeenth century was a concern both to her own English community and to the Native Americans who shared her world. The presence of English women and legal marriages marked out some parts of the British Atlantic world as more 'civilized' than others, at least in English eyes. Colonial power depended on the social stability that such households were thought to provide. In short, there could be no settled empires without the right kinds of households. To lose sight of these households and the individuals who populated them is to miss a critical aspect of the British Atlantic world. Moving outwards from the household to the vast transoceanic shifts, however, also helps historians to be aware of the sway of broader trends as well as the force of local and individual trajectories.

To attend to the complex intermingling of ideals and practices of gender within a larger British Atlantic world is to insist upon a more complete history of the British Atlantic world. At the same time, it is also to recall that that history depends on the multiplicity of individual narratives. While certain trends united the British Atlantic, others separated its regions and populations. An awareness of general trends can help to illuminate the particular trajectories of individuals, families, localities, and nations. The variegated options, contexts, and responses involved in these myriad Atlantic contacts can be fruitfully explored via this perspective. In looking at the tangle of relationships and structures in a smaller setting, it is then possible to generate larger arguments about gender and cultural change.

After all, these shifts did not have wholly positive or negative effects. They form neither a whiggish path to progress, nor a waning of robust early modern opportunities. Separate spheres and golden ages have little place in a British Atlantic history of gender. Rather, a complex concatenation of changes altered landscapes and lives in ways sometimes positive and sometimes negative. If diminishing community intervention meant freedom in some cases for some individuals, it also meant the diminution of the authority of midwives and goodwives who were no longer called by courts to provide authoritative testimony. If the rise of consumerism and trade goods meant greater choices for some, it also meant a shift in labor organization that was damaging for others, especially those caught in the slave system upon which this growth depended. If the rise of literacy and print culture provided liberating new spaces for the self and the imagination, they did so only for certain populations. At the same time they could also serve conservative ends and emphasize old stories about the need for female purity or manly honesty.

The cruel interposition of race and class also affected the story. 'Ladies' and 'gentlemen' won the leisure to participate in newer cultures of print, refinement, and sensibility on the backs of servants and slaves. Margaret Cowper, an elite British-American girl whose letters demonstrate her absorption of the ideals of sensibility and refinement, wrote to her cousin from a Georgia plantation in the late 1790s, complaining of a recent bout of illness. Cowper casually remarked that, as she was recovering, she had gone into the parlor to amuse herself with the harpsichord 'while my Bed was Making.'[61]

Cowper's syntax elided the labor of the slave woman who made up her sickbed, and who had undoubtedly been nursing her through her illness. Her unthinking reliance on a slave woman indicates vividly the variety of experiences of different sorts of women and men, all of whom built and sustained this British Atlantic world, as well as the ways in which some 'gains' required some 'losses'.

7

Class

Keith Wrightson

I

To discuss the problem of 'class' in the British Atlantic world of the early modern period may well appear anachronistic. For most of that period the term itself was little used to describe the structures of inequality in contemporary society. It was only from the mid-eighteenth century that 'class' as a term descriptive of social distinctions 'glided into the language', gradually establishing its dominance in the conventional vocabulary of social description not only in Britain, but throughout the British Atlantic world.[1]

Prior to that time the structures of societies throughout Europe were most commonly conceptualized in terms of a number of functionally differentiated but interdependent 'orders' or 'estates' of mankind. Originally three such estates were distinguished: the clergy, the noble or 'gentle', and the common people, each of which was further subdivided into an internal hierarchy of status. As a model of the social order it was certainly not independent of the structures of power and wealth. But conceptually it distracted attention from such matters, focusing instead upon the honor or esteem accorded to particular social and economic roles. Its purposes were normative rather than descriptive. It was intended to justify and legitimize established structures of authority rather than to subject them to critical analysis.[2]

The language of 'class', as it emerged, had rather different implications. First, its usage was commonly analytic. Its adoption was

133

linked to the efforts of Enlightenment thinkers to explore the nature and historical development of human society, and its initial appeal owed much to its apparent analytical neutrality. As it developed, however, it acquired distinctive resonances of its own. As a terminology of social differentiation it tended to focus attention upon the economic structures of society, tracing social subordination to the unequal distribution of property and anatomizing contemporary society in terms of broad economic interest groups. Discussions of class further tended to reflect a growing sense of the mutability of society and the contingency of its present forms. And finally, the language of class was often either implicitly or explicitly critical of conceptions of society which disguised hereditary privilege in the garb of organic harmony.[3]

The emergence of the 'discourse of class' in the later eighteenth century can thus be held to have embodied a major shift in the underlying principles of social stratification in Europe. The concept of class had become freighted with meaning – a process of development accelerated in the early nineteenth century by those who reflected upon the experience of industrializing Britain as the 'classic ground' of modern class formation.[4] Yet if the language of class appeared to offer a new conception of the social order, this shift was in some respects more apparent than real – not least in the case of Britain. For if the language of class was increasingly current in eighteenth-century Britain, it acquired its dominance not so much by displacing as by subsuming earlier conceptions of the social order.

Three such conceptions were current in seventeenth- and early eighteenth-century Britain, and indeed throughout the emerging British Atlantic world. In the first, society was presented as a finely graded hierarchy of ranks, extending from the titular nobility at one extreme to the poor at the other. This model, which was most frequently rehearsed in formal, literary accounts of English society, had emerged in the late sixteenth century as an adaptation of the medieval notion of the three estates which rendered it more descriptive of English specifics. In effect, the various 'degrees' distinguishable within each of the medieval estates were shuffled together into a single rank order of status. Relative position within that consolidated hierarchy depended partly upon birth, partly upon the esteem accorded to particular professions, and partly upon wealth and style of life. There was thus a certain flexibility in the definition of rank. Individual mobility between ranks was frankly recognized. Nevertheless, if the social hierarchy lacked rigidity, it was also deemed to be unchanging in its essential structures. Individuals might shift their place, but the system endured. And the moral philosophy of the society of estates also endured in the continuing conviction that the social order was God-ordained and in an overriding preoccupation with order, degree, authority, and subordination.[5]

The finely grained hierarchy of 'estates' and 'degrees', however, was not the only conception of society current in early modern England. Two others are frequently encountered in the records of the period, both of which were expressed in what I have called elsewhere the 'language of "sorts of people".' The first of these presented an essentially dichotomous perception of society, sweeping aside the fine gradations of the status hierarchy and emphasizing instead a crude and brutal distinction between the 'better sort' or sometimes 'richer sort' of people, and the 'poorer', 'meaner', 'ruder', or 'vulgar' sort of people. In this dichotomous form, which emerged into prominence in the later sixteenth century, and long endured, the language of 'sorts of people' presented a polarized view of society. It was pregnant with actual or potential conflict. From the early seventeenth century, however, it became increasingly common for contemporaries to recast the language of sorts into a tripartite form by recognizing the existence of a third category, the 'middle' or 'middling' sort of people. This term was probably of urban origin, but by the turn of the eighteenth century it was being generally applied to describe a heterogeneous body of people occupying an intermediate place in the social distributions of wealth, status, and authority.[6]

Whether in its dichotomous or its tripartite form, the language of 'sorts of people' was clearly a language of social simplification. In contrast to the hierarchy of estates and degrees, which emphasized gradations of status within an organic whole, it focused attention on two or three broad social groupings each with its distinctive characteristics and interests, and it recognized that relations between them were as likely to be antagonistic as to be complementary. To this extent the three perceptions of the social order which I have sketched could be said to have been incompatible. Yet clearly they coexisted. And they did so because they represented alternative perspectives on a complex social order. They illustrate what has been described as 'the degree of freedom which in fact exists in the space between social reality and its representation' – the possibility of a variety of credible interpretations of the nature of a given social order.[7]

For present purposes, the essential point is that all three of these pre-existing perceptions of the structure of English society were subsumed in the language of class as it developed in eighteenth-century Britain. The language of class could be applied to distinguish a multiplicity of classes reminiscent of the estates and degrees of the classical Tudor hierarchy. Alternatively, it could echo the language of 'sorts' by taking a dichotomous form – focusing on the 'upper' and 'lower', 'superior' and 'inferior' classes, or the rich and the poor – or a tripartite form, distinguishing 'higher', 'middling', and 'lower', or 'upper', 'middle', and 'industrious' or 'working' classes.[8] 'Class' thus provided not so much a revolution in the ways in which people perceived social inequality as a unifying vocabulary which enabled them to move more easily between a variety of alternative perceptions. It was conceptually muddled, but it was admirably flexible. It could be invoked in different ways for different purposes. And its emergence as the dominant vocabulary of social description did not in itself involve a wholesale reconceptualization of the social order. It introduced no principle of social differentiation that had not already been prefigured in earlier languages of social stratification. Nor did it give expression to wholly new dimensions of social relations.

In short, much of what we understand by the term 'class' as a means of distinguishing social groups or of characterizing social relations was already present in English society before the term itself was widely adopted. It found expression in a variety of discourses of social inequality which had developed in the course of the sixteenth and seventeenth centuries. Their sequential emergence was linked to processes of demographic, economic, cultural, and political change which reconfigured English society between the sixteenth and the eighteenth centuries. Their persistence as alternative perceptions of the social order was because that reconfiguration involved continuities as well as change, a diversification of social realities in a society that was increasingly a mixture of forms. Their diffusion throughout an emergent British Atlantic world was because those processes of continuity and change had an Atlantic dimension – a dimension that vividly reveals the alternative potentials inherent in English society itself, in the interaction of the English with their neighbors, and in the societies that they created in the New World.

II

In the early decades of the sixteenth century it was still possible, even conventional, to conceive of societies throughout Britain in terms of the three estates of medieval social theory. In the case of England, however, this was the last generation in which such a conception of the social order could truly retain its credibility. From the second quarter of the sixteenth century English society was galvanized by processes of demographic and economic change which in the course of a century were to entail a cumulative reconfiguration of the social structure. In the course of the later sixteenth and early seventeenth centuries population growth and price inflation fuelled the momentum of a gathering process of commercialization. Between the 1520s and the 1640s the population of England doubled. In response to increasing demand, prices rose steadily, and sometimes precipitately. Production was gradually expanded in both agriculture and manufacturing industries. The growing population was redistributed towards the larger cities (above all London) and to the smaller towns and villages of expanding rural industrial areas. Networks of internal trade were elaborated and tightened. The horizons of overseas trade expanded, from the narrow focus upon the trading nexus with the Netherlands which had characterized late medieval commerce, to include first the Baltic lands, Iberia, and the Mediterranean, and in the early seventeenth century the East Indies and the Americas.[9]

All this almost inevitably involved social–structural change through its implications for developments in the social distribution of wealth, of power, and of opportunity or 'life chances'. Landlords responded to the pressure of inflation by adopting more commercial estate management policies, and this, together with their acquisition of confiscated church land at the Reformation, produced an expansion of both the size and the collective wealth of the English landed class. Substantial 'yeoman' farmers prospered and came to hold a much greater proportion of tenanted agricultural land. Small farmers, in contrast, often struggled to hold their own, while for both demographic and economic reasons the landless proportion of the rural population grew massively. In the towns, commercial expansion provided the opportunities for some to acquire great wealth. But a greater social distance opened up between the mercantile elite and independent master tradesmen on the one hand and their 'journeyman' employees on the other. For the 'semi-skilled' and 'unskilled' laborers of the growing towns and rural industrial districts, declining real wages and intermittent employment entailed a pinching and insecure existence. In both town and country alike, then, a large minority was able to prosper, seizing new opportunities to acquire and consolidate wealth. Yet a substantial proportion of the English population (perhaps half by the mid-seventeenth century) had become largely or wholly dependent upon the vicissitudes of the market for their labor, a situation which left many enmired in a perennial struggle for economic survival.

Such contrasting fortunes have led many historians to characterize this period as one of 'social polarization', and there is much to support such a view. Yet at the same time this phrase oversimplifies the changes that were taking place in English society. In the first place the period saw not only the enhancement of the opulence of established elites at one end of the social scale and the emergence of severe problems of 'structural poverty' at the other, but also the expansion and elaboration of a composite body of people of inter- mediate wealth. The 'middle sort' of people constituted an increas- ingly distinctive grouping in society, part product and part source of the economic dynamism of the age. Secondly, these complex processes of economic and social differentiation, of diverging life chances and living standards, produced different outcomes in differ- ent local and regional settings. However we might choose to describe the reconfiguration of England's patterns of social inequal- ity, they were experienced in very different ways in specific local contexts.[10]

All of this had implications for perceptions of society and of the relations between its component groups. Throughout the kingdom the medieval conception of the society of estates was losing its rel- evance as an alternative social order emerged, composed along lines determined by new economic fields of force. The notion of the three estates gave way to the hierarchy of 'estates and degrees' as the formal image of society, implying, in its insistence on degree, order, and obedience, a pervasive anxiety about the stability of the social order. At the same time the language of 'sorts of people' in its dichotomous form gave frank expression to both a growing sense of economic and social distance between the 'better' and 'meaner' sorts of people and the antagonisms to which this gave rise. The growing presence of the 'middle sort' was also registered, as we have seen. But as yet the harsh glare of the anxieties and hostilities attending the social polarization of the age cast them into conceptual shadow. Of the dominant discourses of social inequality, one sought to impose order and stability upon a shifting social reality while the other expressed its essential dynamics and attendant tensions, reveal- ing something of what Gerrard Winstanley termed 'the inward bondages of the mind' occasioned by 'the outward bondage that one sort of people lay upon another.'[11]

III

All this formed the immediate context of English overseas expansion in the early seventeenth century. That expansion was in part an extension of and in part a response to the economic and social dynamic that I have sketched above. And from the perspective of the historian of social differentiation and class relations it reveals the different potentialities inherent in the English society of the time. For if England was 'a globally expanding culture,' it was also a society and culture still in a state of becoming.[12] If the American plantations represented 'England on the move,' it was also the case that the 'charter groups' that established them and shaped their distinctive characters represented not a monolithic England but particular variants of Jacobean culture, each carried by a particular type of Jacobean.[13]

Seventeenth-century Virginia exemplifies the transatlantic extension of the commercial dynamic which was transforming England, a dynamic which in the New World found expression in its most uncompromising form. It was a colony led by adventurers – younger sons of the gentry and discharged army officers, men motivated above all by hopes of personal advancement, whose marginal place in the English elite rendered them the more amenable to take risks and to pursue their advantage with the least scruple. Whatever their initial hopes and dreams, by 1620 it had become clear that Virginia was to be a commercial colony: its survival and prosperity would depend upon the cultivation and export of a staple crop – tobacco. And in consequence tidewater Virginia became 'a boom settlement,' an 'extraordinarily individualistic, fiercely competitive and highly materialistic' society, in which 'the reckless and single minded pursuit of individual gain became the animating impulse and chief social determinant.'[14]

The principal requirements of tobacco cultivation were land and labor. Land was abundant and was parceled out to the leading settlers through the 'headright' system, whereby each was granted 50 acres for himself and a further 50 for each of his family and servants. Accordingly, the settlers spread out rapidly, their plantations being described in 1621 as 'placed straglingly and scatteringly ... and further from neighbours the better' – a dispersal motivated by hopes of expansion and an individualism which dictated that no man 'can endure not to have the free use of his own.'[15] Labor was imported through the institution of indentured servitude, whereby migrants received passage to the colony in return for being bound to serve unpaid for a specified period of years before receiving their freedom – a system which has been described as 'a primary force in shaping Chesapeake society.'[16]

The result was 'an aberrant society' which was 'socially primitive but commercially sophisticated.'[17] By the 1660s Virginia was dominated by a ruling elite of wealthy planters, reinforced by governor Sir William Berkeley's policy of recruiting and favoring aspirant younger sons of English gentry families. At the other extreme was a mass of indentured servants, most of them young, male, and of low social origins, recruited in the ports of London and Bristol and in all likelihood taking passage to the New World as an extension of what has been termed 'subsistence migration' from the English countryside to those cities.[18] And there was little middle ground.

Relations between masters and servants were highly exploitative. A servant was 'a thing, a commodity with a price,' to be bought and sold, or even gambled for, 'a machine to make tobacco,' subject to a degree of bondage which as John Rolfe observed, would be 'held in England a thing most intollerable.' They were also 'exceptionally turbulent.' As early as 1610 servants were described as 'full of mutenie and treasonable intendment.' They were prone to acts of insubordination and to desertion, and in return they were subjected to an often brutal discipline. They were not slaves. They had hopes of freedom and even of advancement if they survived the conditions of their servitude and the catastrophic mortality of the early Chesapeake settlements. But the distinction between their situation and that of the small numbers of African slaves introduced into Virginia from Barbados at this time was not necessarily apparent to them. White servants and black slaves sometimes joined in conspiracy or ran away together – a fact which has led some historians to speculate that in early Virginia, as in those Caribbean plantation economies which initially combined servitude and slavery, 'class rather than race may have been the bond that united workers.'[19]

These tensions came to a head in the 1660s and 1670s. By then Virginia was a somewhat more settled society in its institutional structures and developing 'webs of community' among the planters. It was also somewhat less drastically polarized, with a growing population of freedmen who had survived their servitude and become established as small planters or tenants in the settled areas or as farmers in the frontier zones. If anything, however, it was still more troubled. Servant discontent was widespread and found new expression in major conspiracies intended to end their bondage. Freedmen enjoyed little real opportunity, caught as they were between continued dependence upon the planter elite as tenants or as debtors and the insecurities of settlement on marginal frontier land. In Governor Berkeley's famous phrase, they were 'Poore, Endebted, Discontented and Armed.' And whatever the complexities of motive underlying Bacon's rebellion of 1676, it provided an opportunity for both groups to vent their visceral hostility to the colonial establishment, and to engage vigorously and vengefully in plundering the estates of its supporters.[20]

The unfettered commercialism of Virginia's early development had produced a deeply divided and unstable society, riddled with class antagonisms which were expressed in a language of dissociation and contempt. 'Gentlemen of Good condition', or 'the better sort of people', otherwise termed 'the rich', were pitted against the 'common people', otherwise termed 'the meaner sort', 'the poorer sort', 'the basest sort', or 'the Rascality and meanest of the people.'[21] It was a situation which would be resolved only when the pushing back of Indian populations to open more land to settlement and the replacement of white servitude with black slavery as the basis of the labor system created the possibility of an alternative social order: 'a society that would nourish the freeman's freedom and at the same time make possible the unlimited exploitation of labor.'[22]

Virginia thus exemplified the most ruthlessly exploitative dimension of English social relations in the seventeenth century. The New England settlements, in contrast, represented a reaction against the tensions so evident in Jacobean society. Of those tensions, the most explicit were of course religious. As proponents of an austere and demanding Protestant Christianity, the Puritan colonists sought to escape the attentions of an English ecclesiastical hierarchy which was both alarmingly revisionist in its theology and attachment to traditional forms of worship, and aggressively hostile to their own religious practice. At the same time, however, the Puritans' ardent attachment to reformation, their defining godly *activism*, reflected not only their personal religious and ethical anxieties, but also some of the broader social anxieties excited by the strained social relations of many English communities at the turn of the seventeenth century. Puritanism projected a new kind of order for both individual and society. Its passionate emphasis upon personal sanctification presented to the troubled individual opportunities for a redefinition of selfhood, a new and deeply comforting sense of identity and integrity. But it also offered, even required, participation in the building of a new kind of disciplined community, a reconstruction of community on a stable footing at a time when so much seemed out of joint.

The Puritan colonists, then, were radical in their religious, but conservative in their social, ideals. They migrated in family units, recruited from networks of like-minded people within particular English regions.[23] They settled in coherent townships, often reflecting in their institutional structures the familiar patterns of their English regions of origin.[24] They established a family farming economy which closely followed English agricultural norms. This was in part because the New England environment permitted such familiar practices, but it was also a cultural matter, the outcome of deliberate choice. Even Puritans could not live by the Word alone, but they were not primarily motivated by hopes of economic advancement. They chose a family farming system rather than endeavoring to create a cash crop/export economy on the Virginian or Barbadian model. To be sure, some became involved in the fur trade, in commercial fisheries, and in the supply of agricultural produce to the Caribbean colonies. But in the main their economic ambitions were modest and the pace of economic development slow.[25]

A similar cultural choice was evident in the arrangements that gave rise to the patterns of social structure and social relations that characterized New England townships. A clearly defined social structure was desired by the colonists' leaders, as conducive to both order and harmony. Township lands initially deeded to the leaders or proprietors of new settlements were distributed on a variety of criteria, among which pre-existing social status was prominent. In Dedham, Massachusetts, for example, it was based on household size, 'usefulness in either Church or Commonwealth' and 'men's rank and quality.' What has been termed 'a hierarchically structured society of lineal families on small, community-oriented farms' was thus created deliberately.[26] Within those structures, leadership roles were accorded to the 'principall inhabitants', 'men of good rank and quality', and relations between neighbors were conducted in a manner that stressed order, harmony, reconciliation, and the mediation of differences.[27]

Such realities underlie the common view that 'in no part of North America ... was rural England so faithfully recreated than in New England.'[28] Yet this is at best a half-truth. For what the Puritans actually built was not a reproduction of rural England but 'an idealized version of the gentry-cum-yeoman society which they had seen disappearing in England.'[29] For if attention is naturally drawn to what they brought with them and sought to preserve, we must not forget what they left behind. There were no noblemen in New England and relatively few gentlemen of substance. The greater part of the colonists were drawn from the broad middling ranks of English society. If social differences between them were respected and indeed carefully preserved, the range of social distance was not great. This was a relatively egalitarian society in which a very high proportion of householders enjoyed political rights. And above all, it did not perpetuate the sharp distinction between householders of property and the laboring poor that was becoming increasingly evident in England. Not a few of the colonists brought servants with them – young people who could expect a degree of opportunity in New England that they could rarely have envisaged at home. But there were very few laboring men among the colonists. A farming system based upon family labor had no need to recruit a large, cheap, and subservient labor force, and in Essex County, Massachusetts, 'the identifying occupational designation of labourer almost disappeared from county records.'[30] If New England townships, despite their social distinctions, provided no real economic basis for class tensions, that was primarily because they lacked one of the most obvious consequences of social change in old England – a large and permanent class of laboring poor.

IV

By the third quarter of the seventeenth century something of a diversification of social structures had taken place in the English world. The slave plantations of the Caribbean and the farming communities of New England, it has been said, 'represented the outer limits of English social expression in the seventeenth century,'[31] but between those poles lay a considerable diversity of local and regional realities. Nor was this process of differentiation confined to England or its earliest American colonies. It could be found also in the other territories owing allegiance to the 'multiple monarchy' of the Stuarts. Social-structural change in Scotland is poorly documented, but it is at least evident that demographic growth in the northern British kingdom had created by the early seventeenth century severe problems of poverty and rural congestion.[32]

Ireland's experience was more drastic. In the sixteenth century Ireland was already 'a society fragmented in economic, political and social terms.'[33] The 'old English' areas of the east and south resembled the rural societies of England and 'anglicized' Wales, 'with a peasantry ranging from landless labourers and poor cottiers holding one or two acres to prosperous husbandmen and yeomen.'[34] In the

Gaelic north and west, however, as in the western Highlands and islands of Scotland which were part of the same cultural zone, a different social order persisted in effective independence. This was 'an aristocratic culture', 'articulated by warfare', a culture of feuding and feasting in which a man's standing depended upon the 'armed might' of his following of kinsmen and retained fighting men, and in which the lowborn who did not bear arms were of 'little account.' Gaelic society was fairly sharply divided between the chieftains who, together with their kinsmen, exercised lordship over loosely defined and shifting territories and the mass of tenants-at-will who owed them tribute, usually in the form of food renders and labor.[35]

In the course of the later sixteenth and early seventeenth centuries, these realities changed in Ireland in two ways, first by a slow process of 'anglicization' of land tenure and its associated social relations. Some chieftains secured a personal title in English law to defined territories through the process of surrender of their lands to and regrant from the crown. They gradually turned themselves into 'landlords rather than warlords.' Kinsmen who had formerly enjoyed claims to the clan lands were reduced to tenant status. Among the lesser tenantry arbitrary exactions of tribute gave way to the payment of annual rents.[36] Secondly, these processes were consolidated and periodically accelerated by colonization.

In the fraught international situation of the later sixteenth century the quasi-independence of the great Irish lords, who had remained Catholic, posed a security threat that could no longer be tolerated by the English crown. Rebellion was followed by confiscation, first in Munster in the 1580s, then in Ulster after 1607, and the devising of elaborate schemes of systematic plantation which were intended to bring a turbulent Irish society within the bounds of 'civility'. In practice such ambitions were not realized. While 'undertakers' and 'adventurers' could be found readily enough to take Irish lands, they were rarely able to recruit sufficient tenants from England or Scotland to create the ethnically homogeneous colonial societies initially envisaged. Some 'favored' Gaelic landlords were permitted to remain within the areas of settlement and most 'New English' landowners were obliged to accept Irish tenants. Nevertheless, by the 1630s some 22,000 English settlers in Munster had established a society with strong similarities to that of south-western England (to which it was closely linked). In Ulster some 7000 adult male migrants – drawn from England and Scotland in roughly equal proportions – were settled in the counties of plantation by the 1620s, and a less formal process of land acquisition and migration had created a Scottish enclave of some 4000 settlers in Antrim and Down. These hybrid societies added to the complex mosaic of Ireland's composite social order. If they were shaken and depleted by the Irish Rebellion of 1641, and the subsequent civil wars, they were not extinguished. And with the Cromwellian reconquest of 1649–51 and the wholesale displacement of Catholic landowners by grantees of British origin (many of them former military officers) there was a massive extension of that area of Ireland within which a British ruling class and English institutions were superimposed upon a Gaelic peasantry.[37]

V

Throughout what was to become the British Atlantic world, then, the later sixteenth and seventeenth centuries witnessed significant social-structural change. English historians have tended to stress the gradual reconfiguration of English society under the twin pressures of demographic growth and economic development. Irish historians have focused upon the catastrophic impact of growing English dominance and eventual conquest upon the Gaelic social order. Historians of early America have dwelt upon the novelty of the societies created by English settlers in the New World and the tensions that they felt between the cultural inheritance carried with them and the demands of a novel environment. Yet there is a sense in which all these societies were innovative and all also experienced, albeit to different degrees, the stresses generated by the impact of the new upon established social and cultural expectations. Their different dynamics produced different outcomes within a general process of diversification in social structures and social relations.

From the later seventeenth century, however, historians have been more impressed by processes of convergence among these distinctive but interconnected societies. Historians of Britain and Ireland have tended to stress the integrating influence of the intensification from the later seventeenth century of the commercial dynamic that had begun a century earlier: the consolidation and extension of the structures of capitalist agriculture; urban growth; the expansion of extractive and manufacturing industries; the maturation of regional economies which were distinctive in their complexion but bound together into an integrated whole by tighter and more elaborate networks of communication and internal trade.[38] Historians of colonial

America have traced the emergence of more elaborate social institutions and more sharply articulated social structures in both New England and the Chesapeake, a process elaborated in Jack P. Greene's interpretative synthesis into a model of colonial development which involved a 'convergence toward the center' and a closer 'replication' of English society.[39] All these developments were articulated by common participation, either directly or at one remove, in an emergent British economic system in which the Atlantic trades in tobacco, sugar, timber, furs, shipping supplies, provisions, manufactured goods, and slaves had a central place. And they involved flows not only of goods but also of people, ideas, habits of consumption, and so forth within a transatlantic anglophone cultural zone.

These processes of connectedness, of convergence, 'anglicization', or 'social replication', clearly carried implications for the development of social structures and social relations throughout the British Atlantic world of the eighteenth century. But did they imply the emergence of a single social system? A common language of social classification might certainly suggest this. Americans used the terms 'esquire' and 'gentleman' to describe the members of their landed, mercantile, and professional elites, just as the British did. They too spoke and wrote of the richer or better, middling, and lower, poorer, or inferior 'sorts' or 'classes'.[40] But such language can be deceptive. For if there was convergence in social-structural terms it was limited in its nature and degree.

It can certainly be discerned at the level of the social elite. Throughout the British Atlantic world society was headed by landowning elites that had much in common. They were confident of their innate superiority and maintained a patrician attachment to hierarchy and tradition. Yet at the same time they fully appreciated the benefits of commercial enterprise, were adaptive to economic change, conversant with the commercial and financial worlds, and apt to measure one another in terms of their estimated annual incomes. They were cultural amphibians: rooted in the countryside, but participating in the pleasures of the urban season; given to some of the coarser elite traditions of hard drinking, gambling, sexual predation, and violence in defense of their honor, but also cultivating the veneer, and often enough the substance, of politeness, learning, and civility. The ruling class of the British world might be geographically dispersed, and provincially inflected in tone, but it also had a 'cosmopolitan' tone and considerable cultural homogeneity.[41]

Much the same might be said of the commercial and professional 'middling sort' – a group much studied in England, though less so in other contexts. They were a heterogeneous body of people, ranging from independent tradesmen of substance to great merchants and leading professional practitioners who enjoyed effective gentility. But many of them were directly involved in forging or sustaining the commercial links which bound together the societies of the British Atlantic world, and in other respects also they had a good deal in common. They were relatively affluent, though subject to the insecurities attending a commercial living. They nurtured the values of diligence, thrift, prudence, and good management essential to success in the commercial world, and strove to preserve their 'credit' or reputation amongst their peers. As the backbone of the 'consumer revolution' of the late seventeenth and eighteenth centuries, they shared a material culture which expressed their solid worth and respectability. They were heavily involved in the associational lives of their communities, frequently well educated and aware and politically active in local and sometimes national affairs. And if their individual spheres of action were often circumscribed, their collective presence can be said to have been felt throughout the British Atlantic world.[42]

These common elements were important. They gave coherence to a dispersed social world.[43] But at the same time it must be recognized that that world *was* dispersed. The social groups that provided its most obvious lateral connections were also situated within radically different social configurations. And to this extent a common language of 'ranks', 'sorts', and 'classes' obscures more than it reveals.

This is immediately apparent if we consider some of the differences between the social orders of eighteenth-century colonial America and those of Britain and Ireland. If America had a wealthy landed elite that modeled itself on the English gentry, it had no legally privileged hereditary aristocracy. America had a significant urban 'middling sort' engaged in commercial and professional occupations. But only some 5 percent of the population of the 13 colonies lived in towns, whereas in England in 1750 an estimated 21 percent of the population lived in towns of more than 5000 inhabitants, and many more in smaller urban centres.[44] If white American society was becoming more differentiated in the longest settled areas and in the cities, its most obvious characteristic remained its widespread level of solid prosperity. The ideal of a decent independent 'competency' was attainable by most whites on the freehold family farms that typified much of rural America. The range of social differentiation was limited.[45] To be sure, there was poverty – among some of the small tenant farmers of tidewater Virginia, for example, or among those of the urban labor force whose employment was intermittent. But there was no permanently impoverished cottager class. The laboring population was relatively small in both town and country. Wage labor was often a life-cycle phase rather than a permanent condition. The perennial shortage of labor for hire meant that wages were often good.[46] And for those prepared to move, the frontier continued to extend the promise of independence.[47]

In comparison, the peasantry of rural Ireland subsisted on tiny holdings, frequently subject to rack-rents, in what was described by Sir William Petty as a 'brutish, nasty, condition.' George Whitefield was sufficiently impressed by 'the meanness of the poor peoples living' in County Clare to note that 'If my parishioners at Georgia complain to me of hardships, I must tell them how the Irish live.'[48] Much of Lowland Scottish rural society remained a world of small subsistence tenants, or of the cottars who labored for more substantial men in return for access to a few acres and a kailyard. 'The Cottars' slavery is incredible' noted one observer in 1759. Theirs was a world of endemic rural poverty, alleviated by no serious hope of social advancement. As for the Highland peasantry, their scraping existence in the 1720s provoked John Burt's exclamation, 'good God! You could not conceive there was such misery in this island.'[49]

In England social conditions were considerably better. Yet Gregory King could calculate with much plausibility in the 1690s that three-fifths of the families in England (comprising half the total population) were 'decreasing the wealth of the nation' in the sense that their family incomes frequently fell short of their necessary expenses. These were the 'laboring poor' of England's highly commercialized agriculture, growing cities, and agglomerating industrial districts. (By 1750 a third of the population were engaged in 'rural non-agricultural' occupations, primarily in the small towns and villages of the industrial regions.) Their condition varied in accordance with their skills, age, stage of the family cycle, fluctuations in the demand for their labor, and access to such supplementary resources as common rights and industrial perks. Their poverty has been described as 'shallow'. But if relatively few at any one time were wholly destitute and dependant upon parish relief under the Poor Laws, most could be regarded as living at risk of such a fate.[50]

Colonial America had little of all this. But if that was so, it was in large part because of a further social-structural peculiarity. Where there was an economic need for a substantial labor force, it was provided by other means. Two-fifths of the population of the southern colonies in 1760 (and nine-tenths of that of the British West Indies) were African slaves. 'For the free, opportunities were impressive.' But those opportunities were purchased in part by what has been termed 'the great transforming circumstance of American history' – 'a system of racial caste which was totally without precedent in Britain.'[51]

VI

Such varied configurations of the economic structures of inequality provided the contexts for the conduct of class relations in the British Atlantic world. They did not in themselves determine the nature of those relations. But they exerted influence upon the formation of individual and collective identities and on the extent to which those identities found expression in acceptance or rejection of prevailing structures of wealth, status, and power. And just as a common language of class could be employed contextually to describe a variegated set of social realities, so also certain common idioms were deployed in the conduct of social relations – idioms of paternalism and deference, and of independence and resistance – which were more or less resonant in particular social contexts.

Paternalism and deference were perhaps the dominant idiom of social relations throughout the British Isles, certainly in rural society and to a considerable degree in the interactions of what were still conventionally termed 'masters' and 'servants' in the worlds of commerce and industry. Social superiors were expected to treat their subordinates and dependents with consideration, to respect their legitimate interests, and to extend assistance in time of need. And in return they expected an unquestioning acceptance of and deference to their own social authority. All this has been described as 'a description of social relations as they might be seen from above', 'always more potent as a rhetoric serving to legitimize inequalities of wealth and status than as an actual determinant of behaviour.' If its reciprocities suggested 'human warmth in a mutually assenting relationship,' they were markedly unequal in their nature. Behind them lay the cold realities of relative power, and paternalism tended to wither when the interests of the superior were at issue. Nevertheless, where its canons were broadly adhered to, or at least not blatantly abused, it could be an effective technique of rule. It could transmute disparities of rank into a bond of personal identification between inferior and superior, even 'inhibit the growth of alternative horizons and expectations' on the part of the subordinate.[52]

Yet it had its limits. Deference could be and often was a pose, a necessary demeanor, a manipulative claim. The servility of the Irish peasantry in the presence of their Protestant landlords was notorious, but only an optimist would have believed in its sincerity. The deference displayed to their 'betters' by English farm laborers, industrial workers, or tradesmen frequently concealed bitter resentments.[53] Moreover, the very ubiquity of patronage and dependency in the hierarchy of domination and subordination placed a premium on the ideal of 'independence'.

Independence was the principal aspiration of the middling sort. And if many of them remained enmeshed in ties of clientage, it was also the case that among those of them who possessed it, their effective independence could render the respect customarily afforded to their superiors markedly conditional and contingent. It could be asserted quietly in the form of religious dissent, or truculently in the populist politics of the cities.[54] Nor was an attachment to independence peculiar to the middle sort. It was also a powerful element in the self-identity of many laboring people. In part this involved the maintenance of tradition, the retention where possible of those spaces for self-activity that remained to them in the interstices of the prevailing economic and social order: common rights, the customs of the trade. In the crystallizing industrial cultures of the cities and of the manufacturing and mining districts it also meant increasingly the development of forms of organization and action which enabled them either to resist detrimental changes in the terms and conditions of their labor, or to attempt to improve them – journeymen's associations, friendly societies, 'combinations', restrictive practices, absenteeism, riots, strikes. For the most part Britain's plebeians lived with the world as it was, but when what they took to be their independence was threatened, they could and did 'stand on their terms with their masters.'[55]

Such matters are less discussed in the case of colonial America, though they have their place. The assumptions that gradations of rank were necessary to the equilibrium of society and that people of rank and status were fittest to hold positions of authority remained commonplace. Patronage was a widespread feature of the conduct of social relations, and a self-conscious paternalism was part of the gentlemanly culture of the southern planter elite.[56] Yet all were perhaps enacted in contexts that subtly changed their meaning. The paternalism of the southern planters was in the first instance racial – directed less towards the maintenance of their authority amongst white tenants than towards justifying their exploitation of slave labor. And slavery played its part also in their relations with the middling and lower classes who readily accepted their leadership of southern society. Virginia remained 'a layered society' in which social differentiation was everywhere apparent. Yet its once turbulent social relations had been eased by the making available of land to poor freedmen, the substitution of African slavery for white indentured servitude, and the creation of a society in which all whites shared a position of racial superiority. The deference accorded the Virginian gentry was an expression of 'a common social identity that linked whites of all social classes.'[57]

More generally, however, visitors were often struck by the apparent lack of deference in American society, by the easy familiarity of social relations. This too was a society in which independence was valued. But crucially, it was also one in which the ideal of an independent competency had been widely achieved. Even the poorer farmers did not live in conditions of abject dependency and the numerical preponderance of independent freeholders 'gave normative status to their social values.'[58] This is not to say that white society was free of social tensions and conflicts of interest. They reverberated in the long debate in Massachusetts over the desirability of a land bank, in the 'Regulator' movements in the Carolinas in the 1760s and 1770s, in the artisan politics of Boston, Philadelphia, and other cities.[59] Yet in general white American society seems to have witnessed fewer expressions of social conflict in the colonial period than did eighteenth-century Britain. Perhaps, as J. T. Main argued, 'Economic abundance, together with high mobility combined to minimize those conflicts which might have grown out of the class structure and the consolidation of wealth,' or as Gary B. Nash puts it, differences of expectation fostered 'a psychological transformation fraught with implications for notions about the structuring of society.'[60] Where independence was a commonplace reality, fewer people were directly subject to the exploitation of others. Gentlemen could be accorded respect by lesser folk without the galling sense that this involved a forced acknowledgement of their innate superiority. Gentlemen themselves could extend ideals of liberty (to which their

British counterparts were equally attached) to entertain notions of equality. Yeomen and artisans could share those ideals because they were consonant with the world as they perceived it.

VII

This essay has attempted to survey two centuries of change in the English/British Atlantic world insofar as they have bearing on the problem of 'class' (broadly defined as the structures of economic inequality and their social, cultural, and political ramifications). In conclusion one must inevitably ask: what does an Atlantic perspective bring to the discussion of class in history?

First, such a perspective certainly demonstrates that social inequality 'pervaded the early modern Atlantic world.'[61] But that in itself is hardly surprising. Second, and perhaps more importantly, it serves to emphasize that it existed in different forms, was experienced in different degrees, and carried different implications in the component societies of this emergent transatlantic complex. By the mid-eighteenth century the British Atlantic world used an essentially common language to describe social distinctions and to express social tensions; it had certain common idioms in social relations. Yet these common categories concealed a set of very different social configurations. The variegated national and regional societies of mainland Britain were mixtures of forms in terms of both social structure and social relations, despite their growing commercial interconnectedness. The societies of colonial America had imported some patterns of social inequality from Britain, but they developed others that were peculiarly their own. If they were in some respects 'anglicized', they 'both mirrored and distorted the social structure of the homeland.'[62] If they were converging, they still presented a considerable diversity of experience.

Thirdly, an Atlantic perspective serves to underline the importance of historical time as a dimension of social structure. Throughout the Atlantic world the prevailing social realities of the eighteenth century contained layers of time. They represented different outcomes of a dynamic of economic and social change unleashed in the sixteenth century and sustained in part by the emergence of the Atlantic economy. But the social development of the component parts of that emergent whole demonstrate no common trajectory. Some central themes are certainly apparent – notably the fundamental differences in land/labor ratios between the

Old World and the New. Yet even so, there was no predictability in the outcomes observable in particular societies. Their histories are full of unintended consequences, frequently divergent, and repeatedly shaped by the influence of contextual and contingent circumstances. The shared language and family resemblances of the societies of the British Atlantic world are important reminders of the influence of common origins and shared traditions. But the real differences to be observed among them are even more telling testimony to the variety of potentials inherent in any social situation, and the unpredictability of their development over time.

Finally, the larger perspective of the Atlantic world serves, paradoxically, to re-emphasize the significance of the local. It provides a powerful reminder of how little we really know in detail of many of the societies briefly alluded to here. If we seek to understand class in the societies of the British Atlantic world, then we need first to examine more closely the social dynamics of those regional and local cultures within which class identities and class relations were structured and most immediately experienced. That ultimately is the best way of perceiving how those dynamics and those experiences related to a transatlantic whole.

8

Race

Joyce E. Chaplin

Race matters – so much does it matter to us now, that our current conceptions of it may hamper our understanding of how it mattered (or didn't matter) in the past. Tracing the history of ideas of race can make sense of what they may have meant in the past while also showing that the Atlantic dimension of this history is precisely what has shaped our current ideas of race. Indeed, racism in its present form is a specific product of Atlantic history. That is, if race is a perceived physical difference that is assumed to be inherited, is strongly associated with skin color, and is crafted to support systems of human subjugation, this idea was peculiar to the Atlantic world created by European colonization. To be sure, it had precedents in certain theories that had emerged in pre-Columbian Europe. Yet its most distinctive elements would have been alien to Europeans in the classical and medieval worlds, despite their considerable experience with exploitation, xenophobia, and imperialism. Perhaps more than any other set of ideas, race was Atlantic. The history of slavery makes especially clear that racism took strong hold in the western Atlantic, with powerful implications for the populations that mingled in the Americas, for the social structures of colonial societies, and for ideas of political rights on either side of the Atlantic. It is the continuing legacy of these implications that interests us in race and makes it necessary for us to see how it so deeply marked the modern world.

In the first part of my essay, I will survey the range of attitudes Europeans had about race before they crossed the Atlantic, and, by so doing, I will stress that for every tendency that gestured toward a modern concept of race there was an equal and opposite tendency to undercut the potential foundations of race. I will then show how European colonization of the Americas encouraged colonizers to identify labor to exploit and to present reasons for that exploitation as grounded in physical nature; these impulses gave race its foundations, ones that had been lacking before European expansion across the Atlantic.

I will commence with a broad look at European history, then a narrower look at Iberian origins of Atlantic colonization and racism. This will make clear that the English were not at the frontier of these experiences; they came later to the Americas and their decisions reflect knowledge of existing Iberian practices toward Africans and Indians. In relation to Africans, the English were *imitators* of Iberian theory and practice, especially in their adoption of enslaved African laborers for plantation regions; in relation to American Indians, however, the English were *innovators*, establishing ideas about natives' bodily frailty that were distinctive to the British colonies.

I

Though much recent work on the English-speaking Atlantic world claims to discuss race, most of this scholarship in fact discusses questions of status, religious confession, superficial physical appearance, or cultural practice. That is, these studies fail to address the definitive and insidious feature of racism: its grounding in the human body and in lineage, which thus defines it as inescapable, a non-negotiable attribute that predicts socio-political power or lack of power. This idea has a relatively recent history. Indeed, the history of the word 'race' reveals the distance we have traveled since the pre-Columbian era. The term, which originated in several Romance languages during the middle ages, designated a race as any group of people who shared some characteristics, and it did so rather neutrally, much in the way we would describe ethnicity, nationality, language group, or even kin group. It was not until the eighteenth century that race took on a consistently judgmental connotation, indicating differences among peoples meant to describe superiority and inferiority and implying an inheritance of status that was inescapable. Even into the nineteenth century, however, race continued to carry multiple meanings, making it difficult to distinguish what we might now recognize as race from the other connotations the word carried. To find the ancestors of modern conceptions of race, we need to look at a broad set of concerns, only some of which might be congruent with modern ideas.[1]

Most ancient and medieval schemas that distinguished between human populations were concerned with civic and religious status, not bodily difference. Denigration according to skin color, it should be noted, was not a marked feature of ancient or medieval societies. The ancient Greeks (on whose thinking Europeans grounded much of their political theory) were far more concerned to define who belonged to the polity, and therefore had citizenship, than they were to distinguish among differently appearing humans. Civic status was only available to free men who owned property within the *polis*; slaves, servants, women, children, landless men, and aliens all lacked true political character. In ancient Greece and Rome, xenophobia against those with an unfamiliar appearance certainly was present, yet not of paramount interest to ancient theorists of rights or their lack.[2]

Between the fall of Rome and the eighteenth century, European commentators on humanity assented to the orthodox, Christian doctrine of monogenesis, the belief that all people were descended from the originally created parents, Adam and Eve. To a certain extent, monogenesis curbed impulses that otherwise distinguished between human groups: other humans could be only so alien and inferior before realization of their common humanity had to occur. Monsters, who might appear to be partly human, existed in a separate category, indicating God's ability to create fantastic beings yet also serving to demarcate the boundaries of humanity. Against the monstrous, humans existed in their separate and special creation, a status that unified all people as actual or potential worshipers of their true creator.[3]

The lack of meaningful color prejudice and the belief in monogenesis give two cheers for the western tradition's unifying tendencies, but this is not to say that ideas of superiority and inferiority did not exist in the ancient and medieval worlds. A great deal of effort went into the differentiation of people in order to argue for specific social and political arrangements; some arguments also posited that human differences were inherited. This was the case even within otherwise unified cultural groups, in which lineage demarcated predictable social roles. Most obviously, the idea of aristocracy presented privileged position (property and authority) as the result of inherited qualities made manifest in inherited goods and power. The ancient concept of noble lineage is therefore quite possibly the remote ancestor of racial ideas. People other than aristocrats likewise inherited their abilities and position; assertions about peasants' mean nature (and low status) also stressed inheritance. In both cases, aristocrats and peasants were assumed to have physical and mental capacities appropriate for their roles. Thus the deep roots of the assumption that 'breeding will out', and that, however they might dress in each other's garb and wield each other's tools and weapons, persons of different ranks would betray their essentially different natures.[4]

These ideas were closely related to, and indeed probably modeled upon, ideas about sexual difference. Lineage depended, of course, on sexual reproduction, which itself was possible only because men and women were physically different; difference enabled reproduction and was itself reproduced naturally over the generations. Western culture was not content with these phenomena as facts of nature, but embellished them with assumptions about other physical and mental differences between male and female. These cultural embellishments ascribed hierarchical roles to men and women, usually emphasizing men's ability for public roles in war and politics along with women's private roles in childbearing and domestic work. Above all, the primary characteristic of citizens was their maleness. Women lacked political personality; cultural aliens were therefore essentially feminized, as persons external to the *polis*. The expectation that some people would be subordinate and others dominant was therefore deeply embedded in assumptions about social and gender hierarchy within European culture.[5]

These ideas were not identical to the parallel concepts that differentiated between humans who came from varied cultures. Prejudice against cultural outsiders did mark ancient and medieval thought, but people were rarely consistent in arguing that aliens were irreducibly different and inferior in the way that they argued that lineage and sex made people different. Instead, language, custom (what we would call culture), and climate created human variety across the globe. Each of these factors received lavish attention and generated complex literatures. Medical theories and travel accounts, especially, devoted a great deal of attention to the question of why the world's populations presented variety rather than conformity.

Surveys of human types were openly chauvinistic, promoting the qualities of the surveyors over those of the surveyed. Language and climate were measures of one's civility over the uncivilized nature of others. Thus the Greeks had called non-Greeks barbarians because of the way their utterances sounded (as if babbled, 'bar-bar') to the Greek ear; the Greeks and Romans maintained that written language was an essential element of true humanity, meaning legal and political culture. The Greeks had also asserted that a temperate climate was essential for true civilization. Hot climates made people prone to sloth, luxury, and vice; cold climates made humans stoic and stupid. These prejudices survived antiquity, with European commentators insisting that written language and temperate climate were prerequisites to law and civility.[6]

For medieval and early modern Europeans, the paramount categories for humans had to do with religion, meaning Christianity or its absence. Christendom designated the part of the world that was central to Christian cosmography. Conceptualization of Christian Europe as the world's focal point developed especially in the context of the crusades against Muslims in the Near East. During these conflicts, the term 'Frank' became more common as a term to describe a Christian European, as opposed to Jews and Muslims. Religion therefore functioned in some ways as a form of ethnicity and as a foundation of nationality; if lineage and sex indicated where Europeans belonged within their own societies, religion (like climate and language) showed where they belonged in relation to the rest of the world. Religion denoted European belonging and exclusion and indicated terms for persecution and possible exploitation.[7]

Still, as was the case with language, custom, political identity, and climate, religious difference was not irreversible. Indeed, it was precisely because people could learn new languages, convert to new faiths, acquire political capacity, settle in and adapt to new climates, and adopt new customs that these variables lacked the all-important inescapability of lineage and sexual status. In some instances, acquired differences were thought to become heritable. Overall, however, these were characteristics that went under the contemporary heading of accidental: that is, they were accidents of birth (and hence reversible within a generation) rather than intrinsic to a lineage and continuing over the generations.

These bundles of ideas – too polyvalent and flexible to form ideologies comparable to modern racism – continued through much of the eighteenth century. Their variety and persistence demonstrate that ideas about race were not inevitable products of western culture; there were too many possibilities at work earlier. That a rather narrow idea – in which inherited bodily differences justified exploitation of some by others – would triumph over other views would not necessarily have seemed likely during the middle ages, for instance. But careful recent scholarship on attitudes toward two groups, Jews and sub-Saharan Africans, has revealed that medieval and early modern Europeans in the Mediterranean were in fact crafting much more exclusionary explanations of these two peoples that would point in a new and distinctive direction.

Anti-Semitism and anti-African xenophobia accordingly had the clearest resemblances to modern ideas of race, however regional and specialized these attitudes may have been during the middle ages themselves. Prejudice against Jews was perhaps most marked in late medieval Spain. There, religious persecution of Jews (and Muslims) fostered belief among some that even Jews who had converted to Christianity bore some mark of difference and inferiority. Concern over 'purity of blood' led officials in the Inquisition to arrest and interrogate suspect *conversos*, people who had converted from Judaism to Christianity but remained tainted in lineage, despite this cultural and religious transformation. Such suspicion also marked Mediterranean Europeans' views of sub-Saharan Africans, individuals usually brought into Europe under conditions of enslavement and therefore deeply associated with a bondage, physical durability, and cultural inferiority that would pass down to their children.[8]

The hypothesis that Jews and Africans inherited their characteristics was connected to biblical exegesis about the scattered progeny of Noah. Orthodox Christian (like Judaic) belief stressed that the peoples of the world were descended from the sons of Noah who had repopulated the world after the Deluge. Each son was interpreted as traveling to a different part of the globe; in addition, the lineage of one son, Canaan (father of Cham), was supposedly cursed. Explanations of each son's destination, and especially the eventual home of Cham, varied, but some interpretations placed Cham in Africa and described his descendants as cursed. This tracing of Noah's genealogy built upon expectations that lineage and religion designated human status. Obviously we can here detect insidious tremors of the racist earthquake yet to come in mass enslavement and genocide against Africans and Jews. Still, these were developments in the future, and beliefs that Jews and Africans belonged to cursed lineages were not yet put to systematic work in the ways they would be in the nineteenth and twentieth centuries.[9]

In the meantime, attitudes toward disease functioned much more to justify socio-economic exploitation of certain groups, and especially the enslavement of Africans. The experience of the Black Death in medieval Europe gave its residents a shocking reminder of their bodily weakness and an interest in determining who, if anyone, might be resistant to such physical assaults. If the idea of the curse on Cham signified a vague quest to discover who might be hewers of wood and drawers of water, suspicion that West Africans were uniquely fit to bear physical hardship was a much more salient contribution to the pro-slavery arguments eventually based on race. African bodily durability had been a byword since the Roman era. Importation of slaves into the European Mediterranean accelerated after the Black Death and during shortages of labor in Europe. Meanwhile, the Europeans who now knew their bodily weakness in the face of plagues also noticed that they could not thrive in the tropical climates of West Africa, as might natives of this place. These experiences and assumptions about work, body, and disease may very well have reinforced each other to promote a preference for enslaved African labor in certain places. Certainly, Iberian use of African labor on the Atlantic islands they colonized and planted with sugar was a clear step in the development of racial slavery in the Atlantic, that is, a practical association between bodily type and socio-economic status in the Atlantic world, with some to be enslaved and others to be slaveholders.[10]

Before the era of European overseas expansion, therefore, everything that could possibly have been said about human difference had already been said. Some human characteristics were held to be merely accidental differences, incidental features that might change within an individual's time or over the generations, if new customs were introduced or migration to new climates occurred. Other features were inherited, sometimes indicating social status and sexual role, sometimes marking even more strongly different capacities for religious salvation or social mobility. All these ideas existed together, one or another being deployed as circumstances necessitated. That some worked against others (accidents versus lineage, especially) showed that many Europeans were not yet interested in crafting a coherent ideology of inborn differences to help consistently to exploit others. And one idea essential to modern theories of race was entirely absent, a meaningful theory about a mechanism of inheritance. This idea only emerged once Europeans began to colonize the western side of the Atlantic.

II

The Americas presented Europeans with many new opportunities, including intellectual challenges that began to narrow the field of options that described different human populations. From the European perspective, America was a new world, and therefore a problem for their theories about the globe – and the cosmos. That the Americas were not described in either classical or biblical texts was a considerable conundrum. There was no easy way to determine who the peoples of this new world were and where they had originated. Discussions of this problem referred to inquiry into the different lineages of humanity (including debate over Noah's progeny), thus initiating concern in the earliest descriptions of the Americas over bloodlines as distinguishing features of human groups. The theory of monogenesis prevented open speculation that Amerindians were descended from a distinct branch of humanity (or were sub-human), but many other ideas were marshaled to emphasize their cultural and physical alienness.[11]

One idea that Europeans, especially the Spanish, debated was that Amerindians were natural slaves, an inferior category of humanity that Aristotle had postulated as lying outside civil society. Natural slaves had deficient intellectual and moral capacities that required true citizens to rule them by force. In the end, the crown and religious officials declared that Amerindians were not natural slaves but instead fully human and capable of civil and ethical improvement. In the meantime, however, the Spanish and Portuguese tendency to enslave Africans revealed an acceptance, albeit a tacit one, that this population was suited to a form of natural slavery. This assumption built upon processes already in place in the 'old' world, but the scale was different and the arguments for enslavement began to take on permanent and tragic dimensions.[12]

One reason for this acceleration of enslavement was disease. As with the Black Death in Europe earlier, the populations of the Americas (native or recently introduced) suffered differential survival rates in the face of epidemics. Native Americans had particularly high rates of sickness and mortality after their populations, which had no immediate resistance to Old World contagious diseases, came into contact with Europeans. Europeans themselves did not thrive in tropical climates, something they had already noted in Africa. Placing all these Atlantic experiences together, Iberians, then other colonizing Europeans, concluded that Amerindians were strikingly weak and Africans correspondingly tough, with Europeans located at some mid-point between these two extremes; they were more vigorous than Amerindians, yet not so insensibly durable as Africans. Such observations helped support assessments that Amerindians were inadequate as a source for large-scale labor and had little claim to American land, while Africans made ideal and transportable slaves.

These were not idle statements. Development of plantation agriculture in the Americas was the motor that ran the Atlantic slave trade. Here, the Atlantic environment meant everything to the subsequent determination of socio-economic roles, and showed a propensity on the part of Europeans to declare that such roles were grounded in nature itself. Based on these Iberian formulations, a first shift, in which the range of ways to describe others began to narrow, is apparent by the sixteenth century.[13]

III

As they turned their attention to the Americas, the English tended to argue (early and often) that unequal status in their colonies was based on natural differences. The very first English attempt to set up a colony, a 1570s fortified mining camp in the Arctic, elicited speculation about bodily differences that survived removal to new climates, a fundamental challenge to doctines of human difference as accidental. To make this point, George Best in his *True Discourse of the Three Voyages of Discoverie [of Martin Frobisher]* (1578) referred to sub-Saharan Africans' dark skin, hypothesizing that it resulted from an 'infection' carried through the bloodline. Though the colonizing venture in which Best participated failed, his speculations cast a long shadow over subsequent British actions in the Americas.[14]

English colonial policies tended to lack the metropolitan oversight that characterized Spanish colonization. This decentralized pattern gave English colonizers a much freer hand in determining how they would treat aliens. Their actions revealed an early propensity to seek labor and use it by any means possible. Unlike the Spanish, the English did enslave Amerindians freely, kidnapping them from the coast of North America as early as the mid-1500s. A brisk trade in Amerindian slaves continued, especially in regions that had the worst Anglo-Indian warfare, as in the seventeenth century Pequot and King Philip's wars in New England, the roughly contemporary Anglo-Powhatan wars and Bacon's rebellion in Virginia, and the Yamassee and Tuscarora wars in early eighteenth-century South Carolina. In parallel, English attitudes toward Africans reveal an 'unthinking imitation' of Iberian enslavement of Africans, a little-questioned tendency to lean toward enslaved African labor whenever settlers could afford it. Fundamental to this pattern was the belief that Africans were durable and capable of hard work in daunting climates, especially for sugar cultivation in tropical places. As one discussion of New World settlement concluded, the heavy work of American colonization was best done by 'Negroes', who were 'a people strong and able'. During the eighteenth century, the assertion that West Africans were uniquely adapted to tropical and subtropical environments played an active role in their exploitation in plantation agriculture.[15]

But during the seventeenth century, these options were still indeterminate and not yet equivalent to the rigid systems of slavery and racial status that were to come. While captive Amerindians and Africans were notable as subordinate groups, they were mixed into large populations of white indentured servants and into smaller populations of whites who were condemned to slavery for long periods (in rare cases, for life). Exploitation and inferior status were not yet racial but spread over several groups; this variegated socio-economic reality paralleled the variety of ideas about human difference that had existed in pre-Columbian Europe and then crossed the Atlantic.[16]

Uncertainty over the contradictory meanings of these options marked English literature on the Atlantic world during the seventeenth and early eighteenth centuries. In fact, two kinds of texts proliferated: one that discussed the body and climate, and another that considered the low status of non-European peoples as possibly unjust. The former literature continued to stress the accidental and reversible nature of bodily difference; this was true of natural histories of the New World, of medical literature on the colonies, and of discussions of the growth of English populations in the western Atlantic.[17] Within these writings, however, some authors embedded assertions as to the enduring differences between human bodies. Commentary on epidemics among Amerindians, and assumptions that Africans (and the English) displayed contrasting bodily strengths, steadily increased confidence that lineage was destiny. Thus Virginia's governor, Samuel Argall, wrote in 1617 of 'a great mortality among us, [though] far greater among the Indians.' Population studies were especially telling measures of English confidence, and demographic surveys of the colonies were distinctively English ways of charting their increase and Amerindians' demise, providing a running account of whose bodies thrived in the New World, and who therefore could call upon nature itself as vindication for their cultural prowess. As one account of the 1637 Pequot War in New England emphasized, the English had God-given 'facultie' 'to beget and bring forth more children than any other nation of the world.'[18]

Another and in some ways a competing group of texts lamented that some populations of the new Atlantic world suffered at the hands of others. The first examples were directed at European mistreatment of Amerindians. The English adopted this genre, originally meant by the Spanish to prevent enslavement of and warfare on Amerindians, and used it to criticize fellow English people who (unlike the Spanish) continued these practices. One of the most enduring forms of this literature revolved around the Inkle and Yarico story, about an Englishman (Thomas Inkle) who betrays and sells into slavery his Indian lover, Yarico, and their unborn child. These writings did not necessarily dissent from the opinions in the literature that assessed bodies and climates, so in fact their criticisms of exploitation were not yet racialized. Instead, they functioned as generalized doubt over the place of slavery and violence in the Atlantic world or in empires more generally.[19]

The early period of English colonization also saw the final piece of intellectual work that needed to be done before a modern idea of race could be articulated, that is, describing a mechanism of inheritance. In the mid-1600s, natural philosopher William Harvey first indicated the material processes of reproduction that we now accept. Harvey postulated that animals (including humans) reproduced because their females produced eggs, a primordial generative material. He never saw these eggs, but improvement of microscopes toward the end of the seventeenth century confirmed the existence of male gametes and supplied evidence of tangible reproductive material for those who wished to emphasize lineage over other causes of human characteristics. The context for this new inquiry was probably not exclusively colonial; anxiety over paternity was a marked feature of English society in the second half of the seventeenth century. Likewise, these trends were at first evident only among a learned minority of Europeans because Harvey published his findings in Latin. But their rudiments and implications thereafter spread and were well developed by the eighteenth century, the era when ideas about race seemed to take on modern, permanent form. The popularized doctrine of preformation, for instance, which argued that a small, preformed human existed either in egg or sperm, revealed a conviction that human types were fully formed before birth, rather than shaped by climate and custom afterward.[20]

IV

Concern to consider human bodies as natural entities, whose characteristics could be described according to a systematic science, proceeded apace during the eighteenth century. At this point, poly-genesis, the idea that different groups of humans might have been created in different times and places, was publicly discussed in a way that would have been heretical earlier. Philosophers such as Henry Home, Lord Kames, and Voltaire were among those who wrote about polygenesis; in contrast, naturalists were less likely to accept the doctrine. They instead contributed to the construction of tax-onomies that placed humans in relation to the rest of the physical creation, as if their fundamental qualities were no different from those of animals. Swedish botanist Linnaeus (Carl von Linné) was the first (in the 1730s and 1740s) to present humans as part of the animal world, as a species of mammalian bodies with physical characteristics that indicated their place within nature. Linnaeus's taxonomy was followed by that of Johann Friedrich Blumenbach, who was first (in 1759) to use the term 'Caucasian' to indicate a lineage supposedly unique to central and western Europe, and alleged to be aesthetically superior to those of Africa, Asia, America, and other places.[21]

These developments must be placed within the socio-economic context of the greater Atlantic world, which mattered extraordinar-ily to the implications of theories about human superiority and in-feriority. The eighteenth century was, above all, the heyday of the Atlantic slave trade. Burgeoning markets for sugar and other tropical and semi-tropical commodities encouraged investment in their production, including investment in slaves and elaboration of ration-ales for their debasement. In parallel, the different European powers expanded claims to American territories, accelerating dispossession of Native American populations and inflating rhetoric that justified this land grab. At this point, English arguments for the bodily fitness of Africans to labor in hot climates, and complementary assertions that Amerindians were unlikely to survive in and utilize American lands, took on the qualities of conclusions; conviction that Africans and Amerindians must passively inherit these fates justified imperial ambitions.[22]

Such prejudices deeply informed the political constitution of colonial societies. Laws regulating slaves and prohibiting Amerindians and free blacks from equal access to legal and political action became standard in colonial societies, with no intervention from metropolitan authorities. In fact, settlers' insistence that race dictated political identity crossed the Atlantic eastward, making English law itself complicitous with colonial policy.[23] Belief that some humans had bodies and belonged to lineages that gave them subordinate social roles was clearly shaping the worlds that bordered the Atlantic Ocean during the eighteenth century – long before Charles Darwin's theory of evolution and popular conceptions of the 'survival of the fittest'. While racism may have been most visible and virulent in regions heavily invested in slavery or engaged in warfare against Amerindians, racial attitudes and racially defined captives were present throughout the English-speaking world, from Grenada to Glasgow.[24]

At some points, however, whites in British America played a tellingly creative role in defining bodily differences as heritable. This was particularly true for residents of regions with economies dependent on plantation agriculture and slavery. Edward Long, in *History of Jamaica* (1774), his account of his native island, paid elaborate attention to questions of blood and lineage. He provided charts for lines of descent from white and black ancestors and praised 'the genuine English breed, untainted with these heterogeneous mixtures.' Long lamented colonists' use of 'Negro' wet-nurses, whose 'blood may be corrupted' with venereal diseases; he hoped that, in contrast to what he perceived as the amalgamated nature of residents of Spanish America, English settlers would raise 'in honourable wedlock a race of unadulterated beings.'[25] Physician William Wells, who was a native of South Carolina, was first to theorize in writing that skin color was inherited rather than the result of climate – a fundamental challenge to continuing belief that sub-Saharan Africans gained their dark complexion from a burning sun. Wells hypothesized, in a paper presented to the Royal Society in London in 1813 (and published five years later), that African skin color was due to a physical adaptation to disease that was then passed down through the generations – a remarkable restatement of George Best's suppositions two and a half centuries earlier. These manifestly racist opinions contrast with New Englander Samuel Stanhope Smith's emphasis, in his *Essay on the Causes of the Variety of Complexion and Figure in the Human Species* (1787), on monogenesis and on the power of climate and custom to mark superficially the human body. Smith concluded that efforts to classify human races according to physical characteristics were 'a useless labor', so similar were humans to each other.[26]

Smith's lack of racism notwithstanding, body and lineage had come to have overwhelming significance for assignment of rank and role in the English plantations. In the end, it may have mattered little that the English lacked a full-blown racial ideology such as would flourish in the nineteenth century. Inconsistency and contradiction about the body and lineage cost the English nothing; formation of an even partial and incoherent idea of race may have cost a great many Amerindians and Africans everything.

V

The power and function of these arguments about the different populations in the Atlantic world reveal possible differences from other regions that the English colonized. The English never used arguments about disease and population to justify colonization of Ireland, for instance, never stigmatizing the Irish on bodily grounds in as extreme a fashion as they did Amerindians and Africans. In fact, the English perceived Ireland (and Scotland) as overpopulated, to the point that one late seventeenth-century pioneer of political economy, William Petty, proposed that parts of Ireland and Scotland have their populations removed in order to facilitate cattle ranching. This was imperialism, but not one with the same racialized discourse on population, land, and labor that dominated the worlds across the Atlantic.[27]

India presented yet another set of imperial possibilities. Certainly, British colonizers asserted that the peoples of the subcontinent, like those of Asia proper, had languages, religions, customs, and appearance alien to Europe. Further, assertions of a racial difference would eventually mark nearly all British attitudes toward India. But theorizing about India's differences also took a less naturalized route, beginning at least as early as Sir William Jones's examination of Sanskrit. Jones's early 1800s taxonomy of languages postulated ancient connections between India and Europe and suggested a common 'Aryan' ancestry for their languages. This created a genealogy that ignored the human body and physical lineage in favor of cultural factors, and above all it was a genealogy that linked rather than separated Europe and Asia. (It also presents a painful irony in the history of race, given that National Socialism under Hitler would reidentify Aryan as a racial rather than a linguistic category.) That this was a non-racial description of India shows how naturalized descriptions clung more tightly to the Atlantic than to other parts of the British empire; English examination of Native American and African languages was never so painstaking and never reached a comparable conclusion.[28]

If non-Atlantic portions of the British empire emphasize the distinctiveness of colonization in the New World, it is also possible to trace some similarities having to do with race throughout the colonized portions of the Americas. It has long been thought that sexual activity across the 'races' was more characteristic of Iberian and French colonies than of English ones. But the 'lack' of mestizos in Anglo-America now seems suspect. Such people indeed existed, but it has taken determined reinterrogation of the historical record to discover them. Their existence shows that, in British America, mixed-race people were not absent – official recognition of them was. Whereas the state in Spanish America and in New France was alert to the sexual behaviors of Christians, and to the engendering of people of part-Christian parentage, political and religious officials in the anglophone colonies took no such interest. Such behaviors were private, albeit illegitimate, and the children who resulted were likewise regarded as illegitimate and beneath public notice. As with so much of British colonization, the state stood aside and gave local authorities in the colonies vast leeway to dictate social and legal realities and in essence to regard mestizos as invisible. These new discoveries indicate that, however much English-speaking people insisted that Africans and Amerindians had bodies different from their own, this was not a significant curb on either sexual predation or on willingness to make permanent relationships with members of other 'races' despite social disapprobation. A complicated dynamic was therefore in place throughout the Americas, a wish to distinguish between Europeans and others that was both reinforced and undercut by desire to connect their bodies in the most intimate way.[29]

VI

One final question will help tease out the implications of race for Atlantic history: who wasn't racist? That is, who lived along the shores of the Atlantic and confronted the fully modern definition of race – as heritable difference that was hierarchically meaningful – and declared it invalid, intellectually or morally? If race is Atlantic, is anti-racism the product of the same historical context?

A good guess is that those who were the objects of racism were suspicious of its intellectual foundations. We know little, however, about Amerindian and African beliefs that might have resembled European notions of race or that contradicted them. Certainly, West African forms of slavery were rarely heritable or lineal – in strong contrast to European practice. Some Amerindian cultures focused on body and lineage, even emphasizing separate creations of 'red' and 'white' peoples, but it is not clear whether these views preceded extensive contact with Europeans and the experience of war and enslavement at their hands.[30]

Historians have more systematically traced a questioning of racism among populations of European descent. Some Europeans and some white Creoles in North America fiercely contemplated the inequities on the western side of the Atlantic. This was most famously present in the emerging anti-slavery movement, first to abolish the Atlantic slave trade, then to do away with the institution of chattel slavery altogether. It is true, of course, that many critics of slavery were racist; some abolitionists preferred that freed blacks be removed to Africa, lest their perceived physical and cultural inferiority taint metropolitan populations or Creole peoples in America. But sentiments critical of European colonization were also present in a broader rethinking of empires and of political systems during the late eighteenth and early nineteenth centuries, and some advocates of radical reform did question ideas of race and stressed that liberty belonged to all humans who might seek it. William Gordon thus baited his anti-revolutionary opponents with the statement that 'a black, tawny or reddish skin is not so unfavorable an hue to the genuine son of liberty, as a tory complection.'[31]

Many of the objections to slavery had a religious basis. Such arguments followed the old Christian logic of monogenesis: all humans descended from one lineage, were of one blood, and must be allowed to find their way to the true God, a process that slavery (with its violent impositions on body and mind) might impede. Missionaries in the Americas had long been insisting on these precepts; the first doubts about Amerindian dispossession and African enslavement continued and critics began to argue against assertions, like polygenesis or scientific taxonomies, that humans belonged to distinct lineages with distinct fates.[32]

This does not mean, however, that critics of racism were critics of science in its efforts to describe the material world. Nor do I mean that religion and science necessarily teased out substantially different attitudes toward humanity. Some well-known naturalists belonged to radical Protestant sects; they were certainly not anti-scientific, but took instead a different approach to nature, regarding empirical inquiry into it as a form of devotion to God, the omnipotent creator. It is therefore possible that those who insisted on a 'one blood' vision of humans were critical of versions of science that argued otherwise, but did not reject science out of hand. Conversely, descriptions of human inequality, and justifications of New World chattel slavery, continued to rely on scriptural exegeses, particularly emphasis on Noachic lineages. And there are certainly secular philosophical roots for anti-slavery, particularly political and legal theorization about the rights of man that emphasized all of humanity's intrinsic right to be free.[33]

The politics of the era stimulated this questioning of hierarchies, including those built at least in part on race. The American and French revolutions, and the wars of independence in the Caribbean and Latin America, all tested the logic of the rights of man. These tests were trans-Atlantic, as historians have long argued; the revolutions reverberated on either side of the ocean and fundamentally challenged western conceptions of order, authority, and power. They were deeply implicated in concerns over race as well, and this is an Atlantic dimension that has been less celebrated because it raises such serious questions about the power of racism to curb radical social change and to survive – and thrive – into our day.

In some ways, American patriots in what would become the United States sought to loosen racial categorization in order to connect arguments for political independence from Britain to discourse on a hypothetical 'American' physical environment and concomitant bodily type. This argument for a naturalized national character appropriated Amerindian identities while never seriously considering Amerindians as potential fellow citizens. Brief public recognition of mestizo peoples, and valorization of those mestizos who supported the revolution, were white patriots' opportunistic identification with some people of native descent.[34] But the revolution's only provisional promises to African Americans and its exclusion of Native Americans from statements of universal equality among citizens demonstrate how the history of race in the modern Atlantic laid a heavy hand on the history of the west. Additionally, the anti-slavery revolt in the French colony of St Domingue, and the consequent revolutionary creation of the republic of Haiti, revealed the joining together of revolutionary politics and anti-racist claims among people of color. Yet most whites in America and Britain rejected this second American revolution and second Atlantic republic. Anti-racism made sense to those who had suffered from racism but looked like an invitation to disorder even to whites who held otherwise radical opinions.[35]

The best case in point in this regard is perhaps Thomas Jefferson – ardent friend of liberty yet apologist for racial slavery. That his thinking was fully racialized helps explain why he could maintain both positions: liberty and slavery were, as far as he was concerned, based on natural characteristics of different humans. In his *Notes on the State of Virginia* (1787), Jefferson stated straightforwardly that 'the difference [between whites and blacks] is fixed in nature.' He meant that skin color, race's most immediate marker, was a natural fact, yet 'there are other physical distinctions proving a difference of race', including that Africans had less facial hair, secreted more via skin pores than by the kidneys, had differences in their 'pulmonary apparatus', and 'require less sleep', a restatement of the long-standing opinion that blacks were indefatigable workers. Jefferson's racism in regard to Amerindians was more subtle, relying as it did on the idea, again a long-standing one, that their population was doomed to decline, even to the point of extinction: stresses to their populations had made it impossible that sexual 'generation' would make up for their losses. Jefferson's racism was not atypical, and its consequences are still evident in American culture today.[36]

These battles over racism, and their continued resonance within our own politics, should encourage us to consider carefully race's contested meanings in the past and its legacy for our time. We do not yet have a post-racial comprehension of humanity, and continuing debates over race show its deep roots in Atlantic history. The nations of the Americas and of Europe by and large show unwillingness to regard people whose ancestry is not dominantly European as full and equal citizens. And that the Americas, the portion of the modern world that contained most of the first modern revolutions, remain deeply racist is perhaps the ultimate paradox of the modern Atlantic world.

This is a problem even for historians who study that Atlantic world. Some scholarship has recently emerged that describes the early republic of the United States as a 'post-colonial' society. Such an identification deeply misrepresents the racial politics of the past and the present. Post-colonial is a term, originally applied to India after independence, that indicates how colonial populations and regimes have passed away. While the imperial regime of Britain passed away in part of North America after 1776, the colonizing population did not; it, and its descendants, continue to colonize the United States and Canada, to monopolize and control North America's resources and polities. Understanding this is to understand

how theories of race managed to make Native American populations in the United States invisible and to make the subordination of
African-American peoples on both sides of the Atlantic seem to be a
natural state of affairs. Neither Britain nor the United States (nor
Canada) is a post-colonial nation – sadly, we are still too much a
product of the Atlantic history of race for this to be a reality.

Part IV
Politics

9

Empire and State

Elizabeth Mancke

The Atlantic world was defined by states but colonized by empires. The British, no less than the Spanish, Portuguese, French, and Dutch, negotiated their claims beyond Europe through institutions within Europe. However, as latecomers to the race for Atlantic empire, the British had to operate on terms set by their predecessors and competitors. As a result of the regularization of diplomatic relations in the Atlantic basin French and Spanish diplomats developed the concept of lines of amity; to the north and east of them lay Europe, to the south and west lay the extra-European world.[1] The implications of this conceptual distinction were to be profound for the subsequent history of the Atlantic world. Men and women who settled beyond those lines were now thought to be proper subjects of European monarchs. In contrast, the Portuguese and Castilian monarchs had declared millions of Americans, Africans, and Asians to be their subjects. Henceforth, colonization would increasingly foster a distinction between native populations and settler-subjects. Moreover, this division of the world allowed other European powers to challenge Iberian claims, while at the same time creating a very clear distinction between the nature of European empires and of European states. Lines of amity in the Atlantic divided Europe from the rest of the world far more profoundly than did the Mediterranean Sea or an unmapped marchland between Europe and Asia. This distinction was of central importance to the development of tensions between colonists and the British state in the eighteenth century and had a profound impact on the development of the internal structure of the metropolitan state. An Atlantic history of

175

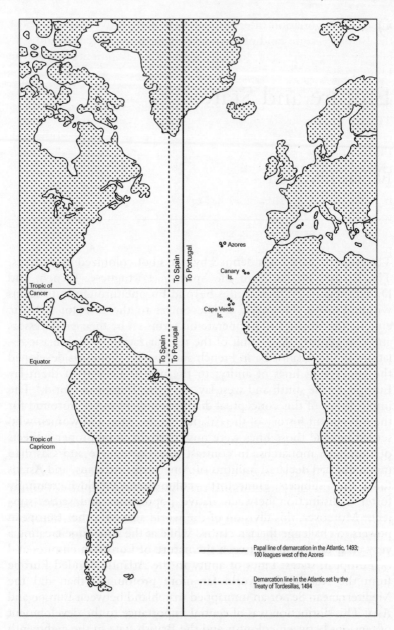

Map 3 The lines of amity, adapted from Max Savelle, *The Origins of American Diplomacy: The International History of Anglo-America, 1492–1763* (New York, 1967), p. 15.

interstate negotiation offers crucial new perspectives both on how the British empire (and others) developed in the sixteenth and seventeenth centuries, and on how imperial developments shaped the United Kingdom and the United States in the eighteenth century.

These developments can be explored through an examination of how early modern empire building affected British state formation. The scholarly literature tends to treat them as quite distinct phenomena, and indeed the two processes can be viewed as antithetical. European states tried to define their territorial boundaries more precisely, though at the same time they issued charters to establish colonies with imprecise boundaries. Overseas expansion spawned new institutional forms, while European authorities worked within their polities to create greater institutional articulation if not uniformity. Monarchs reined in the private armies of the nobility, but gave chartered companies, colonial promoters, and hundreds of sea captains the right to wage war in the Americas, Africa, and Asia. In short, empire building and state formation seem to be parallel more than interdependent phenomena, related coincidentally rather than consequentially.[2]

At the level of foreign policy, however, empire building and state formation were interdependent, and thus international relations offers a starting point for analyzing the dialectical relationship between the two. The restructuring of international relations in response to overseas expansion, this essay argues, reinforced state formation because it reinforced one of the most centralized parts of government, foreign affairs. In the sixteenth and seventeenth centuries, the English metropolitan government initially institutionalized much of the oversight of transoceanic ventures as a part of foreign policy. Thus empire building was not just a problem of how to govern a larger, more dispersed, and more diverse composite polity.[3] As the early institutional manifestations of empire within the metropole suggested, the problem was also one of negotiating a shifting and ambiguous international order. Indeed, a key element in understanding early modern British empire building is to determine the extent to which the metropolitan government treated the overseas activities of British subjects as a problem of external affairs or of internal governance, or some combination of the two.

Empire building also influenced state formation through the networks of economic and political power that overseas expansion engendered.[4] Some of these networks had quasi-public institutional expressions, as colonial ventures or joint-stock companies. Others, such as business partnerships, never did. Scholars have tended to

discount the relationship between private networks and the metropolitan state and to argue instead that they demonstrate the lack of
state involvement in empire building.[5] At the level of the state's
financial commitment this point is, of course, true. Yet at the diplomatic level, state-to-state negotiations frequently focused on new
networks of power in the extra-European world, their relationship
to one or another state, the willingness of a state to regulate, if not
restrain, these networks, and the necessity of some international
coordination in defining the world within which they operated.
Many of those state-level discussions did not find permanent expression in new fiscal extractions or institutions, but they gradually
redefined the international role and relationship of states, especially
those with overseas empires.

The analysis in this essay is in three parts. The first part sketches the
shifting and novel nature of international relations that developed
among the expanding European powers to negotiate their interests in
the extra-European world. The second looks at how the various
sectors of British overseas commerce and colonization reflected different combinations of external affairs and internal governance, and the
implications for the structures of power within the metropolitan state.
The third analyzes why developments in the mid-eighteenth century
unsettled the distribution of power both within the empire and within
the core of the British state itself.

***

Over the course of the early modern era, empire building did begin
to exhibit characteristics associated with state formation. European
states with overseas interests began to control or suppress privatized
violence, to define the boundaries of overseas claims, and to coordinate institutions within and between overseas dependencies. Much
of the impetus for these developments came from diplomatic pressures and negotiations, and thus represents more than just internal
processes of coalescence. This observation applies to all the states
with early modern empires with the following caveat. Initially the
Spanish and Portuguese 'domesticated' overseas expansion by
defining their overseas jurisdictions as extensions of the realms of
Castile and Portugal. The French, English, and Dutch challenged
the Iberians by redefining extra-European space as initially 'foreign'
to all Europeans and which could not be claimed through mere discovery of a whole continent, royal fiat, or papal bull.

The diplomacy that ensued from these oppositional positions produced a distinct chronology of international relations that provides a framework for understanding 300 years of developments. The first period stretches from 1492 to the 1640s, during which time the Iberians refused to recognize non-Iberian rights in the extra-European world. A new period opened in the 1640s when the Iberians began to acknowledge the claims of the Netherlands, England, and France. Diplomacy shifted to multilateral concerns over questions of the control of privatized violence, conflicting land claims, and boundaries. These matters of oversight and regulation were ones that metropolitan states seldom delegated, but handled directly. For the French and British, they complemented the emergence of institutions and policies for governing and defending overseas dependencies.[6] In the eighteenth century, the question of oceanic control and Spain's continued claims to suzerainty, if not sovereignty, over the Atlantic and Pacific oceans resurfaced as an issue of international debate and marks a third period of international relations.[7] The Spanish finally relinquished their claims to the Atlantic and Pacific oceans in 1750 and 1790 respectively, completing the emergence of a global international order defined and controlled by a few European states.[8]

Exclusive Iberian claims to the extra-European world, based on papal bulls issued in 1493 and the Treaty of Tordesillas in 1494, implicitly defined the transoceanic ventures of other Europeans as adversarial. The Portuguese and Spanish division of the extra-European world drew on practices used to adjudicate their conflicting claims to the Canaries, Azores, Madeiras, and Cape Verde Islands. In those cases, they had appealed for adjudication to the pope, whose authority in such disputes had been legitimated, in part, through the precedent of deciding similar cases during the Crusades. Other Europeans accepted Iberian claims to these Atlantic islands, at times validating them in treaty negotiations. There was, however, no immediate reaction to the Treaty of Tordesillas, although Henry VII's charter to John Cabot in 1497 suggests he either did not consider the treaty to apply to north Atlantic waters, or that in those waters he could ignore Iberian claims with relative impunity.[9]

In the 1520s, the French crown began disputing the Iberians' claims in diplomatic exchanges, often precipitated by Iberian complaints about the transoceanic voyages of French subjects. The French, and later the English, challenges undermined the legitimacy of the terms of the Treaty of Tordesillas, the papal bulls that preceded it, and the Luso-Spanish treaties that followed it. Consequently, they also rejected existing practices for sanctioning the extension of European spheres of influence and power. The foreign relations that evolved to address transoceanic expansion were more secular, more exclusive, and more state-oriented than were intra-European foreign relations. The rejection of the papacy's role in adjudicating claims to new lands effectively secularized this branch of European diplomacy a full century before the Peace of Westphalia did the same for continental relations.[10] Over the early modern period, only five states regularly participated in negotiations over transoceanic affairs: Spain, Portugal, France, England, and the Netherlands. While other powers made the occasional overseas foray, such as Scotland and Sweden, they had modest roles in defining this branch of international relations.

The exclusivity of this arena of international relations was further reinforced by the criteria for legitimating overseas land claims. The general outcome is well known: discovery, occupation, or conquest became the three dominant criteria. Discovery could be superseded by occupation, and the abandonment of occupation (as happened on St Lucia in 1605) could extinguish a claim, as could conquest, in which case the conquerors became the acknowledged claimant. The need of the English, French, and Dutch to challenge the Spanish and Portuguese hegemonic claims biased their initial activities in extra-European lands and with non-European peoples. Confronting Iberian claims, they paid little heed to grappling with the rights of native peoples. Rather, the English, French, and Dutch concentrated on establishing their claims vis-à-vis other Europeans. All Europeans excluded non-European claims from multinational negotiations. Instead they were treated as matters of negotiation between agents of the expanding powers and indigenous leaders, and thus not within the arena of European multilateral adjudication and negotiation. The separation of relations between Europeans and non-Europeans from European foreign affairs had the effect of colonizing, if not domesticating, the former, of making them an aspect of internal relations more than external relations. Europeans often expressed the exclusion of non-Europeans in religious terms, but the criteria Europeans used to legitimate sovereignty over land were primarily secular in definition. As well, the institutions of Christianity, whether the papacy or the newly emergent Protestant and national churches, played little direct role in shaping these criteria at the international level.

The distinction between Europe and the extra-European world was expressed spatially with the conceptualization of 'lines of amity'.

During the negotiations for the 1559 Treaty of Câteau-Cambrésis, French negotiators tried to persuade the Spanish to acknowledge the right of French merchants to trade in the Caribbean basin. Spain refused, unwilling to acknowledge non-Spanish rights in the area. France refused, in turn, to recognize Spanish claims and to prohibit French subjects from trafficking in American waters. Rather than have American concerns threaten peace in Europe, Spain and France made an oral agreement that the treaty would only apply within European space, defined by 'lines of amity', one a north–south line west of the Azores and the other an east–west line on the Tropic of Cancer. By defining the Azores, Madeiras, Canaries, and surrounding waters as part of Europe, the treaty obliged France to restrain its corsairs who had been plundering Spanish shipping in these waters. Extra-European space was outside the lines of amity, i.e. west of the Azores and south of the Tropic of Cancer, territory in which the treaty was not applicable.[11]

In the sixteenth century, the most active French, English, and Dutch agents against Spanish and Portuguese claims were merchant adventurers, explorers, privateers, and pirates, men willing to take risks for the promise of wealth and glory. Often operating at the boundaries of legitimacy, they absorbed the risks that governments could not afford directly, but which needed to be taken if France, England, and later the Netherlands were to establish claims to the potential wealth that overseas ventures promised. In turn, adventurers needed a modicum of political backing to legitimate their undertakings and to negotiate with Spain and Portugal over access to markets or the return of seized ships, men, and cargoes.[12] Occasionally crown support included a financial investment. Elizabeth I invested in John Hawkins's slaving voyages to West Africa from 1562 to 1568, a pointed challenge to Portuguese claims to Africa. Foreign policy concerns could also make a monarch cautious. After the death of Philip II of Spain in 1598, Elizabeth I did not charter the East India Company in hopes of improved Anglo-Spanish relations. Within two years relations had worsened rather than improved, and she granted the company its first charter.[13]

Iberian charges of piracy engendered international disputes over trading rights and navigation on the high seas, which in turn required governments to define their role in protecting the observation of those rights. One of the most consequential incidents of piracy occurred in 1603 when the Dutch East India Company (VOC) seized a Portuguese vessel in the Straits of Malacca. The Spanish, who controlled the Portuguese throne at the time, charged the Dutch with violating Portuguese waters. The VOC hired the legal theorist Hugo Grotius to defend their interests. His resulting treatise, *Mare Liberum* (1609), argued for freedom of the seas, and became the foundational text in shaping the modern debate over the international law of the sea, especially freedom of navigation, the extent of territorial waters, and fishing rights. As well, the Iberian–Dutch dispute had an immediate collateral impact on Anglo-Dutch relations. The English interpreted the Dutch position, as articulated in *Mare Liberum*, as an ill-disguised attempt to redefine territorial waters in such a way that Dutch fishermen could fish in English waters.[14]

While international debates over the criteria for land claims, the extent of territorial waters, or the rights of freedom of navigation did not increase appreciably the costs of state infrastructures, they did redefine a state's functions relative to other states and to the activities of subjects outside a state's territorial boundaries. The relationship between overseas expansion and the reordering of international society is under-studied and under-theorized.[15] These international debates contributed to the increasing regulation of foreign trade by states, and thus enhanced central state authority. In the sixteenth and early seventeenth centuries, trading rights in foreign countries were negotiated primarily by associations of merchants, often under royal charter, rather than by crown-appointed diplomats. Among the English, a chief reason for chartering firms such as the Spanish Company (1577), the Eastland Company (1579), and the Muscovy Company (1555) was so they could negotiate commercial rights with foreign governments, a privilege which the crown also granted to chartered companies organized for transoceanic ventures. By the late seventeenth century, chartered companies operating within Europe had been disbanded largely because commercial diplomacy had been assumed by state-appointed diplomats.[16] The expanded scope of international relations that trade negotiations represented may not have substantially increased the costs of a central government, but it did enlarge its power as governments became involved in regulating economies. Merchants participated in that shift of diplomatic responsibilities because it transferred the cost of commercial diplomacy onto the state, as well as created the conditions for transferring more expensive protection costs to states.[17]

Europeans operating in the extra-European world also relied on the appearance of a strong state. The non-governmental funding of English overseas commerce and colonization has been interpreted as weak state involvement in expansion, which, of course, it was in a direct sense. But the willingness of investors to undertake that financial risk was predicated, in part, on some confidence in the crown's diplomatic support and its unwillingness to accept Iberian charges of piracy. Indeed, maintaining those mutual bonds of confidence between a metropolitan government and its overseas subjects was critical to sustaining expansion. Retaining overseas possessions depended, in part, on people believing that a metropolitan government had the power to protect overseas interests and the will to use it, even if it seldom did.[18]

In the 1640s, civil war in England diverted government and commercial interests from overseas concerns, and in turn encouraged an existing propensity for colonists in the Caribbean and the Chesapeake to rely on Dutch shipping and financial services. Parliament passed the 1651 Navigation Act partly in response to aggressive Dutch competition with English shipping and commerce both in Europe and overseas. The English government recognized that if it did not define a trade policy that provided essential services to colonists by English subjects and directed colonial products into English ports then it risked losing those colonies to nations that could provide reliable services. Conversely, lack of colonial observance of those regulations could also jeopardize the long-term maintenance of colonies. In 1651, the Commonwealth government sent naval forces to Barbados and Virginia to oblige colonists to recognize Parliament's suzerainty and the Navigation Act; colonists accepted the first but not the second and negotiated free trade. Charles II was more insistent that colonists obey the Navigation Acts, which he partially achieved without an overt show of force. Colonial acceptance of metropolitan policy without coercion was, of course, preferred, but there was also an awareness that the application of metropolitan policy might include the use of force, though always with the attendant risk of colonial resistance.[19]

The English capture of New Netherland in 1664 was facilitated by the persistently weak support of the colony by both the Dutch West India Company and the Dutch metropolitan government. For Dutch colonists in New Netherland, resisting an English invasion was pointless if neither the company nor the government could come to their aid.[20] Thus the belief of colonists in the strength of their home state and the ability and willingness of that state to craft policy to support colonists was probably as critical to imperial development as the manifestation of state strength in measures such as the deployment of troops overseas.

Diplomatic negotiations frequently dealt with the responsibility of states for the actions of their subjects in extra-European arenas. Throughout the sixteenth century, the Iberians resisted acknowledging the legitimacy of any non-Iberian ventures and generally interpreted all of them as some form of piracy. In negotiations for the Treaty of Vervins (1598) and the Treaty of London (1604), diplomats for Henri IV and James I respectively pressed the Spanish to recognize the rights of their subjects to engage in commerce and colonization in those parts of the extra-European world where the Iberians were not physically present. The Spanish refused.[21] Nevertheless, Spain's weakening power after long years of international war and continuing civil war in the Netherlands allowed the French and the English to exploit the inroads their privateers and merchants had made in the 1580s and 1590s. Henri IV began issuing charters for overseas commerce and colonization, and by 1608 the French had established permanent settlements in Acadia and Canada. James I chartered the Virginia Company in 1606 and the Newfoundland Company in 1610.[22]

The success of some overseas ventures by the French, English, and Dutch shifted international dynamics. In the first instance, success created more volatility, particularly in the Atlantic basin. The French, English, and Dutch now attacked each other, as well as the Spanish and Portuguese. For example, Samuel Argall, sailing out of Virginia in 1612, attacked the French in Acadia. In 1623, the Dutch killed ten East India Company employees at Amboina. Sir William Alexander, a Scot with a charter to Nova Scotia, seized Port Royal, Acadia, in 1627. The Kirke brothers, sons of the English merchant Gervais Kirke, occupied Canada from 1629 to 1632 when the Treaty of St Germain-en-Laye returned it to the French.[23] These new incidences of violence created the diplomatic conditions for the English, French, and Dutch to negotiate their respective claims without involving the Iberians. Thus even if the Iberians would not recognize their legitimacy, they now legitimated each other.

French, English, and Dutch successes, coupled with Iberian problems in Europe, finally forced the Portuguese and the Spanish to abandon their hegemonic claims to the extra-European world. In 1641, the Portuguese negotiated treaties with the French and the Dutch that recognized their overseas commercial and colonial rights in partial exchange for legitimating the 1640 Portuguese revolt against the Spanish and the restoration of the Portuguese crown. The English followed suit in a 1642 Anglo-Portuguese treaty. Spain first acknowledged non-Iberian claims in the 1648 Treaty of Munster when it recognized both Dutch independence and overseas claims. That treaty served as the basis for the Spanish acknowledgement of English claims in the 1667 Treaty of Madrid.[24] The Iberian recognition of non-Iberian claims shifted the focus of diplomatic negotiations among expanding states. The right of non-Iberians to engage in overseas commerce and colonization ceased to be the primary issue. Rather, shared concerns such as privatized violence, conflicting claims, and ambiguous boundaries became matters of multilateral negotiation.

Resolving these concerns in a transoceanic context posed enormous problems for European governments, which often found themselves maneuvering between diplomatic commitments and overseas subjects who had enormous autonomy of action. One of Spain's objectives in recognizing English claims to Jamaica in 1667 was to oblige the English government to restrain privateering attacks on Spanish shipping in the Caribbean. The governor of Jamaica, Thomas Modyford, ignored metropolitan orders to refrain from issuing letters of marque, contending that the security of the island depended on the protection provided by privateers. The 1686 Treaty of Whitehall established Anglo-French neutrality in the Americas, but did not keep French naval forces in Canada from attacking Hudson's Bay Company forts. International pressure, as well as complaints from the East India Company, contributed to the crackdown on piracy spearheaded by the Board of Trade after the Treaty of Ryswick in 1697. It expanded the power of the admiralty courts in the colonies, and when colonial courts proved unwilling to help curb piracy, Parliament passed the Act for the More Effectual Suppression of Piracy (1700), which allowed for the transportation to England of persons charged with piracy in the colonies. The legislation had its intended effect, though within a year renewed hostilities with France prompted a royal pardon that released men in prison to return to the high seas.[25]

The Treaty of Utrecht ending the War of the Spanish Succession (1713) marked a significant transition in international relations. It was the first major multilateral treaty in which the expanding powers attempted to sort out their conflicting overseas claims, and critical issues of the previous two centuries were resolved.[26] Spain and Portugal were forced to accept French and British contentions that colonization and conquest, and at times discovery of a specific place, should be the bases of land claims in the extra-European world, not the papal bulls of 1493 or the 1494 Treaty of Tordesillas. In turn, the French and British enacted stricter legislation and policies to regulate, if not to police, the exercise of privatized force overseas.

At the international level France, Great Britain, and the Netherlands had become imperial states by 1713, along with Spain and Portugal, even if many of their internal policies for governing overseas territories were not commensurate with imperial status. As an international community, however, these European states were not juridically equal, because Spain persisted in claiming hegemony over the western half of the Atlantic Ocean and all of the Pacific, and thereby arrogated superior status over her competitors. In the eighteenth century, rights of navigation on the high seas remained a highly contentious issue. In the sixteenth century, the English had been advocates of freedom of the seas, but in the seventeenth century the Stuart monarchs had made expansive claims to the 'Western Sea', at times as far west as North America. After the accession of William and Mary in 1689, the English returned to their sixteenth-century contention that navigation on the high seas could not be restricted.[27]

The Spanish resuscitation of their oceanic claims in the early eighteenth century served as a check on encroachments by the French and the British. The Spanish contended that they had never ceded their maritime claims, but only claims to land, and that they had only granted non-Iberians rights of passage between an overseas colony and the mother country, or between one colony and another. Thus, for example, Spain claimed that British vessels could sail from Jamaica to Britain or from Jamaica to Massachusetts without infringing Spain's rights, but British vessels could not sail in waters between Jamaica and Panama. Spain's particular concern was to keep the French and the British out of the South Atlantic and the Pacific Ocean, but at a practical level the Spanish could exercise their claims most forcefully in the Caribbean basin.[28] Spain's aggressive policing of Caribbean waters, beginning in the 1720s, contributed to the War of Jenkins's Ear in 1739, which then extended into the War of the Austrian Succession (1742–8). In 1750 Spain and Portugal negotiated a treaty that made 'null and void' those parts of the Treaty of Tordesillas pertaining to the 'line of demarcation', and thus ended Spain's claims to the Atlantic.[29]

It took another 40 years of pressure by the British, the French, and then the Russians before Spain would relinquish its claims to the Pacific Ocean. The erosion of Spanish claims of hegemony in the

Pacific, however, happened quite differently from the erosion of Iberian claims in the rest of the extra-European world. In the Atlantic and Indian Ocean basins the pressure had started to build in the sixteenth century and had largely been achieved through non-state agents, albeit generally operating under an official charter. In the Pacific Ocean, in contrast, most of the important expeditions had been directly planned and funded by the French or British navies. While the Anglo-Spanish confrontation over Nootka Sound had been precipitated by the presence of British merchants, and not the British navy, the expeditions of exploration that demonstrated the viability of commercial ventures in the Pacific, particularly James Cook's third voyage (1776–81), had been state funded and sponsored.[30] As well, even though the Nootka Sound Agreement was bilateral, by the end of the eighteenth century these agreements had multilateral implications based on international practices worked out in the Atlantic.

Over three centuries a global system of international relations emerged that was strikingly different from the two hegemonic systems that the Iberians had defined at the end of the fifteenth century. In many respects it was an extension of the European inter-state system with its emphasis on the equality of sovereign states. Yet the global system did not emerge from the coalescence of states within Europe, but rather from a protracted struggle over the terms of empire building in the extra-European world. Significantly, most of the issues had been articulated in the sixteenth or early seventeenth centuries, in particular the principles for claiming overseas territory and freedom of navigation, though it took two centuries of contestation before they were applied globally. The combination of their early articulation and their eventual application make them seem foregone conclusions, and hence scholars have done little to analyze the impact of international negotiations on early modern empire building or on how expanding powers understood the evolving functions of the state at the international level.

While the principles underlying international negotiations were defined relatively early, great ambiguity existed over how European polities should be internally structured in response to the challenges posed by overseas expansion. Indeed, to the extent that the five European powers with large overseas empires – Spain, Portugal, France, Great Britain, and the Netherlands – developed 'imperial states' in the early modern era, they were widely divergent. Within Britain the political and constitutional integration of overseas expansion was a slow, highly differentiated, and generally reactive process.

Unlike the Iberians, and particularly the Spanish, the Tudor–Stuart monarchs could not effectively declare extra-European space an extension of the realm and thereby establish *dominium* by royal fiat. As well, English overseas expansion did not produce the immediate wealth that the gold and silver from the Americas and the pepper from Asia generated for Spain and Portugal respectively, and which allowed for the relatively rapid centralization of those states.

For the English, the beginnings of empire were closely tied to foreign policy. Early overseas ventures were generally challenges to the Portuguese and Spanish, whether directly, such as the voyages of Sir Francis Drake, or indirectly, such as the Arctic explorations to find a northern passage to Asia that the Iberians did not control. Through the seventeenth century, the granting of most charters was calibrated against foreign policy concerns. The voyages of Hawkins to Africa and the Caribbean in the 1560s under the auspices of the Guinea Company were an explicit challenge to the Portuguese and the Spanish. As we have seen, Elizabeth I delayed from 1598 to 1600 in granting a charter to the East India Company in hopes of improved relations with Spain. The Virginia Company received its charter in 1606, two years after the Treaty of London ended the war with Spain. James I revoked the Amazon Company charter in 1619 to appease Spain. English adventurers planted proprietary colonies in the Caribbean in the 1620s while Spain was preoccupied with war in Europe. Charles II gave his brother, the Duke of York, the authority to attempt taking the colony of New Netherland from the Dutch. The Hudson's Bay Company (established 1670) challenged French dominance in the North American fur trade, while the Royal African Company (established 1663) challenged Dutch dominance in the slave trade. In a few instances, the crown granted charters where the English already had claims: Maryland was carved out of Virginia, and the land granted to the Massachusetts Bay Company had previously been granted to the Council of New England. Even in these colonies, the problems of foreign challengers could not be ignored.[31]

A number of issues derive from this basic observation about the connection between empire building and foreign affairs, but three are important here. First, for the British the early stages of empire building depended on multilateral state pressure on the Iberians. Thus empire building was linked to the international redefinition of the community of states. For now, it is enough to note that the ability of colonies to wage wars of independence depended on their being able to claim a right to membership in that community of states that was the creation of Europe, but not confined to Europe. Second, foreign affairs were a matter of crown prerogative, and thus the growing involvement of the English in overseas expansion re-inforced the central executive authority of the state. Adventurers needed connections in court that would yield royal charters, if not financial support, as well as diplomatic backing in the event of seizure of people or property. Success did not obviate foreign policy concerns, as colonists in places such as St Christopher, Jamaica, or New York knew. Thus for the English, empire building required a concomitant increase in the departments of state concerned with foreign affairs. Third, and more problematically, ongoing ventures, whether the East India Company, the colony of Virginia, or sugar colonies in the West Indies, had to be domesticated, connected to domestic affairs rather than just foreign affairs. The English govern-ment had no plan or policy for that transformation, and the diversity of overseas ventures made the formulation of policies and their effective application extremely difficult.[32]

In the early seventeenth century, neither the crown nor its ministers foresaw the extent to which many of the newly chartered ventures, such as those to Virginia or Massachusetts, would deviate institution-ally from existing overseas ventures. Rather, crown officials assumed that new overseas ventures would have an institutional presence in London, such as the Muscovy Company, the Levant Company, and the East India Company had with a governing council in England, as well as subsidiary councils overseas. Indeed, the Virginia Company did have a governor and directors resident in England, and when it was royalized in 1624, James I (*d.* 1625) and then Charles I drew on the company model to envisage two governing councils, one in London and one in Virginia. The former, however, never evolved beyond a temporary commission.[33] So accepted was the perception that colonies needed an institutional presence in England that when the Puritans took the Massachusetts Bay Company's charter to North America in 1630 royal officials immediately saw it as an affront to royal authority. Indeed, Puritans in New England sought institutional autonomy, but other colonies achieved it through unintended developments. Whether colonial autonomy developed intentionally or unintentionally, in the early modern era the metropolitan government never devised adequate ways to overcome it. When the King's Bench tried to revoke the Massachusetts charter in the 1630s it could not complete the proceedings because the charter was not physically present in England and Governor John Winthrop would not send it back. Crown attorneys faced the same problem in the 1680s, though this time the King's Bench succeeded in revoking the Massachusetts Bay Company charter on a procedural technicality.[34] Beginning in the early seventeenth century, commercial and colonial expansion had divergent patterns of institutional development relative to the metropolitan government.

Commercial ventures that did not rely on colonies promised greater returns on investments than did colonial ventures. Only from the Caribbean colonies could absentee investors anticipate any profit-taking, and consequently West Indian colonists had closer ties with England than did North American colonists. The cost of settling North American colonies quickly exhausted the working capital of metropolitan-based ventures, discouraged further investment, shifted the costs of long-term capital investments onto the colonists themselves, and thus attenuated the already fragile ties with England. No export commodity from the mainland colonies ever produced wealth comparable to that in many other sectors of overseas trade. Tobacco dominated mainland colonial trade, but on the eve of the revolution it accounted for only 29.5 percent of British North American exports. The average annual value of tobacco shipped from the Chesapeake from 1768 to 1772 was £756,128; the value of sugar, by comparison, was £3,910,600.[35]

From the perspective of the metropole, as overseas ventures North American colonies were economically and politically marginal. Not until the end of the seventeenth century did these colonies begin to send agents to London to represent their interests.[36] In contrast, merchants involved in the fishery, the African trade, the Asian trade, and the Caribbean trade had long had agents in London who manipulated all the levers of power in Whitehall and Westminster to protect their interests. The profitability of these trades engendered fierce commercial competition and particularly heated political contests if monopoly rights or other restrictions on trade were at stake. By the early eighteenth century, the Newfoundland fishery, the African trade, and the East India Company operated under parliamentary legislation or charters, and a diverse range of governing bodies, including the Privy Council, Parliament, the Treasury, and the navy, participated in the regulation and oversight of one or more of them. In 1698, Parliament revoked the Royal African Company's monopoly on the slave trade and opened it to all English merchants. From then until the dissolution of the company in 1750, Parliament made most governmental policy affecting trading in Africa. The Newfoundland fishery came under parliamentary legislation in 1699 with the passage of the Newfoundland Act, and every summer the navy sent out a fleet to provide governance for the fishing season. In 1709, Parliament chartered the United East India Company after the debilitating competition of two rival companies threatened their financial survival and the solvency of the British government, which had come to rely on East India Company loans.[37]

By the early eighteenth century, overseas commercial ventures had been politically and institutionally linked to governing bodies within Britain, largely as a result of merchant pressure and by expanding the use of existing governmental institutions – such as the Royal Navy's involvement in the fishery – rather than on the creation of new institutions. Forging institutional links with colonies was far more problematic and was complicated by their transatlantic separation from Britain, the lower profitability of most colonial ventures, and the need for civilian (and not just company) governance. British claims to land overseas also created jurisdictional ambiguity, particularly over questions of sovereignty and whether it was vested in the crown or the crown-in-Parliament. So long as colonies remained politically and economically marginal as overseas ventures, the implications of the jurisdictional and institutional ambiguities could be contained as the problem of a particular colony or ignored without serious short-term consequences. The vesting of colonial oversight in the Board of Trade, created in 1696 after a series of committees, commissions, and councils, symbolizes that tension.[38] A subcommittee of the Privy Council, the Board of Trade reported to the Secretary of State for the Southern Department, who handled foreign affairs with Spain, Portugal, and France, thus underscoring the intersection of colonization and overseas trade with international relations. Keeping colonial affairs under ministerial oversight had developed after James I and Charles I rebuffed Parliament's suggestions that it provide some oversight. Charles II and James II followed suit during the Restoration. William founded the Board of Trade to maximize his control over the colonies and to minimize Parliament's.[39] One consequence of ministerial oversight, however, was to keep colonies in a conceptual marchland between foreign and domestic affairs.

As more merchants plied Atlantic waters and as the colonies grew, the intensifying complexities of the Atlantic world spawned tensions and conflicts that could not be contained within a single colony, sector of trade, or empire. Multi-state negotiations to resolve shared problems contributed to the tendency of the imperial powers to delegate fewer and fewer responsibilities to quasi-private agents, as had been the practice in the sixteenth and seventeenth centuries. In the eighteenth century, the British government appointed a broadening range of metropolitan officials to handle matters such as boundary disputes and relations with native peoples. Structural stresses within the empire demanded new solutions. When British traders from North American colonies began selling surplus provisions to planters in the foreign West Indies, the Caribbean lobby in London convinced Parliament to pass the Molasses Act (1733), which put high (though uncollectable) duties on foreign sugar products. Spain's policing of Caribbean shipping routes led to merchant demands for naval intervention. At the end of the War of the Austrian Succession the British decided to establish a new naval port at Halifax, Nova Scotia, which complemented the ones in Bermuda and Antigua.[40]

The Seven Years War (1756–63) fed on, if it was not caused by, the growing tensions and complexities in the Atlantic world, and Britain's straddling of European and overseas commitments further strained the points of stress.[41] Ministerial decisions to fight the war at all costs created an enormous public debt. Treaty negotiations fueled vociferous political debates within Britain over the fidelity of negotiators to British interests. The acquisition of new colonies and territories with non-British peoples forced an examination of the nature of subjecthood and civil governance in the empire. The North American colonies assumed new importance as a reserve of military manpower, a vast consumer market, a source of settlers for new colonies such as Nova Scotia and Quebec, and a trove of potential revenues for a seriously indebted government. The magnitude and number of problems, however, meant that piecemeal and reactive decision-making could no longer be used to make plumb the structural misalignments in the extra-European world. The ensuing upheavals in the Atlantic world exposed both the strengths and weaknesses of the previous 250 years of empire building and state formation within Britain, within the larger British world, and within the international community of states.

Within Britain, attempts to address the problems engendered by the Seven Years War, especially those associated with the empire, reconfigured and challenged the distribution of power among the ministry, Parliament, and the Treasury.[42] For decades the Treasury had shaped policy to maximize the self-financing of colonies and to minimize expenses paid by the metropole. That policy was pursued as part of a broader practice of separating decision-making on

revenue generation derived from acts of Parliament, from the hereditary revenues of the crown, and from the colonies. Then in the
1760s, it became necessary for the Treasury to involve Parliament in
the raising of revenue from sources that had been left to colonial dis-
cretion. While the immediate impetus for the change arose from the
financial exigencies of the Seven Years War, it also represents a relin-
quishment of Treasury and ministerial power over the colonies to
Parliament, a legacy of the crown's attempt, whether under the
Stuart kings or under William and Mary, to minimize Parliament's
influence in shaping colonial policy. Partially in response to the
ensuing colonial resistance to parliamentary legislation, the offices of
the secretaries of state were reorganized. Colonial oversight was
removed from the Secretary of State for the Southern Department
and a third office of Secretary of State for the Colonies was created.
That latter office lasted from 1768 to 1782, when the Board of
Trade was abolished and the offices of the secretaries of state were
again reorganized and a Home and Colonial Secretary and a Foreign
Secretary were appointed. After nearly two centuries of the overseas
settlement of British subjects, the oversight of colonies was institutionalized within Britain as a matter of domestic governance.[43]

The acquisition of numerous new colonies and territories in the
Seven Years War, including the Trans-Appalachian West, Quebec, East
and West Florida, the Ceded Islands (Dominica, Grenada, St Vincent,
and Tobago), and Bengal exposed the differential and asymmetrical
ways in which empire building had affected state formation within
Britain. The practice of regulating overseas colonies and territories
through the Privy Council raised serious questions about the power it
concentrated in the hands of a few ministers and the prerogative they
had to govern more people overseas than lived in England, Wales,
Scotland, and Ireland combined. The debates over the passage of the
1773 Regulating Act (which provided some civil institutions and
royally appointed officials for Bengal) and the 1774 Quebec Act
(which granted political rights to Catholics and preserved French civil
law in Quebec) returned again and again to this problem.[44]

Supporters of both pieces of legislation argued that the acquisition of Quebec and Bengal, alone, intolerably increased the potential
for both ministerial abuse and the violation of the rights of non-
British subjects. One pamphleteer argued that the question of parliamentary involvement in defining a civil government for Bengal was
whether Indians should live under the 'despotic authority in a few?
or *limited* authority in many?' Drawing an analogy to acquisitions of

the Spanish kingdoms under Ferdinand and Isabella, he argued that concentrating too much power in the crown would contribute to the undermining of the country. In the parliamentary debates on Quebec, the Solicitor-General noted that only the Romans and the English engaged in the 'cruel and barbarous policy' of forcing 'their laws on the conquered.' Sir William Meredith, in a pamphlet styled a 'letter to the Earl of Chatham', who opposed the Quebec Act, noted that 'a government by proclamation' (i.e. the Proclamation of 1763) left the welfare of the Canadians to the whim of the crown. Parliamentary legislation, or *imperium legis*, would be superior to *imperium hominis*.[45] At the heart of these debates were substantive issues about the distribution of power between the crown and Parliament and the control of patronage, as well as just ways to govern non-British people. After protracted debates inside and outside of Westminster, Parliament passed legislation for Quebec and Bengal which provided a political and constitutional domestication of these new territories in a way that had never happened with the colonies settled in the seventeenth century.

In the old British colonies, the domestication of the political culture had occurred almost entirely within the colonies, and in the long run had been more conducive to local state formation than empire building. For many metropolitan observers, the colonies were dependent polities; in the most negative analogy, they were little different from municipal corporations in Britain, and thus by definition incomplete polities. Politically and constitutionally, they believed, the colonies needed the British connection to be complete. In contrast, colonists throughout British America argued that colonies were discrete dominions of the crown and should have commensurate political autonomy. As resistance to parliamentary legislation deepened, North American colonists came to believe that they had acquired many of the characteristics of states, and in 1776, 13 of them claimed that status.[46]

Ironically, the transatlantic community of states in which the United States claimed a right of membership was also a product of empire building. One of the distinctive characteristics of the overseas empires that English, French, and Dutch built is that they depended on a reconfiguration of state relations at the international level. The international competition for empire contributed to redefining the role of governments in the oversight and regulation of commercial affairs, whether through intentional centralizing, as happened in France, or unintentional centralizing, as happened in Britain when merchants put pressure on Whitehall and Westminster to protect their interests. In Britain, the establishment of colonies overseas gave monarchs the illusion of the possibility of overseeing them without the undue involvement of Parliament, in ways that overseas commerce alone did not. Three factors abetted the crown. Overseas colonies could be defined as part of foreign affairs (and hence treated under the crown prerogative) as much as domestic affairs in which Parliament would have to be consulted. The political and economic marginality of colonies limited the ability of colonists to support agents in London and hence to draw in Parliament in the ways that merchants had involved Parliament in the regulation of long-distance trade. The Treasury kept the colonies largely self-financing so that Parliament did not have to raise monies for them, but it also meant that the crown received no revenues within the colonies, except insofar as colonies paid royally appointed officials. The financial and political autonomy of transatlantic colonies subtly reinforced the centralization of executive power within Britain, but it also proved to be the fatal flaw in empire building.

British-American colonists had long known that the Atlantic served as both a buffer against the metropolitan government and a conceptual marchland between Europe and the extra-European world, between the foreign and the domestic, between empires and states. In the late eighteenth century, colonists throughout the Americas challenged that conceptual divide, as they broke down empires and created new states. The Atlantic still served as a cultural divide between Europe and the extra-European world, but revolutionaries claimed successfully that states could exist not only within the imperial boundaries once defined by the lines of amity, but also beyond them in the Americas.

10

Revolution and Counter-Revolution

Eliga H. Gould

Few historians would dispute the interconnectedness of what they now describe as the 'three British revolutions' of 1641, 1688, and 1776.[1] Each convulsion affected the entire British archipelago,[2] with the course of events in England repeatedly being dictated by developments in Scotland and Ireland.[3] Although only the American Revolution had its origins in the colonies, all three revolutions were transatlantic in scope, triggering upheavals of varying magnitude throughout North America and the Caribbean. The so-called First British Empire – considered both as a set of political institutions and as an ideological construct – was largely a product of the two seventeenth-century revolutions,[4] and the radical principles of the American Revolution reverberated within the remaining portions of Britain's Atlantic empire well into the nineteenth century.[5] Taken together, this revolutionary lineage highlights the integrative tendencies of Atlantic history, with a geographically dispersed British community being bound ever more closely by a common heritage of law, religion, language, education, constitutional government, and economic opportunity.

If the trend toward writing unified histories of the British Atlantic has been beneficial, however, it raises several difficult questions, among them how to reconcile this unity with the fact that the English-speaking Atlantic was also deeply fragmented. Until the parliamentary unions with Scotland (1707) and Ireland (1801), the British monarchy was itself a composite entity, with England, Scotland, and Ireland each maintaining its own Parliament, laws, and established church. Colonists in North America and the West Indies were inclined to extend this composite model still further, claiming Ireland's coordinate relationship with England as an appropriate model for 'ancient' colonies like Virginia, Massachusetts, and Barbados.[6] Adding yet another level of complexity, men and women throughout the British empire regarded those parts that lay in the western and southern Atlantic as existing 'beyond the line' – in stateless, racially diverse regions full of wonder (as well as social and economic opportunity) but outside the pale of European civil society.[7] For the three British kingdoms of Charles I no less than the greater British nation of George III, the forces dividing the British Atlantic's component realms and provinces were at least as conspicuous as those that held them together.

Because of this complex structure, the revolutions and counter-revolutions that swept the early modern British Atlantic operated in two partially distinct contexts. The first of these was the internal context that framed the dispute (or series of disputes) over conditions of government in England, Scotland, Ireland, and America – what the Progressive historian of the American Revolution Carl Becker called the 'struggle over who should rule at home.' With growing intensity, however, Britain's revolutions were also contests over the structure of the British Atlantic community as a whole, with English – as well as Scottish and, after 1707, British – claims to imperial pre-eminence clashing (in Becker's typology) with colonial and provincial aspirations to 'home rule' of varying degrees.[8] Without discounting the significance of the former, practitioners of British and Atlantic history have tended to emphasize the latter. From this wider context, it is clear that the British dynamics of revolution and counter-revolution ultimately strengthened the imperial capacity of the Anglo-British state. Among the more important consequences was the displacement of the main theaters of revolution to Britain's archipelagic and trans-atlantic periphery. In a sense, empire helped insulate England – and, eventually, Britain – from revolutionary upheaval elsewhere in the Atlantic world, even as the British empire's expanding power ensured that revolution and the quest for home rule remained a viable and necessary form of politics in each of its outlying regions.

I

This geography of revolution had its origins in the uneven nature of political authority within the Three British Kingdoms of England,

Scotland, and Ireland, an entity that included the principality of
Wales, the Isle of Man, the Hebrides, and the Orkney, Shetland, and
Channel Islands. At the time of Charles I's accession (1625), British
rule over the whole archipelago was less than a quarter-century old,
the key pillars being Henry VIII's elevation of Ireland to an independent kingdom subordinate to the English crown (1541); the Anglo-
Welsh Acts of Union (1536 and 1543), which imposed English
shires and justices of the peace in the marcher lordships; and the
Anglo-Scottish union of crowns (1603) under Charles's father, James
VI and I. Of these, only the union between England and Scotland
was regarded as one between equals, with each claiming to be an
'empire' whose monarch (and people) owed allegiance to no other
earthly power.[9] However, the composite structure of the Anglo-
Scottish relationship was emblematic of a more general pattern of
decentralization. Throughout the British archipelago – in London
no less than Edinburgh and Dublin – the ability of metropolitan
authorities to control events on the periphery was tenuous, a weakness amply illustrated by the loyalty of Charles's English subjects
toward their county or, as it was often rendered, their 'country'.[10]

Although Charles I's 'triple Diadem' inspired occasional flights of
fancy,[11] it proved unable to withstand either the European crisis of
the Thirty Years War (1618–48) or the king's own imperial ambitions. In England, Charles managed (barely) to dispense with
Parliament after 1629, using the prerogative tax known as ship
money to compel towns and counties on the coast – and, after 1636,
inland – to build a navy and enforce his claim to lordship of the
'British seas' as far as the shores of Holland and France. The osten-
sible reason for this assertion of maritime lordship was to secure
Britain and Ireland from 'thieves, pirates, and robbers of the seas';
Charles also hoped to use the revenue to help recover the German
Palatinate for his nephew Frederick V of Bohemia, a project that
required a secret (and highly unpopular) alliance with Catholic
Spain.[12] Under the firm hand of Sir Thomas Wentworth, similar
success greeted Charles's policies in Ireland, which consisted of
strengthening bishops, ignoring Parliament, and arming Catholics.
In Scotland, however, the king's assault on local privileges was
explosive. Outraged by royal attempts to remake the Presbyterian-
controlled kirk in the image of its Anglican cousin, the Scots
responded with destructive riots in Edinburgh, a National Covenant
(1638) denouncing the reform's 'popish' tendencies, and a provisional government whose leaders – known as 'the Tables' – began

raising the army that thwarted an English invasion during the First Bishops' War (1639) and mounted its own invasion during the second (1640). Faced with a hostile army in the north of England, Charles was forced to summon two separate English parliaments in 1640, setting off the chain of events that resulted in the Irish rebellion of 1641 and the outbreak of the English Civil War in 1642.

During the succeeding conflicts, now known collectively as the Wars of the Three Kingdoms (1639–52),[13] two characteristics stand out. The first was the persistence beyond England's borders of an imperial, pan-British vision. Of the various conflicts that convulsed the British archipelago during the 1640s and 1650s, only the Catholic rebellion in Ulster (1641) approximated a straightforward quest for rights within the existing structure of the Three British Kingdoms.[14] By contrast, the Scottish resistance to Charles's religious policies was much more than a defensive movement in the face of an aggressive neighbor. From the outset, subscribers to the National Covenant displayed imperial tendencies of their own, as was evident from the close correspondence that developed in 1640 between the Scottish army at Newcastle and the king's Puritan opponents in Parliament.[15] As ratified in the Solemn League and Covenant of 1643, the Scots' ambitions entailed offering Parliament military assistance in exchange for English guarantees that 'the reformation of religion in the kingdoms of England and Ireland' would proceed on a Scottish Presbyterian model.[16] With the emergence of Oliver Cromwell's New Model Army, Parliament became less dependent on Scottish aid and was consequently able to renege on its earlier promise. Nonetheless, Scotland's British aspirations continued to haunt politics to the south, most conspicuously in the aftermath of Charles I's execution (1649) when the Presbyterian earl of Argyll courted an English invasion by having the younger Charles Stuart proclaimed 'king of Great Britain', as opposed to the less elevated (and threatening) title king of Scotland.[17]

The second defining feature of the Wars of the Three Kingdoms was the vulnerability of England's political institutions to such external upheavals. In terms of the crown's ability to control events beyond England's borders, the most intractable of Britain's outlying regions were Lowland Scotland and the Irish Pale. In the former, the imperial status of Scotland's crown precluded all forms of English intervention but war and diplomacy; in the latter, Anglo-Irish Protestant settlers could claim the same rights as the crown's subjects in England, including the right to be governed by a parliament of their own choosing.

This weakness was further aggravated by the lawlessness that plagued the Celtic hinterlands of Scotland, Ireland, and Wales, turning large stretches into 'zones of war' whose inhabitants' 'delight in rapine' (as an English traveler wrote of the Highlands in 1689) placed them beyond the reach of the king's justice.[18] Complementing the apparent barbarism of Britain's periphery was the chaos of its surrounding seas. Despite Stuart assertions of maritime sovereignty, coastal communities lived in dread of raids like the one inflicted by Barbary corsairs on the Irish port of Baltimore in 1631, during which 200 of the king's subjects were carried into slavery.[19]

None of these obstacles to English hegemony was insurmountable, as became brutally clear during the Cromwellian conquest of Ireland (1650) and Scotland (1651). As the ship money controversy of the 1630s demonstrated, however, projecting the power of the crown beyond England's borders – whether by land or sea – threatened to distort its power at home. The result was a direct confrontation between royal claims to sovereignty over the British archipelago and the English right to make no 'gift, loan, benevolence, [or] tax ... without common consent by Act of Parliament.'[20] Between 1637 and 1642, this conflict rendered Charles powerless to expel the Scots or subdue the Irish. Although England clearly possessed superior resources, Parliament refused to grant the king the funds necessary to raise an army and build a navy. Only with the creation of the English republic was this conflict temporarily resolved, opening the way for Cromwell's devastating victories at Drogheda (1649), Dunbar (1650), and Worcester (1651). With the Navigation Ordinance of 1651, the Commonwealth achieved another of Charles's unrealized goals, building a 77-ship navy, regulating England's foreign trade, and forcing the Dutch Republic – during the First Anglo-Dutch War (1652–4) – to acknowledge its lordship of the British seas.[21] In England, the costs of such achievements were considerable, especially in the form of heavy taxation.[22] Still, under the union of common-wealths devised in 1652, the Parliament of England, Scotland, and Ireland showed itself to be a far more efficient instrument of British government than the triple crown of Charles I.

Of course, the wider transformation wrought by Cromwell's British triumphs was only one dimension of the English Revolution. Equally significant was the revolution's impact on England itself. Compared to the French Revolution of 1789, the English Revolution of the 1640s was an ambivalent affair, with divisions between sectarians committed to uprooting the old order 'root and branch' and republican pragmatists whose main goal was to preserve as much of England's ancient constitution as possible.[23] Despite these fissures, Parliament's abolition of bishops in 1646, followed three years later by the monarchy and the House of Lords, produced a brief but intense period of social, political, and religious experimentation, especially on the part of groups like the Quakers and the Levellers.[24] With its hostility to unchecked military and political power, this revolution was only partly compatible with the Irish and Scottish conquests that ended the Wars of the Three Kingdoms. Not surprisingly, one of Cromwell's more enduring legacies was to entrench a hatred of standing armies throughout the British archipelago and, eventually, North America.[25] Yet insofar as the English Revolution confirmed the power of the nation's landed and commercial interests, its internal goals were at one with its external.[26] Nowhere was this relationship more conspicuous than in Ireland. Following the campaigns of 1649 and 1650, commissioners appointed by the English Parliament confiscated nearly two-thirds of the island's property, transferring the estates of the Stuarts' predominantly Catholic supporters to Protestant soldiers, settlers, and adventurers, many of them English.[27] In the space of a decade, the English Republic achieved what a century of rule by the British crown had not: Ireland's subjugation as an English colony of settlement, in fact if not in name.

Following the restoration of the monarchy in 1660, Charles II sought to undo much (though by no means all) of this transformation, in England no less than Scotland and Ireland. As an indication of these counter-revolutionary objectives, the king's ministers reinstated the tripartite monarchy of his father, replete with episcopal churches and tests against nonconformity. However, despite the low-grade rebellion that the regime's reactionary Anglicanism induced among Protestant dissenters in all three kingdoms, Charles continued the quest for imperial power in the manner of Cromwell's Protectorate, both within the British archipelago and, increasingly, in the wider Atlantic world. Toward that end, Parliament renewed the Navigation Act (1663 and 1673), ensuring England's continued ability to contest the Dutch Republic's naval power during the second and third Anglo-Dutch Wars (1665–7, 1672–4).[28] No less important, Parliament clarified the military and fiscal powers of the English crown, affirming the king's right to sole command of the militia while abolishing the feudal tenures that had enabled Charles I to raise supplies without convening Parliament. Whereas the English crown had lacked professional soldiers to subdue the Scottish and

Irish insurrections of 1637–42, it was never without a standing army after 1660. Although Charles II used his power to very different ends, the Cromwellian (and revolutionary) lineage of his monarchy was unmistakable.

Despite the crown's growing imperial capacity, the Restoration monarchy was unable to avoid the crisis brought on by the open Catholicism of Charles's brother and eventual successor, James VII and II (1685–8). Unlike the monarchy's collapse under Charles I, the Glorious Revolution (1688–9) did not plunge England into civil war; nor did it precipitate another round of social upheaval. Had James's heavily Irish Catholic army attempted to repulse the forces of his Protestant nephew William of Orange, events undoubtedly would have followed the English pattern of 1642–9. However, thanks to the defection of James's English officers at Torbay and the king's subsequent loss of nerve, William's intervention opened the way for a transfer of power whose bloodless character in England left the crown's capacity for empire intact.[29] Indeed, in several fundamental respects the so-called Revolution Settlement enhanced that power. By replacing the Catholic James with the Protestant co-monarchy of William and Mary (who was also the deposed king's daughter), Parliament removed the chief religious obstacle to English government based on the conjoint authority of crown, lords, and commons; by passing the Toleration Act (1689), Parliament helped ensure the loyalty of English dissenters, though at the expense of High Church Anglican support; and by agreeing to fund William III's European campaigns against Louis XIV, Parliament made the military and fiscal revolution begun by Cromwell a permanent, if unwelcome, part of the English state.[30]

Outside England, of course, the accession of William and Mary was anything but bloodless. Because Louis XIV continued to recognize the title of James and his Catholic heirs, William's war with France – the Nine Years War (1688–97) – was, among other things, the first in a series of European and colonial wars over the British succession. One effect of these wars was to consolidate English domination of the British archipelago, especially in Ireland where the Catholic majority remained militantly loyal to James. During the Jacobite War (1689–91), an English-backed army of Irish, Scottish, English, and Dutch soldiers reduced the island to submission, notably at the battle of the Boyne (1690) and the siege of Limerick (1691). This was followed by a fresh round of confiscations at the hands of the Protestant-controlled Parliament, together with a string of anti-Catholic laws banning marriage with Protestants, forbidding the observation of most Catholic holidays, and banishing Catholic bishops and regular clergy. By drawing so heavily on English resources, however, the kingdom's Protestant settlers found themselves also reduced to the status of 'colonial subjects' of the English crown.[31] During the eighteenth century, the British Parliament affirmed its supremacy over the island by regulating the Irish economy to England's advantage, interfering in internal Irish matters such as the disposition of confiscated estates, and enacting the Declaratory Act of 1720. Notwithstanding critics like the Anglo-Irish William Molyneux, who insisted that the kingdom's 'people' were 'the Progeny of the English and Britains' and thus entitled to the same rights of self-government, the Glorious Revolution completed Ireland's subordination as a British dependency.[32]

Initially, Scotland experienced a different fate, as William sought recognition of his claim to the Scottish crown by restoring the kirk's Presbyterian structure and abolishing the Lords of the Articles that had kept the kingdom's parliament subservient to the crown.[33] Although Scotland was also the scene of fighting, notably at the battle of Killiecrankie (1689) and the massacre of Glencoe (1692), the settlement opened the way for the first truly independent parliaments in Scottish history. The more significant accomplishments included growing support for economic 'improvement' throughout the kingdom; an act mandating universal primary education (for girls as well as boys) under the kirk's auspices; and the Company of Scotland's ill-fated attempt to establish a colony on Panama's Isthmus of Darién.[34] With the Darién scheme, however, Scotland's status as an imperial kingdom once again clashed with England's own imperial standing, a conflict greatly exacerbated by the Edinburgh Parliament's refusal to second the Act of Settlement (1701), which transferred the English and Irish succession to the German house of Hanover. During the ensuing dispute, Scots like Andrew Fletcher of Saltoun freely admitted England's growing political and economic dominance, even as they continued to insist on the independence of their own institutions. Nonetheless, most came to the conclusion that the only way to realize Scotland's imperial aspirations – both in the sense of national autonomy and of overseas dominion – was through an incorporating union of parliaments with its more powerful neighbor. According to the Anglo-Scottish Treaty of Union (1707), the Edinburgh Parliament agreed to its own abolition in return for provisions ensuring the kirk's Presbyterian structure, the continued autonomy of Scots law, and access to England's overseas trade and colonies. As John Robertson has written, the British union was, indeed, 'a union for empire'.[35]

By the time of George I's accession in 1714, the Three British Kingdoms of Charles I had thus metamorphosed into a partially unified British nation. As a consequence of the two European wars with Louis XIV – the second being the War of the Spanish Succession (1702–13) – the government had at its disposal a standing army and navy, a permanent revenue, and an enormous public debt, all of which helped speed the growth of single-party government under the premiership of Sir Robert Walpole and the Court Whigs (1722–42).[36] No less significant, the Hanoverian regime showed itself capable of quelling rebellions by the exiled Stuarts' Scottish supporters in 1715 and 1745, the latter of which produced the one-sided victory at Culloden (1746) followed by the Highlands' brutal 'pacification' at the hands of the duke of Cumberland's army of occupation. If the British nation was a polity 'forged' by war and revolution, however, it was one whose libertarian underpinnings commanded broad allegiance, not only in England but also (increas-ingly) in Scotland and Ireland.[37] During the Anglo-French wars of the 1740s and 1750s, Highland regiments served with distinction in America, while the loyalism of Irish Catholics during the opening phase of the American Revolution prompted the government of George III to contemplate easing anti-Catholic penalties throughout the British archipelago.[38] Equally important, in the Wars of the British Succession and the War of American Independence, the gov-ernment managed to keep armed hostilities well away from English, Irish, and (after 1746) Scottish soil.[39] Although Georgian Britons typically took a dim view of what the earl of Clarendon called the 'troubles' of the previous century, they were, without question, among the principal beneficiaries of Britain's first two revolutions.

II

Despite their archipelagic origins, the effects of Britain's seventeenth-century revolutions extended well beyond the vicinity of England, Scotland, and Ireland. Between the late 1620s and 1640s, New England was the preferred destination for Puritans fleeing Archbishop Laud's reforms; in 1637 the Providence Island Company, chartered to contest Spanish power in the West Indies, helped sponsor John Hampden's unsuccessful suit challenging the crown's right to levy ship money in England; and Cromwell had to dispatch warships in the early 1650s to subdue the royalist colonies of Barbados, Maryland, and Virginia. This transatlantic context appeared with equal force during the Glorious Revolution, as the collapse of James II's authority in England triggered insurrections in Massachusetts, New York, and Maryland.[40] During each of these upheavals, the religious conflict that beset the British archipelago was conspicuous in the colonies as well, from the destruction of Catholic estates during Ingle's Rebellion in Maryland (1645) to the Salem witch trials of 1692.[41] In the 1640s, ties between the Old World and the New were sufficiently close for Hugh Peter to proclaim New England's godly experiment as a model for England's own Puritan revolution; two generations later, colonists assumed that the principles enshrined in the Bill of Rights (1689) applied equally throughout the English-speaking Atlantic.[42]

Taken together, these connections would seem to validate the current trend – evident most recently in the work of Peter Linebaugh and Marcus Rediker – toward conceiving of the 'revolutionary Atlantic' as a natural (if many-headed) extension of the revolutions that swept the British archipelago from the 1640s onward.[43] Despite the temptation to describe the English-speaking Atlantic as a continuous zone of revolution, however, the British recognized important distinctions between metropolitan Europe – including the British archipelago – and the lands and seas that lay beyond. Within Europe, the civil wars and revolutions that beset the Stuart monarchy were subject (albeit with brutal consequences) to the law of nations, as well as the municipal law of England, Scotland, and Ireland. By contrast, convulsions in North America and the West Indies occurred south and west of the so-called 'lines of amity', in regions (along with sub-Saharan Africa) where European treaties and international agreements often possessed little or no authority (see map 3, page 176).[44] In the words of the German natural jurist Samuel Pufendorf, European belligerents typically acknowledged the distinction between these two spheres by concluding 'truce[s] to be observed in Europe', while continuing hostilities 'in the East or West Indies'.[45] Occasionally, governments reversed this relationship by negotiating extra-European pacts of neutrality, in effect permitting their overseas colonies to adopt policies inimical to metropolitan interests. Either way, most Europeans subscribed in their dealings with each other to the principle that 'might makes right beyond the line', a maxim that applied equally to relations with the indigenous peoples of Africa and the Americas.[46] Although settlers who colonized the Americas brought the municipal law of England with them, the Atlantic world's lines of demarcation created significant differences between their own political condition (internal as well as external) and political conditions in the British archipelago.

These differences were readily apparent from the English republic's foreign policy during the 1650s, especially the 'Western Design' against Spanish power in the Caribbean.[47] In Ireland and Scotland, Cromwell's armies operated at least ostensibly within the European law of nations, confiscating Irish property under the customary rules of war and offering the defeated Scots a union that acknowledged their residual rights as an independent nation.[48] By contrast, the conquest of Jamaica in 1655 was little more than a thinly veiled act of piracy, with the Protectorate undertaking the expedition on the (mistaken) assumption that attacking Spain in the Americas would not start a war between the two powers in Europe.[49] In keeping with such perceptions, both North America and the West Indies served as dumping grounds during the 1650s for the victims of Cromwell's revolution, including nearly 10,000 Irish, Scottish, and English prisoners of war condemned to colonial servitude.[50] Although both Puritan morality and English common law were hostile to slaveholding in England, the Interregnum also witnessed growing English participation in the African slave trade to the West Indies, an involvement formalized by Charles II's creation of the Company of Royal Adventurers to Africa (1663) and its successor, the Royal African Company (1672).[51] Despite its growing importance to British interests, the extra-European Atlantic was a zone of impunity, where Britons believed themselves free to behave in ways that were unacceptable within the British archipelago.

Complementing these assumptions about the lawlessness of the Americas was the success of the colonies' own quest for autonomy. Although New Englanders like Hugh Peter greeted the outbreak of the English Civil War by returning home, more typical was the response of Barbados and Virginia, where royalists and parliamentarians alike used the crisis of the 1640s to gain greater control over their own political and economic affairs.[52] Despite subsequent attempts by the English Commonwealth and Charles II to reassert metropolitan authority, most colonies continued to chart their own course, with Massachusetts, Plymouth, Connecticut, and Rhode Island openly refusing to obey the Navigation Acts until their brief subjugation to James II's Dominion of New England (1686–9).[53] Significantly, the two great colonial upheavals of the later seventeenth century – King

Philip's War in New England (1675) and Bacon's rebellion in Virginia (1676) – made little difference to the conduct of politics in England, although they carried dire implications for the status of Indians and the growth of African slavery in North America.[54] Whereas political unrest in Scotland and Ireland repeatedly encroached on English affairs, the American colonies were juridically and geographically remote.

From the 1690s, two developments, both connected to the Glorious Revolution, began to counteract these centrifugal tendencies. The first of these was the emergence of Parliament as an adjunct to the imperial authority of the English/British crown. In a pattern closely related to the growth of parliamentary authority in the British archipelago, the decades following the accession of William and Mary produced a series of initiatives designed to tighten colonial administration, including a revised Navigation Act authorizing colonial vice-admiralty courts (1696), legislation suppressing piracy (1700) and regulating privateers (1708), and the creation of a general post office (1710) with branches in Scotland, Ireland, and each of the American colonies.[55] No less significant, the British government became increasingly involved in the colonies' internal affairs, clarifying the role of English common law in settled and conquered colonies, passing a colonial Naturalization Act (1740) that offered the rights of natural-born British subjects to foreign Protestants and Jews, and compelling colonial assemblies – often in the face of substantial opposition – to enact laws granting religious liberty modeled on the English Toleration Act (1689).[56] In a sense, Britain's colonial policy during the first half of the eighteenth century amounted to a protracted (if uneven) series of attempts to implement the Revolution Settlement that had transformed political conditions in the British archipelago in the western reaches of the British Atlantic.

The Glorious Revolution's other consequence for the colonies was to extend the Wars of the British Succession to North America and the West Indies. In Ireland and Scotland, armed hostilities with James's adherents ended, respectively, in 1691 and 1746. By contrast, although there was little support for the Jacobite cause in America, the British effort to secure the Protestant succession by curbing the power of France produced fighting in the colonies right up to the fall of Quebec (1760). This 'military revolution' considerably enhanced Britain's responsibility for colonial defense, especially in the strategically and economically vital sugar islands of the Caribbean. During the Nine Years War and the War of the Spanish Succession, Whitehall garri-

soned regiments in Barbados, Jamaica, and the Leeward Islands; the
Royal Navy also established a permanent station in the West Indies,
from which its ships helped enforce the Navigation Act and cleared the
seas of pirates following the Peace of Utrecht (1713).[57] Despite the
creation of a North American station in 1745, the mainland colonies
continued to rely more heavily on their own forces until the outbreak
of the Seven Years War (1756–63); however, there, too, parliamentary
funds helped pay for wartime levies like the New England soldiers who
captured French Louisbourg on Cape Breton Island in 1745. Although
hardly comparable to that in Ireland or the Scottish Highlands, Britain's
military presence in the colonies nonetheless partook of the same
centralizing impulses.

In none of these attempts at consolidation did Britain meet with
unqualified success. During the first half of the eighteenth century,
disagreements over the respective rights of metropolitan and colonial authorities affected disputes ranging from the Parson's Cause
over clergy stipends in Virginia (1759) to the impressment of colonial seamen during the Anglo-French wars of the 1740s and 1750s.
Indeed, one consequence of the Hanoverian regime's increased
assertiveness was a countervailing effort to formulate an 'imperial
constitution' – in the apt words of Jack Greene – based on the
proposition that British colonists in North America and the West
Indies were entitled to the same rights of self-government as British
subjects in Ireland and Scotland (before 1707).[58] To British officials
like Governor Shirley of Massachusetts, such efforts appeared to
threaten 'the nature of Government in general, and [to be] contrary
to the Practice of it in the English Constitution.'[59] By making their
claims in terms of fundamental English rights and the British constitution, however, the government's colonial opponents under-
scored the English-speaking Atlantic's growing political unity.
Where England's colonies in North America and the West Indies
had been situated in a zone of perpetual violence and chaos, the
British Atlantic increasingly resembled what Bernard Bailyn has
called a vast 'interior ocean', subject to a common set of laws and
political institutions.[60]

Without this development, there could have been no American
Revolution, or at least no revolution in the sense of an upheaval
whose consequences were felt throughout the Atlantic world. During
the Anglo-French wars of the 1740s and 1750s, the economic and
strategic potential of Britain's Atlantic empire attracted growing interest in England and Scotland, within Parliament as well as without.[61]

Although some of this imperial sentiment had a 'libertarian' cast, it helped prepare the way for the Stamp Act (1765), whereby Parliament attempted to fund a new American establishment of 10,000 regulars by taxing the colonists on the same terms as George III's subjects in England, Scotland, and Wales.[62] Over the next two decades, the British engaged in a protracted debate over the Americans' precise relationship to the British crown and Parliament. According to some (especially the proponents of parliamentary taxation), the colonies were analogous to English 'counties palatine' – jurisdictions without parliamentary representation but integral members of the English body politic; to others (especially radicals like Richard Price and John Cartwright), the colonies were 'distinct states' with the same rights as Ireland or (less frequently) Scotland before the parliamentary union of 1707.[63] What no one doubted was that the colonists were 'fellow subjects' whose resistance to parliamentary taxation carried momentous implications for the entire British archipelago, to say nothing of Europe generally.

To the king's American subjects, of course, there was no question that colonists were entitled to the fruits of England's revolutionary legacy, including the right to no taxation without representation. Even as Americans became convinced that they were victims of a conspiracy of vast, transatlantic proportions, the most conspicuous feature of their response was the depth of their identification as British subjects.[64] In his *Summary View of the Rights of British America* (1774), Thomas Jefferson gave voice to widespread hopes that the dispute over colonial taxation could be resolved within a British context; for that to happen, Jefferson argued, the empire had to be understood, not as a unitary state subject to an all-powerful Parliament, but as a confederation of coordinate realms and provinces bound together, like the Three British Kingdoms of Charles I, by their common allegiance to George III.[65] As late as the summer of 1776, Washington wrote his wife that 'I love my king'.[66] By then, of course, the Continental Congress was moving toward renouncing its allegiance to the British crown, but many worried with Pennsylvania's John Dickinson that the colonies were about to destroy 'a House before We have got another, In Winter, with a small Family.'[67] Although Americans eventually decided that Britain's actions gave them no choice but to declare independence, they did so less out of convictions of their own separateness than because they refused to abandon what they took to be their rights under English common law and the British constitution.

III

Although the American Revolution was a product of the growing unity of the British empire, its outcome precipitated yet another transformation in the structure of the Atlantic world, one at least as far-reaching as the English Revolution of the 1640s and, in many ways, more self-conscious and deliberate in its radical intentions. As laid down in the Declaration of Independence (1776), the crux of this transformation was the creation of independent nations and states where none had previously existed.[68] On the Revolution's eve, the extra-European Atlantic was still inherently colonial space, within which the maritime powers of Europe could only interact by establishing colonies, monopolizing trade, practicing slavery, and waging war on each other's commerce and possessions. Between 1776 and 1825, the United States, Haiti, and the republics of Latin America challenged key elements of this conception, achieving independence from their colonial masters and turning the western and southern Atlantic into an extension of the European state system. Even with this transformation, Europe's colonial empires did not vanish from the Americas. Nonetheless, the Atlantic Wars of Independence inaugurated by the American Revolution – together with the European upheavals of revolutionary and Napoleonic France – rendered their prospects significantly less certain.

Ironically, Britain weathered this international transformation far better than Europe's other maritime powers. Within the metropolitan confines of England, Scotland, and Wales, the War of American Independence generated enormous burdens in the form of massive debts, escalating taxes, and intrusive recruiting.[69] Except for the English county association movement of 1780, however, the fighting overseas never threatened to engulf Britain itself.[70] Although the American Revolution opened deep fissures in the political nation, both the North ministry's supporters and its critics managed to keep their differences within the bounds of civil society, preferring the roles of armchair patriots and radicals to the violence in America.[71] When the radical historian Catharine Macaulay compared a parliamentary speech by John Wilkes in 1775 to 'some of her favorite Speeches in 1639 etc.', she was clearly expressing strong support for the revolutionaries in the colonies; however, neither she nor Wilkes had any intention of playing the part of Charles I's Puritan opponents to Washington's Covenanting army.[72] Despite the growing radicalism of the 1790s – in the cotton mills of Lancashire no less than the London Corresponding Society –

the same pattern held during the wars with revolutionary France.[73] Even in defeat, the parliamentary monarchy of George III was less susceptible to revolution, rebellion, and civil war than the triple crown of its Stuart predecessor; as Linda Colley has written of the ultimately victorious effort against Napoleon, Britain's rulers proved adept at mobilizing 'the support of all Britons – not just Englishmen, or Anglicans, or the propertied, or men of conservative views, but Britons generally.'[74]

British policies within the wider Atlantic revealed a similar determination to resist the radicalism of the American and French revolutions. In the Canada Act (1791), the government sought to inoculate the new provinces of Upper and Lower Canada from the republicanism to the south by legislating strong governors, appointive councils, and established churches (Anglican and Catholic respectively).[75] Between 1792 and 1815, British officials replicated this counter-revolutionary imperialism elsewhere in the Atlantic, encouraging what Christopher Bayly has called a policy of 'proconsular despotism' from Trinidad to the Cape of Good Hope.[76] Hostility to revolution was no less conspicuous in Britain's relations with the United States, as the government maintained British regulars and Indian auxiliaries in territory ceded to the American Republic by the Peace of Paris (1783). Despite the protests of the West India lobby, Parliament refused to modify the Navigation Act to permit American merchants to continue trading in the British Caribbean. Likewise, following the outbreak of war with revolutionary France, the Royal Navy showed scant regard for the republic's maritime rights, searching American vessels for enemy goods, violating American territorial waters, and impressing American seaman.

Even as the British Atlantic underwent an imperial Thermidor, however, Britain had to modify this counter-revolution with two far-reaching concessions. The first was the Declaratory Act of 1778, whereby Parliament permanently renounced its right to tax colonies for revenue (as opposed to levying taxes for regulation of trade under the Navigation Act).[77] The second was Westminster's acceptance (amid considerable pressure from the Irish Volunteers) of the repeal of Poynings' Law in 1782, which effectively placed Ireland on the same constitutional footing with Britain as Scotland had been with England before the parliamentary union of 1707.[78] In both instances, the government acted out of apprehensions that such concessions were necessary to make British provincials less likely to follow the

Americans' subversive example – in Canada and the West Indies no less than in Ireland.[79] Although Ireland's independence lasted barely two decades, the colonial rights enshrined in the legislation of 1778 remained in force until the formation of the British Commonwealth. Despite the felt need to hold republicanism at bay everywhere, the rights of white settlers throughout the British empire remained grounded in the political and constitutional legacy of Britain's two seventeenth-century revolutions.

If Britain was not the counter-revolutionary hegemon that historians have sometimes imagined, its imperial capacity was still formidable. In part, this power came from the unrivaled military and fiscal resources of the British state – resources that the government used to devastating effect during the French-backed Irish rebellion of 1798 and subsequent Anglo-Irish Union (1801). To a surprising degree, though, Britain's continued mastery of the Atlantic world lay in its ability to turn the dynamics of revolution to its own advantage. During the Latin American wars of independence, British diplomats and merchants used the collapse of Spanish and Portuguese power to fashion an informal empire based on free trade and British commercial dominance.[80] Notwithstanding the Anglo-American War of 1812, the government gradually adopted a similar policy of accommodation with the United States, opening markets even as it tacitly accepted the principles of the Monroe Doctrine (1823).[81] Even the abolition of the slave trade (1807) left the British empire in a stronger position than the measure's critics feared, with the Royal Navy using its new powers to disrupt the shipping of Britain's maritime rivals, just as anti-slavery legitimated new imperial forays into Africa and South America.[82] Although the walls of the great Atlantic empires had been breached, the age of Atlantic empire was not yet over.

★★★

Despite its counter-revolutionary image, Britain at Victoria's accession (1837) was thus no less a product of revolution than the Britain of William and Mary or Oliver Cromwell. By the 1830s, of course, the British Atlantic was only one part of a larger English-speaking region. Even with the international fragmentation wrought by American independence, however, the nineteenth-century Atlantic was, in many respects, far more integrated than its seventeenth- and eighteenth-century predecessors, with a zone defined by perpetual war between European empires yielding to a community of nations at least potentially at peace. Unlike the Indian and Pacific oceans, which remained (in British eyes) inherently colonial space, the nineteenth-century Atlantic seemed to be a region amenable to free trade, mutually beneficial diplomacy, and expanding individual rights (indigenous as well as Creole). In terms of formal relations between the British empire and the United States, this quasi-liberal international order ultimately proved far more durable than the one that preceded it, but the governments of the two English-speaking empires were not its only beneficiaries. In areas as varied as women's rights, evangelical revival, electoral reform, industrial change, and the movement to abolish slavery, the independence of the Americas was a prelude to new and, more often than not, closer contact among peoples throughout the Atlantic.

In a very real sense, the modern field of Atlantic history is itself the child (or perhaps the grandchild) of this last phase of Britain's early modern revolutions. As long as the western and southern Atlantic lay beyond the line, its affairs could be disregarded as juridically and politically irrelevant to those of Europe. By contrast, as citizens of sovereign states at least potentially within the pale, Americans everywhere – in Latin America no less than the United States – gained a new voice in matters common to the Atlantic as a whole, even as they became internationally accountable for their own actions, especially with regard to slavery and the dispossession of indigenous peoples. Because of Britain's capacity for displacing revolution onto its periphery, the impact of this transformation was less immediately evident within the nineteenth-century British empire. But it was there nonetheless, with the partially repressed memory of the United States' successful war for independence providing a counterpoint to metropolitan assertions of absolute supremacy throughout Britain's remaining Atlantic empire, even in a dependency as apparently integral to the United Kingdom as Ireland.[83] Only with the toppling of the early modern empires did the underlying unity of the wider Atlantic world become evident in its legal and political structure – and only at that point could its character as a zone of revolution become fully manifest.

11

The Politics of Slavery

Christopher L. Brown

The last two decades have brought a burst of new scholarship on slavery in the British Americas. The historiography displays a depth and sophistication it lacked 20 years ago. Taking note in 1980 of the disproportionate focus on the antebellum era, Ira Berlin concluded that students of American slavery had tended to '[hold] time constant and ignore the influence of place.' Now, a generation later, we have, at the very least, satisfactory studies of slavery in every British colony where it mattered, as well as fine studies of slavery in those settlements where it scarcely existed. Historians of the British Caribbean have yet to produce overviews comparable to the massive surveys published recently by Berlin and Philip Morgan on slavery in North America, but thoughtful work has emerged on each of the key sugar islands, and for most time periods. At the same time, Robin Blackburn's provocative grand narrative of the rise and fall of new world slavery has clarified the history of British plantation societies by situating it in a wider international context. If the most recent scholarship has not quite rectified the overemphasis in Anglo-American studies on the first half of the nineteenth century, there is now a more proportionate attention to what Berlin has properly called the first two centuries of slavery in British America.[1]

Most of this new work has focused on social, economic, and, to a lesser extent, cultural history. The questions important to researchers concern the work that slaves performed, the commodities that they produced, the lives that they lived, the worlds that slaveholders and slaves made together, and made apart. The political history of slavery, with a few crucial exceptions, has been served less well.[2] Historians interested in the antebellum period of American history cannot ignore the politics of slavery since those contests culminated in the 1860s in a bloody civil war. Without a crisis of comparable magnitude to explain, historians of the British empire have treated the political history of slavery during the colonial era in a less sustained, more fragmentary fashion, as isolated episodes detached from the central themes in imperial history. In important respects the subject is in its infancy, though its outlines may be dimly traced and certain elements have been studied in depth. A rich body of work, for example, details slave resistance and Anglo-American anti-slavery movements. But these subjects typically are studied in foreshortened time spans, and treated as separate topics.[3] It becomes clear, moreover, that an exclusive focus on resistant slaves and abolitionists underestimates the complexity of the conflicts in question. Recent work on the Spanish frontier, the American Revolution, and the Haitian Revolution have established the pertinence of military history to the study of slavery. At the same time, a renewed attention to imperial contexts has highlighted the import-ance of contests between colonial slaveholders and the British state, conflicts pregnant with consequence for the institution of slavery throughout British America.[4] The necessary pieces take shape. But scholars and students do not yet have a connected account of the po-litical history of slavery in the early British empire, from the first years of colonial settlement through the last years of colonial slaveholding.

Even more to the point, few have a clear picture of what such a history might look like, the structure it might take, or the themes it could develop. If a political history of slavery must encompass more than the history of slave resistance and the history of abolitionism, what are the proper boundaries of the subject? What historical prob-lems should such work address? Words written a half-century ago by Frank Tannenbaum, a pioneer in the comparative study of slavery, may provide a clue:

> Slavery changed the form of the state, the nature of property, the system of law, the organization of labor, the role of the church as well as its character, the notions of justice, ethics, ideas of right and wrong. Slavery influenced the architecture, the cooking, the politics, the literature, the morals of the entire group – white and black, men and women, old and young … Nothing escaped … nothing and no one.[5]

Tannenbaum knew that understanding the history of slavery meant comprehending its external history as well as its internal dynamics, the difference it made in the broader Atlantic world as well as within specific colonies. Because of the work of Eric Williams, and the controversy that his 1944 study *Capitalism and Slavery* inspired, scholars have come to appreciate the ways human bondage in the colonies affected economic change in the British Isles.[6] Yet, as things stand, it is more difficult than it should be to characterize the impact of colonial slavery on the political life of the British Atlantic world during the early modern era. And this is a shame because in at least five very basic ways the institution of slavery in the colonies made a profound difference: it produced political power, defined political interests, generated political conflicts, shaped political thought, and, by the late eighteenth century especially, influenced the political culture.

I

The ownership of slaves gave British men power, as well as wealth. It figured in the rise of a social group distinctive to the subtropical colonies in the Americas – the planter class. Distinguished by their command of outsized quantities of land and labor, the planters dominated by the early eighteenth century each of the provincial governments in the British Caribbean and the southern mainland.[7] The renowned stability of these colonies in the half-century before the American Revolution owed much to the political supremacy of the slaveholding gentry, which managed, with a few important exceptions in these years, to prevent effective challenge to their authority from below. Slaveholding not only empowered men on the peripheries – in some instances it gave them influence in the metropole. In the present state of research it is not easy to determine the extent to which slave-produced wealth heightened the political standing of merchants in outports like Glasgow, Liverpool, and Bristol where trade with West Africa and British America was brisk.[8] Clearer is the success of absentee planters in transforming sugar profits into political power. By the middle decades of the eighteenth century, the West India interest represented the most influential colonial lobby in London, and absentee sugar planters held several dozen seats in the House of Commons.[9] A political history of slavery, then, would need to assess the political power of the planter class and certain overseas merchants, both in the colonies and at home, and chart the ebb and flow of their influence as it changed over time.

A comprehensive account would have to consider as well the role of slavery in state formation during the seventeenth and eighteenth centuries. For slavery produced public wealth as well as private wealth and, as a consequence, figured significantly in the enhancement of national power. Duties collected by the customs service represented between a fifth and a third of the revenues collected by the state between 1690 and 1790, and throughout this era tobacco and sugar remained among the most heavily taxed of commodities.[10] The increased revenue helped Britain finance the wars that opened up foreign markets and expanded imperial possessions. Unfortunately, the history of the British government's relation to the development and evolution of slavery – unlike the US government's[11] – remains unwritten. Nonetheless, it is clear that the process of empire building during the seventeenth century depended heavily on state investment in the Atlantic slave trade and the control of slave-produced commodities. To win wars in Europe and North America the British sometimes sacked French and Spanish plantations to deprive those empires of colonial wealth. And the state exhausted enormous resources in money and men during the wars with revolutionary France in the 1790s to attain supremacy in colonial trade. Slaves served the British army in the Americas during the Seven Years War, the American Revolution, and in great numbers during the French Revolution. Throughout the early modern era, slavery affected how wars were fought, and sometimes where and when. Acquiring and sustaining international power during the eighteenth and early nineteenth centuries meant, in many instances, commanding the territories where the slaves were, even if that required the reduction of commitments elsewhere.[12]

Slavery, therefore, not only produced political power, it also defined political interests, for individuals as well as for the state. Most propertied men in the Americas, to some degree, sought wealth, autonomy, security, and mastery in their households. The institution of slavery gave these common ambitions a distinctive shape. As the owners of factories in the field, planters favored, as a rule, ready credit, low production costs, protection from foreign competition, high consumer prices for their commodities, and extensive markets in which to sell. They dedicated much of their formal political activity to attaining economic policies that served these ends. In slave societies, mastery meant ruling a small army of laborers, not merely a household. And so planters throughout the slave societies of British America established elaborate slave codes that, in unprecedented ways, made public authorities the guarantors of quasi-feudal powers. The risk of revolt from within, moreover, made British plantations attractive targets for seizure in time of war. Thus, far more than elsewhere in British America, the colonial elite in slave-holding societies proved consistently reluctant to play a prominent role in Britain's colonial wars. In the Caribbean, moreover, planters actively sought during the eighteenth century a standing army capable of defending the colonies from their own slaves. In other respects, though, slaveholders possessed an unusual preoccupation with securing independence from metropolitan oversight. Not only did they resent impositions of imperial authority, as other British colonists did. They also tried to prevent Church of England missionaries and sectarian enthusiasts from challenging the customs and values fundamental to the plantation regime. As must be stressed, and as the present histori-ography well reflects, the producers of tobacco, rice, indigo, and sugar had varying experiences and needs. At no time before the American Revolution did they think of themselves as a unitary slaveholding interest. Nonetheless, as the owners of colonial plantations and as the masters of women and men they had common interests and therefore, in ways too frequently neglected, a common history.

The contours of this common history become clearer if we con-sider the variety of political conflicts that slaveholding inspired. The British Atlantic planter class not only had shared interests, they also shared a common set of antagonists. Most prominent were the enslaved themselves who challenged slavery from within, from its moment of inception through emancipation in 1834 and the abolition of apprenticeship four years later. In several instances, slave resistance culminated in insurrections or mass desertions. More commonly, it crystallized as local, private struggles for rights and freedom. In either case, slave resistance defined the choices available to slaveholders. In times of peace, planters sustained local militias or soldiers to discour-age collective rebellion. In times of war, slaveholders faced the risk of a fight on two fronts, against an internal enemy within the colonies as well as rivals without. Enslaved men and women, moreover, some-times benefited from the assistance of dissidents in the colonies, free blacks or whites without slaves who resented the political supremacy of the slaveholders and, as a consequence, could prove unreliable allies in the defense of human bondage. Internal opposition coordinated by slaves and other dissidents, of course, created opportunities for hostile outsiders – Native Americans, maroons, the French, and the Spanish – to pose as armed liberators, and thus threaten the survival of slavery from without. The slave societies of British America often faced their greatest danger when enemies stood poised to exploit their vulnera-bility to revolution from below.

Competing economic interests in the metropole or in the northern and middle colonies in North America could also present significant threats to the planters' welfare. Planters often wanted an exclusive right to supply their goods to markets within the empire, but merchants, refiners, and consumers sometimes found it in their interest to obtain tropical commodities from elsewhere if they could be had at a better price. A colossal contest emerged in the early nineteenth century between the planters of the West Indies and the metropolitan merchants trading to the east who wished to import sugar from India for sale in markets in Britain. Less spectacular conflicts with British creditors occurred with some regularity, since planters in the colonies often purchased land, slaves, equipment, goods, and provisions upon the expectation of producing a substantial crop. Now and again, moreover, planters found themselves at odds with both the shipowning interests and the state when they looked to foreign carriers, such as the Dutch in the seventeenth century or Americans after the war for independence, who were willing to carry off their commodities for sale in foreign markets. In numerous instances, indeed, planters found that their interests conflicted with the agendas of Parliament or the crown. The state raised duties when the planters wanted them reduced. Whitehall sometimes chose war when planters would have been happier with peace. Over time, British officials proved less reliable in defending white supremacy than slaveholders would have liked. They established regiments of enslaved black soldiers to fight in the Americas during the 1790s and, in the process, ignored the many planters who preferred to keep arms out of the hands of African slaves. These conflicts over economic and strategic policy sometimes merged, especially at the end of the era, with concurrent contests between metropolitan and colonial values. Throughout the early modern era there were British critics, often clergy, who denounced the way planters treated enslaved men and women and pushed for the conversion of the enslaved to Christianity. Typically, they wanted to make slavery better. At the end of the eighteenth century, they were followed by an emerging anti-slavery movement that insisted that planters should not keep slaves at all.

These threats to British slave societies, from within and from without, gave rise to a distinctive set of political ideas. In general, at present, we know far too little about how the defense of colonial slavery affected the development of Anglo-American political thought.[13] Nonetheless, at least five claims originated by the slaveholders and rehearsed frequently in their formal political literature proved especially consequential. One concerned the value of the slaveholding colonies to the empire. The owners of plantations sought favor and favorable legislation by insisting on their economic importance. In the process they helped generate a rival set of ideas attractive to those suspicious of the planters' influence on commercial policy, ideas that questioned the benefits of the American colonies and that promoted, as an alternative, an empire based primarily on trade. The rise of free trade ideology in the late eighteenth and early nineteenth centuries is incomprehensible without reference to the concurrent attack on the privileged position of the West India interest. Planters also affected attitudes towards property in persons by insisting on a right to hold human chattel. Masters of households and employers of labor had long possessed extensive power over their dependents. But the planter class was the first to suggest that, with respect to slaves, these powers should be absolute and unqualified, a claim that over time raised more general questions about the appropriate limits of patriarchal authority. Planters buttressed their professed right to slave property by insisting on the inferiority of African peoples. If the slaveholding elite did not originate the idea of race, they gave it a salience and currency in Anglo-American political thought it otherwise would have lacked. Repeatedly, pro-slavery argument had unforeseen consequences. Colonial slaveholders were the first to suggest that the entire nation, not merely the owners of slaves, bore responsibility for the slave system in British America – a claim which, ironically, proved of great value to abolitionists in the 1780s hoping to make anti-slavery a public concern by describing colonial slavery as a national sin. And the owners of slaves were the first to suggest that workers in industrializing Britain lived no better, and in some respects lived worse, than the enslaved men and women for whom the abolitionists expressed concern. Planters called attention to the prevalence of wage slavery in the British Isles to silence metropolitan critics. But in the process, and again inadvertently, they helped pave the way for later nineteenth-century critiques of free labor.

In a similar way, the campaigns against colonial slavery touched off broader transformations in British political culture. Abolitionism helped unite a nation recovering from the loss of North America and the political divisions that conflict had caused. It allowed Members of Parliament to express their commitment to reform when discouraging institutional change at home. At the same time, the anti-slavery movement initiated significant change in public politics. The campaigns provided an unprecedented opportunity for political participation among disenfranchised groups. It helped the marginalized, particularly Quakers and Anglican evangelicals, achieve social respectability. The movement brought thousands of British women into formal political canvassing. And they in turn expanded the established repertoire of political agitation by organizing consumer boycotts of slave-grown sugar. At times between 1787 and 1838, the issue of slavery dominated national politics. The formal debates in Parliament generated extensive discussion out-of-doors, an astounding number of anti-slavery petitions, and a substantial corpus of controversial literature. A bibliography published in 1932 identified more than 500 pamphlets published on slavery in the late eighteenth and early nineteenth centuries. An updated search likely would turn up a good deal more. Most fundamentally, British abolitionism helped establish opposition to slavery as an expression of collective virtue, a tradition that would exercise significant influence over British political life into the early twentieth century and help it become a fundamental component of national identity, as well as the moral basis for the exertion of imperial power.[14]

In all of these ways – by producing power, shaping interests, generating conflicts, inspiring debate, and forming identities – slavery mattered to the political history of the British Atlantic world. A simple enumeration of the key topics, however, can tell us little about the dynamic aspects of this history, the way contests for power within and over slavery changed over time, or how the political history of slavery reflected and figured in the broader political developments of the era. It becomes a relatively simple task to develop a chronology for the half-century after the American Revolution, when conflicts between abolitionists and the slaveholding interest take center stage. More difficult is devising a chronology for the first century and a half of colonial slavery, since, at first glance, the political experience of the slaveholding colonies in this period would seem to be defined by their individual histories rather than by a common struggle. Yet, as I have tried to suggest, the British Atlantic planter class often had shared interests and a shared set of antagonists. And it is these shared interests and antagonists that make it possible to treat aspects of the political history of slavery as a single story. The questions helpful for the era after American independence, as it happens, serve equally well for the decades before: in the struggle to establish, profit from, and preserve colonial slavery, what were British planters up against? When and how did those challenges change during the course of the colonial era?

II

Chattel slavery represented a substantial departure in English social and economic history when established in the colonies during the early seventeenth century. The colonists that settled in the Chesapeake and the Caribbean had no experience with the operation of large-scale plantations or the management of slave labor. The settlers had in front of them, it is true, the example of other European colonists, the Spanish and the Portuguese especially, who, by the late sixteenth century, had begun to use slave labor extensively. And enslaved African men and women were available in the Americas to those who could afford the purchase from merchants, primarily Dutch in this period, engaged in the Atlantic slave trade. But it took several decades for slavery to emerge in the new English colonies, in part because of the adjustment slavery required to English customs. The founders did not set out to establish slave societies. The trading companies and individual proprietors thought of the first settlers as employees rather than entrepreneurs and expected them to work for metropolitan investors rather than for themselves. As tenants rather than landowners, the first colonists lacked the incentive to invest in plantation agriculture. It took time for settlers to identify a viable crop and cultivate it successfully. And in the Chesapeake, in St Kitts, and on Providence Island colonists were vulnerable in the early years to raids by the neighboring Powhatans, Caribs, or Spanish. But in the development of colonial slavery the first significant political struggle that mattered took place between colonists seeking property rights in land and the metropolitan promoters seeking a return on their investment. The emergence of slavery in the English colonies depended heavily upon the liberation of the English colonists from the control of metropolitan overseers, a process that began for some colonies shortly after their founding and was completed for all during the turmoil of the Civil War and the Interregnum which removed the last vestiges of proprietorial control over the plantation economies.

If the ownership of land and command of the colonial economy represented the first political victory for the planters, the reduction of labor into a commodity represented the second. Profitably exploiting the land meant intensifying the exploitation of labor. In the Chesapeake and on Barbados especially, planters abandoned the 'pre-capitalistic, moral-paternalistic ideological superstructure of traditional servitude', as historian Hilary Beckles put it, in favor of a system that transformed indentured servants into 'temporary chat-tels'. Servants in seventeenth-century England, it is true, also endured arduous labor, physical punishment, and recapture when they fled from an employer. They too were unfree in critical respects. What made service in the Chesapeake and the West Indies different in the early and mid-seventeenth century for both volun-tary and involuntary migrants was their almost complete transforma-tion into private property. In early Barbados, according to Beckles, planters routinely 'bought, sold, gambled away, mortgaged, taxed as property, and alienated in their wills their indentured servants.' There, as in the other plantation colonies, the institutions that might have protected laborers from maltreatment – the courts particularly – lay under the control of the planters. The English state, moreover, was an unreliable guardian. Acts of Parliament in 1652 and 1654 licensed the shipment of the defenseless poor to the colonies. And combatants during the mid-century wars in the British Isles added to the total by exiling the defeated to the Americas. The indepen-dence that allowed the early colonial elite to establish private owner-ship in land also allowed them to exploit the human flotsam dispersed by political conflict at home. The supply of servants avail-able to the plantation colonies declined in the late seventeenth century as the number of migrants to the Americas fell, as the indentured looked for opportunity elsewhere, as an intensifying concern with the rights of the freeborn gradually discouraged the reduction of English nationals into near slavery, and as an emerging English trade in the eastern Atlantic made more African slaves avail-able. But when planters in the Caribbean turned decisively to the employment of Africans after the Restoration, they had already established for themselves the nearly unrestricted right to employ and govern human property as they saw fit.[15]

In the first half-century of colonial settlement, then, the nascent planter class waged a successful fight to control land and labor. The 50 years that followed, from 1660 to 1713, were characterized by a struggle to persist through a series of setbacks that destabilized the emerging plantation regime. Slavery in English America first took root when the overseas settlements lay outside the constant scrutiny of rulers in the metropole. Its future became less certain as the crown began to recognize the commercial and strategic importance of the colonies. Before the 1650s, the plantation colonists depended heavily on Dutch merchants for manufactured goods and the export of their produce to Europe. Because of the Navigation Acts, English planters lost their short-lived liberty to find the best market for their goods. At the same time, new duties imposed on sugar and tobacco threatened to reduce their profits just as the first boom years for tropical commodities passed. Royal government, moreover, threatened not only a loss of wealth but also a decline in political power. A campaign inaugurated by Charles II and extended during the short reign of James II threatened to reduce the independence of the colonies and the authority of the colonial elite. Royal governors sent by the crown to Virginia and the English West Indies in this period tried to stifle the lower houses of assembly and tighten the enforcement of the acts of trade. To make matters worse, the planters stood to lose a great deal from the colonial wars conducted by the state. England spent half of the era between the Restoration and the Treaty of Utrecht at war with the Netherlands or France. These conflicts, in the short run, had a disastrous effect on property holdings in the plantation colonies. Enemies wreaked havoc on each of the English Caribbean islands at least once during this period. St Kitts alone was sacked seven times. In becoming valuable to the empire, the slave colonies became as well a chief prize in the high stakes contests for local political authority and international supremacy.[16]

The planters were especially vulnerable in such contests. Settlements in South Carolina, Jamaica, and the Leeward Islands would achieve social stability and consistent economic success only after the achievement of a lasting peace in Europe. Planters lost white servants to the army and navy by the hundreds. When the French and Dutch invaded, they often carried off slaves from the English plantations by the thousands. Predictably, the frequent unrest endangered the already uncertain authority that landowners held over their servants. Revolts by Irish laborers in Barbados in the 1630s and 1640s led several colonies to limit, as they could, subsequent Irish immigration. The Catholic workers, the planters believed, represented not only a disgruntled labor force but also a potential fifth column. Royal governors sent by James II to the British West Indies in the late 1680s turned to Irish servants as well as small landowners and (in Jamaica) buccaneers to humble the English planter class. With the encouragement of the Jacobite governor-general Nathaniel Johnson, Irish workers on St Kitts destroyed the English plantations in June of 1689, clearing the way for a French conquest of the island months later. Seditious behavior, of course, followed as much from the resentments of class as from the fault lines of religion and politics. English servants oppressed by their employers in St Kitts welcomed a

Spanish invasion force in 1628 with grateful cries for liberty. Nathaniel Bacon famously rallied servants, slaves, and others among the dispossessed in a rebellion against the Virginia elite in 1676. Interracial conspiracies, such as the aborted 1692 plot in Barbados, especially unnerved planters because they threatened to unite the black majority with the disgruntled and landless unsympathetic to the plantation regime. Enslaved men and women, though, did not need the assistance of white servants to seek their freedom. And the growth of slaveholding throughout the plantation colonies in the late seventeenth century led to repeated attempts among the enslaved to overthrow human bondage.[17]

If slaveholders faced a genuine threat to their social and political position between 1713 and 1763, from the Treaty of Utrecht until the end of the Seven Years War, it came from the slaves themselves. The demographic imbalances that resulted from the growth of the slave trade helped make slave plots and conspiracies a frequent occurrence. Unconquered maroon communities prevented planters from achieving supremacy in Jamaica and negotiated terms of peace that gave them legal recognition. Although Britain seized Jamaica from Spain in 1655, nearly a century and a half would pass before it could claim authority over the entire island. In some instances, the enslaved found allies in the enemies of the slaveholders. The Spanish in Florida compromised the security of British low-country settlements by offering liberty to slaves who escaped to St Augustine, a policy that precipitated the famous Stono Rebellion in South Carolina in 1739. For reasons that need more research, the 1730s and 1740s witnessed an unparalleled cycle of plots and conspiracies. Some climaxed in open rebellion, most notably the New York conspiracy of 1741.[18] Planters in the British colonies escaped a revolution from below in the decades before the American Revolution, but only by responding with brutal reprisals.

Outside the constant threat of insurrection, the planters faced few serious challenges to their interests during the first six decades of the eighteenth century. In this period, they consolidated their authority in the colonial assemblies and all but silenced local dissent. Greater political security in the colonies led to a more energetic engagement with politics in the metropole. Because of a dependence on the state for military protection, and because of a need for protection from competing producers of sugar in the French West Indies, planters sought influence within the empire rather than independence from it. Slaveholders won substantial victories over competing economic interests in the first half of the eighteenth century. They assisted the successful campaign that culminated in 1714 against the Royal African Company's monopoly in the British slave trade. An increasingly influential West Indian lobby achieved an important victory with the passage of the Excise Tax of 1733, which severely restricted the North American and Irish trade for rum, and other commodities with the French Caribbean colonies. Over the objections of shipowners, refiners, and metropolitan grocers, the sugar planters managed in 1739 to drive up the price of sugar in Britain by winning the privilege to sell directly to purchasers in Europe. And in the 1740s, South Carolina slaveholders would figure critically in the successful campaign in colonial Georgia for the introduction of chattel slavery. The half-century following the Peace of Utrecht represented the heyday of the planting interest. There was little reason by the 1760s to think that the planters, or the slave system, would find their political fortunes reversed.[19]

Those who opposed slavery on moral grounds in these years scarcely looked like a credible threat. From the beginning, from the establishment of the first slaveholding colonies in English America, planters had faced critics both in the colonies and in the metropole discomfited by the practice of human bondage. Exceptionally pious men and women numbered heavily among the critics. What angered them was not only the enslavement of human bodies but also the neglect of redeemable souls. Slaveholders in the British colonies, almost as a rule, showed no interest in converting enslaved men and women to Christianity or exhibiting the paternal values which, the critics said, would encourage loyal service among the enslaved. As a consequence, the devout, on their own initiative, tried to promote Christianity on the plantations. Quaker settlers in Barbados began this missionary work first in the late seventeenth century. The Church of England, through the auspices of the newly founded Society for the Propagation of the Gospel (SPG), sponsored a more comprehensive program conceived for all of plantation America in the early eighteenth. Scholars have tended to dismiss this campaign to Christianize slavery because it failed spectacularly. There were few Protestant Christians among the nearly half million enslaved men and women in the colonies on the eve of the American Revolution. The commitment to missionary work within the Church of England was inconsistent at best. But the Christianization initiatives failed because planters had no desire to reform the ethos of the labor system, raise the expectations of the enslaved, or permit outsiders to patrol the plantations spreading potentially subversive ideas. And in this regard, until the early nineteenth century, when their evident hostility to the clergy began to enrage metropolitan opinion, the planters got their way.[20]

Alongside the effort among some clergy to make slaves Christians, a more secular critique of slavery also took shape during the first three-quarters of the eighteenth century. Evidence of distaste for human bondage in the Americas is littered through the literary record of the period. Historians often have focused on the pronouncements of well-known Scottish intellectuals such as Frances Hutcheson, Adam Smith, and John Millar. But, as the planters knew, a discomfort with colonial slavery ran widely, if not deeply, through polite society in the British Isles. A pamphlet published in London had challenged the morality of slavery on the grounds of natural rights as early as 1709. And in the 1730s the Reverend Robert Robertson of Nevis was bemoaning the 'current and longstanding Humour' in England of judging planters 'by the most rigorous severity'.[21] The critiques intensified during the 1750s and 1760s, as social and commercial connections with the colonies deepened, as the newspaper and pamphlet literature reported on events in British America with greater frequency, as poets and novelists increasingly used colonial settings to explore the themes of civility and barbarism, virtue and savagery. The growth of anti-slavery sentiment in the second half of the eighteenth century followed in large part from the internal logic of cultural change, from the growing value placed on sensibility, charity, and enlightenment. It reflected broader trends in the intellectual culture of western Europe, trends that had little to do with the specifics of Anglo-American politics. But it was the conflict over the rights of the colonies in the years before the American Revolution that galvanized anti-slavery sentiment into an organized movement.

If American colonists had presented their case for independence in more parochial terms, if they had argued only for the customary rights and liberties of Englishmen, perhaps, as before, few would have thought about the rights of Africans. However, by invoking purportedly universal principles rather than established law or custom, by describing liberty as a natural right, and by defining their political crusade as a campaign against slavery, they inadvertently drew attention to the dubious justice of holding men, women, girls, and boys in lifelong bondage. Defenders of imperial authority eager to expose the hypocrisy of American planters – Samuel Johnson most famously – condemned colonial slavery in the 1770s to discredit the colonial movement for political liberties. And several of the growing number of commentators on imperial affairs decided that the overgrown authority of slaveholders in the plantation colonies of Virginia and South Carolina had contributed directly to their pursuit of independence. As a consequence, the first emancipation schemes circulated in Britain during the 1770s aimed not only to liberate slaves but also to subject the slaveholding colonies to greater metropolitan control.[22]

Predictably, the rise of anti-slavery sentiment and the threat of coercion by the imperial state put slaveholders on the defensive.[23] Typically, planters reacted by insisting on self-government and property in slaves as fundamental to the rights of Englishmen. Sometimes they held British slave traders responsible for the growth of slavery in the colonies. The possibility that metropolitan intervention might overturn the power of planters in the colonies figured significantly in the calculations made by the provincial elite in the months before the outbreak of war with Britain in 1775. When royal governors threatened to turn slaves against their owners to restore imperial authority, it helped drive landholding elites in South Carolina and Virginia into revolution. The war for American independence ruined the plantation colonies on the southern mainland in the short term, as thousands of enslaved men and women fled to the British for liberty and protection. In the long run, though, liberation from imperial oversight freed planters in the south to win greater security for slavery under a new federal union. Although the American Revolution spawned anti-slavery agitation in the northern states as well as in the British Isles, it paved the way for a substantial expansion of the slaveholding empire in the southern territories of the newly independent United States. As before, a weak central government facilitated the extension of private property in slaves.

In the British West Indies, the impact of the American Revolution was very different. Instead of strengthening colonial slavery, it inaugurated a series of conflicts that culminated in its destruction. For many years historians understood the declining fortunes of the Caribbean planter class during the early nineteenth century in economic terms. In an influential study (1928), Lowell Joseph Ragatz contended that beneath the complex sequence of events that led to emancipation in 1838 seemed to lie the steady erosion of the planters' economic position. During the last half-century of British West Indian slavery, he argued, the soil of the old Caribbean colonies had declined in productivity. And this occurred just as new lands were opening for sugar cultivation, both in neigh-boring French colonies and within the British empire after the Seven Years War. The West India lobby in London could discourage to an extent the migration of sugar planting to new settlements, but they had almost no control over the quantity or quality of sugar pro-duced elsewhere in the Americas. As a consequence, the planters of Barbados and the Leeward Islands, especially, found themselves increasingly uncompetitive in European markets, a situation made much worse in 1784 by restrictions imperial officials placed on trade with the newly independent United States and in 1807 by the aboli-tion of the British slave trade. The planter class, according to Ragatz, was caught in a death spiral of low profitability and high debt by the 1820s. The campaign to abolish colonial slavery succeeded in 1833, Ragatz intimated, because the plantations were no longer econom-ically viable. Building on this theme 16 years later, Eric Williams argued that the abolitionists had not only benefited from changing economic conditions, but themselves represented economic interests in disguise.[24]

Most scholars now believe that the decline of the West Indian economies was as much a consequence as a cause of the anti-slavery movements that emerged in the 1780s.[25] The abolitionists have re-emerged in recent accounts as the deciding influence in the fall of British slavery. If no doubt now remains about their significance, however, too many continue to overlook the broader political context that allowed the abolitionists to succeed. As the planters knew well, the opponents of the West India interest multiplied in the decades after the American Revolution. What declined steadily and perceptibly after the American war was less the planters' econ-omic position than their political standing. Time and again in the later eighteenth and early nineteenth centuries, the slaveholders found it difficult to get their way on what they regarded as matters of importance. The imperial state emerged after the American Revolution as an almost constant antagonist rather than a reliable ally. Relations between planters and Parliament broke down first over the admission of United States ships to West Indian ports. The mercantilists at Whitehall had established doctrine on their side when they banned American carriers from the British Caribbean colonies in the 1780s. But the West Indians experienced the prefer-ence given to military and metropolitan commercial interests as a sacrifice of the plantation economy. The restrictions on inter-American trade would remain a lingering grievance among the

planters until 1822, when Parliament finally opened Caribbean ports
to American ships. But by that time, as far as slaveholders were
concerned, the evidence of official betrayal was indisputable. Import
duties increased by the state during the American and French
revolutions remained high in times of peace. And, in several
instances, imperial officials displayed a cavalier attitude toward the
enforcement of white supremacy. Planters opposed the decision by
the British army to put slaves in arms during the French revolutionary and Napoleonic wars. Even more ardently, they opposed the
tendency of British military officials to put blacks and whites on an
equal footing. Just when the slave uprising in Saint Domingue
seemed to show the dangers of unsettling racial hierarchies, the state
seemed all too willing to blur differences between white and black.
For these reasons, the abolition of the slave trade in 1807 looked to
planters like only the most concrete proof of their rapid decline in
political influence.[26]

The abolitionists represented the best organized of the several
metropolitan interest groups that took on the slaving interest after
the American Revolution. The origins of the movement lay in the
disastrous experience of the American war, which directed new
attention to the character of overseas empire and fostered new efforts
to bring colonial institutions in line with concepts of national virtue
and English liberty. Quakers and Anglican evangelicals, the leaders
of the movement, thought of abolitionism as a way to make religion
matter in politics and public life. And they succeeded by the early
1790s in making moral opposition to the slave trade an essential
aspect of what it meant to be British. The movement achieved note-
worthy peaks of influence between 1814 and 1816, during the effort
to ban the international slave trade and regulate the intercolonial slave
trade, and after 1823 when British slaveholding itself came under
sustained attack. In these campaigns, the abolitionists benefited from
the cooperation of a diverse set of economic interests – merchants,
shipowners, and grocers particularly – that had grown resentful of the
privileged position West India sugar producers held in the imperial
economy. A merger of these moral and economic interests took
shape during the 1820s in the offices of the Liverpool East India
Association, the leaders of which hoped to substitute cheaper sugar
produced by 'free labor' in India for the more expensive, slave-grown
sugar produced in the West Indies.[27]

If this was not enough, planters also faced new threats to their
supremacy from within the colonies. An emerging class of mixed-

raced freedmen in the early nineteenth century pushed for the political and economic rights of white men and played a critical role in the dissemination of Protestant Christianity through the British West Indies. Moravian and Methodist preachers had established religious meetings on the Caribbean plantations in the last decades of the eighteenth century, and Baptist and Anglican clergy joined them in the decades that followed. But an emerging network of black and mixed-race ministers would prove to be the chief exponents of Christianity in the slave quarters, and their version of Christianity placed far less emphasis on submission to earthly authority than on the promise of divine redemption. Three major slave rebellions occurred in the British West Indies in the early nineteenth century, on Barbados in 1816, in Demerara in 1823, and on Jamaica in 1831 and 1832. In each instance the enslaved acted upon rumors that planters were withholding rights granted to them by Parliament. In each instance privileged and Christian slaves provided the leadership for the revolt. In each instance the planter class responded with savage reprisals designed to restore order to plantation society. And in each instance the brutal suppression of the rebellions intensified metropolitan distaste for the slaveholding class in the colonies. Slavery came to an end in the British empire because the reformed Parliament of 1832, itself unusually responsive to the expression of public opinion, abolished slavery in 1834. But emancipation almost certainly would have come much later if the enslaved engaged in freedom struggles in the British West Indies had not eroded the institution of slavery from within.[28] British slavery took shape in an era when planters enjoyed almost complete independence from contending political factions in the metropolis. It collapsed before a bevy of hostile strategic, economic, religious, moral, and revolutionary agendas that, taken together, left British planters by the late 1820s without a significant political ally.

***

The political history of slavery, then, might be told as the rise and fall of the British Atlantic planter class, as the history of their efforts to establish, command, and sustain the institution of human bondage through a series of internal and external challenges from the reign of James I to the accession of Victoria more than 200 years later. There are, of course, other ways that the intersection between politics and slavery might be approached. In his outstanding study of slave revolts in the British West Indies, Michael Craton has shown how the evolving fortunes of British slavery might be explored through patterns of resistance among the enslaved.[29] I have concentrated on the planters because of the broad perspective that their experience provides. The planters were the men in between, at once the elite in the colonies where they lived and the subjects of an imperial state over which they had little control. With a focus on the planters it becomes possible to see how local conflicts between masters and slaves shaped the broader history of the British empire, and how macro-political crises in the empire affected the relationship between masters and slaves 'on the ground'. The history of British slavery took place outside the plantation colonies as well as in those territories where the slaves were. The task at hand involves relating these realms of experience to each other and tracing them out from beginning to end. At that point the political history of slavery in the British Atlantic world may be written.

Afterword
Atlantic History:
A Circumnavigation

J. H. Elliott

In the rousing words of David Armitage, 'We are all Atlanticists now.'[1] But, if so, what Atlantic are we talking about? For most of the eighteenth century the Atlantic meant, for the English, only the North Atlantic. Anything further south was called the 'Ethiopian Sea',[2] that vast Iberian Atlantic which scarcely figures in this volume. While the theme of the volume and the fields of expertise of its contributors make this understandable, it is well to bear in mind that there are alternative perspectives from which to view the current trend towards the reconceptualization of British and North American history in terms of 'Atlantic history'.

For early modern Spaniards the Atlantic was the 'Mar Océano' – the Ocean Sea – and they do not seem to have drawn the distinction made by English mapmakers between two separate seas. Their Atlantic was a single ocean, as no doubt it also was for the English captains who sailed to the Gambia to collect their slave cargoes for sale in the West Indies, or to the Rio de la Plata to unload their shipments of contraband goods in exchange for the silver of Potosí. Similarly, it is in terms of a unified ocean that historians are being encouraged to think today, as indeed they were already in the 1950s and 1960s by such historians as Charles Verlinden, Jacques Godechot, and Robert Palmer.[3]

It would scarcely seem a coincidence that those early pleas for Atlantic history followed in the wake of the publication by Fernand Braudel in 1949 of *La Méditerranée et le Monde Méditerranéen à l'époque de Philippe II*. Here was an attempt, breathtaking in its ambition, to embrace in a unified conceptual framework an entire sea and the lands that bordered it. The flaws in that grand Braudelian design have become increasingly apparent as the years have passed. In particular, it may legitimately be asked whether Braudel did not use his mystical conception of the Mediterranean to impose an artificial unity on two very different civilizations, those of Latin Christendom and Ottoman Islam, submerging their distinctive characteristics and historical trajectories in a geographical determinism created by their shared proximity to the same strip of water. If 'Mediterranean history' is itself problematic, we may justifiably wonder how much more problematic is the history not of an inland sea but of a vast ocean, bordered by three different continents.

One answer, indicated here by David Armitage,[4] is that, unlike the Mediterranean, or, for that matter, the Indian Ocean, both of which had for centuries been navigated by peoples from different civilizations and societies, the Atlantic was a purely European construct. Essentially it was a fifteenth- and sixteenth-century invention, the end product of innumerable voyages whose point of departure was the ports of northern and Iberian Europe. Here, unlike in the Indian Ocean, there were no pre-existing oceanic trading systems into which European ships and merchants irrupted. The Atlantic began its historical existence as a European lake.[5]

If the Atlantic is a purely European construct, albeit one that was all too soon to acquire an African dimension, there would on the face of it seem to be a strong case for a unified approach to its history. But against the pan-Atlantic approach it could be argued, in line with D. W. Meinig's formulation, that there was not one Atlantic – at least during the sixteenth and seventeenth centuries – but a minimum of three, defined by different climatic and environmental conditions and different movements of winds and currents. There was a North European Atlantic linking the societies of northern Europe to the Newfoundland fishing banks, the cluster of settlements running down the eastern American seaboard, and a few West Indies outposts; a Spanish Atlantic of the *carrera de Indias*, linking Seville to the Caribbean and the American mainland; and a Luso-Atlantic, linking Lisbon to Brazil.[6] Only in the later seventeenth and eighteenth centuries did all three Atlantic systems begin seriously to merge, in a process of mutual interaction in which the African slave was an involuntary and all too prominent participant.

Insofar as Atlantic history has been written, it has tended to be an Atlantic history compartmentalized into these three zones of European settlement, trade, and colonial rule. Because of the physical and logistical differentiation of the zones over the first two to three centuries following Columbus's landfall, this historical compartmentalization is comprehensible and to some extent justified. Not even historians can join together what God put asunder. A further constraint on the adoption of a pan-Atlantic approach, perhaps less justified but no less comprehensible, has been the tradition of a historiography defined in terms of nationality and national experience. Not surprisingly, Atlantic history has so far consisted largely of British, French, Dutch, Spanish, and Portuguese Atlantic history, divided into neat national packages.

This national approach – national in the sense of concentrating on the history of a single state or nation and its transatlantic extensions – has led to a long line of distinguished works. These works have primarily been concerned with two aspects of the transatlantic relationship – imperial or institutional connections, and commercial connections – although they have also, by a logical progression, moved into the sphere of international relations. As far as imperial connections are concerned, Bernard Bailyn rightly reminds us in his 1996 article in *Itinerario* on 'The Idea of Atlantic History' of the important contributions of Charles Andrews for the British transatlantic empire, and of Clarence Haring for the Spanish. Similarly, it is not hard to think of major works on the commercial connections between metropolis and colonies: Richard Pares, for instance, on Britain and the West Indies,[7] or the *magnum* – not to say *maximum* – *opus* of the Chaunus on the Spanish Atlantic economy.[8]

Yet in this age of globalization we are all uneasily aware that national history is no longer enough. Indeed, the spate of outstanding works on African slavery and the slave trade over recent decades, running from Philip Curtin to Robin Blackburn and David Eltis, has opened up exciting perspectives that suggest the dawn of a new era of pan-Atlantic history.[9] The same can be said of the growing number of books and articles on the fascinating topic of migration, like that of Alison Games, one of the contributors to this volume, on *Migration and the Origins of the English Atlantic World*.[10] But it could be argued that some topics lend themselves better than others to a multinational, and multicontinental, approach. Slavery and migration, both voluntary and involuntary, are particularly appropriate for a pan-Atlantic treatment precisely because, by their very nature as the story of people in movement, they transcend the history of single nations and continents, and effectively force historians to adopt a perspective that embraces as a single unit of study the Atlantic and the societies that border it.

Writing about imperial government or bilateral trade, on the other hand, historians are inevitably driven back to the primarily national contexts in which they operated. The same is largely true of a number of concepts and constructs, such as race, class, and gender, which possess enormous resonance in the contemporary world. As the essays in this volume indicate, these, too, can be treated effectively within the context of the history of a British – or for that matter Iberian – Atlantic, providing in the process a bifocal perspective from both sides of the Atlantic on a phenomenon which at once unites and separates societies linked by common origins but divided by the sea.

In spite of this, however, Atlantic history lends itself particularly well to two distinctive approaches, not necessarily mutually exclusive, but complementary. It encourages historians to trace *connections*. But it also encourages them – or should encourage them – to draw *comparisons*. The drawing of comparisons in an Atlantic context is not itself a new phenomenon, as can be seen from Frank Tannenbaum's path-breaking *Slave and Citizen: The Negro in the Americas*, published as long ago as 1946. Once again slavery, as a phenomenon transcending national boundaries, helped to open the way to cross-cultural approaches. But this is only one among many Atlantic themes that can lend themselves to fruitful comparison, and in recent years interest has been growing in comparative approaches to the history of the Atlantic world. For example, Anthony Pagden, in his *Lords of All the World*, has compared the ideologies of empire in Spain, Britain, and France,[11] while Patricia Seed has examined the varying ways in which explorers, conquerors, and settlers from different European nations laid ceremonial claim to the American lands on which they so unceremoniously intruded.[12]

As one who is currently grappling with a comparative Atlantic project, in this instance a comparison of the transatlantic societies created by British and Spanish settlers on American soil, I would be the first to recognize the limitations inherent in a comparative approach. It is technically very demanding, the act of comparison itself is all too liable to deliver less than it appears to promise, and there is a danger either of placing too much emphasis on similarities at the expense of differences, or else of emphasizing the differences to create – as it could be argued that Patricia Seed tended to create – national stereotypes.

On the other hand, comparison as applied to Atlantic history offers wonderful possibilities for identifying both the similarities and the differences in the responses of different European societies to the challenges of overseas colonization and confrontation with the indigenous inhabitants of America. This can only expand and enrich our vision of the great transatlantic migration. Even recognizing the constraints of space under which the contributors to this volume were forced to operate, it would have benefited from more comparative comments allowing glimpses of regions that lie outside an exclusively Anglo-American landscape. A useful one, for instance, is provided by Alison Games, when she uses the work of historians of the Andes to suggest that, in an Atlantic world made up of migrants, Native Americans can be seen as 'the consummate migrants'.[13] Joyce Chaplin, in her bold attempt to trace the development of British attitudes to race, refers to late medieval and early modern Spanish attitudes to the Moors and the Jews. To this it might be added that, in Covarrubias's Castilian dictionary of 1611, the entry under *raza* begins with pure-blooded horses, but then goes on to say that 'in matters of lineage *raza* is taken as pejorative, as containing some *raza* of Moor or Jew.'[14] There is, however, some reason for skepticism about the degree to which metropolitan attitudes to the Moors and the Jews influenced Spanish perceptions of the indigenous peoples of America, where questions of climate, status, Christianity, and civility also came into play.

There are other opportunities, too, for such cross-referencing. Sarah Pearsall, for instance, writes that 'the colonial world was full of European men and their Native American wives.'[15] But how far is this true of the English colonial world? The available evidence suggests that cohabitation in British America, at least in the seventeenth century, did not occur on anything like the scale to be found in the Spanish or French colonial worlds. If not, why not?[16]

Adopting a comparative pan-Atlantic approach, it is not therefore impossible to envisage a general treatment even of such complex topics as race, class, and gender, although it would take a bold historian to embark on them. But by and large Atlantic history is always likely to remain a history framed more in terms of connections than of comparisons – connections both trans-Atlantic and circum-Atlantic. An Atlantic history conceived in terms of connections, however, also has its problems, not the least of which is the space over which connections are traced. If we look at the ripple effects of transatlantic migration, for example, we find that they reach far beyond the societies located on the Atlantic rim. Do the Indians of the Great Plains fall into the sphere of Atlantic history as the patterns of their lives are touched, disturbed, and eventually revolutionized by the settlement of European colonists on the Atlantic seaboard? Does the history of Peru, which is so rapidly integrated into an Atlantic economy, form part of Atlantic history? If so, a country bordering the Pacific finds itself subjected to a dramatic geographical displacement; the Atlantic becomes the most expansive of oceans, and Atlantic history the most expansive of concepts.

The contributions to this volume offer, above all, a history, not of Atlantic comparisons but of transatlantic connections, operating within a predominantly anglophone world. In view of this, the question that immediately suggests itself to outsiders to Anglo-American history is likely to be: what, then, is new?

Between 1918 and 1934 the distinguished Harvard historian Roger B. Merriman published a four-volume work under the title of *The Rise of the Spanish Empire in the Old World and the New*. In Merriman's volumes the history of metropolitan Spain and of Spain in America run alongside each other. A discussion of Spanish campaigns in the Mediterranean, for example, is followed by an account of the Spanish settlement of Florida. In the same way, standard histories of sixteenth- and seventeenth-century Spain by Spanish historians have traditionally incorporated, as a matter of course, chapters on the conquest, colonization, and government of Spain's American possessions. While these were primarily devoted to narratives of conquest, followed by institutional and administrative history, Jaume Vicens Vives, perhaps the outstanding Spanish historian of the twentieth century, planned and edited a five-volume work, published in 1957, entitled *The Social and Economic History of Spain and America*.[17]

The history of Spanish America during the colonial period, therefore, has conventionally been regarded as a natural concomitant of the history of metropolitan Spain, and vice versa.[18] The same can hardly be said of general histories of England, nor for that matter of histories of the British colonies in America, strongly preoccupied with the kind of society into which they were to evolve. To some extent, therefore, it is difficult to avoid the suspicion that the new Atlantic history, insofar as it is subsumed into British Atlantic history, represents a piece of historical catching-up. It is, of course, no less welcome for that. English history and American history have all too often gone their separate ways, without any consistent or sustained dialog between the two. Now, with American historians moving away from their teleological preoccupations and exceptionalist assumptions, and with English historians moving away from their localist concerns, the mid-Atlantic is a good place to meet. The encounter has been greatly facil-

itated by the historiographical transformation of recent years, which
has seen the ending of the automatic equation of English with British
history, and the deconstruction of English history into the history of
the so-called 'British archipelago', of which the British settlements on
the further side of the Atlantic form remote but essential component
elements.[19] In particular, Ireland, as an important part of that archipelago, becomes at once a way-station and a laboratory for the planting
of settlements in America.[20]

Again it could be argued that Spanish historians got there first, by
seeing the conquest of America as a logical extension, and in many
respects a replication, of the *reconquista* of southern Spain from the
Moors. But it would be wise not to exaggerate the achievements of
Spanish historiography any more than to minimize the achievements of
a long line of Anglo-American historians who have illuminated many
aspects of the ties, both formal and informal – like the interest groups
studied by Alison Olson[21] – which bound together the British Atlantic
community. The treatment of the Hispanic Atlantic community has in
fact suffered from many of the same weaknesses as that of the British
Atlantic community. Spanish historians and those of the various Latin
American states have tended to follow their own paths, with the latter
preferring to concentrate on the internal development of their own
societies rather than the ties that bound them to the metropolis, while
historians of Spain, even if incorporating Spanish America into their
histories, have tended to limit themselves to a few standard themes,
treated as parallel, rather than integral, to their master-narrative.[22]

The mere juxtaposition of metropolitan history and 'colonial'
history does not constitute the integrated Atlantic history whose
arrival Bernard Bailyn celebrated in his article in *Itinerario*. This
requires both a more expansive geographical framework and a more
wide-ranging approach to the past, which makes space for those
aspects of history – such as gender history and the history of *mentalités*
– that have excited so much interest in recent years. One purpose of
this volume is to do precisely this.

The new Atlantic history might be defined as the history, in the
broadest sense, of the creation, destruction and re-creation of communities as a result of the movement, across and around the Atlantic
basin, of people, commodities, cultural practices, and ideas. It is not
the history of the advent – or non-advent – of modernity, a concept
which has bedevilled the history of the Americas, but rather of
change and continuity in the face of new experiences, new circumstances, new contacts, and new environments. Both the change and

the continuity only become understandable if set into the context of an Atlantic that is seen as at once a unifying element, connecting peoples and events across the great expanses of the ocean, and a divisive element, fragmenting and distancing communities through space and time, and promoting, in a multiplicity of different environments, a whole spectrum of responses.

This would seem to be the thrust of David Armitage's 'cis-Atlantic history', which aims to study the interplay between a particular place or places and a wider, interconnected Atlantic world of which they form a part. It is clear that this is an extremely challenging assignment, as some of the authors of these essays explicitly recognize. Eliga Gould, for instance, writes: 'If the trend toward writing unified histories of the British Atlantic has been beneficial, however, it raises several difficult questions, among them how to reconcile this unity with the fact that the English-speaking Atlantic was also deeply fragmented.'[23] There is a natural temptation to exaggerate the extent to which one side of the Atlantic influenced developments on the other, perhaps in an effort to prove the writer's Atlanticist credentials. But it needs to be recognized that there is no need to find a consistency, and still less a progressive development, of interaction over time and space. At some times and in some places the Atlantic component will figure strongly, while at others it may well occupy a subordinate position. Tracing and explaining the fluctuations in the degree of interaction between the whole and the parts is a necessary element in the writing of Atlantic history.

These general pronouncements may help to suggest a number of ways in which lines of inquiry might be usefully extended or approaches modified.

The relationship between empire building and state formation is an important subject, stimulated not least by the work of David Armitage on the *Ideological Origins of the British Empire*,[24] but the nature of this relationship is still far from clear. One of the problems is that the whole notion of state formation is at present in a state of flux among European historians, who have become increasingly aware of the composite nature of European monarchies, including the British.[25] What was once described as 'state formation' is now more likely to be seen as attempts to enhance the authority of the crown or the central executive, both on the national and the international level, rather than to bring centralization and uniformity to composite monarchies composed of distinct units possessing their own distinctive characteristics and constitutional arrangements.

Viewed from this perspective, how should we assess what Elizabeth Mancke calls 'the dialectical relationship' between empire building and state formation?[26] Here a British–Spanish comparison may be of some value. The Spanish crown, having come unexpectedly into the position of lordship over vast Indian populations and silver-rich territories largely as a result of privately sponsored initiatives, moved swiftly and with considerable success to impose its authority over its new American territories. These in turn brought it wealth, and an extension of power, on an almost unimaginable scale. This acquisition of American empire had two domestic consequences of enormous long-term significance. First, thanks to the steady remittance of silver from the mines of Mexico and Peru to Seville, it gave the crown far more room for maneuver than it would otherwise have enjoyed. In particular, it was able to conduct a highly expensive foreign policy and sustain the Spanish monarchy's pre-eminent position in Europe without being excessively constrained by the objections of representative institutions. In other words, overseas empire tilted the domestic balance decisively in favour of the royal prerogative. Secondly, because the American territories were seen as Castilian acquisitions, and were therefore formally incorporated into the Crown of Castile, their possession tipped the balance of forces within the Spanish composite monarchy heavily in favor of Castilian preponderance. As result, Castile and Spain, at least in Castilian eyes, were equated as one and the same.

England's transatlantic expansion brought it neither large Indian populations nor deposits of precious metals. Even if it had possessed the strength, the English crown therefore had less immediate interest than the Spanish crown in asserting effective authority over the new settlements. This in itself suggests possibilities for another form of Atlantic history, hitherto hardly attempted: counter-factual Atlantic history, which might run somewhat as follows.

Columbus, as is well known, takes service with Henry VII. Following his 1492 landfall, English West Countrymen from Devon, Cornwall, and Somerset swarm into the Caribbean, hopping from one island to the next and leaving devastation in their wake. In 1519 an expedition of 500 of them lands on the coast of Mexico, and with great skill and daring conquers the empire of Montezuma, which is renamed New England. Ten years later another expedition, again led by West Countrymen, conquers Peru. Vast Indian populations now become the subjects of the English crown, and with the discovery of vast silver deposits in the newly created viceroyalties of New England and Peru, Henry VIII becomes the wealthiest monarch in Christendom.

Let us now look at some of the consequences of these dramatic events:

1. Bristol becomes the sole port of embarkation for the New World, and the receiving point for the regular annual remittances of silver from the mines of New England and Peru. With considerations of security dictating the need for tight control over emigration and the silver trade, none of the free trade and open competition described in this volume by Nuala Zahedieh proves to be feasible.

2. The Privy Council sets up a Committee for America, with close responsibility for oversight over all American affairs, and for the maintenance and extension of royal authority over the two viceroyalties.

3. Henry VIII, now guaranteed a regular flow of American silver into the exchequer, can safely relegate Parliament to a marginal position in the body politic. No representative assemblies are allowed in the American territories. The crown buys off the English elite by providing jobs for the sons of the gentry in a rapidly expanding imperial bureaucracy. While Henry VIII's matrimonial problems lead him to the brink of a break with Rome, a lavish gift of silver to the pope enables him at the last moment to resolve them to the satisfaction of both parties. The effective master of a powerful state church, he has no need to dispose at one fell swoop of the monastic estates, thanks to his American revenues and the patronage opportunities available to him for keeping the nobility contented.

4. With vast Indian populations to be converted, the Henrician church embarks on a systematic missionary effort, which enhances its authority both at home and in America. Sir Thomas More speaks out on behalf of the Indians oppressed by English settlers.

5. Since these large indigenous populations provide an adequate labor force, there is no overriding need for massive English emigration to America. Over the course of the sixteenth century a total of some 200,000 emigrants cross the Atlantic. As the Indian population is decimated by diseases brought by the English, the gaps are filled by the importation into the viceroyalties of slaves from Africa, through arrangements negotiated with Portuguese merchants.

6. Henry's American silver allows him to engage in an aggressive European foreign policy, which enables him to recover large parts of Gascony for the English crown. Surplus English males

find an outlet in military service in the English armies on the continent which fight over the course of two centuries to preserve the Gascon territories.

7. The Irish rebel against a predatory English ruling class, but the rebellion is rapidly and permanently suppressed, and the Irish reduced to civility. Scotland remains a fringe region of the Stuart composite monarchy, until its conquest during the war with England over the Hanoverian succession. Thereafter it continues to be largely marginal to the imperial enterprise, although increasing numbers of Scots are permitted to emigrate to America through the port of Bristol, to help fill border territories threatened by the encroachments of rival European powers.

8. A settler elite gradually forms in the American viceroyalties, and secures a considerable degree of control over land and labor, although it remains subject to an intrusive royal bureaucracy. During the seventeenth century, however, as the crown's resources are depleted by its European wars, the elite infiltrates the American bureaucracy and achieves effective self-government at the king's command.

9. In the eighteenth century, England's control over its American territories is gravely weakened by its rivalries with European powers, and particularly with Spain, which – coming late to overseas empire – has occupied the north-eastern American seaboard and a number of Caribbean islands, and has created a vibrant commercial society based on a rapidly expanding Atlantic economy.

10. In the mid-eighteenth century, its defeats in the war with Spain force the English crown to embark on a program of reform in the Americas. The resulting reforms alienate the settler elites, who pride themselves on being more English than the English, and resent their relegation to the status of colonials.

11. In 1776 the viceroyalties of New England and Peru declare their independence from the crown.

This counter-factual scenario may perhaps raise some suggestive questions, not least about the transfer of English culture and values to America. What are those values in the heavily monarchical and bureaucratized English imperial state that has here been described? How prominent, in the spectrum of values transported to America, are liberty and commerce?

Returning from the counter-factual to the world of the factual, we find that when the British crown does belatedly, and still fitfully, attempt in the later seventeenth century to impose its authority, it is already too late. A new balance of forces had been established at home in which the royal prerogative was hemmed in by forces in society which found their expression in Parliament. It therefore seems hard to argue convincingly that the possession of empire gave new latitude to the royal prerogative in England, as it did in Castile. Overseas empire did, however, as Michael Braddick makes clear,[27] help to reinforce the fiscal–military state as it emerged out of the upheavals of the middle and later seventeenth century – a state that was neither fully royal nor parliamentary, but mixed. The warfare waged by this increasingly rich and successful state in defense of Britain's interests, both in Europe and overseas, inevitably led to a concentration of power in ministerial hands. In an adversarial parliamentary society this could be interpreted by opponents of the government as a dangerous new assertion of the power of the crown. But it never really threatened a constitutional system based on the sovereignty of king in Parliament.

A closer resemblance between the impact of empire on Britain and Spain is to be found in the way in which it reconfigured the balance of interests in the composite monarchy at large. In both composite monarchies it reinforced the predominance of the centre at the expense of the peripheral kingdoms and territories. The fiscal–military state, with its increasingly imperial aspirations, was essentially an English state; and in the same way as Castile, the possessor of empire, equated Castilian with Spanish, so England was encouraged by its imperial pre-eminence to equate English with British. In both the British and Hispanic Atlantic communities, this equation would create intense resentments at home, and generate a powerful backlash in their overseas dependencies in the later eighteenth century.

For all the importance of such attitudes, it has to be said that in both instances the projection overseas of the crown's imperial authority was heavily complicated by local circumstances and considerations, although royal authority was far more intrusively present in Spanish than in British America. Yet in spite of this, the Spanish crown in America was, and remained, heavily dependent on the collaboration of local elites, drawing on a form of mutually interested partnership which Michael Braddick sees as the key to government and political stability in the British composite monarchy also.

The effectiveness of the royal writ in the colonies was everywhere constricted by the need to acquire the cooperation, or at least the acquiescence, of local elites in its enforcement. Inevitably, where their perceived interests were at stake they displayed a marked reluctance to obey; and the crown, lacking the means to persuade, found to its chagrin that only the option of coercion remained. But at this point anyone acquainted with the Spanish Atlantic world is likely to ask why the British crown seems to have played the game in its colonies with so little skill. Why did it not do more to manipulate the settler elites, following its practice in Scotland and Ireland, where it won over the elites through the judicious use of patronage? Why, for instance, did it not confer titles on leading colonial planters and settlers who remained resident in the colonies? May its unwillingness to do so suggest that it saw the colonies as different from the British periphery, and treated them as such?

Assuming that the crown had chosen to distribute titles, there is room for speculation about the impact of this on the social structure of the colonies. Would it have come to resemble more closely the class structure in the metropolitan society, as described in the chapter by Keith Wrightson, or would other features of the American environment have effectively militated against any such development?

While the inner workings of transatlantic imperial relationships depended on an uncertain partnership between the metropolitan government and colonial elites, that partnership also impinged on questions of war, peace, and international relationships, in ways which deserve to be factored into Atlantic history. Elizabeth Mancke provides instances of the overseas projection of military and naval force by imperial states, as when they sought to grapple with the problem of Caribbean piracy.[28] But there was frequently a disjunction between the foreign and commercial policies adopted by the metropolis, and the reactions to those policies in transatlantic societies. The inhabitants of Spain's American possessions, for example, had no compunctions about trading with the merchants of nations officially at war with the mother country, and the same was true of the English colonists. No peace beyond the line could also be transformed, if the colonists so wished, into no war beyond the line.

In her study of seventeenth-century Anglo-Dutch relations in an Atlantic context, *Atlantische Welten*,[29] Claudia Schnurmann describes how neither the Navigation Acts nor open war between England and the Dutch Republic were allowed to interfere with the commercial operations of Dutch merchants supplying the needs of English colonists. Her book effectively shows how interregional and intercolonial networks were developing in the Americas, taking little or no account of metropolitan policy when it was seen to be in conflict with colonists' perceptions of where their best interests lay. In this instance, local concerns take precedence over trans-Atlantic loyalties, while in other instances – for example, when colonial populations require protection by the metropolitan power against aggressive neighbors – the traditional nexus of loyalty that binds colony to metropolis reasserts itself.

We have, then, a circum-Atlantic community which consists of continuously fluctuating relationships along both an east–west and a north–south axis. Sometimes metropolitan governments and colonial elites collaborated closely. A notable example of this occurred in the English Atlantic community during the course of the Seven Years War following William Pitt's assumption of office, as Fred Anderson makes clear in his *Crucible of War*, an outstanding example of genuinely Atlantic history which traces a complex chain of connections and interactions running all the way from Prussian hussars to the Shawnee Indians.[30] When this happened, the imperial state functioned well. At other times a process of distancing occurred, either as a result of conflicts of interest, or because of the preoccupation of one society or the other with pressing concerns nearer home. As far as Britain is concerned, Eliga Gould is right to remind us that 'whereas political unrest in Scotland and Ireland repeatedly encroached on English affairs, the American colonies were juridically and geographically remote.'[31] This remoteness was reduced after the 1690s, for the reasons he suggests: the emergence of Parliament as an adjunct to the imperial authority of the crown, and the extension of the War of the Spanish Succession to North America and the West Indies.

The remoteness was also dramatically reduced by the extraordinary growth from the later seventeenth century of a British Atlantic economy, the subject of Nuala Zahadieh's essay in Part II, 'Connections'. This provides a clear and well-documented account of the developing process of economic interdependence between metropolis and colonies, which was to realize Hakluyt's grand vision of an empire of commerce. But the British Atlantic system of the eighteenth century, as she describes it, was less enclosed than it tends to appear. In practice, the economies of Britain and Europe were dependent on the constant supply of Brazilian gold and Spanish-American silver, of which England received nearly 9 million *pesos* in 1745 alone.[32] The gold and silver coins that circulated in the colonies – like the silver piece of eight, or dollar – were of Iberian origin.[33] It was the ineffably porous character of the Spanish Atlantic economy that created the context in which the British Atlantic economy of the eighteenth century could flourish and expand.[34]

Economically at least, the British, Spanish, and Portuguese Atlantics were merging in the eighteenth century into an integrated Atlantic system.

But within this system, the English Atlantic, as described by Ian Steele in a book revealingly subtitled 'An Exploration of Communication and Community',[35] may well stand out from the other European Atlantics in terms of the degree and intensity of the process of exchange and communication between metropolis and colonies. A nexus of political, commercial, psychological, and personal ties had developed which – even during the moments of distancing or self-absorption – made the transatlantic relationship an essential point of reference, affecting attitudes and responses on both sides of the ocean. There was an unending process of movement – that movement of people, commodities, and cultural beliefs and practices that are integral to Atlantic history.[36] Migration, as Alison Games writes, was 'an ordinary activity' in the Atlantic societies, and it carried with it, as she also shows, a spectrum of attitudes, assumptions, and patterns of behavior.[37]

For all the advances that have been made over the past few years in the study of British Atlantic migration, we so far lack – perhaps because the documentation has simply not survived – those personal testimonials whose publication in recent years has brought Spanish Atlantic migration so vividly to life. James Lockhart and Enrique Otte's *Letters and People of the Spanish Indies*[38] is only a small sample, in English translation, of the vast body of letters now available in print, exchanged between migrants to America and their relatives back home.[39] These letters illustrate the desire for 'betterment',[40] which also figures alongside economic necessity as one of the motivating forces behind migration from Britain. Occasionally, too, they suggest the transforming impact of the transatlantic passage to a new environment, as when an emigrant to Peru writes to a cousin that on returning home to Spain he will seem 'so different that those who knew me will say that I am not I.'[41]

These words raise the difficult question, touched on by Alison Games with reference to its demographic context, of the extent to which Atlantic migration brought about a transformation, as distinct from a transfer, of cultural values, practices, and assumptions. This is a question that deserves more attention than it receives in these essays, and there are clues about the process of cultural transfer in George Foster's *Culture and Conquest* which deserve to be followed up by historians of the English Atlantic.[42]

The question of cultural transfer is implicit in the study of American religion. While it is important to trace the shared nature of religious experience on both sides of the Atlantic, it is no less import-ant to examine the degree of divergence as well as convergence of religious beliefs and practices. What was different, and what was the same, about Puritanism or the eighteenth-century evangelical revival on the two sides of the Atlantic, and how are the differences to be explained? It is also necessary to take into account the religious inter-action of metropolitan and colonial society as a result of the crossing and recrossing of the Atlantic by ministers. Did the American back-ground or experience of those returning ministers, or of Harvard graduates in search of preferment or expanded opportunities – like the seven of nine members of the class of 1642 – make a distinctive con-tribution to the effervescent religious life of England in the years of the Civil War and Commonwealth?[43] If so, what was it?

Both 'Identities' and 'Politics', the subjects of the last two sections of the book, are concerned with cultural attitudes and constructs in their various forms, including political culture. Both start from a fact of fundamental importance, to which the essays of Joyce Chaplin and Christopher Brown allude:[44] because of the lack of close metropolitan oversight, the settlers – unlike their Spanish equivalents – enjoyed absolute control over land and (in the southern colonies) of labor. This gave them, in Joyce Chaplin's words, 'a much freer hand in determin-ing how they would treat aliens.' English settlers brought with them a set of cultural preconceptions and values derived from a common European heritage, but tempered by national experience. In their new American environment they found themselves in close proximity, first to an indigenous population of whose societies they knew nothing, and subsequently to growing numbers of Africans, a race about which a whole series of assumptions had already been formed.

Joyce Chaplin seeks to show how the Atlantic environment fostered the gradual development of 'a coherent ideology of inborn differences', which was to be at the heart of modern notions of race.[45] The English settlers were not alone in their contribution to the formation of this ideology, as Jorge Cañizares-Esguerra has recently demonstrated in an article tracing the development of ideas about the supposed innate characteristics of the Indian population of Spanish America in the course of the seventeenth century.[46] But what still needs explanation is why the English, unlike the Spaniards, the Portuguese, and the French, should have erected such strong barriers of exclusion, both physical and psychological, to separate themselves from peoples of other races. They seem to have possessed a deep-rooted fear of cultural degeneration as a consequence of living at close quarters with peoples perceived as inferior to themselves. This fear may perhaps be attributable to their centuries of uneasy coexistence with the Irish, and to their belief that the settlers in Ulster either had been, or were in imminent danger of being, dragged down to the level of the barbarous people among whom they lived. The equation of the Indians with the 'wild Irish' was all too easily made.[47]

The long-standing European belief in their 'bodily durability', in Joyce Chaplin's phrase,[48] placed Africans in a different category from the Native Americans, and made them more appropriate for work on the plantations as slaves. Christopher Brown's essay provides a valuable programmatic statement about possible approaches to the political history of slavery and what it should include. In a sense, his story too is about the formation of identity, this time primarily among the holders of slaves rather than among the slaves themselves. His essay, in demonstrating how power over slaves generated a series of attitudes and interests in the planter class that were at odds with the sentiments of a growing body of opinion in the British Atlantic community, brings home the fact that there is more to Atlantic history than the story of progressive, if not always consistent, integration of the two sides of the Atlantic, which is then politically ruptured in the late eighteenth century by the series of revolutionary movements in the Americas. It is no less a story of fragmentation, as Eliga Gould reminds us when he observes that the American revolution was itself 'a product of the growing unity of the British empire.'[49]

This is a story in which paradoxes abound – integration and fragmentation, the ties that bind and the forces that divide. As Keith Wrightson remarks, the differences to be found in the evolution of the anglophone Atlantic societies are 'telling testimony to the variety of potentials inherent in any social situation and the unpredictability of their development over time.'[50] This unpredictability, the vast range of variations created by Wrightson's 'contextual and contingent circumstances', is one of the elements that make Atlantic history at once so stimulating and yet so difficult both to conceptualize and to write. Yet the effort has notably expanded horizons; and while it is possible to remain skeptical about the degree to which large elements of the history of the peoples who live around the Atlantic basin can be encompassed within a conceptual framework of this magnitude, it is reasonable to hope, in the light of what has been accomplished to date, that the enterprise will continue to exercise the best historical minds.

Notes

The following abbreviations are used in this section and the next:

AHR   *American Historical Review*
AQ   *American Quarterly*
HJ   *Historical Journal*
JAH   *Journal of American History*
JICH   *Journal of Imperial and Commonwealth History*
PP   *Past and Present*
WMQ   *William and Mary Quarterly*

Preface

1. Bernard Bailyn, 'The Idea of Atlantic History', *Itinerario*, 20 (1996) 19–44.

Chapter 1: Three Concepts of Atlantic History

For successive opportunities to define and refine my argument I am very grateful to Bernard Bailyn, Elizabeth Mancke, James Thompson, Richard Drayton, Franz Bosbach, Jim Williams, Anupama Rao, Jessica Harland-Jacobs, Burke Griggs, Ariane Koek, David Cannadine, and Eliga Gould.

1. J. H. Elliott, *Do the Americas Have a Common History? An Address* (Providence, RI, 1998), p. 19.
2. Adam Smith, *An Inquiry into the Nature and Causes of the Wealth of Nations* (1776), ed. R. H. Campbell and A. S. Skinner, 2 vols. (Oxford, 1976), vol. 1, p. 448; Karl Marx and Friedrich Engels, *The Communist Manifesto* (1848), introd. Eric Hobsbawm (London, 1998), p. 35.
3. Martin W. Lewis and Kären Wigen, *The Myth of Continents: A Critique of Metageography* (Berkeley, Calif., 1997).
4. Martin W. Lewis, 'Dividing the Ocean Sea', *Geographical Review*, 89 (1999) 188–214.
5. Daniel Walker Howe, *American History in an Atlantic Context* (Oxford, 1993); Daniel T. Rodgers, *Atlantic Crossings: Social Politics in a Progressive Age* (Cambridge, Mass., 1998); Kevin H. O'Rourke and Jeffrey G. Williamson, *Globalization and History: The Evolution of a Nineteenth-Century Atlantic Economy* (Cambridge, Mass., 1999).
6. Bernard Bailyn, 'The Idea of Atlantic History', *Itinerario*, 20 (1996) 19–44.
7. Mark Silk, 'Notes on the Judeo-Christian Tradition in America', *AQ*, 36 (1984) 65–85.

8. Carlton J. H. Hayes, 'The American Frontier – Frontier of What?', *AHR*, 51 (1946) 215.
9. Jacques Godechot, *Histoire de l'Atlantique* (Paris, 1947); Michael Kraus, *The Atlantic Civilization: Eighteenth-Century Origins* (New York, 1949); Godechot and R. R. Palmer, 'Le problème de l'Atlantique du XVIIIème au XXème siècle', in 10th International Congress of Historical Sciences, *Relazioni*, 6 vols. (Florence, 1955), vol. 5, pp. 173–239; Palmer, *The Age of the Democratic Revolution*, 1: *The Challenge*; 2: *The Struggle* (Princeton, NJ, 1959–63).
10. W. E. B. Du Bois, *The Suppression of the African Slave-Trade to the United States of America, 1638–1870* (New York, 1896); C. L. R. James, *The Black Jacobins: Toussaint L'Ouverture and the San Domingo Revolution* (London, 1938); Eric Williams, *Capitalism and Slavery* (London, 1944).
11. Victoria de Grazia, *The White Atlantic: American Market Culture in the Making of Twentieth-Century Europe* (Cambridge, Mass., forthcoming).
12. Kevin Whelan, 'The Green Atlantic: Radical Reciprocities between Ireland and America, 1776–1815', in Kathleen Wilson, ed., *Crossings: The New Imperial History* (Cambridge, forthcoming).
13. Peter Linebaugh and Marcus Rediker, *The Many-Headed Hydra: Sailors, Slaves, Commoners, and the Hidden History of the Revolutionary Atlantic* (Boston, Mass., 2000); David Armitage, 'The Red Atlantic', *Reviews in American History*, 29 (2001) 479–86.
14. Paul Gilroy, *The Black Atlantic: Modernity and Double Consciousness* (Cambridge, Mass., 1993).
15. Joseph Roach, *Cities of the Dead: Circum-Atlantic Performance* (New York, 1996), pp. 4–5.
16. M. N. Pearson, 'Introduction I: The State of the Subject', in Ashin Das Gupta and Pearson, eds., *India and the Indian Ocean, 1500–1800* (Calcutta, 1987), pp. 9–10.
17. David Eltis, 'Atlantic History in Global Perspective', *Itinerario*, 23 (1999) 142; Kevin H. O'Rourke, *When Did Globalization Begin?*, National Bureau of Economic Research, Working Paper 7632 (Cambridge, Mass., 2000).
18. Gilroy, *The Black Atlantic*, p. 2; Roach, *Cities of the Dead*, p. 5.
19. J. H. Elliott, 'A Europe of Composite Monarchies', *PP*, 137 (November 1992) 48–71; compare Elizabeth Mancke's essay below, Chapter 9.
20. Dennis O. Flynn and Arturo Giráldez, 'Born with a "Silver Spoon": The Origin of World Trade in 1571', *Journal of World History*, 6 (1995) 201–21.
21. Fernand Braudel, *The Mediterranean and the Mediterranean World in the Age of Philip II*, trans. Siân Reynolds, 2 vols. (London, 1973), vol. 1, p. 231.
22. Bailyn, 'The Idea of Atlantic History', 20; Nicholas Canny, 'Writing Atlantic History, or, Reconfiguring the History of Colonial British America', *JAH*, 86 (1999) 1106–7.

23. Pearson, 'Introduction', in Das Gupta and Pearson, eds., *India and the Indian Ocean*, p. 5.

24. John Wilkes, *The Observer* (25 November 1779), in *The Correspondence of the Late John Wilkes, with his Friends*, ed. John Almon, 5 vols. (London, 1805), vol. 5, p. 212; Richard Watson, *A Sermon Preached before the University of Cambridge, on Friday, February 4th, 1780* (Cambridge, 1780), p. 15 (my thanks to Eliga Gould for this reference); Charles Henry Arnold, *The New and Impartial History of North and South America, and of the Present Trans-Atlantic War* (London, 1781).

25. Jeremy Bentham, *An Introduction to the Principles of Morals and Legislation* (1780/89), ed. J. H. Burns and H. L. A. Hart, introd. F. Rosen (Oxford, 1996), pp. 6, 296.

26. [Jeremy Bentham], 'Short Review of the Declaration', in [John Lind and Bentham], *An Answer to the Declaration of the American Congress* (London, 1776), pp. 119–32; David Armitage, 'The Declaration of Independence and International Law', *WMQ*, 3rd ser., 59 (2002) 39–54.

27. See Mancke, 'Empire and State', Chapter 9 in this volume.

28. Frank Tannenbaum, *Slave and Citizen: The Negro in the Americas* (New York, 1946); Herbert Klein, *Slavery in the Americas: A Comparative Study of Virginia and Cuba* (Chicago, 1967); J. H. Elliott, *National and Comparative History* (Oxford, 1991); Elliott, *Britain and Spain in America: Colonists and Colonized* (Reading, 1994); Elliott, 'Empire and State in British and Spanish America', in Serge Gruzinski and Nathan Wachtel, eds., *Le Nouveau Monde – Mondes Nouveaux: L'expérience américaine* (Paris, 1996), pp. 365–82.

29. John Clive and Bernard Bailyn, 'England's Cultural Provinces: Scotland and America', *WMQ*, 3rd ser., 11 (1954) 200–13; Jack P. Greene, *Peripheries and Center: Constitutional Development in the Extended Polities of the British Empire and the United States, 1607–1788* (Athens, Ga., 1986).

30. Linda Colley, *Britons: Forging the Nation, 1707–1837* (New Haven, Conn., 1992).

31. Charles Royster, 'Founding a Nation in Blood: Military Conflict and American Nationality', in Ronald Hoffman and Peter J. Albert, eds., *Arms and Independence: The Military Character of the American Revolution* (Charlottesville, Va., 1984), pp. 25–49; John Murrin, 'A Roof Without Walls: The Dilemma of American National Identity', in Richard Beeman, Stephen Botein, and Edward C. Carter III, eds., *Beyond Confederation: Origins of the Constitution and American National Identity* (Chapel Hill, NC, 1987), pp. 333–48.

32. Colin Kidd, *British Identities before Nationalism: Ethnicity and Nationhood in the Atlantic World, 1600–1800* (Cambridge, 1999), pp. 261–79.

33. Eliga H. Gould, *The Persistence of Empire: British Political Culture in the Age of the American Revolution* (Chapel Hill, NC, 2000), pp. 181–214.

34. Lester D. Langley, *The Americas in the Age of Revolution, 1750–1850* (New Haven, Conn., 1996).

35. Thomas Jefferson, *Notes on the State of Virginia* (1785), ed. William Peden (Chapel Hill, NC, 1982), p. 63.
36. Thomas Jefferson to James Monroe, 24 October 1823, in *The Writings of Thomas Jefferson*, ed. Albert Ellery Bergh, 20 vols. (Washington, DC, 1907), vol. 15, p. 477.
37. Huguette Chaunu and Pierre Chaunu, *Seville et l'Atlantique, 1504–1650*, 8 vols. (Paris, 1955–9).
38. D. W. Meinig, *Atlantic America, 1492–1800* (New Haven, Conn., 1986); E. Estyn Evans, *Ireland and the Atlantic Heritage: Selected Writings* (Dublin, 1996); Barry Cunliffe, *Facing the Ocean: The Atlantic and its Peoples, 8000 BC–AD 1500* (Oxford, 2001).
39. David Armitage, 'Greater Britain: A Useful Category of Historical Analysis?', *AHR*, 104 (1999) 427–45.
40. David Harris Sacks, *The Widening Gate: Bristol and the Atlantic Economy, 1450–1700* (Berkeley, Calif., 1991).
41. Ignacio Gallup-Diaz, 'The "Door of the Seas and the Key to the Universe": Indian Politics and Imperial Rivalry in the Darién, 1640–1750', Ph.D. dissertation, Princeton University, 1999.
42. Richard White, *The Middle Ground: Indians, Empires and Republics in the Great Lakes Region, 1650–1815* (Cambridge, 1991).
43. David Hancock, '"A Revolution in the Trade": Wine Distribution and the Development of the Infrastructure of the Atlantic Market Economy, 1703–1807', in John J. McCusker and Kenneth Morgan, eds., *The Early Modern Atlantic Economy* (Cambridge, 2000), pp. 105–53.
44. Jane Ohlmeyer, 'Seventeenth-Century Ireland and the New British and Atlantic Histories', *AHR*, 104 (1999) 446–62.
45. Hiram Morgan, 'Mid-Atlantic Blues', *Irish Review*, 11 (1991–2) 50–5; Raymond Gillespie, 'Explorers, Exploiters and Entrepreneurs: Early Modern Ireland and its Context, 1500–1700', in B. J. Graham and L. J. Proudfoot, eds., *An Historical Geography of Ireland* (London, 1993), p. 152.
46. Ned C. Landsman, 'Nation, Migration, and the Province in the First British Empire: Scotland and the Americas, 1600–1800', *AHR*, 104 (1999) 463–75; Landsman, ed., *Nation and Province in the First British Empire: Scotland and the Americas, 1600–1800* (Lewisburg, Pa., 2001).
47. Sir John Clotworthy, April 1638, cited in Kevin Sharpe, *The Personal Rule of Charles I* (New Haven, Conn., 1992), p. 821.
48. Andrew Mackillop, *'More Fruitful than the Soil': Army, Empire and the Scottish Highlands, 1715–1815* (East Linton, 2000), p. 241.
49. Peter Clark, 'Migration in England during the Late Seventeenth and Early Eighteenth Centuries', in Clark and David Souden, eds., *Migration and Society in Early Modern England* (London, 1987), pp. 213–52; Nicholas Canny, 'English Migration Into and Across the Atlantic During the Seventeenth and Eighteenth Centuries', in Canny, ed., *Europeans on the Move: Studies on European Migration, 1500–1800* (Oxford, 1994), pp. 39–75; Alison Games, *Migration and the Origins of the English Atlantic World* (Cambridge, Mass., 1999); Games, 'Migration', Chapter 2 below.

50. Michael J. Braddick, *State Formation in Early Modern England, c. 1550–1700* (Cambridge, 2000), pp. 397–419; Braddick, 'Civility and Authority', Chapter 5 below.
51. Braudel, *The Mediterranean and the Mediterranean World in the Age of Philip II*, trans. Reynolds, vol. 1, p. 167.

Chapter 2: Migration

For their assistance, I wish to thank the other contributors to this volume, the participants in the conference at Harvard, Trevor Burnard, Erick Langer, Peter Mancall, Larry Poos, Adam Rothman, Jim Williams, and Karin Wulf. James Horn and Philip D. Morgan generously shared with me their forthcoming chapter, 'Settlers and Slaves: European and African Migrations to Early Modern British America', in Carole Shammas and Elizabeth Mancke, eds., *The Creation of the British Atlantic World* (Baltimore, forthcoming). I am particularly grateful for their statistical labors and for Jim Horn's patient answers to my queries. My considerable debt to their work will be clear throughout this chapter.

1. Mary O'Dowd, 'Gaelic Economy and Society', in Ciaran Brady and Raymond Gillespie, eds., *Natives and Newcomers: Essays on the Making of Irish Colonial Society, 1534–1641* (Dublin, 1986), p. 124; R. A. Houston and I. D. Whyte, eds., *Scottish Society, 1500–1800* (Cambridge, 1989), p. 5.
2. L. R. Poos, *A Rural Society after the Black Death: Essex, 1350–1525* (Cambridge, 1991), pp. 162, 170, 290; Ian D. Whyte, *Migration and Society in Britain, 1550–1830* (London, 2000), pp. 23–5.
3. Peter Clark, 'The Migrant in Kentish Towns, 1580–1640', in Clark and Paul Slack, eds., *Crisis and Order in English Towns, 1500–1700* (Toronto, 1972), pp. 117–63, quotation at p. 145.
4. Whyte, *Migration*, p. 65.
5. A. L. Beier and Roger Finlay, eds., *London, 1500–1700: The Making of the Metropolis* (New York, 1986); Roger Finlay, *Population and Metropolis: The Demography of London, 1580–1650* (Cambridge, 1981), pp. 129–30 (age-specific mortality), 156 (1625 plague), 139–42 (sex ratios); John Landers, *Death and the Metropolis: Studies in the Demographic History of London, 1670–1830* (Cambridge, 1993).
6. Ian D. Whyte, 'Population Mobility in Early Modern Scotland', in Houston and Whyte, eds., *Scottish Society*, p. 41.
7. Whyte, *Migration*, pp. 66–7; T. M. Devine, *The Transformation of Rural Scotland: Social Change and the Agrarian Economy, 1660–1815* (Edinburgh, 1994), p. 34.
8. T. C. Smout, Ned C. Landsman, and T. M. Devine, 'Scottish Emigration in the Seventeenth and Eighteenth Centuries', p. 85, and Nicholas Canny, 'English Migration Into and Across the Atlantic during the

Seventeenth and Eighteenth Centuries', p. 62, in Nicholas Canny, ed., *Europeans on the Move: Studies on European Migration, 1500–1800* (Oxford, 1994).

9. Bernard Bailyn, *Voyagers to the West: A Passage in the Peopling of America on the Eve of the Revolution* (New York, 1986); Nicholas Canny, 'Migration and Opportunity: Britain, Ireland and the New World', *Irish Economic and Social History*, 12 (1985) 7–32.

10. Louis M. Cullen, 'Irish Diaspora', in Canny, ed., *Europeans on the Move*, pp. 139, 140.

11. Nicholas Canny, 'Fashioning "British" Worlds in the Seventeenth Century', in Canny, Joseph E. Illick, Gary B. Nash, and William Pencak, eds., *Empire, Society, and Labor: Essays in Honor of Richard S. Dunn, Pennsylvania History*, 64 (1997) 26–45; and Canny, *Making Ireland British, 1580–1650* (Oxford, 2001).

12. Canny, 'English Migration', p. 64.

13. L. M. Cullen, 'Scotland and Ireland', in Houston and Whyte, eds., *Scottish Society*, p. 231.

14. David Souden, 'English Indentured Servants and the Transatlantic Colonial Economy', in Shula Marks and Peter Richardson, eds., *International Labour Migration: Historical Perspectives* (Hounslow, Middlesex, 1984), pp. 19–33; John Wareing, 'Migration to London and Transatlantic Emigration of Indentured Servants, 1683–1775', *Journal of Historical Geography*, 7 (1981) 356–78.

15. Alison Games, *Migration and the Origins of the English Atlantic World* (Cambridge, Mass., 1999), ch. 1; P. J. Marshall, *East Indian Fortunes: The British in Bengal in the Eighteenth Century* (Oxford, 1976), pp. 15–24.

16. Smout, Landsman, and Devine, 'Scottish Emigration', pp. 77–85; statistics from p. 85.

17. Horn and Morgan, 'Settlers and Slaves'.

18. Letter from Peter Hay, quoted in J. H. Bennett, 'Peter Hay, Proprietary Agent in Barbados, 1636–1641', *Jamaican Historical Review*, 5 (1965) 10–11; Peter Hay to James Hay, Barbados, 15 October 1636, GD34/923/3, Scottish Record Office.

19. Games, *Migration*, pp. 28–30, 213.

20. European statistics from Horn and Morgan, 'Settlers and Slaves'; on the Highlands see Houston and Whyte, *Scottish Society*, p. 5.

21. Aaron Spencer Fogleman, *Hopeful Journeys: German Immigration, Settlement, and Political Culture in Colonial America, 1717–1775* (Philadelphia, 1996), p. 2; Appendix 2, p. 163; Georg Fertig, 'Transatlantic Migration from the German-Speaking Parts of Central Europe, 1600–1800: Proportions, Structures, and Explanations', in Canny, ed., *Europeans on the Move*, p. 203.

22. Thomas Klingebiel, 'Huguenot Settlements in Central Europe', in Hartmut Lehmann, Hermann Wellenreuther and Renate Wilson, eds., *In Search of Peace and Prosperity: New German Settlements in Eighteenth-*

Century Europe and America (University Park, Pa., 2000), pp. 39–40; Finlay, *Population and Metropolis*, p. 67.

23. Ralph A. Austen, 'The Trans-Saharan Slave Trade: A Tentative Census', in Henry A. Gemery and Jan S. Hogendorn, eds., *The Uncommon Market: Essays in the Economic History of the Atlantic Slave Trade* (New York, 1979), p. 66; Paul E. Lovejoy, *Transformations in Slavery: A History of Slavery in Africa*, 2nd edn (Cambridge, 2000), ch. 3, esp. Tables 3.1, 3.9; David Eltis, *The Rise of African Slavery in the Americas* (Cambridge, 2000), pp. 95–100; Eltis, 'The Volume and Structure of the Transatlantic Slave Trade: A Reassessment', *WMQ*, 58 (2001) 38; Table III, p. 45.

24. Eltis, 'Volume and Structure', Table IV, p. 46.

25. W. Shakespeare, *As You Like It*, II.iv.16.

26. Trevor Burnard, 'European Migration to Jamaica, 1655–1780', *WMQ*, 53 (1996) 769–94.

27. Games, *Migration*, p. 47; Eltis, *Rise of African Slavery*, p. 95; Table 4.2, p. 97 (quotation).

28. For mortality in transit, see Horn and Morgan, 'Settlers and Slaves'.

29. John Thornton, 'African Dimensions of the Stono Rebellion', *AHR*, 96 (1991) 1101–13.

30. See especially Nicolás Sánchez-Albornoz, *Indios y tributos en el Alto Peru* (Lima, 1978); Karen Vieira Powers, *Andean Journeys: Migration, Ethnogenesis, and the State in Colonial Quito* (Albuquerque, 1995).

31. Virginia DeJohn Anderson, *New England's Generation* (Cambridge, 1991); James Horn, 'Moving on in the New World: Migration and Out-migration in the Seventeenth-century Chesapeake', in Peter Clark and David Souden, eds., *Migration and Society in Early Modern England* (Totowa, NJ, 1988), pp. 172–212; Games, *Migration*, ch. 6; Fogleman, *Hopeful Journeys*, pp. 93–5.

32. J. M. Bumsted, 'Resettlement and Rebellion', in Phillip A. Buckner and John G. Reid, eds., *The Atlantic Region to Confederation: A History* (Toronto, 1994), p. 162.

33. Games, *Migration*, pp. 190–206; David Cressy, *Coming Over: Migration and Communication between England and New England in the Seventeenth Century* (Cambridge, 1987); Marion Nelson Winship, 'The Land of Connected Men: A New Migration Story from the Early American Republic', in Canny, Illick, Nash, and Pencak, eds., *Empire, Society, and Labor*, pp. 88–104.

34. Lorena S. Walsh, *From Calabar to Carter's Grove: The History of a Virginia Slave Community* (Charlottesville, Va., 1997), p. 210; Gail S. Terry, 'Sustaining the Bonds of Kinship in Trans-Appalachian Migration, 1790–1811', in John Saillant, ed., *Afro-Virginian History and Culture* (New York, 1999), pp. 61–84; and James Sidbury, *Ploughshares into Swords: Race, Rebellion, and Identity in Gabriel's Virginia, 1730–1810* (Cambridge, 1997), pp. 14–49.

35. James H. Merrell, 'The Indians' New World: The Catawba Experience', *WMQ*, 41 (1984) 537–65.
36. Daniel K. Richter, *The Ordeal of the Longhouse: The Peoples of the Iroquois League in the Era of European Colonization* (Chapel Hill, NC, 1992); and Richard White, *The Middle Ground: Indians, Empires, and Republics in the Great Lakes Region, 1650–1815* (Cambridge, 1991).
37. Jane Landers, 'Gracia Real de Santa Theresa de Mose: A Free Black Town in Spanish Colonial Florida', *AHR*, 95 (1990) 9–30.
38. Quoted in Merrell, 'The Indians' New World', 543.
39. Bailyn, *Voyagers*, p. 26; Table 1.
40. Peter Marshall, 'British North America, 1760–1815', in Marshall, ed., *The Eighteenth Century*, p. 376 (Nova Scotia population).
41. Bailyn, *Voyagers*, Table 6.1, pp. 206–7; David Eltis, Stephen D. Behrendt, David Richardson, and Herbert S. Klein, eds., *The Trans-Atlantic Slave Trade: A Database on CD-ROM* (Cambridge, 1999).
42. Marshall, 'British North America', p. 382.
43. Michael Craton and Gail Saunders, *Islanders in the Stream: A History of the Bahamian People*, vol. 1 (Athens, Ga., 1992), ch. 12.
44. Allan Kulikoff, 'Uprooted Peoples: Black Migrants in the Age of the American Revolution', in Ira Berlin and Ronald Hoffman, eds., *Slavery and Freedom in the Age of the American Revolution* (Charlottesville, Va., 1983), p. 144; Ira Berlin, *Many Thousands Gone: The First Two Generations of Slavery in North America* (Cambridge, Mass., 1998), p. 304.
45. Sylvia R. Frey, *Water from the Rock: Black Resistance in a Revolutionary Age* (Princeton, NJ, 1991).
46. Colin G. Calloway, *The American Revolution in Indian Country: Crisis and Diversity in Native American Communities* (Cambridge, 1995).
47. Kulikoff, 'Uprooted Peoples', pp. 143–4; Berlin, *Many Thousands Gone*, p. 265; Adam Rothman, 'The Contest for Sovereignty in the Mississippi Territory, 1790–1820', unpublished paper, Philadelphia, 2001; Aaron S. Fogleman, 'From Slaves, Convicts, and Servants to Free Passengers: The Transformation of Immigration in the Era of the American Revolution', *JAH*, 85 (1998) 43–76.

Chapter 3: Economy

1. Richard Hakluyt, 'A Particular Discourse Concerning the Greate Necessitie and Manifolde Comodyties that are like to grow to this Realme of England by the Westerne Discoveries lately attempted', *Maine Historical Society Collections*, 2 (1877).
2. Nicholas Canny, 'English Migration Into and Across the Atlantic during the Seventeenth and Eighteenth Centuries', in Nicholas Canny, ed., *Europeans on the Move: Studies on European Migration, 1500–1800* (Oxford, 1994), pp. 39–75. See Games, 'Migration', Chapter 2 in this volume.

3. Robert Brenner, *Merchants and Revolution: Commercial Change, Political Conflict and London's Overseas Traders, 1550–1653* (Cambridge,1993); Keith Wrightson, *Earthly Necessities: Economic Lives in Early Modern Britain* (New Haven, Conn., 2000).

4. Edward A. Wrigley and Roger S. Schofield, *The Population History of England, 1541–1871* (Cambridge, 1981).

5. Kenneth R. Andrews, *The Spanish Caribbean: Trade and Plunder, 1530–1630* (New Haven, Conn., 1978); Nuala Zahedieh, 'Trade, Plunder and Economic Development in Early English Jamaica, 1655–89', *Economic History Review*, 47 (1986) 205–22.

6. John J. McCusker and Russell R. Menard, *The Economy of British America, 1607–1789* (Chapel Hill, NC, 1985). Nuala Zahedieh, 'Overseas Expansion and Trade in the Seventeenth Century', in Nicholas Canny, ed., *The Oxford History of the British Empire*, vol. 1, *The Origins of Empire: English Overseas Activity to the Close of the Seventeenth Century* (Oxford, 1998), pp. 398–422; Jacob M. Price, 'The Imperial Economy, 1700–1776', in P. J. Marshall, ed., *The Oxford History of the British Empire*, vol. 2, *The Eighteenth Century* (Oxford, 1998), pp. 78–104.

7. Walter E. Minchinton, ed., *The Growth of English Overseas Trade in the Seventeenth and Eighteenth Centuries* (London, 1969).

8. Charles Davenant, 'On the Protection and Care of Trade', in Charles Whitworth, ed., *The Political and Commercial Works of that Celebrated Writer Charles Davenant*, 2 vols. (London, 1771), vol. 1, p. 397.

9. George P. Insh, *Scottish Colonial Schemes, 1620–86* (Glasgow, 1922); Insh, *The Company of Scotland Trading to Africa and the Indies* (London, 1932); T. C. Smout, *Scottish Trade on the Eve of Union, 1660–1707* (Edinburgh, 1963).

10. For detailed accounts of the legislation see Lawrence A. Harper, *The English Navigation Laws: A Seventeenth Century Experiment in Social Engineering* (New York, 1939); George L. Beer, *The Origins of the British Colonial System, 1578–1660* (New York, 1908).

11. Ralph Davis, *The Rise of the English Shipping Industry in the Seventeenth and Eighteenth Centuries* (Newton Abbot, 1962); Davis, 'English Foreign Trade, 1770–1774', *Economic History Review*, 15 (1962) 285–303.

12. David Ormrod, *The Rise of Commercial Empires: England and the Dutch Staplemarket in the Age of Mercantilism, 1670–1770* (Cambridge, 2002).

13. Patrick K. O'Brien, 'Inseparable Connections: Trade, Economy, Fiscal State, and the Expansion of Empire, 1688–1815', in Marshall, ed., *The Oxford History of the British Empire*, vol. 2, pp. 53–77.

14. Edmund S. Morgan, *American Slavery, American Freedom: The Ordeal of Colonial Virginia* (New York, 1975); Russell R. Menard, 'The Tobacco Industry in the Chesapeake Colonies, 1617–1730: An Interpretation', *Research in Economic History*, 5 (1980) 109–77.

15. Joan Thirsk, 'New Crops and their Diffusion: Tobacco Growing in Seventeenth Century England', in Thirsk, *The Rural Economy of England: Collected Essays* (London, 1984), pp. 259–85.
16. David Harley, 'The Beginnings of the Tobacco Controversy: Puritanism, James I and the Royal Physicians', *Bulletin of the Society for the History of Medicine*, 67 (1993) 28–50; Jordan Goodman, *Tobacco in History: The Culture of Dependence* (London, 1993).
17. Menard, 'Tobacco Industry'; Robert C. Nash, 'The English and Scottish Tobacco Trades in the Seventeenth and Eighteenth Centuries: Legal and Illegal Trade', *Economic History Review*, 35 (1982) 354–72.
18. Gregory King, *Natural and Political Observations and Conclusions upon the State and Condition of England, 1696* (London, 1804), pp. 48–9.
19. Thomas Tryon, *The Way to Health, Long Life and Happiness* (London, 1691), pp. 126–8.
20. Carole Shammas, *The Pre-Industrial Consumer in England and America* (Oxford, 1990), pp. 77–80. Nash, 'English and Scottish Tobacco Trades'.
21. Menard, 'Tobacco Industry'.
22. Russell R. Menard, 'Transport Costs and Long-Range Trade, 1300–1800: Was there a European "Transport Revolution" in the Early Modern Era?', in James D. Tracy, ed., *The Political Economy of Merchant Empires* (Cambridge, 1991), pp. 228–75.
23. Nuala Zahedieh, 'The Capture of the Blue Dove, 1664: Policy, Profits and Protection in Early English Jamaica', in Roderick A. McDonald, ed., *West Indies Accounts: Essays on the History of the British Caribbean and the Atlantic Economy in Honour of Richard Sheridan* (Kingston, Jamaica, 1996), pp. 29–47; James F. Shepherd and Gary M. Walton, *Shipping, Maritime Trade and the Economic Development of Colonial North America* (Cambridge, 1972).
24. Carl and Roberta Bridenbaugh, *No Peace Beyond the Line: The English in the Caribbean, 1624–1690* (New York, 1972). Richard S. Dunn, *Sugar and Slaves: The Rise of the Planter Class in the English West Indies, 1624–1713* (Chapel Hill, NC, 1972).
25. Richard Ligon, *A True and Exact History of Barbadoes* (London, 1657), pp. 24–5.
26. Joan Thirsk, *Alternative Agriculture: A History from the Black Death to the Present Day* (Oxford, 1997), pp. 75, 91.
27. Richard B. Sheridan, *Sugar and Slavery: An Economic History of the British West Indies, 1623–1775* (Barbados, 1974).
28. Kenneth G. Davies, *The Royal African Company* (London, 1957).
29. David W. Galenson, 'White Servitude and the Growth of Black Slavery in Colonial America', *Journal of Economic History*, 61 (1981) 39–49; Hilary McD. Beckles, 'The Economics of Transition to the Black Labour System in Barbados, 1630–1680', *Journal of Interdisciplinary History*, 18 (1987) 227–8.

30. Trevor Burnard, 'A Failed Settler Society: Marriage and Demographic Failure in Early Jamaica', *Journal of Social History*, 28 (1994) 63–82; Burnard, 'European Migration to Jamaica, 1655–1780', *WMQ*, 3rd ser., 53 (1996) 769–94.

31. McCusker and Menard, *Economy of British America*, pp. 153–4. See Games, 'Migration', Chapter 2 in this volume.

32. Noel Deerr, *The History of Sugar*, 2 vols. (London, 1949–50).

33. Dalby Thomas, *An Historical Account of the Rise and Growth of the West-India Colonies and the Great Advantage they are to England in Respect of Trade* (London, 1690), p. 8.

34. 'The Political Conclusions of Gregory King', p. 67, in *Pioneers of Demography: The Earliest Classic Works by G. Graunt and G. King* (1973).

35. Sidney W. Mintz, *Sweetness and Power: The Place of Sugar in Modern History* (New York, 1985), p. 37; Shammas, *The Pre-Industrial Consumer*, pp. 81–6.

36. Peter Mathias, *The Brewing Industry in England, 1750–1830* (Cambridge, 1959), p. 375.

37. Mintz, *Sweetness and Power*, pp. 151–86.

38. McCusker and Menard, *Economy of British America*, pp. 169–88.

39. Ibid., p. 108.

40. Ibid., p. 199.

41. Davenant, *Works*, vol. 2, p. 24.

42. Jacob M. Price, 'A Note on the Value of Colonial Exports of Shipping', *Journal of Interdisciplinary History*, 6 (1976) 701–9.

43. Davies, *The Royal African Company*.

44. Hakluyt, 'Particular Discourse', p. 160.

45. For a recent restatement of the importance of extensive growth in explanations of Europe's precocious industrialization see Kenneth Pomeranz, *The Great Divergence: China, Europe, and the Making of the Modern World Economy* (Princeton, NJ, 2000).

46. McCusker and Menard, *Economy of British America*, pp. 267–70.

47. Patrick K. O'Brien and Stanley L. Engerman, 'Exports and the Growth of the British Economy from the Glorious Revolution to the Peace of Amiens', in Barbara L. Solow, ed., *Slavery and the Rise of the Atlantic System* (Cambridge, 1991), pp. 177–209.

48. Adam Smith, *An Inquiry into the Nature and Causes of the Wealth of Nations*, vol. 2 (London, 1776).

49. Jean O. McLachlan, *Trade and Peace with Old Spain, 1667–1750: A Study of the Influence of Commerce on Anglo-Spanish Diplomacy in the First Half of the Eighteenth Century* (Cambridge, 1940).

50. Frances Armytage, *The Free Port System in the British West Indies: A Study in Commercial Policy, 1766–1822* (London, 1953), p. 58.

51. Nuala Zahedieh, 'The Merchants of Port Royal, Jamaica, and the Spanish Contraband Trade, 1655–1692', *WMQ*, 3rd ser., 43 (1986) 570–93.

52. Francis Hanson, ed., *The Laws of Jamaica* (London, 1683), introduction.
53. Ann Storrow to her sister, 24 April 1792, Storrow family papers, Massachusetts Historical Society, Boston.
54. Josiah Child, *A New Discourse of Trade* (London, 1692), pp. 207–8.
55. Victor S. Clark, *History of Manufactures in the United States*, 3 vols. (Washington, DC, 1929); Simon D. Smith, 'The Market for Manufactures in the Thirteen Continental Colonies', *Economic History Review*, 51 (1998) 676–708.
56. Memorial of Sir Thomas Lawrence, 25 June 1695, *Calendar of State Papers Colonial, America and the West Indies, 1695*, No. 1916.
57. David Corner, 'The Tyranny of Fashion: The Case of the Felt-Hatting Trade in the Late Seventeenth and Eighteenth Centuries', *Textile History*, 22 (1991) 153–78; Ian K. Steele, 'The Anointed, the Appointed, and the Elected: Governance of the British Empire, 1689–1784', in Marshall, ed., *Oxford History of the British Empire*, vol. 2, pp. 105–27.
58. Benjamin Franklin, quoted in McCusker and Menard, *The Economy of British America*, pp. 278–9.
59. Marion Tinling, ed., *The Correspondence of Three William Byrds of Westover, Virginia, 1684–1779*, 2 vols. (Charlottesville, Va., 1977), vol. 1, pp. 29–30, 64.
60. Geraldine Mozley, *Letters to Jane from Jamaica, 1788–1796* (London, 1938), pp. 98–9.
61. Timothy H. Breen, 'Narrative of Commercial Life: Consumption, Ideology, and Community on the Eve of the American Revolution', *WMQ*, 3rd ser., 50 (1993) 471–501.
62. Brenner, *Merchants and Revolution*.
63. Davenant, *Works*, vol. 1, p. 98.
64. Jacob M. Price and Paul G. E. Clemens, 'A Revolution of Scale in Overseas Trade: British Firms in the Chesapeake Trade, 1675–1775', *Journal of Economic History*, 47 (1987) 1–43; Nuala Zahedieh, 'Credit, Risk, and Reputation in Late Seventeenth Century Colonial Trade', *Research in Maritime History*, 15 (Newfoundland, 1998) 53–74.
65. David Hancock, *Citizens of the World: London Merchants and the Integration of the British Atlantic Community, 1735–1785* (Cambridge, 1995).
66. Zahedieh, 'Credit, Risk, and Reputation'.
67. Peter J. Cain and Anthony G. Hopkins, *British Imperialism: Innovation and Expansion, 1688–1914* (London, 1993).
68. James A. Williamson, 'England and the Opening of the Atlantic', in J. Holland Rose, A. P. Newton, and E. A. Benians, eds., *The Cambridge History of the British Empire*, 8 vols. (Cambridge, 1929–61), vol. 1, pp. 207–38.
69. For a survey of the debate see 'Editor's Introduction', in Joel Mokyr, ed., *The British Industrial Revolution: An Economic Perspective* (Oxford, 1993), pp. 1–131.

70. Patrick K. O'Brien, 'European Economic Development: The Contribution of the Periphery', *Economic History Review*, 35 (1982) 1–18.
71. Patrick K. O'Brien, 'Mercantilism and Imperialism in the Rise and Decline of the Dutch and British Economies, 1585–1815', *De Economist*, 148 (2000) 469–501.
72. Robert P. Thomas and Donald N. McCloskey, 'Overseas Trade and Empire, 1700–1860', in Roderick C. Floud and McCloskey, eds., *The Economic History of Britain since 1700*, 2 vols. (Cambridge, 1981), vol. 1, pp. 87–102.

Chapter 4: Religion

I would like to thank Richard Shiels and John Brooke, who discussed this essay with me, as well as the many colleagues who responded to my inquiries about scholarly literature and historical fact.

1. David George Mullan, *Episcopacy in Scotland: The History of an Idea, 1560–1638* (Edinburgh, 1986); Samantha A. Meigs, *The Reformation in Ireland: Tradition and Confessionalism, 1400–1690* (London, 1997); Alan Ford, James McGuire, and Kenneth Milne, eds., *As by Law Established: The Church of Ireland Since the Reformation* (Dublin, 1995).
2. On the SPG's focus see Michael A. Mullett, *Catholics in Britain and Ireland, 1558–1829* (New York, 1998), pp. 95–6. Harry S. Stout, *The Divine Dramatist: George Whitefield and the Rise of Modern Evangelicalism* (Grand Rapids, Mich., 1991).
3. Richard S. Dunn, 'The Glorious Revolution and America', in Nicholas Canny, ed., *The Oxford History of the British Empire*, vol. 1, *The Origins of Empire: British Overseas Enterprise to the Close of the Seventeenth Century* (Oxford, 1998), pp. 445–66.
4. Linda Colley, *Britons: Forging the Nation, 1707–1787* (New Haven, Conn., 1992); Kathleen Wilson, *The Sense of the People: Politics, Culture and Imperialism in England, 1715–1785* (Cambridge, 1995).
5. Henry Méchoulan and Gerard Nahon, 'Introduction', *Menasseh Ben Israel: The Hope of Israel*, trans. Richenda George (Oxford, 1987), pp. 56–61.
6. Jon Butler, *The Huguenots in America: A Refugee People in a New World Society* (Cambridge, Mass., 1983); Hartmut Lehman et al., eds., *In Search of Peace and Prosperity: New German Settlements in Eighteenth-Century Europe and America* (University Park, Pa., 2000), esp. part IV.
7. Judith Maltby, *Prayer Book and People in Elizabethan and Early Stuart England* (Cambridge, 1998).
8. These examples are drawn from my study *The English Atlantic in an Era of Revolution, 1640–1661* (Cambridge, Mass., forthcoming).
9. Sylvaine Diouf, *Servants of Allah: African Muslims Enslaved in the Americas* (New York, 1998).

10. Glanmor Williams, *Recovery, Reorientation and Reformation: Wales, c. 1415–1642* (Oxford, 1987), and Williams, *The Welsh and Their Religion: Historical Essays* (Cardiff, 1991).

11. Roger Williams, *The Hireling Ministry None of Christs* (London, 1652), p. 13.

12. Jon Butler, *Awash in a Sea of Faith: Christianizing the American People* (Cambridge, Mass., 1990), p. 108.

13. John F. Sensbach, *A Separate Canaan: The Making of an Afro-Moravian World in North Carolina, 1763–1840* (Chapel Hill, NC, 1998); Dee E. Andrews, *The Methodists and Revolutionary America, 1760–1800: The Shaping of an Evangelical Culture* (Princeton, NJ, 2000).

14. Leigh Eric Schmidt, *Holy Fairs: Scottish Communions and American Revivals in the Early Modern Period* (Princeton, NJ, 1989).

15. Thomas Prince's *Christian History* was a precocious early example, appearing in 1744 and 1745 in support of the revivals. An upsurge in religious periodicals in Britain and the US occurred in the later eighteenth century. On the role of print generally, see Hugh Amory and David D. Hall, eds., *The History of the Book*, vol. 1, *The Colonial Book in the Atlantic World* (New York, 2000).

16. Boyd Stanley Schlenther, 'Religious Faith and Commercial Empire', in P. J. Marshall, ed., *The Oxford History of the British Empire,* vol. 2, *The Eighteenth Century* (Oxford, 1998), pp. 128–50; Frank Lambert, *'Pedlar in Divinity': George Whitefield and the Transatlantic Revivals, 1737–1770* (Princeton, NJ, 1994).

17. Nathaniel B. Shurtleff, ed., *Records of the Governor and Company of the Massachusetts Bay,* 5 vols. (Boston, 1853), title page.

18. Neal Salisbury, '"I Loved the Place of my Dwelling": Puritan Missionaries and Native Americans in Seventeenth-Century Southern New England', in Carla Gardina Pestana and Sharon V. Salinger, eds., *Inequality in Early America* (Hanover, NH, 1999), pp. 111–33, and Salisbury, 'Red Puritans: The "Praying Indians" of Massachusetts Bay and John Eliot', *WMQ,* 3rd ser., 31 (1974) 27–54; James Axtell, *Invasion Within: The Contest of Cultures in Colonial North America* (Oxford, 1985).

19. Richard W. Cogley, *John Eliot's Mission to the Indians before King Philip's War* (Cambridge, Mass., 1999).

20. On the Georgia mission plans, Sydney E. Ahlstrom, *A Religious History of the American People* (New Haven, Conn., 1972), p. 242.

21. Peter Burke, 'America and the Rewriting of World History', in Karen Ordahl Kupperman, ed., *America in European Consciousness, 1493–1750* (Chapel Hill, NC, 1995), esp. pp. 41–5.

22. Stephen Marshall et al., dedication to Thomas Shepard's *Clear Sunshine of the Gospel Breaking Forth upon the Indians of New-England* (London, 1648), n.p.; Karen Ordahl Kupperman, *Indians and English: Facing Off in Early America* (Ithaca, NY, 2000), ch. 4; Elaine G. Breslaw, *Tituba, Reluctant Witch of Salem: Devilish Indians and Puritan Fantasies* (New York, 1996).

23. The most famous case for this period involved a woman who became a Catholic, but other 'unredeemed captives' did not; John Demos, *The Unredeemed Captive: A Family Story from Early America* (New York, 1994). For later cases of settlers who took up their new community's faith see James E. Seaver, *A Narrative of the Life of Mrs. Mary Jemison*, new edn with introduction by June Namias (Norman, Okla., 1992), p. 58; and Joel W. Martin, *Sacred Revolt: The Muskogees' Struggle for a New World* (Boston, Mass., 1991), p. 78.

24. Sylvia R. Frey and Betty Wood, *Come Shouting to Zion: African-American Protestantism in the American South and British Caribbean to 1830* (Chapel Hill, NC, 1998); Mechal Sobel, *Trabel' On: The Slave Journey to an Afro-Baptist Faith* (Princeton, NJ, 1988); Michael A. Gomez, *Exchanging our Country Marks: The Transformation of African Identities in the Colonial and Antebellum South* (Chapel Hill, NC, 1998).

25. Philip D. Morgan, 'The Black Experience in the British Empire, 1680–1810', in Marshall, ed., *Oxford History of the British Empire*, vol. 2, pp. 481–3; Gary B. Nash, *Forging Freedom: The Formation of Philadelphia's Black Community, 1720–1840* (Cambridge, Mass., 1988), pp. 192–202.

26. Ole Peter Grell, Jonathan I. Israel, and Nicholas Tyacke, eds., *From Persecution to Toleration: The Glorious Revolution and Religion in England* (Oxford, 1991).

27. Karen Ordahl Kupperman, *Providence Island, 1630–1641: The Other Puritan Colony* (Cambridge, 1993).

28. Mullett, *Catholics in Britain and Ireland*.

29. Edmund S. Morgan, *Roger Williams: The Church and the State* (New York, 1967); Thomas E. Buckley, *Church and State in Revolutionary Virginia, 1776–1787* (Charlottesville, Va., 1987); Colin Kidd, 'Civil Theology and Church Establishments in Revolutionary America', *HJ*, 42 (1999) 1007–26.

30. Stephen Foster, 'English Puritanism and the Progress of New England Institutions, 1630–1660', in David D. Hall, John M. Murrin, and Thad W. Tate, eds., *Saints and Revolutionaries: Essays on Early American History* (New York, 1984), pp. 3–37.

31. Rhys Isaac, 'Evangelical Revolt: The Nature of the Baptists' Challenge to the Traditional Order in Virginia, 1765 to 1775', *WMQ*, 3rd ser., 31 (1974) 345–68.

32. Anthony F. C. Wallace, *The Death and Rebirth of the Seneca* (New York, 1969); Gregory Evans Dowd, *A Spirited Resistance: The North American Indian Struggle for Unity, 1745–1815* (Baltimore, 1992); Douglas R. Egerton, *Gabriel's Rebellion: The Virginia Slave Conspiracies of 1800 and 1802* (Chapel Hill, NC, 1993); James Sidbury, *Ploughshares into Swords: Race, Rebellion, and Identity in Gabriel's Virginia, 1730–1810* (Cambridge, 1997).

33. J. C. D. Clark, *The Language of Liberty, 1660–1832: Political Discourse and Social Dynamics in the Anglo-American World* (Cambridge, 1994).

34. Nancy L. Rhoden, *Revolutionary Anglicanism: The Colonial Church of England Clergy during the American Revolution* (New York, 1999); Stephen J. Stein, *The Shaker Experience in America: A History of the United Society of Believers* (New Haven, Conn., 1992).
35. Ruth H. Bloch, *Visionary Republic: Millennial Themes in American Thought, 1756–1800* (Cambridge, 1985).
36. David Hempton and Myrtle Hill, *Evangelical Protestantism in Ulster Society, 1740–1890* (London, 1992), pp. 27–9.
37. James H. Merrell, *The Indians' New World: Catawbas and their Neighbors from European Contact through the Era of Removal* (Chapel Hill, NC, 1989).

Chapter 5: Civility and Authority

Earlier versions of this chapter were delivered at the workshop in Harvard in September 2001 and at a conference on 'Shaping the Stuart World, 1603–1714', at the Huntington Library, California, in January 2001; and to seminars at the universities of Harvard, Pennsylvania State, and Keele. The author would like to thank the audiences on those occasions for their helpful comments. He is also particularly grateful to David Armitage, Joyce Chaplin, and Karen Harvey for their comments on earlier drafts of this chapter.

1. Michael J. Braddick, *State Formation in Early Modern England* (Cambridge, 2000), esp. ch. 2.
2. Ibid., pp. 71–85; Michael J. Braddick and John Walter, 'Grids of Power: Order, Hierarchy and Subordination in Early Modern Society', in Braddick and Walter, eds., *Negotiating Power in Early Modern Society: Order, Hierarchy and Subordination in Britain and Ireland* (Cambridge, 2001), esp. pp. 11–13.
3. Quoted from Barry Coward, *Social Change and Continuity in Early Modern England, 1550–1750* (London, 1988), pp. 104–6.
4. HAP 15 (8), Henry E. Huntington Library, San Marino, California.
5. The implicit reference is to the sociology of Erving Goffman. For an introduction see Goffman, 'The Interaction Order', *American Sociological Review*, 48 (1983) 1–17; Tom Burns, *Erving Goffman* (London, 1992), esp. ch. 2.
6. N. B. Harte, 'State Control of Dress and Social Change in Pre-industrial England', in D. C. Coleman and A. H. John, eds., *Trade, Government and Economy in Pre-Industrial England* (London, 1976), pp. 132–65.
7. Michael J. Braddick, *Parliamentary Taxation in Seventeenth Century England: Local Administration and Response* (Woodbridge, 1994), p. 33.
8. Quoted in Michael J. Braddick, 'Administrative Performance: The Representation of Political Authority in Early Modern England', in Braddick and Walter, eds., *Negotiating Power*, pp. 166–87.
9. Richard Gough, *The History of Myddle*, ed. David Hey (Harmondsworth, 1981), p. 111.

10. Penelope J. Corfield, 'Dress for Deference and Dissent: Hats and the Decline of Hat Honour', *Costume: Journal of the Costume Society*, 23 (1989) 64–79.

11. Justin Champion and Lee MacNulty, 'Making Orthodoxy in Late Restoration England: The Trials of Edmund Hickeringill, 1662–1710', in Braddick and Walter, eds., *Negotiating Power*, pp. 227–48.

12. John Rushworth, *Historical Collections ...*, 6 vols. (London, 1680 edn), vol. 2, p. 88.

13. Paul Slack, 'The Public Conscience of Henry Sherfield', in John Morrill, Paul Slack, and Daniel Woolf, eds., *Public Duty and Private Conscience in Seventeenth-Century England* (Oxford, 1992), pp. 151–71. Not all activists were motivated by this kind of godliness, of course, and not all the godly were able, or willing, to promote this kind of activism.

14. Patrick Collinson, quoted from Braddick and Walter, 'Grids of Power', p. 12.

15. Braddick, *State Formation*, pp. 260–3.

16. Anna Bryson, *From Courtesy to Civility: Changing Codes of Conduct in Early Modern England* (Oxford, 1998), p. 73.

17. Braddick, *State Formation*, part V.

18. Andrew McRae, *God Speed the Plough: The Representation of Agrarian England, 1500–1600* (Cambridge, 1996); Richard Helgerson, *Forms of Nationhood: The Elizabethan Writing of England* (Chicago, 1992).

19. Samuel Hartlib, *The reformed common-wealth of bees. Presented in severall letters and observations to Sammuel Hartlib Esq. With The reformed Virginian silk-worm* (London, 1655). The Hartlib circle placed a particular Baconian interpretation on these ideas, associating them with a religious impulse to make full use of natural resources. For this larger vision see Charles Webster, *The Great Instauration: Science, Medicine and Reform, 1626–1660* (London, 1975).

20. Braddick, *State Formation*, pp. 340–7.

21. Ibid., pp. 344–6, 405–10.

22. McRae, *God Speed*; Helgerson, *Forms of Nationhood*, ch. 3.

23. Michael Mac Carthy-Morrogh, 'The English Presence in Early Seventeenth-Century Munster', in Ciaran Brady and Raymond Gillespie, eds., *Natives and Newcomers: Essays on the Making of Irish Colonial Society, 1534–1641* (Dublin, 1986), quotation at p. 190.

24. Raymond Gillespie, 'Negotiating Order in Early Seventeenth-Century Ireland', in Braddick and Walter, eds., *Negotiating Power*, quotation at p. 197.

25. Mary Beth Norton, *Founding Mothers and Fathers: Gendered Power and the Forming of American Society* (New York, 1996), p. 5. For a full discussion of this issue see Pearsall, 'Gender', Chapter 6 in this volume.

26. Karen Ordahl Kupperman, 'Presentment of Civility: English Reading of American Self-Presentation in the Early Years of Colonization',

WMQ, 3rd ser., 54 (1997) 193–228. In other respects, as Joyce Chaplin has shown, early commentators resorted to a kind of racial 'idiom': 'Natural Philosophy and an Early Racial Idiom in North America: Comparing English and Indian Bodies', *WMQ*, 3rd ser., 54 (1997) 229–52. This made the prospect of assimilating Indians to civil society seem more distant. See, on these issues, Chaplin, 'Race', Chapter 8 in this volume.

27. David Armitage, *The Ideological Origins of the British Empire* (Cambridge, 2000), ch. 3; Edward Johnson, *A history of New-England: From the English planting in the yeere 1628. untill the yeere 1652* (London, 1654).

28. David Hancock, *Citizens of the World* (Cambridge, 1995); Perry Gauci, *The Politics of Trade: The Overseas Merchant in State and Society, 1660–1720* (Oxford, 2001).

29. Timothy H. Breen, 'Creative Adaptations: Peoples and Cultures', in Jack Greene and J. R. Pole, eds., *Colonial British America: Essays in the New History of the Early Modern Era* (London, 1984), pp. 195–232. For migration see Games, 'Migration', Chapter 2 in this volume.

30. Ian K. Steele, 'Empire of Migrants and Consumers: Some Current Atlantic Approaches to the History of Colonial Virginia', *Virginia Magazine of History and Biography*, 99 (1991) 489–512.

31. Bernard Bailyn and Philip D. Morgan, eds., *Strangers Within the Realm: Cultural Margins of the First British Empire* (Chapel Hill, NC, 1991).

32. James Walvin, *Fruits of Empire: Exotic Produce and British Taste, 1660–1800* (Basingstoke, 1997).

33. Jack P. Greene and J. R. Pole, 'Reconstructing British-American Colonial History: An Introduction', in Greene and Pole, eds., *Colonial British America*, pp. 1–17.

34. For full references see Braddick, *State Formation*, pp. 368, 371–3.

35. Nicholas Canny, *Making Ireland British, 1580–1650* (Oxford, 2001); S. J. Connolly, *Religion, Law and Power: The Making of Protestant Ireland, 1660–1760* (Oxford, 1992).

36. Jack P. Greene, *The Intellectual Construction of America: Exceptionalism and Identity from 1492–1800* (Chapel Hill, NC, 1993); Greene, *Imperatives, Behaviors and Identities: Essays in Early American Cultural History* (Charlottesville, Va., 1992); Richard L. Bushman, *The Refinement of America: Persons, Houses, Cities* (New York, 1992); C. Dallett Hemphill, *Bowing to Necessities: A History of Manners in America, 1620–1860* (Oxford, 1999).

37. For variations in social structure see Wrightson, 'Class', Chapter 7 in this volume.

38. For anti-slavery see Brown, 'The Politics of Slavery', Chapter 11 in this volume.

39. For example, see Zahedieh, 'Economy', Chapter 3 in this volume, p. 65.

40. Margaret R. Hunt, *The Middling Sort: Commerce, Gender, and the Family in England, 1680–1780* (Berkeley, Calif., 1996).

41. Michael J. Braddick, 'The English State, War, Trade and Settlement, c. 1625–1688', in Nicholas Canny, ed.,*The Oxford History of the British Empire*, vol. 1,*The Origins of Empire: English Overseas Enterprise to the Close of the Seventeenth Century* (Oxford, 1998), pp. 286–308.
42. For the navigation system, and its relationship to the economy as a whole, see Zahedieh, 'Economy', Chapter 3 in this volume.
43. David Armitage, 'The Declaration of Independence and International Law',*WMQ*, 3rd ser., 59 (2002) 39–54.

Chapter 6: Gender

The author would like to thank Laurel Thatcher Ulrich and Rab Houston, as well as David Armitage and Michael Braddick, for insightful critiques of earlier drafts. She also thanks Mary O'Dowd for graciously sharing her work on Ireland. Finally, she would like to acknowledge the helpful comments from fellow contributors and the audience at the British-Atlantic Workshop at Harvard University, September 2001.

1. Keith Wrightson, *English Society, 1580–1680* (Rutgers, NJ, 1982), p. 149. See Braddick, 'Civility and Authority', Chapter 5 in this volume, as well as Paul Griffiths, Adam Fox, and Steve Hindle, eds., *The Experience of Authority in Early Modern England* (Basingstoke, 1996).
2. Lord Falkland as quoted in Mary O'Dowd, 'Women and the Colonial Experience in Sixteenth and Seventeenth Century Ireland', in Terry Brotherstone, Deborah Simonton, and Oonagh Walsh, eds., *Gendering Scottish History: An International Approach* (The Mackie Occasional Colloquia Series 1, Glasgow, 1999), pp. 156–71.
3. O'Dowd develops the point about language and culture in her 'Women and the Colonial Experience'.
4. This debate over women's nature is in Katherine Usher Henderson and Barbara F. McManus, *Half Humankind: Contexts and Texts of the Controversy about Women in England, 1540–1640* (Urbana, Ill., 1985).
5. Joseph Swetnam, quoted in ibid., pp. 189–216, quotation at p. 201.
6. Ester Sowernam, quoted in ibid., pp. 217–43, quotation at p. 220.
7. Amy Erickson, *Women and Property in Early Modern England* (London, 1993).
8. Susan Dwyer Amussen, *An Ordered Society: Gender and Class in Early Modern England* (Oxford, 1988).
9. E. A. Wrigley and R. S. Schofield, *The Population History of England, 1541–1871: A Reconstruction in Social and Demographic History* (Cambridge, Mass., 1981) and R. A. Houston, *The Population History of Britain and Ireland, 1500–1750* (Basingstoke, 1992).
10. Paul Seaver, *Wallington's World: A Puritan Artisan in Seventeenth-Century London* (Stanford, Calif., 1985).

11. See Wrightson, 'Class', Chapter 7 in this volume.
12. Francis Mauriceau, *The Diseases of Women with Child And in Child-Bed*, trans. Hugh Chamberlen (London, 1710). See also Jane Sharp, *The Midwives Book* (London, 1671).
13. Laura Gowing, 'Language, Power, and the Law: Women's Slander Litigation in Early Modern London', in Jenny Kermode and Garthine Walker, eds., *Women, Crime and the Courts in Early Modern England* (London, 1994), pp. 26–47, quotation at p. 30.
14. J. A. Sharpe, *Defamation and Sexual Slander in Early Modern England: The Church Courts at York* (Borthwick Papers 58, York, 1980); Martin Ingram, *Church Courts, Sex and Marriage in England, 1570–1640* (Cambridge, 1987); Gowing, 'Language, Power, and the Law', and also her 'Gender and the Language of Insult in Early Modern London', *History Workshop Journal*, 35 (1993) 1–21.
15. Wrightson, *English Society*, and Wrightson and David Levine, *Poverty and Piety in an English Village: Terling, 1525–1700*, rev. edn (Oxford, 1995).
16. David Underdown, 'The Taming of the Scold: The Enforcement of Patriarchal Authority in Early Modern England', and Susan Amussen, 'Gender, Family, and the Social Order, 1560–1725', both in Anthony Fletcher and John Stevenson, eds., *Order and Disorder in Early Modern England* (Cambridge, 1985), pp. 196–217. Also J. A. Sharpe, 'Witchcraft and Women in Seventeenth-Century England: Some Northern Evidence', *Continuity and Change*, 6 (1991) 179–99. Martin Ingram argues against this view, but still points out the fear of disorderly women in his '"Scolding Women Cucked or Washed?": A Crisis in Gender Relations in Early Modern England?', in Kermode and Walker, eds., *Women, Crime and the Courts*, pp. 48–80.
17. Ingram, '"Scolding Women"', p. 67.
18. Linda K. Kerber, 'Separate Spheres, Female Worlds, Woman's Place: The Rhetoric of Women's History', *JAH*, 75 (1988) 9–39, and her and others' contributions in 'Beyond Roles, Beyond Spheres: Thinking About Gender in the Early Republic', *WMQ*, 3rd ser., 46 (1989) 565–85; Amanda J. Vickery, 'Golden Age to Separate Spheres: A Review of the Categories and Chronology of English Women's History', *HJ*, 36 (1993) 383–414; and Kathleen M. Brown, 'Brave New Worlds: Women's and Gender History', *WMQ*, 3rd ser., 50 (1993) 311–27.
19. Kathleen M. Brown, *Good Wives, Nasty Wenches, and Anxious Patriarchs: Gender, Race, and Power in Colonial Virginia* (Chapel Hill, NC, 1996), p. 33.
20. Edmund Spenser as quoted in Mary O'Dowd, 'Women and the Law in Early Modern Ireland', in Christine Meek, ed., *Women in Renaissance and Early Modern Europe* (Dublin, 2000), pp. 95–108.
21. Willy Maley, as quoted in O'Dowd, 'Women and the Law'.
22. Ann Marie Plane, *Colonial Intimacies: Indian Marriage in Early New England* (Ithaca, NY, 2000).

270   *Notes*

23. David Hume, 'Of the Rise and Progress of the Arts and Sciences', in Hume, *Essays Moral, Political, and Literary*, ed. Eugene F. Miller (Indianapolis, 1987), p. 133.
24. Adam Ferguson, *An Essay on the History of Civil Society*, ed. Fania Oz-Salzberger (Cambridge, 1995), p. 82.
25. James Adair as quoted in Richard Godbeer, 'Eroticizing the Middle Ground: Anglo-Indian Sexual Relations along the Eighteenth-Century Frontier', in Martha Hodes, ed., *Sex, Love, Race: Crossing Boundaries in North American History* (New York, 1999), pp. 91–111.
26. William Wood as quoted in Plane, *Colonial Intimacies*, p. 38.
27. Godbeer, 'Eroticizing the Middle Ground', p. 92.
28. O'Dowd, 'Women and the Colonial Experience'; Lois Green Carr and Lorena S. Walsh, 'The Planter's Wife: The Experience of White Women in Seventeenth-Century Maryland', *WMQ*, 3rd ser., 34 (1977) 542–71; Brown, *Good Wives*; and Trevor Burnard, 'Inheritance and Independence: Women's Status in Early Colonial Jamaica', *WMQ*, 3rd ser., 48 (1991) 93–114 and Burnard, 'Family Continuity and Female Independence in Jamaica, 1665–1734', *Continuity and Change*, 7 (1992) 181–98.
29. Jennifer L. Morgan, '"Some Could Suckle over Their Shoulder": Male Travelers, Female Bodies, and the Gendering of Racial Ideology, 1500–1770', *WMQ*, 3rd ser., 54 (1997) 167–92.
30. Edward Long, *The History of Jamaica*, 2 vols. (London, 1774), vol. 2, p. 383.
31. G. Ugo Nwokeji, 'African Conceptions of Gender and the Slave Trade', *WMQ*, 3rd ser., 58 (2001) 47–68, and David Eltis, *The Rise of African Slavery in the Americas* (Cambridge, 2000), ch. 10.
32. Brown, *Good Wives*.
33. Long, *The History of Jamaica*, and Bryan Edwards, *The History, Civil and Commercial, of the British Colonies in the West Indies* (London, 1793).
34. Barbara Bush, *Slave Women in Caribbean Society, 1650–1838* (London, 1990); Richard S. Dunn, 'A Tale of Two Plantations: Slave Life at Mesopotamia in Jamaica and Mount Airy in Virginia, 1799 to 1828', *WMQ*, 3rd ser., 34 (1977) 32–65; Philip D. Morgan, 'Three Planters and Their Slaves: Perspectives on Slavery in Virginia, South Carolina, and Jamaica, 1750–1790', in Winthrop D. Jordan and Sheila L. Skemp, eds., *Race and Family in the Colonial South* (Jackson, Miss., 1987), pp. 37–80; Sharon Block, 'Lines of Color, Sex, and Service: Comparative Sexual Coercion in Early America', in Hodes, ed., *Sex, Love, Race*, pp. 141–63.
35. Hilary McD. Beckles, 'White Women and Slavery in the Caribbean', *History Workshop Journal*, 36 (1993) 66–82.
36. Maxine Berg, *The Age of Manufactures, 1700–1820: Industry, Innovation, and Work in Britain*, 2nd edn (London, 1994); Margot Finn, 'Men's Things: Masculine Possession in the Consumer Revolution', *Social*

History, 25 (2000) 133–55, and Carole Shammas, *The Pre-Industrial Consumer in England and America* (Oxford, 1990).

37. Benjamin Franklin, *Autobiography and Other Writings*, ed. Ormond Seavey (Oxford, 1993), p. 71.

38. Toby L. Ditz, 'Shipwrecked, or, Masculinity Imperiled: Mercantile Representations of Failure and the Gendered Self in Eighteenth-Century Philadelphia', *JAH*, 81 (1994) 51–80.

39. Richard L. Bushman, *The Refinement of America: Persons, Houses, Cities* (New York, 1992); Lawrence E. Klein, *Shaftesbury and the Culture of Politeness: Moral Discourse and Cultural Politics in Early Eighteenth-Century England* (Cambridge, 1994); John Brewer, *The Pleasures of the Imagination: English Culture in the Eighteenth Century* (London, 1997); and David S. Shields, *Civil Tongues and Polite Letters in British America* (Chapel Hill, NC, 1997).

40. Carol F. Karlsen and Laurie Crumpacker, eds., *The Journal of Esther Edwards Burr* (New Haven, Conn., 1984), p. 192.

41. Philip D. Carter, *Men and the Emergence of Polite Society, Britain, 1660–1800* (Harlow, 2001).

42. Felicity Heal, *Hospitality in Early Modern England* (Oxford, 1990).

43. Maria Nugent to Lady Temple, dated 'Penn. Sunday Feby 14th. 1802—', STG Box 8, Grenville Correspondence, Stowe Collection, Huntington Library, San Marino, California.

44. G. J. Barker-Benfield, *The Culture of Sensibility: Sex and Society in Eighteenth-Century Britain* (Chicago, 1992).

45. David Cressy, *Literacy and the Social Order: Reading and Writing in Tudor and Stuart England* (Cambridge, 1980); Kenneth A. Lockridge, *Literacy in Colonial New England* (New York, 1974); Gloria L. Main, 'An Inquiry Into When and Why Women Learned to Write in Colonial New England', *Journal of Social History*, 24 (1991) 579–89; Joel Perlmann and Dennis Shirley, 'When Did New England Women Acquire Literacy?', *WMQ*, 3rd ser., 48 (1991) 50–67.

46. Cathy N. Davidson, *Revolution and the Word: The Rise of the Novel in America* (Oxford, 1986); Sharon M. Harris, 'Early American Women's Self-Creating Acts', *Resources for American Literary Study*, 19 (1993) 223–45; and Shari Benstock, ed., *The Private Self: Theory and Practice of Women's Autobiographical Writings* (London, 1988).

47. Sarah M. S. Pearsall, '"After All These Revolutions": Epistolary Identities in an Atlantic World, 1760–1815', Ph.D. dissertation, Harvard University, 2001.

48. Mary Wollstonecraft, *A Vindication of the Rights of Woman*, ed. Ashley Tauchert (London, 1995), and Judith Sargent Murray, *Selected Writings of Judith Sargent Murray*, ed. Sharon M. Harris (Oxford, 1995).

49. John Tharp (Sr) to John Tharp (Jr), dated 'Good Hope 3d Octr 1802', R55.7.22 (a), Tharp Family Papers, Cambridgeshire County Record Office, Cambridge.

50. Edward Brathwaite, *The Development of Creole Society in Jamaica, 1770–1820* (Oxford, 1971).

51. See Chaplin, 'Race', Chapter 8 in this volume.

52. Thomas Laqueur, *Making Sex: Body and Gender from the Greeks to Freud* (Cambridge, Mass., 1990).

53. Rebecca Larson, *Daughters of Light: Quaker Women Preaching and Prophesying in the Colonies and Abroad, 1770–1775* (New York, 1999).

54. Susan Juster, *Disorderly Women: Sexual Politics & Evangelism in Revolutionary New England* (Ithaca, NY, 1994).

55. See Pestana, 'Religion', Chapter 4 in this volume.

56. Ronald Hoffman and Peter J. Albert, eds., *Women in the Age of the American Revolution* (Charlottesville, Va., 1989).

57. Ruth H. Bloch, 'The Gendered Meaning of Virtue in Revolutionary America', *Signs*, 13 (1987) 37–58, and Rosemarie Zagarri, 'Morals, Manners, and the Republican Mother', *AQ*, 44 (1992) 192–215.

58. Linda Kerber, *Women of the Republic: Intellect & Ideology in Revolutionary America* (New York, 1980); Jan Lewis, 'The Republican Wife: Virtue and Seduction in the Early Republic', *WMQ*, 3rd ser., 44 (1987) 689–721; Susan Branson, *Those Fiery Frenchified Dames: Women and Political Culture in Early National Philadelphia* (Philadelphia, 2001), and Catherine Allgor, *Parlor Politics: In Which the Ladies of Washington Help Build a City and a Government* (Charlottesville, Va., 2000).

59. Allgor, *Parlor Politics*, p. 99.

60. Elizabeth Smith Shaw as quoted in Mary Beth Norton, *Liberty's Daughters: The Revolutionary Experience of American Women, 1750–1800* (Boston, Mass., 1980), p. 42.

61. Margaret Cowper to Eliza McQueen and Mary Ann Cowper, undated [1796], Mackay-Stiles Papers, Southern Historical Collection, University of North Carolina, Chapel Hill.

Chapter 7: Class

1. Peter Calvert, *The Concept of Class: An Historical Introduction* (London, 1982), ch. 1; Penelope J. Corfield, 'Class by Name and Number in Eighteenth-Century Britain', in Corfield, ed., *Language, History and Class* (London, 1991), p. 103.

2. Peter Burke, 'The Language of Orders in Early Modern Europe', and William Doyle, 'Myths of Order and Ordering Myths', both in M. L. Bush, ed., *Social Orders and Social Classes in Europe since 1500: Studies in Social Stratification* (London, 1992), pp. 1–12 and 218–29.

3. Calvert, *Concept of Class*, pp. 15ff; Corfield, 'Class by Name and Number', pp. 105–9, 114, 126–8.

4. For the subsequent development of the concept of class see Calvert, *Concept of Class*; Patrick Joyce, ed., *Class* (Oxford, 1995); Rosemary Crompton, *Class and Stratification: An Introduction to Current Debates*, 2nd edn (Cambridge, 1998).

5. Keith Wrightson, *English Society, 1580–1680* (London, 1982), ch. 1; Wrightson, 'Estates, Degrees and Sorts: Changing Perceptions of Society in Tudor and Stuart England', in Corfield, ed., *Language, History and Class*, pp. 32–44.

6. Keith Wrightson, '"Sorts of People" in Tudor and Stuart England', in Jonathan Barry and Christopher Brooks, eds., *The Middling Sort of People: Culture, Society and Politics in England, 1550–1800* (London, 1994), pp. 28–51.

7. Dror Wahrman, *Imagining the Middle Class: The Political Representation of Class in Britain, c. 1780–1840* (Cambridge, 1995), p. 6.

8. Corfield, 'Class by Name and Number', pp. 116–21.

9. Keith Wrightson, *Earthly Necessities: Economic Lives in Early Modern Britain* (New Haven, Conn., 2000), chs. 1–7.

10. Ibid., ch. 8.

11. Quoted in Michael Macdonald, *Mystical Bedlam: Madness, Anxiety and Healing in Seventeenth-Century England* (Cambridge, 1981), p. 40.

12. J. G. A. Pocock, 'The New British History in Atlantic Perspective', *AHR*, 104 (1999) 492.

13. James T. Lemon, 'Spatial Order: Households in Local Communities and Regions', and T. H. Breen, 'Creative Adaptations: Peoples and Cultures', both in Jack P. Greene and J. R. Pole, eds., *Colonial British America: Essays in the New History of the Early Modern Era* (Baltimore, 1984), pp. 86, 205; Breen, *Puritans and Adventurers: Change and Persistence in Early America* (New York, 1980), pp. 107–8.

14. Breen, *Puritans and Adventurers*, p. 109; Jack P. Greene, *Pursuits of Happiness: The Social Development of Early Modern British Colonies and the Formation of American Culture* (Chapel Hill, NC, 1988), p. 10.

15. Breen, *Puritans and Adventurers*, pp. 111–12.

16. Greene, *Pursuits of Happiness*, p. 10.

17. Breen, *Puritans and Adventurers*, p. 109; Carole Shammas, 'English Commercial Development and American Colonization', in K. R. Andrews, Nicholas P. Canny, and P. E. H. Hair, eds., *The Westward Enterprise: English Activities in Ireland, the Atlantic and America, 1480–1650* (Liverpool, 1978), p. 152.

18. David W. Galenson, 'The Settlement and Growth of the Colonies: Population, Labor and Economic Development', in Stanley L. Engerman and Robert E. Gallman, eds., *The Cambridge Economic History of the United States*, vol. 1, *The Colonial Era* (Cambridge, 1996), p. 141; Richard S. Dunn, 'Servants and Slaves: The Recruitment and Employment of Labor', in Greene and Pole, eds., *Colonial British America*, p. 162. James Horn, *Adapting to a New World: English Society in the Seventeenth-century Chesapeake* (Chapel Hill, NC, 1994), pp. 62ff. See Games, 'Migration', Chapter 2 in this volume.

19. Edward S. Morgan, *American Slavery, American Freedom: The Ordeal of Colonial Virginia* (New York, 1975), pp. 126–9, 327; Nicholas Canny,

'The Permissive Frontier: The Problem of Social Control in English Settlements in Ireland and Virginia', in Andrews, Canny, and Hair, eds., *The Westward Enterprise*, pp. 27, 28, 34, 41; Horn, *Adapting*, pp. 268–76; Breen, *Puritans and Adventurers*, pp. 133ff; Breen, 'Creative Adaptations', p. 204.

20. Morgan, *American Slavery, American Freedom*, chs. 11–13; Breen, *Puritans and Adventurers*, pp. 128–38; Horn, *Adapting*, pp. 151–60, 373–9.

21. Terms quoted in Morgan, *American Slavery, American Freedom*, pp. 258, 261, 264, 279, 305, and Breen, *Puritans and Adventurers*, pp. 136, 137.

22. Morgan, *American Slavery, American Freedom*, pp. 291–2.

23. Richard S. Dunn, 'Experiments Holy and Unholy, 1630–1', in Andrews, Canny, and Hair, eds., *The Westward Enterprise*, pp. 273–5; Breen, *Puritans and Adventurers*, pp. 49–50.

24. David Grayson Allen, *In English Ways: The Movement of Societies and the Transferral of English Local Law and Custom to Massachusetts Bay in the Seventeenth Century* (Chapel Hill, NC, 1981).

25. J. H. Parry, 'Introduction: the English in the New World', in Andrews, Canny, and Hair, eds., *The Westward Enterprise*, p. 5; Gary B. Nash, 'Social Development', in Greene and Pole, eds., *Colonial British America*, p. 240.

26. Galenson, 'Settlement and Growth', p. 149; Kenneth A. Lockridge, *A New England Town: The First Hundred Years. Dedham, Massachusetts, 1636–1736* (New York, 1979); Nash, 'Social Development', pp. 236–7.

27. Allen, *In English Ways*, p. 120; Breen, *Puritans and Adventurers*, pp. 85–6; Greene, *Pursuits of Happiness*, p. 25.

28. Nash, 'Social Development', p. 236.

29. Hugh Kearney, 'The Problem of Perspective in the History of Colonial America', in Andrews, Canny, and Hair, eds., *The Westward Enterprise*, p. 301.

30. Dunn, 'Experiments', p. 275; Dunn, 'Servants and Slaves', p. 184; Breen, *Puritans and Adventurers*, pp. 17, 49–52, 73, 74, 85; Lockridge, *New England Town*, p. 4; Greene, *Pursuits of Happiness*, p. 25; T. N. Ingersoll, '"Riches and honour were rejected by them as loathesome vomit": The Fear of Levelling in New England', in Carla Gardina Pestana and Sharon V. Salinger, eds., *Inequality in Early America* (Hanover, NH, 1999), p. 47; Galenson, 'Settlement and Growth', pp. 167–8.

31. Dunn, 'Experiments', p. 269.

32. Ian D. Whyte, *Scotland Before the Industrial Revolution* (London, 1995), pp. 113, 119, 121–5.

33. Raymond Gillespie, *The Transformation of the Irish Economy, 1550–1700* (Dublin, 1991), p. 3.

34. Steven G. Ellis, *Ireland in the Age of the Tudors, 1447–1603: English Expansion and the End of Gaelic Rule* (London, 1998), p. 36.

35. R. F. Foster, *Modern Ireland, 1600–1972* (London, 1988), pp. 10, 26; Mary O'Dowd, 'Gaelic Economy and Society', in Ciaran Brady and

Raymond Gillespie, eds., *Natives and Newcomers: Essays on the Making of Irish Colonial Society, 1534–1641* (Dublin, 1986), pp. 125–9; Ellis, *Ireland in the Age of the Tudors*, pp. 40–4; Gillespie, *Transformation*, pp. 20–1. For the Scottish Highlands see R. A. Dodgshon, *From Chiefs to Landlords: Social and Economic Change in the Western Highlands and Islands, c. 1493–1820* (Edinburgh, 1998), chs. 2–4.

36. Ellis, *Ireland in the Age of the Tudors*, p. 58; O'Dowd, 'Gaelic Economy', pp. 131–44; Gillespie, *Transformation*, pp. 10, 20–2, 58.

37. Foster, *Modern Ireland*, chs. 3–5; Michael Mac Carthy Morragh, 'The English Presence in Early Seventeenth-Century Munster', in Brady and Gillespie, eds., *Natives and Newcomers*, pp. 171–90; Nicholas Canny, *Making Ireland British, 1580–1650* (Oxford, 2001).

38. Wrightson, *Earthly Necessities*, chs. 10–14; Gillespie, *Transformation*, pp. 25ff.

39. Greene, *Pursuits of Happiness*, chs. 3–4, 6–8, quoting pp. 167–8, 170–2.

40. J. T. Main, *The Social Structure of Revolutionary America* (Princeton, NJ, 1965), pp. 8, 157, 158, 164, 166, 198, 229–35.

41. Wrightson, *Earthly Necessities*, ch. 12; S. J. Connolly, *Religion, Law and Power: The Making of Protestant Ireland, 1660–1760* (Oxford, 1992), pp. 59–72; Greene, *Pursuits of Happiness*, pp. 84, 93–4, 98, 118–19, 147, 168, 175, 187; Breen, *Puritans and Adventurers*, ch. 8; Darrett R. and Anita H. Rutman, *A Place in Time: Middlesex County, Virginia, 1650–1750* (New York, 1984), pp. 156–7; Rhys Isaac, *The Transformation of Virginia, 1740–1790* (Chapel Hill, NC, 1982), pp. 118–19, 131; Gordon S. Wood, *The Radicalism of the American Revolution* (New York, 1993), pp. 31–42; Richard B. Sheridan, 'The Formation of Caribbean Plantation Society, 1689–1748', in P. J. Marshall, ed., *The Oxford History of the British Empire*, vol. 2, *The Eighteenth Century* (Oxford, 1998), pp. 404–5.

42. Wrightson, *Earthly Necessities*, ch. 13; Barry and Brooks, *The Middling Sort, passim*; David Hancock, *Citizens of the World: London Merchants and the Integration of the British Atlantic Community, 1735–1785* (Cambridge, 1995).

43. For the notion of a 'dispersed society', see Lemon, 'Spatial Order', p. 86.

44. Nash, 'Social Development', p. 247. Estimates of English population distribution are provided in E. A. Wrigley, 'Urban Growth and Agricultural Change: England and the Continent in the Early Modern Period', *Journal of Interdisciplinary History*, 15 (1985) 683–728.

45. Main, *Social Structure*, pp. 11, 17, 18ff, 27, 34ff, 42, 49, 54, 60, 73–4, 166, 271ff; Greene, *Pursuits of Happiness*, pp. 186, 195; Galenson, 'Settlement and Growth', p. 206.

46. Main, *Social Structure*, pp. 112–13, 185ff; Richard B. Sheridan, 'The Domestic Economy', in Greene and Pole, eds., *Colonial British America*, pp. 46–7; Rutmans, *Place in Time*, pp. 134–8, 154, 195ff; James A. Henretta, 'Wealth and Social Structure', in Greene and Pole, eds.,

Colonial British America, pp. 275–6, 284; Galenson, 'Settlement and Growth', p. 143.

47. Main, *Social Structure*, pp. 11, 168ff; Sheridan, 'Domestic Economy', p. 57; Russell R. Menard, 'Economic and Social Development of the South', in Engerman and Gallman, eds., *Cambridge Economic History*, p. 271.

48. Connolly, *Religion, Law and Power*, pp. 45–6, 50, 55, 128–9.

49. T. M. Devine, *The Transformation of Rural Scotland: Social Change and the Agrarian Economy* (Edinburgh, 1994), pp. 7, 11ff, quoting p. 14; Whyte, *Scotland Before the Industrial Revolution*, p. 161; R. A. Dodgshon, *Land and Society in Early Scotland* (Oxford, 1981), p. 306.

50. Wrightson, *Earthly Necessities*, p. 270 and ch. 14.

51. Galenson, 'Settlement and Growth', pp. 173, 207; Philip D. Morgan, 'Rethinking Early American Slavery', in Pestana and Salinger, eds., *Inequality*, p. 240; Greene, *Pursuits of Happiness*, p. 100.

52. E. P. Thompson, 'The Patricians and the Plebs', in *Customs in Common* (London, 1991), pp. 21, 22, 74, 86, and Connolly, *Religion, Law and Power*, pp. 128–9.

53. Connolly, *Religion, Law and Power*, pp. 140–1; K. D. M. Snell, 'Deferential Bitterness: The Social Outlook of the Rural Proletariat in Eighteenth- and Nineteenth-Century England', in Bush, ed., *Social Orders and Social Classes*, pp. 158–84; E. P. Thompson, 'The Crime of Anonymity', in D. Hay et al., *Albion's Fatal Tree: Crime and Society in Eighteenth-Century England* (London, 1975), pp. 255–344.

54. For varying perspectives on the social identity and alignments of the middling sort, see e.g. Thompson, 'Patricians and the Plebs', pp. 32, 87–90; Dror Wahrman, 'National Society, Communal Culture: An Argument about the Recent Historiography of Eighteenth Century Britain', *Social History*, 17 (1992) 43–72; Barry and Brooks, *The Middling Sort*, esp. chs. 3, 4, 6, 7; Kathleen Wilson, *The Sense of the People: Politics, Culture and Imperialism in England, 1715–1785* (Cambridge, 1995); H. R. French, 'The Search for the "Middle Sort of People" in England, 1600–1800', *HJ*, 58 (2000) 277–93.

55. Wrightson, *Earthly Necessities*, pp. 320–30.

56. Gary B. Nash, *The Urban Crucible: Social Change, Political Consciousness and the Origins of the American Revolution* (Cambridge, Mass., 1979), pp. 7, 33; Wood, *Radicalism of the American Revolution*, chs. 1, 3, 4.

57. Rutmans, *Place in Time*, pp. 128–9, 143–54; Morgan, *American Slavery, American Freedom*, chs. 16–17; Greene, *Pursuits of Happiness*, pp. 84, 93–4.

58. Main, *Social Structure*, pp. 166, 222; Greene, *Pursuits of Happiness*, pp. 188, 195. Quoting Henretta, 'Wealth and Social Structure', pp. 281–2.

59. Ingersoll, 'Riches and Honour', pp. 55–7; Menard, 'Economic and Social Development of the South', pp. 292–3; Nash, *Urban Crucible, passim*.

60. Main, *Social Structure*, p. 163; Nash, *Urban Crucible*, p. 10.

61. Ronald Schultz, 'A Class Society? The Nature of Inequality in Early America', in Pestana and Salinger, eds., *Inequality*, p. 203.
62. David Cannadine, *Class in Britain* (New Haven, Conn., 1998), pp. 18–19.

Chapter 8: Race

The author thanks John Bezís Selfa and her two editors for advice on this essay.

1. Eric Voegelin, 'The Growth of the Race Idea', *Review of Politics*, 2 (1940) 283–317; John C. Greene, *The Death of Adam: Evolution and Its Impact on Western Thought* (Ames, Iowa, 1959), chs. 6, 8; Pat Shipman, *The Evolution of Racism: Human Differences and the Use and Abuse of Science* (New York, 1994); Ivan Hannaford, *Race: The History of an Idea in the West* (Baltimore and Washington, DC, 1996), pp. 3–9.
2. A. N. Sherwin-White, *Racial Prejudice in Imperial Rome* (Cambridge, 1967); Frank M. Snowden, Jr, *Before Color Prejudice: The Ancient View of Blacks* (Cambridge, Mass., 1983); Hannaford, *Race*, pp. 10–20, 52–7, 64–72.
3. D. C. Allen, *The Legend of Noah: Renaissance Rationalism in Art, Science, and Letters* (Urbana, Ill., 1963); Hannaford, *Race*, ch. 5; Lorraine Daston and Katharine Park, *Wonders and the Order of Nature, 1150–1750* (New York, 1998), ch. 5.
4. Paul Freedman, *Images of the Medieval Peasant* (Stanford, Calif., 1999), ch. 4.
5. Paul Cartledge, *The Greeks: A Portrait of Self and Others* (Oxford, 1993), ch. 4; Joan Cadden, *Meanings of Sex Difference in the Middle Ages: Medicine, Science, and Culture* (Cambridge, 1993); Ian Maclean, *The Renaissance Notion of Woman: A Study in the Fortunes of Scholasticism and Medical Science in European Intellectual Life* (Cambridge, 1980), ch. 3.
6. Margaret Hodgen, *Early Anthropology in the Sixteenth and Seventeenth Centuries* (Philadelphia, 1964), pp. 386–404; Clarence J. Glacken, *Traces on the Rhodian Shore: Nature and Culture in Western Thought from Ancient Times to the End of the Eighteenth Century* (Berkeley, Calif., 1967), pp. 429–60; Hannaford, *Race*, pp. 20–30, 76–83; Roxann Wheeler, *The Complexion of Race: Categories of Difference in Eighteenth-Century British Culture* (Philadelphia, 2000), pp. 21–8.
7. Denys Hay, *Europe: The Emergence of an Idea*, rev. edn (Edinburgh, 1993); Linda Colley, *Britons: Forging the Nation, 1707–1837* (New Haven, Conn., 1992), ch. 1; Hannaford, *Race*, pp. 89–96; Wheeler, *Complexion of Race*, pp. 14–17.
8. Hannaford, *Race*, pp. 115–26.
9. Benzion Natanyahu, *The Origins of the Inquisition in Fifteenth-Century Spain* (New York, 1995); Benjamin Braude, 'The Sons of Noah and the Construction of Ethnic and Geographical Identities in the Medieval

and Early Modern Periods', *WMQ*, 3rd ser., 44 (1997) 103–42; Robin Blackburn, *The Making of New World Slavery: From the Baroque to the Modern, 1492–1800* (London, 1997), ch. 1.

10. Philip D. Curtin, 'Epidemiology and the Slave Trade', *Political Science Quarterly*, 83 (1968) 198–211; James H. Sweet, 'The Iberian Roots of American Racist Thought', *WMQ*, 3rd ser., 14 (1997) 143–66; Joyce E. Chaplin, *Subject Matter: Technology, the Body, and Science on the Anglo-American Frontier, 1500–1676* (Cambridge, Mass., 2001), pp. 122–3, 128–9.

11. Allen, *Legend of Noah*, ch. 6; L. E. Huddleston, *Origins of the American Indians: European Concepts, 1492–1729* (Austin, Tex., 1967); Anthony Grafton, *New Worlds, Ancient Texts* (Cambridge, Mass., 1992), pp. 210–12, 234–5.

12. Anthony Pagden, *The Fall of Natural Man*, rev. edn (Cambridge, 1986), chs. 3, 5, 6.

13. Curtin, 'Epidemiology and the Slave Trade', pp. 198–211.

14. George Best, *A True Discourse* (1578), in Richard Collinson, ed., *The Three Voyages of Martin Frobisher* (London, 1867), pp. 54, 65; Chaplin, *Subject Matter*, p. 52.

15. Winthrop D. Jordan, *White over Black: American Attitudes toward the Negro, 1550–1812* (New York, 1969), ch. 2; Joyce E. Chaplin, 'Enslavement of Indians in Early America: Captivity without the Narrative', in Elizabeth Mancke and Carole Shammas, eds., *The Creation of the British Atlantic World* (Baltimore, forthcoming); draft of an act for baptizing 'Negroes & Infidells', referring to the West Indies, MS Tanner 447, fol. 53, Bodleian Library, Oxford; Peter H. Wood, *Black Majority: Negroes in Colonial South Carolina from 1670 through the Stono Rebellion* (New York, 1974), ch. 3; Joyce E. Chaplin, *An Anxious Pursuit: Agricultural Innovation and Modernity in the Lower South, 1730–1815* (Chapel Hill, NC, 1993), pp. 117–22.

16. Richard S. Dunn, *Sugar and Slaves: The Rise of the Planter Class in the English West Indies, 1624–1713* (New York, 1973), pp. 226–9, 239–40; Edmund S. Morgan, *American Slavery, American Freedom: The Ordeal of Colonial Virginia* (New York, 1975), ch. 11; Hilary McD. Beckles, *White Servitude and Black Slavery in Barbados, 1627–1715* (Knoxville, Tenn., 1989); Blackburn, *Making of New World Slavery*, ch. 6.

17. Chaplin, *Subject Matter*, ch. 4; P. J. Marshall and Glyndwr Williams, *The Great Map of Mankind: Perceptions of New Worlds in the Age of Enlightenment* (Cambridge, Mass., 1982), chs. 1, 2.

18. Governor Argall to Virginia Company of London, March 10, 1618, in Susan Myra Kingsbury, ed., *The Records of the Virginia Company of London* (Washington, DC, 1906–35), vol. 3, p. 92; [Philip Vincent], *A True Relation of the Late Battell* (London, 1637), 21; Chaplin, *Subject Matter*, chs. 4, 5, 8.

19. David Brion Davis, *The Problem of Slavery in Western Culture* (Ithaca, NY, 1966), pp. 11–13; Peter Hulme, *Colonial Encounters: Europe and the Native Caribbean, 1492–1797* (New York, 1992), esp. chs. 5, 6; Joseph Roach, *Cities of the Dead: Circum-Atlantic Performance* (New York, 1996), ch. 4; Frank Felsenstein, ed., *English Trader, Indian Maid: Representing Gender, Race, and Slavery in the New World: An Inkle and Yarico Reader* (Baltimore, 1999), introduction.
20. Elizabeth B. Gasking, *Investigations into Generation, 1651–1828* (Baltimore, 1967), chs. 2–4, 9; Clara Pinto-Correia, *The Ovary of Eve: Egg and Sperm and Preformation* (Chicago, 1997).
21. Greene, *Death of Adam*, chs. 7, 8; Hannaford, *Race*, pp. 205–13; Wheeler, *Complexion of Race*, pp. 28–33; Stephen Jay Gould, *The Mismeasure of Man* (New York, 1981).
22. Jordan, *White over Black*, ch. 6; Marshall and Williams, *Great Map of Mankind*, chs. 7, 8.
23. A. Leon Higginbotham, *In the Matter of Color: Race and the American Legal Process: The Colonial Period* (New York, 1978), pp. 160–2; Jack P. Greene, *Peripheries and Center: Constitutional Development in the Extended Polities of the British Empire and the United States, 1607–1788* (Athens, Ga., 1986), pp. 1–76; Jonathan A. Bush, 'Free to Enslave: The Foundations of Colonial American Slave Law', *Yale Journal of Law and the Humanities*, 5 (1993) 417–70.
24. Alden T. Vaughan, 'Trinculo's Indian: American Natives in Shakespeare's England', in Peter Hulme and William H. Sherman, eds., *The Tempest and Its Travels* (London, 2000), pp. 49–59; Philip D. Morgan, 'British Encounters with Africans and African-Americans, circa 1600–1780', in Bernard Bailyn and Philip D. Morgan, eds., *Strangers within the Realm: Cultural Margins of the First British Empire* (Chapel Hill, NC, 1991), pp. 157–219; Wheeler, *Complexion of Race*, esp. chs. 1, 5.
25. Edward Long, *A History of Jamaica* (London, 1774), vol. 2, pp. 260–1, 274, 276–7, 327; Davis, *Slavery in Western Culture*, pp. 459–64; Wheeler, *Complexion of Race*, pp. 210–32.
26. John C. Greene, *American Science in the Age of Jefferson* (Ames, Iowa, 1984), pp. 322–7 (Smith quotation on p. 324), 335–6 (Wells).
27. Chaplin, *Subject Matter*, pp. 318–20.
28. Thomas R. Trautman, 'The Lives of Sir William Jones', in Alexander Murray, ed., *Sir William Jones, 1746–1794: A Commemoration* (Oxford, 1998), pp. 105–10.
29. Brewton Berry, 'America's Mestizos', in Noel P. Gist and Anthony Gary Dworkin, eds., *The Blending of Races: Marginality and Identity in World Perspective* (New York, 1972), pp. 194–7; Gary B. Nash, 'The Hidden History of Mestizo America', *JAH*, 82 (1995) 941–62.
30. Gregory Evans Dowd, *A Spirited Resistance: The North American Indian Struggle for Unity, 1745–1815* (Baltimore, 1992), pp. 21, 30, 41–2, 63, 141, 175.

31. David Brion Davis, *The Problem of Slavery in the Age of Revolution, 1770–1823* (Ithaca, NY, 1975), pp. 299–306, quotation at p. 302.
32. Davis, *Slavery in Western Culture*, chs. 10–12; idem, *Slavery in the Age of Revolution*, ch. 5.
33. Margaret C. Jacob, *The Newtonians and the English Revolution, 1689–1720* (Hassocks, Sussex, 1976), ch. 7; Peter Lineham, 'Methodism and Popular Science in the Enlightenment', *Enlightenment and Dissent*, 17 (1998) 104–25; Davis, *Slavery in Western Culture*, chs. 13, 14 (secular anti-slavery); idem, *Slavery in the Age of Revolution*, ch. 11 (scriptural pro-slavery).
34. Antonello Gerbi, *The Dispute of the New World: The History of a Polemic, 1750–1900*, trans. Jeremy Moyle (Pittsburgh, Pa., 1983), chs. 1–5; Philip J. Deloria, *Playing Indian* (New Haven, Conn., 1998), ch. 1.
35. C. L. R. James, *The Black Jacobins: Toussaint L'Ouverture and the San Domingo Revolution* (London, 1938); Davis, *Slavery in the Age of Revolution*; Jordan, *White over Black*, ch. 10.
36. Thomas Jefferson, *Notes on the State of Virginia* (1785), ed. William Peden (Chapel Hill, NC, 1982), pp. 96 (Indians), 138–9 (Africans); Jordan, *White over Black*, ch. 12.

Chapter 9: Empire and State

At various points in the writing of this essay I have benefited from the thought-provoking comments of David Armitage, Huw Bowen, Michael Braddick, Stephen Conway, John H. Elliott, Peter J. Marshall, James Muldoon, Malyn Newitt, and Christopher Tomlins. To each I am grateful for the improvements their suggestions prompted, while I alone am responsible for any shortcomings.

1. Frances Gardiner Davenport, ed., *European Treaties Bearing on the History of the United States and its Dependencies*, 4 vols. (Washington, DC, 1917–37), vol. 1, p. 3.
2. James Muldoon, *Empire and Order: The Concept of Empire, 800–1800* (New York, 1999), pp. 139–49, and David Armitage, *The Ideological Origins of the British Empire* (Cambridge, 2000), pp. 3–4.
3. Jack P. Greene, 'Negotiated Authorities: The Problem of Governance in the Extended Polities of the Early Modern Atlantic World', in *Negotiated Authorities: Essays in Colonial Political and Constitutional History* (Charlottesville, Va., 1994), pp. 1–24; John H. Elliott, 'A Europe of Composite Monarchies', *PP*, 137 (1992) 48–71; and Elliott, 'Empire and State in British and Spanish America', in Serge Gruzinski and Nathan Wachtel, eds., *Le Nouveau Monde – Mondes Nouveaux: L'expérience américaine* (Paris, 1996), pp. 365–82.
4. The ideas in this paragraph are derived from Michael J. Braddick, *State Formation in Early Modern England, c. 1550–1700* (Cambridge, 2000), pp. 9–100.

5. K. R. Andrews, *Trade, Plunder and Settlement: Maritime Enterprise and the Genesis of the British Empire, 1480–1630* (Cambridge, 1984), pp. 10–17.

6. Michael J. Braddick, 'The English Government, War, Trade, and Settlement, 1625–1688', in Nicholas P. Canny, ed., *The Oxford History of the British Empire*, vol. 1, *The Origins of Empire: British Overseas Enterprise to the Close of the Seventeenth Century* (Oxford, 1998), pp. 286–308; Philip B. Boucher, *Les Nouvelles Frances: France in America, 1500–1815: An Imperial Perspective* (Providence, RI, 1989), pp. 43–60.

7. Suzerainty is the highest authority over a territory, while sovereignty implies the highest authority over and ultimate ownership of a territory.

8. Max Savelle, *The Origins of American Diplomacy: The International History of Angloamerica, 1492–1763* (New York, 1967), *passim*, and Elizabeth Mancke, 'Oceanic Space and the Creation of a Global International System, c.1450–1800', paper presented at the Anglo-American Conference of Historians, London, July 2001.

9. Davenport, *European Treaties*, vol. 1, pp. 56–100.

10. Scholarship on the ideology of empire often emphasizes manifestations of Christian mission in the extra-European world. For example, see Anthony Pagden, *Lords of All the World: Ideologies of Empire in Spain, Britain and France, c. 1500–1800* (New Haven, Conn., 1995). The intellectual underpinnings of state formation were also strongly influenced by Europe's Roman Catholic heritage; see Muldoon, *Empire and Order, passim*, and Thomas B. Brady, 'The Rise of Merchant Empires, 1400–1700: A European Counterpoint', in James D. Tracy, ed., *The Political Economy of Merchant Empires: State Power and World Trade, 1350–1750* (Cambridge, 1991), pp. 117–60. In the diplomatic arena, however, state authority superseded religious institutions in the sixteenth century.

11. Davenport, *European Treaties*, vol. 1, pp. 219–22.

12. Anne Pérotin-Dumon, 'The Pirate and the Emperor: Power and the Law on the Seas, 1450–1850', in Tracy, ed., *The Political Economy of Merchant Empires*, pp. 196–227.

13. M. N. Pearson, 'Merchants and States', in Tracy, ed., *The Political Economy of Merchant Empires*, pp. 87–94.

14. C. G. Roelofsen, 'Grotius and the International Politics of the Seventeenth Century', in Hedley Bull, Benedict Kingsbury, and Adam Roberts, eds., *Hugo Grotius and International Relations* (Oxford, 1990), pp. 95–131; Armitage, *The Ideological Origins of the British Empire*, pp. 109–16; and Savelle, *The Origins of American Diplomacy*, pp. 193–231.

15. See Adam Watson, 'European International Society and Its Expansion', in Hedley Bull and Adam Watson, eds., *The Expansion of International Society* (Oxford, 1984), pp. 13–32.

16. Braddick, 'The English Government, War, Trade, and Settlement, 1625–1688', pp. 292–6.

17. On the emergence of political economy see Armitage, *The Ideological Origins of the British Empire*, pp. 146–69. Diplomacy is largely unstudied

282 Notes

as a transaction cost. For other transaction costs see Russell R. Menard,
'Transport Costs and Long-Range Trade, 1300–1800: Was There a
European "Transportation Revolution" in the Early Modern Era?', in
Tracy, ed., *The Political Economy of Merchant Empires*, pp. 228–75; and
Jacob M. Price, 'Transaction Costs: A Note on Merchant Credit and
the Organization of Private Trade', in ibid., pp. 276–97.

18. See Joyce Lorimer, ed., *English and Irish Settlement on the River Amazon,
1550–1646* (London, 1989); and Robert Bliss, *Revolution and Empire:
English Politics and the American Colonies in the Seventeenth Century*
(Manchester, 1990), pp. 86–92.

19. Bliss, *Revolution and Empire*, pp. 86–92; Ian K. Steele, 'The British
Parliament and the Atlantic Colonies to 1760: New Approaches to
Enduring Questions', in Philip Lawson, ed., *Parliament and the Atlantic
Empire* (Edinburgh, 1995), pp. 36–8. The French had the same
problem with colonists using Dutch shipping and financial services; see
Boucher, *Les Nouvelles Frances*, pp. 44–8.

20. Robert C. Ritchie, *The Duke's Province: A Study of New York Politics
and Society, 1664–1691* (Chapel Hill, NC, 1977), pp. 9–24.

21. Davenport, *European Treaties*, vol. 1, pp. 246–57.

22. W. J. Eccles, *France in America*, rev. edn (Markham, Ont., 1990),
pp. 12–17; David B. Quinn, 'James I and the Beginnings of Empire in
America', *JICH*, 2 (1974) 235–52.

23. Eccles, *France in America*, pp. 17–18, 29–33; Philip Lawson, *The East
India Company: A History* (London, 1993), pp. 31–2.

24. Savelle, *The Origins of American Diplomacy*, pp. 46–50; Davenport,
European Treaties, vol. 2, pp. 329–46.

25. Richard S. Dunn, *Sugar and Slaves: The Rise of the Planter Class in the
English West Indies, 1624–1713* (Chapel Hill, NC, 1972), pp. 155–7;
Eccles, *France in America*, pp. 98–9; Robert C. Ritchie, *Captain Kidd
and the War against the Pirates* (Cambridge, Mass., 1986), pp. 170–8; and
Ian K. Steele, *The Politics of Colonial Policy: The Board of Trade in
Colonial Administration, 1696–1720* (Oxford, 1968), pp. 42–59.

26. The Treaty of Ryswick, which ended the Nine Years War (1689–97),
had also been multilateral, but in most instances it provided for a return to
status quo antebellum – and thus ambiguity – rather than a reconciliation
of claims; see Savelle, *The Origins of American Diplomacy*, pp. 135–40.

27. Armitage, *The Ideological Origins of the British Empire*, pp. 109–16.

28. Alan Frost, 'The Spanish Yoke: British Schemes to Revolutionise Spanish
America, 1739–1807', in Alan Frost and Jane Samson, eds., *Pacific Empires:
Essays in Honour of Glyndwr Williams* (Vancouver, 1999), pp. 33–52.

29. Richard Pares, *War and Trade in the West Indies, 1739–1763* (Oxford,
1936), pp. 1–64; Davenport, *European Treaties*, vol. 4, pp. 78–80.

30. Glyndwr Williams, 'The Pacific: Exploration and Exploitation', in
P. J. Marshall, ed., *The Oxford History of the British Empire*, vol. 2, *The
Eighteenth Century* (Oxford, 1998), pp. 552–75.

31. Andrews, *Trade, Plunder and Settlement, passim*; Quinn, 'James I and the Beginnings of Empire in America', pp. 235–52.
32. Much of the argument of the next four paragraphs is developed at greater length in Elizabeth Mancke, 'Negotiating an Empire: Britain and its Overseas Peripheries, c.1550–1780', in Christine Daniels and Michael Kennedy, eds., *Negotiated Empires: Centers and Peripheries in the New World, 1500–1820* (New York, 2002).
33. Wesley Frank Craven, *The Dissolution of the Virginia Company: The Failure of a Colonial Experiment* (Oxford, 1932), pp. 251–336; Bliss, *Revolution and Empire*, pp. 13–15, 18–23.
34. Charles M. Andrews, *The Colonial Period of American History*, 4 vols. (New Haven, Conn., 1934), vol. 1, pp. 419–24; Philip S. Haffenden, 'The Crown and the Colonial Charters, 1675–1688', *WMQ*, 3rd ser., 15 (1958) 297–311, 452–66.
35. John J. McCusker and Russell R. Menard, *The Economy of British America, 1607–1789* (Chapel Hill, NC, 1985), pp. 108, 130, 160, 174, 199.
36. Alison Gilbert Olson, *Making the Empire Work: London and American Interest Groups, 1690–1790* (Cambridge, Mass., 1992), pp. 1–50.
37. P. E. H. Hair and Robin Law, 'The English in Western Africa to 1700', in Canny, ed., *Oxford History of the British Empire*, vol. 1, pp. 255–9; Ralph Greenlee Lounsbury, *The British Fishery at Newfoundland, 1634–1763* (New Haven, Conn., 1934), pp. 149–203; Lawson, *The East India Company*, pp. 38–40.
38. Steele, *Politics of Colonial Policy*, pp. 3–18.
39. Bliss, *Revolution and Empire*, pp. 3–15, 18–23, 112, 193; Steele, *Politics of Colonial Policy*, pp. 17–18.
40. Richard B. Sheridan, *Sugar and Slavery: An Economic History of the British West Indies, 1623–1775* (Baltimore, 1973), pp. 218–22; Pares, *War and Trade in the West Indies*, pp. 77–85; and Jack P. Greene, '"A Posture of Hostility": A Reconsideration of Some Aspects of the Origins of the American Revolution', *Proceedings of the American Antiquarian Society*, 87 (1977) 27–68. On the ideological shifts in conceptions of empire during this period see Armitage, *The Ideological Origins of the British Empire*, pp. 170–98.
41. Eliga H. Gould, *The Persistence of Empire: British Political Culture in the Age of the American Revolution* (Chapel Hill, NC, 2000), pp. 35–71.
42. There is almost no scholarship on the impact of the Seven Years War on the balance of power within Britain. Rather, it all concentrates on the dislocations it caused in the empire. Scholars do debate the impact of the American Revolution on political reform in Britain; see Stephen Conway, *The British Isles and the War of American Independence* (Oxford, 2000), pp. 203–38.
43. Dora Mae Clark, *The Rise of the British Treasury: Colonial Administration in the Eighteenth Century* (New Haven, Conn., 1960), pp. 14, 107–10, 167; Mark A. Thomson, *The Secretaries of State, 1681–1782* (Oxford, 1932).

44. Huw V. Bowen, *Revenue and Reform: The Indian Problem in British Politics, 1757–1773* (Cambridge, 1991); and Philip Lawson, *The Imperial Challenge: Quebec and Britain in the Age of the American Revolution* (Kingston and Montreal, 1989), pp. 126–45.
45. [George Johnstone], *Thoughts on our Acquisitions in the East Indies, Particularly Respecting Bengal* (London, 1771), iv, xiii; 'Proceedings in the Commons on the Bill for the Government of Quebec', *Parliamentary History*, vol. 17, col. 1362; and Sir William Meredith, *A Letter to the Earl of Chatham on the Quebec Bill* (London, 1774).
46. Jack P. Greene, *Peripheries and Center: Constitutional Development in the Extended Polities of the British Empire and the United States, 1607–1788* (Athens, Ga., 1986), pp. 55–180.

Chapter 10: Revolution and Counter-Revolution

I wish to thank David Armitage, Bernard Bailyn, Michael Braddick, Sir John Elliott, Nicoletta Gullace, Elizabeth Mancke, and Carla Pestana for their helpful suggestions; thanks also to my parents for timely assistance on the home front.

1. J. G. A. Pocock, ed., *Three British Revolutions: 1641, 1688, 1776* (Princeton, NJ, 1980).
2. British and Irish historians increasingly use 'Atlantic archipelago' as a less metro-centric term for what is popularly known as the British Isles. Because the term has yet to take hold with American historians (or students), I have opted for the more familiar, if slightly less satisfactory, phrase 'British archipelago'.
3. Conrad Russell, *The Fall of the British Monarchies, 1637–1642* (Oxford, 1991); Robert Beddard, ed., *The Revolutions of 1688* (Oxford, 1996); Stephen Conway, *The British Isles and the War of American Independence* (Oxford, 2000).
4. Michael J. Braddick, 'The English Government, War, Trade, and Settlement, 1625–1688', in Nicholas Canny, ed., *The Oxford History of the British Empire*, vol. 1, *The Origins of Empire: British Overseas Enterprise to the Close of the Seventeenth Century* (Oxford, 1998), pp. 286–308; David Armitage, *The Ideological Origins of the British Empire* (Cambridge, 2000).
5. Eliga H. Gould, 'A Virtual Nation: Greater Britain and the Imperial Legacy of the American Revolution', *AHR*, 104 (1999) 476–89.
6. Jack P. Greene, *Peripheries and Center: Constitutional Development in the Extended Polities of the British Empire and the United States, 1607–1788* (Athens, Ga., 1986), pp. 117, 139–40.
7. J. H. Elliott, *The Old World and the New, 1492–1650* (Cambridge, 1970); Stephen Greenblatt, *Marvelous Possessions: The Wonder of the New World* (Chicago, 1991); Jack P. Greene, *The Intellectual Construction of America: Exceptionalism and Identity from 1492 to 1800* (Chapel Hill, NC, 1993), esp. chs. 5 and 6.

8. Carl Lotus Becker, *The History of Political Parties in the Province of New York, 1760–1776* (Madison, Wisc., 1909), p. 22.

9. John Robertson, 'Empire and Union: Two Concepts of the Early Modern European Political Order', in Robertson, ed., *A Union for Empire: Political Thought and the Union of 1707* (Cambridge, 1995), p. 8.

10. John Morrill, *The Revolt of the Provinces: Conservatives and Radicals in the English Civil War, 1630–1650* (London, 1976), pp. 13–51.

11. James Maxwell, *Carolanna* (London, n. d.), sig. C3r, quoted in Arthur H. Williamson, *Scottish National Consciousness in the Age of James VI* (Edinburgh, 1979), p. 106.

12. Thomas Wemyss Fulton, *The Sovereignty of the Sea: An Historical Account of the Claims of England to the Dominion of the British Seas, and of the Evolution of the Territorial Waters* (Edinburgh, 1911), p. 254.

13. The period from the First Bishops' War to the Cromwellian conquest of Scotland; see esp. J. C. Beckett, *The Making of Modern Ireland, 1603–1923* (London, 1963), ch. 4.

14. Ibid., p. 82.

15. Edward M. Furgol, 'The Military and Ministers as Agents of Presbyterian Imperialism in England and Ireland, 1640–1648', in John Dwyer et al., eds., *New Perspectives on the Politics and Culture of Early Modern Scotland* (Edinburgh, 1982), pp. 95–132.

16. 'A solemn league and covenant for reformation and defense of religion, the honour and happiness of the King, and the peace and safety of the three kingdoms of England, Scotland and Ireland', in J. P. Kenyon, ed., *The Stuart Constitution: Documents and Commentary* (Cambridge, 1966), p. 264.

17. Derek Hirst, 'The English Republic and the Meaning of Britain', in Brendan Bradshaw and John Morrill, eds., *The British Problem, c. 1534–1707: State Formation in the Atlantic Archipelago* (London, 1996), pp. 197–8.

18. J. G. A. Pocock, 'The Limits and Divisions of British History: In Search of the Unknown Subject', *AHR*, 87 (1982) 322–3; comments of Thomas Morer, quoted in T. C. Smout, *A History of the Scottish People, 1560–1830* (1969; London, 1972), p. 205.

19. Fulton, *The Sovereignty of the Sea*, p. 247.

20. 'The Petition of Right, 1628', in Kenyon, ed., *The Stuart Constitution*, p. 84.

21. Daniel Baugh, 'Maritime Strength and Atlantic Commerce: The Uses of "A Grand Marine Empire"', in Lawrence Stone, ed., *An Imperial State at War: Britain from 1689 to 1815* (London, 1994), pp. 185–223; Steven C. A. Pincus, *Protestantism and Patriotism: Ideologies and the Making of English Foreign Policy, 1650–1668* (Cambridge, 1996).

22. Hirst, 'The English Republic and the Meaning of Britain', pp. 218–19.

23. John Morrill, *The Nature of the English Revolution* (London, 1993), pp. 23–9; Mark Kishlansky, *A Monarchy Transformed: Britain, 1603–1714* (London, 1996), pp. 189–91.

24. Christopher Hill, *The World Turned Upside Down: Radical Ideas during the English Revolution* (London, 1972).
25. Lois Schwoerer, '*No Standing Armies!': The Anti-Army Ideology in Seventeenth-Century England* (Baltimore, 1974); J. G. A. Pocock, *The Machiavellian Moment: Florentine Political Thought and the Atlantic Republican Tradition* (Princeton, NJ, 1975).
26. Lawrence Stone, 'The Results of the English Revolutions of the Seventeenth Century', in Pocock, ed., *Three British Revolutions*, p. 51.
27. T. C. Barnard, *Cromwellian Ireland: English Government and Reform and Ireland, 1649–1660* (Oxford, 1975).
28. For the Navigation Acts see Zahedieh, 'Economy', Chapter 3 in this volume.
29. John Childs, *The Army, James II and the Glorious Revolution* (Manchester, 1980).
30. J. G. A. Pocock, 'The Significance of 1668: Some Reflections on Whig History', in Beddard, ed., *The Revolutions of 1688*, pp. 271–92.
31. Patrick Kelly, 'Ireland and the Glorious Revolution: From Kingdom to Colony', in Beddard, ed., *The Revolutions of 1688*, pp. 184–90.
32. William Molyneux, *The Case of Ireland's Being Bound by Acts of Parliament in England, Stated* (Dublin, 1698), p. 35.
33. William Ferguson, *Scotland: 1689 to the Present* (Edinburgh, 1968), ch. 1.
34. Smout, *A History of the Scottish People*, pp. 261–81; David Armitage, 'The Scottish Vision of Empire: Intellectual Origins of the Darién Venture', in Robertson, ed., *A Union for Empire*, pp. 97–118.
35. The phrase comes from the title to Robertson's edited volume, *A Union for Empire*, but see esp. Robertson's own essay, 'Empire and Union', pp. 3–36.
36. J. H. Plumb, *The Growth of Political Stability in England, 1675–1725* (London, 1967).
37. Linda Colley, *Britons: Forging the Nation, 1707–1837* (New Haven, Conn., 1992), ch. 1.
38. For Catholic loyalism in Ireland during the American Revolution see esp. Conway, *The British Isles and the War of American Independence*, p. 184.
39. Eliga H. Gould, *The Persistence of Empire: British Political Culture in the Age of the American Revolution* (Chapel Hill, NC, 2000), esp. ch. 1.
40. David S. Lovejoy, *The Glorious Revolution in America* (New York, 1972); Richard S. Dunn, 'The Glorious Revolution and America', in Canny, ed., *Oxford History of the British Empire*, vol. 1, pp. 445–66.
41. Historians of colonial America typically emphasize the gendered, religious, and economic origins of the Salem persecutions; however, a contributing factor was the disarray of the colony's courts brought on by the collapse of the Dominion of New England.
42. Christopher Hill, *The Century of Revolution* (Edinburgh, 1961), p. 70; Jack P. Greene, 'The Glorious Revolution and the British Empire, 1688–1783', in Greene, *Negotiated Authorities: Essays in Colonial Political and Constitutional History* (Charlottesville, Va., 1994), pp. 78–92.

43. Peter Linebaugh and Marcus Rediker, *The Many-Headed Hydra: Sailors, Slaves, Commoners, and the Hidden History of the Revolutionary Atlantic* (Boston, Mass., 2000).

44. The lines of amity were intersecting lines of longitude and latitude customarily situated along the Tropic of Cancer and a meridian lying somewhere to the west of the Azores: see Max Savelle, *The Origins of American Diplomacy: The International History of Angloamerica, 1492–1763* (New York, 1967), esp. ch. 4; see also Mancke, 'Empire and State', Chapter 9 in this volume.

45. Samuel Pufendorf, *De Jure Naturae et Gentium* (1688), vol. 2, 'On the Law of Nature and Nations', trans. C. H. Oldfather and W. A. Oldfather, Carnegie Endowment for International Peace, 2 vols. (Oxford, 1934), bk viii, ch. vii, sect. 3 (p. 1318).

46. Savelle, *Origins of American Diplomacy*, p. 21.

47. David Armitage, 'The Cromwellian Protectorate and the Languages of Empire', *HJ*, 35 (1992) 531–55.

48. On the Irish conquest see Jacqueline Hill, 'Ireland without Union: Molyneux and his Legacy', in Robertson, ed., *A Union for Empire*, pp. 277–84; on the Scottish union see Hirst, 'The English Republic and the Meaning of Britain', in Morrill, ed., *The British Problem*, pp. 199–201.

49. Savelle, *The Origins of American Diplomacy*, pp. 89–90.

50. David Eltis, *The Rise of African Slavery in the Americas* (Cambridge, 2000), pp. 50–2, 236–7.

51. Brown, 'The Politics of Slavery', Chapter 11 in this volume; Robin Blackburn, *The Making of New World Slavery: From the Baroque to the Modern, 1492–1800* (London, 1997), pp. 239, 243–50, 254–5; for the legal status of slaves and slavery in England see David Brion Davis, *The Problem of Slavery in Western Culture* (Oxford, 1966), pp. 207–8.

52. Hilary McD. Beckles, 'The "Hub of Empire": The Caribbean and Britain in the Seventeenth Century', in Canny, ed., *Oxford History of the British Empire*, vol. 1, p. 238; Edmund S. Morgan, *American Slavery, American Freedom: The Ordeal of Colonial Virginia* (New York, 1975), pp. 146–7.

53. Dunn, 'The Glorious Revolution and America', in Canny, ed., *The Origins of Empire*, vol. 1, pp. 447–8.

54 Jill Lepore, *The Name of War: King Philip's War and the Origins of American Identity* (New York, 1998); Morgan, *American Slavery, American Freedom*, esp. chs. 15–16.

55 Ian K. Steele, 'The Anointed, the Appointed, and the Elected: Governance of the British Empire, 1689–1784', in P. J. Marshall, ed., *The Oxford History of the British Empire*, vol. 2, *The Eighteenth Century* (Oxford, 1998), pp. 109–10.

56. James H. Kettner, *The Development of American Citizenship, 1608–1870* (Chapel Hill, NC, 1978), ch. 4; Patricia U. Bonomi, *Under the Cope of Heaven: Religion, Society, and Politics and Colonial America* (Oxford, 1986), pp. 156, 166, 182–3.

57. Robert C. Ritchie, *Captain Kidd and the War against the Pirates* (Cambridge, Mass., 1986); Marcus Rediker, *Between the Devil and the Deep Blue Sea: Merchant Seamen, Pirates, and the Anglo-American Maritime World, 1700–1750* (Cambridge, 1987).

58. Greene, *Peripheries and Center*, p. xi.

59. William Shirley to Henry Fox, March 8, 1756, Huntington Library, San Marino, California, Loudoun Papers LO 867.

60. Bernard Bailyn, 'The Idea of Atlantic History', *Itinerario*, 20 (1996) 26.

61. T. H. Breen, 'Ideology and Nationalism on the Eve of the American Revolution: Revisions *Once More* in Need of Revising', *JAH*, 84 (1997) 13–39; Kathleen Wilson, *The Sense of the People: Politics, Culture, and Imperialism in England, 1715–1785* (Cambridge, 1995), ch. 3.

62. Gould, *The Persistence of Empire*, ch. 4.

63. Ibid.

64. Bernard Bailyn, *The Ideological Origins of the American Revolution* (Cambridge, Mass., 1967).

65. Peter S. Onuf, *Jefferson's Empire: The Language of American Nationhood* (Charlottesville, Va., 2000), pp. 153–4.

66. George Washington to Martha Washington, June 24, 1776, in *Letters from General Washington to Several of his Friends in the Year 1776* (London, 1777), p. 35.

67. John Dickinson, 'Arguments against the Independence of the Colonies …' (July 1, 1776), in Jack P. Greene, ed., *Colonies to Nation, 1763–1789: A Documentary History of the American Revolution* (New York, 1967), p. 295.

68. Eliga H. Gould, 'American Independence and Britain's Counter-Revolution', *PP*, 154 (1997) 124–7; Peter S. Onuf, 'A Declaration of Independence for Diplomatic Historians', *Diplomatic History*, 22 (1998) 71–83; David Armitage, 'The Declaration of Independence and International Law', *WMQ*, 3rd ser., 59 (2002) 39–54.

69. Conway, *The British Isles and the War of American Independence*, p. 346 and *passim*.

70. To Herbert Butterfield, the association movement was the 'revolution we escaped': *George III, Lord North, and the People, 1779–80* (London, 1949), p. iv.

71. Gould, *The Persistence of Empire*, ch. 5.

72. Thomas Wilson to John Wilkes, November 4, 1775, British Library, Add. MS 30871, fol. 248.

73. Colley, *Britons*, ch. 7; but see E. P. Thompson, 'The Making of a Ruling Class', *Dissent*, 40 (1993) 377–82.

74. Colley, *Britons*, p. 317.

75. David Milobar, 'Conservative Ideology, Metropolitan Government, and the Reform of Quebec, 1782–1791', *International History Review*, 12 (1990) 45–64; see also P. J. Marshall, 'Empire and Authority in the Later Eighteenth Century', *JICH*, 15 (1987) 105–22.

76. C. A. Bayly, *Imperial Meridian: The British Empire and the World, 1780–1830* (London, 1989), pp. 193–209.
77. Gould, *The Persistence of Empire*, p. 212.
78. James Kelly, *Prelude to Union: Anglo-Irish Politics in the 1780s* (Cork, 1992).
79. This was certainly Lord Sheffield's opinion: see John [Holroyd], Lord Sheffield, *Observations on the Commerce of the American States*, rev. edn (New York, 1970), pp. 174–9, esp. 177; see also Andrew Jackson O'Shaughnessy, *An Empire Divided: The American Revolution and the British Caribbean* (Philadelphia, 2000).
80. Peter J. Cain and Anthony G. Hopkins, *British Imperialism: Innovation and Expansion, 1688–1914* (London, 1993), ch. 9.
81. Ibid., p. 90; John E. Crowley, *The Privileges of Independence: Neomercantilism and the American Revolution* (Baltimore, 1993), ch. 4.
82. David Brion Davis, *The Problem of Slavery in the Age of Revolution, 1770–1823* (Ithaca, NY, 1975), pp. 373–85; Christopher L. Brown, 'Empire without Slaves: British Concepts of Emancipation in the Age of the American Revolution', *WMQ*, 3rd ser., 56 (1999) 273–306.
83. Gould, 'A Virtual Nation', pp. 485–9; D. George Boyce, *Decolonization and the British Empire, 1775–1997* (New York, 1999), ch. 2.

Chapter 11: The Politics of Slavery

Research for this essay was facilitated by a Senior Fellowship at the Gilder Lehrman Center for the Study of Slavery, Resistance, and Abolition at Yale University and a research fellowship at the Huntington Library sponsored by the Omohundro Institute for Early American History and Culture (OIEAHC). Early drafts drew helpful comments from David Armitage, Bernard Bailyn, Kristen Block, Eliga Gould, Jane Ohlmeyer, Simon Newman, Sarah Pearsall, Carla Pestana, and the audience for the panel on 'Aspiration and Experience in the British Atlantic World' at the seventh annual conference of the OIEAHC in July 2001. I owe special thanks to Kristen Block and Lesley Doig of Rutgers University for assistance in tracking down the pertinent scholarship.

1. Ira Berlin, 'Time, Space, and the Evolution of Afro-American Society in British Mainland North America', *AHR*, 85 (1980) 45; Berlin, *Many Thousands Gone: The First Two Centuries of Slavery in North America* (Cambridge, Mass., 1998); Philip D. Morgan, *Slave Counterpoint: Black Culture in the Eighteenth-Century Chesapeake and Lowcountry* (Chapel Hill, NC, 1998); Robin Blackburn, *The Overthrow of Colonial Slavery* (London, 1988); Blackburn, *The Making of New World Slavery: From the Baroque to the Modern* (New York, 1997).
2. James Oakes, 'Slaves Without Contexts', *Journal of the Early Republic*, 19 (1999) 103–9.

3. Merton Dillon, *Slavery Attacked: Southern Slaves and their Allies, 1619–1865* (Baton Rouge, Ind., 1990) represents a notable exception.
4. David Geggus, *Slavery, War, and Revolution: The British Occupation of Saint Domingue* (Oxford, 1982); Sylvia Frey, *Water From the Rock: Black Resistance in a Revolutionary Age* (Princeton, NJ, 1991); Jane G. Landers, *Black Society in Spanish Florida* (Urbana, Ill., 1999); Robert Olwell, *Masters, Slaves, and Subjects: The Culture of Power in the South Carolina Low Country* (Ithaca, NY, 1998); Woody Holton, *Forced Founders: Indians, Debtors, Slaves and the Making of the American Revolution in Virginia* (Chapel Hill, NC, 1997); Jeffrey Robert Young, *Domesticating Slavery: The Master Class in Georgia and South Carolina, 1607–1837* (Chapel Hill, NC, 1999); Andrew J. O'Shaughnessy, *An Empire Divided: The American Revolution and the British Caribbean* (Philadelphia, 2000).
5. Frank Tannenbaum, *Slave and Citizen: The Negro in the Americas* (Boston, Mass., 1946) p. 117.
6. Eric Williams, *Capitalism and Slavery* (Chapel Hill, NC, 1944); Stanley L. Engerman and Barbara L. Solow, eds., *British Capitalism and Caribbean Slavery: The Legacy of Eric Williams* (Cambridge, 1987).
7. For the planter class at the apex of its political power in the eighteenth century see Olwell on South Carolina, O'Shaughnessy on the British Caribbean, and, for Virginia, Allan Kulikoff, *Tobacco and Slaves: The Development of Southern Cultures in the Chesapeake, 1680–1800* (Chapel Hill, NC, 1986), esp. ch. 7.
8. David Hancock has shown how fortunes earned from trade with the colonies helped several men from modest backgrounds attain seats in the House of Commons during the middle decades of the eighteenth century. Hancock, *Citizens of the World: London Merchants and the Integration of the British Atlantic Community, 1735–1785* (Cambridge, 1995).
9. Richard B. Sheridan, *Sugar and Slavery: An History of the British West Indies, 1623–1775 (Barbados, 1974)*, p. 60.
10. John Brewer, *The Sinews of Power: War, Money, and the English State, 1688–1783* (New York, 1989), p. 98.
11. Don E. Fehrenbacher, *The Slaveholding Republic: An Account of the United States Government's Relations to Slavery* (Oxford, 2001).
12. In addition to the works by Geggus and O'Shaughnessy cited in n. 4 above, see Richard Pares, *War and Trade in the West Indies, 1739–1763* (Oxford, 1936); Michael Duffy, *Soldiers, Sugar, and Seapower: The British Expeditions to the Caribbean and the War against Revolutionary France* (Oxford, 1987); and Roger N. Buckley, *Slaves in Red Coats: The British West India Regiments, 1795–1815* (New Haven, Conn., 1979).
13. Dale H. Porter, *The Abolition of the Slave Trade in England, 1784–1807* (Hamden, Conn., 1974); Joyce E. Chaplin, *An Anxious Pursuit: Agricultural Innovation and Modernity in the Lower South, 1730–1815* (Chapel Hill, NC, 1993); Gordon K. Lewis, *Main Currents in Caribbean*

Thought: The Historical Evolution of Caribbean Society in its Ideological Aspects (Baltimore, 1983), chs. 2, 3; Larry Tise, *Proslavery: A History of the Defense of Slavery in America, 1701–1840* (Athens, Ga., 1987).

14. Linda Colley, *Britons: Forging the Nation, 1707–1838* (New Haven, Conn., 1992), pp. 350–5; David Brion Davis, *The Problem of Slavery in the Age of Revolution, 1770-1823* (Ithaca, NY, 1975); Davis, *Slavery and Human Progress* (Oxford, 1984); Clare Midgley, *Women Against Slavery in the British Campaigns, 1788–1870* (London, 1992); Seymour Drescher, *Capitalism and Antislavery: British Mobilization in Comparative Perspective* (London, 1987); Lowell Joseph Ragatz, *A Guide to the Study of British Caribbean History, 1763–1834, Including the Abolition and Emancipation Movements* (Washington, DC, 1932).

15. Hilary McD. Beckles, *White Servitude and Black Slavery in Barbados, 1627–1715* (Knoxville, Tenn., 1975); Beckles, 'The Concept of "White Slavery" in the English Caribbean during the Early Seventeenth Century', in John Brewer and Susan Staves, eds., *Early Modern Conceptions of Property* (London, 1995), pp. 572–83; Robert J. Steinfeld, *The Invention of Free Labor: The Employment Relation in English and American Law and Culture, 1350–1870* (Chapel Hill, NC, 1991), chs. 2 and 3.

16. Richard S. Dunn, *Sugar and Slaves: The Rise of the Planter Class in the English West Indies, 1624–1713* (Chapel Hill, NC, 1972).

17. Beckles, *White Servitude and Black Slavery in Barbados*, pp. 38–9; Dunn, *Sugar and Slaves*, pp. 88–100, 133–4, 156–63; Kathleen M. Brown, *Good Wives, Nasty Women, and Anxious Patriarchs: Gender, Race, and Power in Colonial Virginia* (Chapel Hill, NC, 1996), pp. 137–86.

18. For the British Caribbean, see Michael Craton, *Testing the Chains: Resistance to Slavery in the British West Indies* (Ithaca, NY, 1982). On South Carolina see Peter Wood, *Black Majority: Negroes in Colonial South Carolina* (New York, 1975), pp. 308–26. The cycle of unrest in the 1730s and 1740s is detailed in Peter Linebaugh and Marcus Rediker, *The Many-Headed Hydra: Sailors, Slaves, Commoners, and the Hidden History of the Revolutionary Atlantic* (Boston, Mass., 2000), pp. 193–8.

19. Frank Wesley Pitman, *The Development of the British West Indies, 1700–1763* (New Haven, Conn., 1917); Sheridan, *Sugar and Slavery*, pp. 54–74; Tim Keirn, 'Monopoly, Economic Thought, and the Royal African Company', in Brewer and Staves, eds., *Early Modern Conceptions of Property*, pp. 427–45; K. G. Davies, *The Royal African Company* (London, 1957), pp. 97–152; Rebecca Starr, *A School for Politics: Commercial Lobbying and Political Culture in Early South Carolina* (Baltimore, 1998), pp. 28–9.

20. Jon Butler, *Awash in a Sea of Faith: Christianizing the American People* (Cambridge, Mass., 1990), pp. 132–51; Sylvia R. Frey and Betty Wood, *Come Shouting to Zion: African American Protestantism in the American South and British Caribbean to 1830* (Chapel Hill, NC, 1998), pp. 63–79.

21. Jack P. Greene, "'A Plain and Natural Right to Life and Liberty'": An Early Natural Rights Attack on the Excesses of the Slave System in Colonial British America', *WMQ*, 3rd ser., 57 (2000) 793–803; *The Gentleman's Magazine*, 11 (March 1741) 145–7.
22. Christopher L. Brown, 'The Ends of Innocence: Slavery, Politics, and the Idea of Moral Responsibility, 1764–1783', paper prepared for the International Seminar on the History of the Atlantic World, 1500–1800 at Harvard University, Cambridge, Massachusetts, August 17, 2000; Brown, 'Empire Without Slaves: British Concepts of Emancipation in the Age of the American Revolution', *WMQ*, 3rd ser., 56 (1999) 273–306.
23. Jack P. Greene, 'Liberty, Slavery, and the Transformation of British Identity in the Eighteenth-Century West Indies', *Slavery and Abolition*, 21 (2000) 1–31; Michal J. Rozbicki, 'The Curse of Provincialism: Negative Perceptions of Colonial American Plantation Gentry', *Journal of Southern History*, 43 (1997) 727–52.
24. Lowell Joseph Ragatz, *The Fall of the Planter Class in the British Caribbean* (New York, 1928); Williams, *Capitalism and Slavery*, pp. 169–96.
25. Seymour Drescher, *Econocide: British Slavery in the Age of Abolition* (Pittsburgh, Pa., 1977); Drescher, *From Slavery to Freedom: Comparative Studies in the Rise and Fall of Atlantic Slavery* (New York, 1999), pp. 87–115, 379–98; David Eltis, *Economic Growth and the Ending of the Transatlantic Slave Trade* (Oxford, 1987).
26. Ragatz, *The Fall of the Planter Class in the British Caribbean*, pp. 173–285; Buckley, *Slaves in Red Coats*.
27. Roger Anstey, *The Atlantic Slave Trade and British Abolition, 1760–1810* (Atlantic Highlands, NJ, 1975), parts 2, 3 and 4; Drescher, *Capitalism and Antislavery*.
28. Frey and Wood, *Come Shouting to Zion*, pp. 129–39; Michael Craton, *Empire, Enslavement, and Freedom in the Caribbean* (Jamaica, 1997), pp. 263–305.
29. Michael Craton, *Testing the Chains: Resistance to Slavery in the British West Indies* (Ithaca, NY, 1982).

Afterword: Atlantic History: A Circumnavigation

1. See above p. 11.
2. Ian K. Steele, *The English Atlantic, 1675–1740* (Oxford, 1986), pp. 14–15.
3. For the pre-history of the concept, see Bernard Bailyn, 'The Idea of Atlantic History', *Itinerario*, 20 (1996) 19–44.
4. Above, p. 12.
5. In this, and passages that follow, I repeat or develop points that I made in a lecture (October 2000) to a Spanish-speaking audience and published as a booklet, *En búsqueda de la historia atlántica* (Ediciones del Cabildo de Gran Canaria, Las Palmas de Gran Canaria, 2001).

6. D. W. Meinig, *The Shaping of America*, vol. 1, *Atlantic America, 1492–1800* (New Haven, Conn., 1986), esp. pp. 55–65.

7. Richard Pares, *War and Trade in the West Indies, 1739–1763* (Oxford, 1936); Pares, *A West-India Fortune* (London, 1950).

8. Huguette and Pierre Chaunu, *Séville et l'Atlantique, 1504–1650*, 8 vols. (Paris, 1955–9).

9. Philip D. Curtin, *The Atlantic Slave Trade: A Census* (Madison, Wis., 1969); Robin Blackburn, *The Making of New World Slavery: From the Baroque to the Modern, 1492–1800* (London, 1997); David Eltis, *The Rise of African Slavery in the Americas* (Cambridge, 2000).

10. Alison Games, *Migration and the Origins of the English Atlantic World* (Cambridge, Mass., 1999).

11. Anthony Pagden, *Lords of All the World* (New Haven, Conn., 1995).

12. Patricia Seed, *Ceremonies of Possession in Europe's Conquest of the New World, 1492–1640* (Cambridge, 1995).

13. Games, 'Migration', p. 44 above.

14. Sebastián de Covarrubias, *Tesoro de la lengua castellana o española*, ed. Martín de Riquer (Barcelona, 1989).

15. Pearsall, 'Gender', p. 121 above.

16. For a possible approach to this question see John Elliott, *Britain and Spain in America: Colonists and Colonized* (The Stenton Lecture, University of Reading, 1994), pp. 8–12.

17. J. Vicens Vives, *Historia social y económica de España y de América* (Barcelona, 1957–9).

18. The Chilean historian Mario Góngora is an outstanding example of a Latin American historian concerned to relate the histories of metropolis and colonies. See in particular his *Studies in the Colonial History of Spanish America* (Cambridge, 1975).

19. J. G. A. Pocock, 'British History: A Plea for a New Subject', *Journal of Modern History*, 47 (1975) 601–24.

20. See for example David Beers Quinn, *The Elizabethans and the Irish* (Ithaca, NY, 1966), and Nicholas Canny, *Kingdom and Colony: Ireland in the Atlantic World, 1560–1800* (Baltimore, 1988).

21. Alison Gilbert Olson, *Making the Empire Work: London and American Interest Groups, 1690–1790* (Cambridge, Mass., 1992).

22. See my *En búsqueda de la historia atlántica* for suggestions of possible ways of widening the approach to the study of the Hispanic Atlantic community.

23. Gould, 'Revolution and Counter-Revolution', p. 196 above.

24. David Armitage, *The Ideological Origins of the British Empire* (Cambridge, 2000).

25. See J. H. Elliott, 'A Europe of Composite Monarchies', *PP*, 137 (1992) 48–71.

26. Mancke, 'Empire and State', p. 177 above.

27. Braddick, 'Civility and Authority', p. 109 above.

28. Mancke, 'Empire and State', pp. 181–2 above.
29. Claudia Schnurmann, *Atlantische Welten* (Cologne, 1998).
30. See Fred Anderson, *Crucible of War: The Seven Years' War and the Fate of the Empire in British North America, 1754–1766* (New York, 2000), esp. ch. 32.
31. Gould, 'Revolution and Counter-Revolution', p. 207 above.
32. Michel Morineau, *Incroyables Gazettes et Fabuleux Métaux* (Cambridge and Paris, 1985), Table 57 (p. 377).
33. John J. McCusker and Russell R. Menard, *The Economy of British America, 1607–1789* (Chapel Hill, NC, 1985), p. 339.
34. See Stanley J. Stein and Barbara H. Stein, *Silver, Trade and War: Spain and America in the Making of Early Modern Europe* (Baltimore, 2000).
35. Steele, *The English Atlantic*.
36. See above, p. 238.
37. Games, 'Migration', p. 46 above.
38. James Lockhart and Enrique Otte, *Letters and People of the Spanish Indies* (Cambridge, 1976).
39. Enrique Otte, *Cartas privadas de emigrantes a Indias* (Seville, 1988), from which the letters in Lockhart and Otte are taken; Isabelo Macías and Francisco Morales Padrón, *Cartas desde América, 1700* (Seville, 1991); Rocío Sánchez Rubio and Isabel Testón, *El hilo que une* (Junta de Extremadura, Mérida, 1999).
40. Games, 'Migration', p. 34 above.
41. Otte, *Cartas privadas*, letter 571 (January 20, 1584).
42. George M. Foster, *Culture and Conquest: America's Spanish Heritage* (Chicago, 1960).
43. See William L. Sachse, 'The Migration of New Englanders to England, 1640–1660', *AHR*, 53 (1948) 251–78; Sachse, 'Harvard Men in England, 1642–1714', *Publications of the Colonial Society of Massachusetts*, 35 (*Transactions*, 1942–6) 119–44.
44. Chaplin, 'Race', p. 162 above; Brown, 'The Politics of Slavery', pp. 222–3 above.
45. Chaplin, 'Race', p. 162 above.
46. Jorge Cañizares-Esguerra, 'New World, New Stars: Patriotic Astrology and the Invention of Indian and Creole Bodies in Colonial Spanish America, 1600–1650', *AHR*, 104 (1999) 33–68.
47. See Elliott, *Britain and Spain in America*, and John Canup, *Out of the Wilderness: The Origins of an American Identity in Colonial New England* (Middletown, Conn., 1990), pp. 79–81.
48. Chaplin, 'Race', p. 190 above.
49. Gould, 'Revolution and Counter-Revolution', p. 210 above.
50. Wrightson, 'Class', p. 153 above.

Further Reading

Chapter 1: Three Concepts of Atlantic History

The history of the British Atlantic world cannot be separated from Atlantic history as a whole or from oceanic history more generally. Useful introductions to the problems and prospects of Atlantic history can be found in three recent collections of journal articles: 'The Nature of Atlantic History', *Itinerario*, 23/2 (1999); 'Forum: The New British History in Atlantic Perspective', *AHR*, 104/2 (1999) 426–500; and 'Oceans Connect', *Geographical Review*, 89/2 (April 1999). For magisterial overviews see Bernard Bailyn, 'The Idea of Atlantic History', *Itinerario*, 20 (1996) 19–44, Jack P. Greene, 'Beyond Power: Paradigm Subversion and Reformulation and the Re-Creation of the Early Modern Atlantic World', in Greene, *Interpreting Early America: Historiographical Essays* (Charlottesville, Va., 1996), pp. 17–42, and Nicholas Canny, 'Writing Atlantic History, or, Reconfiguring the History of Colonial British America', *JAH*, 86 (1999) 1093–114. For other models of oceanic history see, for example, Fernand Braudel, *The Mediterranean and the Mediterranean World in the Age of Philip II*, trans. Siân Reynolds, 2 vols. (London, 1973), O. H. K. Spate, *The Pacific Since Magellan*, vol. 1, *The Spanish Lake* (London, 1979), and Ashin Das Gupta and M. N. Pearson, eds., *India and the Indian Ocean, 1500–1800* (Calcutta, 1987).

For varying approaches to the black Atlantic see Paul Gilroy, *The Black Atlantic: Modernity and Double Consciousness* (Cambridge, Mass., 1993), Joseph Roach, *Cities of the Dead: Circum-Atlantic Performance* (New York, 1996), John Thornton, *Africa and Africans in the Making of the Atlantic World, 1400–1800*, 2nd edn (Cambridge, 1999), and David Eltis, *The Rise of African Slavery in the Americas* (Cambridge, 2000); Robin D. G. Kelley, '"But a Local Phase of a World Problem": Black History's Global Vision, 1883–1950', *JAH*, 86 (1999) 1045–77 traces its earlier history. For contrasting versions of the history of the white Atlantic see D. W. Meinig, *Atlantic America, 1492–1800* (New Haven, Conn., 1986), Paul Butel, *The Atlantic*, trans. Iain Hamilton Grant (London, 1999), and David Hancock, *Citizens of the World: London Merchants and the Integration of the British Atlantic Community, 1735–1785* (Cambridge, 1995).

The three outstanding circum-Atlantic histories of the anglophone Atlantic world are Alison Games, *Migration and the Origins of the English Atlantic World* (Cambridge, Mass., 1999), Ian K. Steele, *The English Atlantic: An Exploration of Communication and Community, 1675–1740* (New York, 1981), and Bernard Bailyn, *Voyagers to the West: A Passage in the Peopling of America on the Eve of the American Revolution* (New York, 1987). Trans-Atlantic studies have tended to treat religious, commercial, and intellectual connections, as in the work of

Stephen Foster, *The Long Argument: English Puritanism and the Shaping of New England Culture, 1570–1700* (Chapel Hill, NC, 1991), Leigh Eric Schmidt, *Holy Fairs: Scottish Communions and American Revivals in the Early Modern Period* (Princeton, NJ, 1989), T. H. Breen, '"Baubles of Britain": The American and Consumer Revolutions of the Eighteenth Century', *PP*, 119 (1988) 73–104, Carole Shammas, *The Pre-Industrial Consumer in England and America* (Oxford, 1990), Bernard Bailyn, *The Ideological Origins of the American Revolution*, 2nd edn (Cambridge, Mass., 1992), and J. G. A. Pocock, *The Machiavellian Moment: Florentine Political Thought and the Atlantic Republican Tradition* (Princeton, NJ, 1975). Cis-Atlantic histories remain few and largely confined to studies of port towns: see, for example, Franklin W. Knight and Peggy Liss, eds., *Atlantic Port Cities: Economy, Culture, and Society in the Atlantic World, 1650–1850* (Knoxville, Tenn., 1991) and David Harris Sacks, *The Widening Gate: Bristol and the Atlantic Economy, 1450–1700* (Berkeley, Calif., 1991).

Chapter 2: Migration

The study of migration is first and foremost the study of population: for England, the definitive work remains E. A. Wrigley and R. S. Schofield, *Population History of England, 1541–1871* (Cambridge, 1981). On the intersection between population growth, migration, and urbanization, see the classic formulation by E. A. Wrigley, 'A Simple Model of London's Importance in Changing English Society and Economy', *PP*, 37 (1967) 44–70. For the study of British migration more generally in this period, a wonderful starting point is Ian D. Whyte's recent synthesis, *Migration and Society in Britain, 1550–1830* (London, 2000). Whyte's focus is internal migration within Britain, but his volume can be supplemented with a number of essays on British migration overseas. See especially Nicholas Canny, 'English Migration Into and Across the Atlantic in the Seventeenth and Eighteenth Centuries', T. C. Smout, Ned C. Landsman, and T. M. Devine, 'Scottish Emigration in the Seventeenth and Eighteenth Centuries', and Louis M. Cullen, 'The Irish Diaspora of the Seventeenth and Eighteenth Centuries', all in Nicholas Canny, ed., *Europeans on the Move: Studies on European Migration, 1500–1800* (Oxford, 1994). James Horn has written several essays on British migration in all parts of the Atlantic world, including 'British Diaspora: Emigration from Britain, 1680–1815', in P. J. Marshall, ed., *The Oxford History of the British Empire*, vol. 2, *The Eighteenth Century* (Oxford, 1998).

British (especially English) migration to America has been treated in a variety of specialized studies of particular regions in America. For broad overviews, see for the seventeenth century Alison Games, *Migration and the Origins of the English Atlantic World* (Cambridge, Mass., 1999), and for the eighteenth century Bernard Bailyn, *Voyagers to the West: A Passage in the Peopling of America on the Eve of the Revolution* (New York, 1986). Non-British European migrants to British America are the focus of Aaron Spencer Fogleman's study, *Hopeful Journeys: German Immigration, Settlement, and Political Culture in Colonial America, 1717–1775* (Philadelphia, 1996), and a number of other books focus on German-speaking migrants, including Marianne S. Wokeck's twin study of German and Irish migration, *Trade in Strangers: The Beginning of Mass Migration to North America* (University Park, Pa., 1999). Scholarship on the migration of Africans within the British Atlantic world tends to be subsumed within larger works on the transatlantic slave trade as a whole, but for those interested especially in the British Atlantic world, David Eltis, *The Rise of African Slavery in the Americas* (Cambridge, 2000), is the definitive starting point.

Efforts to accommodate Africans and Native Americans within a larger story of migration in the British Atlantic are at a formative stage. David Eltis has done much to point the way in this regard. Similarly, James Horn's and Philip D. Morgan's 'Settlers and Slaves: European and African Migrations to Early Modern British America', in Carole Shammas and Elizabeth Mancke, eds., *The Creation of the British Atlantic World* (Baltimore, forthcoming) provides an initial formulation of the contours of migration and the fruitful possibilities for considering different migrant populations in tandem. Scholars who have insisted on the conceptualization of Native Americans as migrants include especially Colin G. Calloway, who has explicitly posited Native Americans as migrants in a number of studies, particularly *The Western Abenakis of Vermont, 1600–1800: War, Migration, and the Survival of an Indian People* (Norman, Okla., 1990) and *New Worlds for All: Indians, Europeans, and the Remaking of Early America* (Baltimore, 1997), particularly ch. 7; and James H. Merrell, *The Indians' New World: Catawbas and Their Neighbors from European Contact through the Era of Removal* (Chapel Hill, NC, 1989). Migration and displacement are central themes of Merrell's study.

The relationship between migration patterns, the endurance of Old World cultural forms, and the configuration of colonial cultures is complicated and contested. For good starting points to the issues raised briefly in this essay see for Africans in the Americas Sidney W. Mintz and Richard Price, *The Birth of African-American Culture: An Anthropological Perspective* (Boston, Mass., 1992); for Native Americans and Europeans together see especially Calloway, *New Worlds for All*; and for all three populations of British America see particularly T. H. Breen, 'Creative Adaptations: Peoples and Cultures', in Jack P. Greene and J. R. Pole, eds., *Colonial British America: Essays in the New History of the Early Modern Era* (Baltimore, 1984), pp. 195–232.

Chapter 3: Economy

The British Atlantic economy took firm shape in the seventeenth century but rested on earlier initiatives. Kenneth R. Andrews offers a comprehensive account of early English enterprise in *Trade, Plunder and Settlement: Maritime Enterprise and the Genesis of the British Empire* (Cambridge, 1984). Nuala Zahedieh's chapter in Nicholas Canny, ed., *The Oxford History of the*

British Empire, vol. 1, *The Origins of Empire: English Overseas Enterprise from the Beginning to the Close of the Seventeenth Century* (Oxford, 1998) provides an overview of the British Atlantic economy in the seventeenth century, and Jacob M. Price's chapter in P. J. Marshall, ed., *The Oxford History of the British Empire,* vol. 2, *The Eighteenth Century* (Oxford, 1998) does the same for the eighteenth century. The colonial export trades are used to provide an organizational framework for John J. McCusker and Russell R. Menard, *The Economy of British North America, 1607–1789* (Chapel Hill, NC, 1985), which provides an excellent introduction to its subject, a large amount of valuable statistical material, and a useful bibliography, updated in a second edition of 1991.

The most thorough introduction to the institutional framework within which Britain's imperial economy operated remains Lawrence A. Harper, *The English Navigation Laws: A Seventeenth Century Experiment in Social Engineering* (New York, 1939). The European context for British imperial expansion and interstate rivalry is covered in Kenneth G. Davies, *The North Atlantic World in the Seventeenth Century* (Oxford, 1974), Ralph Davis, *The Rise of the Atlantic Economies* (1973), and Patrick K. O'Brien's chapter in Marshall, ed., *Oxford History of the British Empire,* vol. 2.

For sectoral approaches to the British Atlantic economy see Ralph Davis, *The Rise of the English Shipping Industry in the Seventeenth and Eighteenth Centuries* (Newton Abbot, 1962) and David Richardson's chapter on the slave trade in Marshall, ed., *Oxford History of the British Empire,* vol. 2. Jordan Goodman, *Tobacco in History: The Culture of Dependence* (London, 1993) and Sidney W. Mintz, *Sweetness and Power: The Place of Sugar in Modern History* (New York, 1985) provide economic, social, and cultural insights into the rise of Atlantic commodities, and this is placed into the wider context of changing consumption patterns in Carole Shammas, *The Pre-Industrial Consumer in England and America* (Oxford, 1990).

The daily routines of Atlantic trade are well captured in Jacob M. Price, 'What Did Merchants Do?: Reflections on British Overseas Trade, 1660–1790', *Journal of Economic History,* 49 (1989) 267–84. The importance of trust and reputation is detailed in Nuala Zahedieh, 'Credit, Risk, and Reputation in British Atlantic Trade in the Seventeenth Century', in Olaf Janzen, ed., *Merchant Organization and Maritime Trades: Research in Maritime History* (Newfoundland, 1994), pp. 53–74, and 'Making Mercantilism Work: London Merchants and Atlantic Trade in the Seventeenth Century', *Transactions of the Royal Historical Society,* 9 (1999) 143–58. For a vivid reconstruction of the business and social worlds of a group of eighteenth-century London merchants operating on a global scale see David Hancock, *Citizens of the World: London Merchants and the Integration of the Atlantic Community, 1735–1785* (Cambridge, 1995).

The debate about the links between empire, trade, and the industrial revolution is summarized in the 'Editor's Introduction' to Joel Mokyr, ed.,

The British Industrial Revolution (Oxford, 1993), Kenneth Morgan, *Slavery, Atlantic Trade and the British Economy, 1660–1800* (Cambridge, 2000), Patrick K. O'Brien and Stanley Engerman, 'Exports and the Growth of the British Economy from the Glorious Revolution to the Peace of Amiens', in Barbara Solow, ed., *Slavery and the Rise of the Atlantic System* (Cambridge, 1991), and Patrick K. O'Brien, 'The Reconstruction, Rehabilitation and Reconfiguration of the British Industrial Revolution as a Conjuncture in Global History', *Itinerario*, 24 (2000) 117–34.

Chapter 4: Religion

The history covered in this essay has been pieced together from many books and articles, most of which cover one locale, one faith tradition, and shorter spans of time. A few authors provide a broader view. For a general survey of Britain but not Ireland or the colonies see Sheridan Gilley and W. J. Sheils, eds., *A History of Religion in Britain: Practice and Belief From Pre-Roman Times to the Present* (Oxford, 1994). Another general treatment can be found in David Hempton, *Religion and Political Culture in Britain and Ireland: From the Glorious Revolution to the Decline of the Empire* (Cambridge, 1996). See also Nicholas Tyacke, ed., *England's Long Reformation, 1500–1800* (London, 1988). Surveys of colonial religion (focused on the mainland North American colonies) include Patricia Bonomi, *Under the Cope of Heaven: Religion, Society and Politics in Colonial America* (New York, 1986) and Jon Butler, *Awash in a Sea of Faith: Christianizing the American People* (Cambridge, Mass., 1990). To aid in rethinking the interaction of Native American and European religion see the essay by Joel W. Martin, 'Indians, Contact and Colonialism in the Deep South: Themes for a Postcolonial History of American Religion', in Thomas A. Tweed, ed., *Retelling U.S. Religious History* (Berkeley, Calif., 1997), pp. 149–80. For an essay on eighteenth-century British Atlantic religion see Boyd Stanley Schlenther, 'Religious Faith and Commercial Empire', in P. J. Marshall, ed., *The Oxford History of the British Empire*, vol. 2, *The Eighteenth Century* (Oxford, 1998), pp. 128–50.

For specific faith traditions or locations, the following sources supplement those cited in the essay itself. Quaker missionaries are placed in an Atlantic context in Rebecca Larson's *Daughters of Light: Quaker Women Preaching and Prophesying in the Colonies and Abroad, 1700–1775* (New York, 1999). On Ireland, and for a good model foregrounding lay devotion, see Raymond Gillespie, *Devoted People: Belief and Religion in Early Modern Ireland* (Manchester, 1997). On Scotland see Callum G. Brown, *Religion and Society in Scotland since 1707* (Edinburgh, 1997). For the importance of devotional literature in Wales see Geraint H. Jenkins, *Literature, Religion and Society in Wales, 1660–1730* (Cardiff, 1978). Rhys Isaac's *The Transformation of Virginia, 1740–1790* (Chapel Hill, NC, 1982) remains the starting point for understanding Anglicans and Baptists in Virginia. Little has been written on religion in the West Indies prior to the late eighteenth century; for general coverage of European Christianity in the early years see Arthur Charles Dayfoot, *The Shaping of the West Indian Church, 1492–1692* (Gainesville, Fla., 1999). Also see Shirley C. Gordon, *God Almighty, Make Me Free: Christianity in Preemancipation Jamaica* (Bloomington, Ind., 1996). Much has been written on religion and society in New England, but no accessible single volume exists to introduce students to the region. The second volume of Perry Miller's *The New England Mind*, entitled *From Colony to Province* (Cambridge, Mass., 1953) magisterially surveys the religious politics of the middle colonial period; James F. Cooper's *Tenacious of their Liberties: The Congregationalists in Colonial Massachusetts* (New York, 1999) treats lay-clerical relations; Michael J. Crawford's *Seasons of Grace: Colonial New England's Revival Tradition in Its British Context* (New York, 1991) provides an Atlantic framework for eighteenth-century revivalism in the region. For a broader context still, but one that is focused largely on leadership, see W. R. Ward, *The Protestant Evangelical Awakening* (Cambridge, 1992). Southern religion in the late eighteenth century and beyond is covered in Christine Leigh Heyrman, *Southern Cross: The Beginnings of the Bible Belt* (New York, 1997).

Chapter 5: Civility and Authority

This chapter develops some themes first explored in Michael J. Braddick, *State Formation in Early Modern England, c. 1550–1700* (Cambridge, 2000), which contains full references to secondary literature, and in the editor's introduction and Braddick's essay in Michael J. Braddick and John Walter, eds., *Negotiating Power in Early Modern Society: Order, Hierarchy and Subordination in Britain and Ireland* (Cambridge, 2001). The latter collection contains a number of essays relevant to the themes of this chapter. The micro-sociological perspective of this essay owes much to the work of Erving Goffman: see especially Goffman, 'The Interaction Order', *American Sociological Review*, 48 (1983) 1–17 and Tom Burns, *Erving Goffman* (London, 1992). For a classic study of the relationship between taste, social distinction, and power see Pierre Bourdieu, *Distinction: A Social Critique of the Judgement of Taste* (London, 1984).

The best discussion of the crucial concept of civility is Anna Bryson's *From Courtesy to Civility: Changing Codes of Conduct in Early Modern England* (Oxford, 1998). For discussions of landscape see Andrew McRae, *God Speed the Plough: The Representation of Agrarian England, 1500–1600* (Cambridge, 1996) and Richard Helgerson, *Forms of Nationhood: The Elizabethan Writing of England* (Chicago, 1992). For politeness and eighteenth-century manners see Philip D. Carter, *Men and the Emergence of Polite Society: Britain, 1660–1800* (Harlow, 2001) and Lawrence E. Klein, *Shaftesbury and the Culture of Politeness: Moral Discourse and Cultural Politics in Early Eighteenth-*

Century England (Cambridge, 1994). The relationship between these values and the assertiveness of the middling sort is a central theme of Margaret R. Hunt, *The Middling Sort: Commerce, Gender, and the Family in England, 1680–1780* (Berkeley, Calif., 1996). Merchant society and culture are the subject of David Hancock, *Citizens of the World: London Merchants and the Integration of the Atlantic Community, 1735–1785* (Cambridge, 1995) and Perry Gauci, *The Politics of Trade: The Overseas Merchant in State and Society, 1660–1720* (Oxford, 2001).

The importance of these ideas to the legitimation of the empire at an abstract level is discussed in David Armitage, *The Ideological Origins of the British Empire* (Cambridge, 2000). Much of the material relevant to political and social practice in Ireland is discussed by Nicholas Canny, *Making Ireland British, 1580–1650* (Oxford, 2001) and, for the later period, by S. J. Connolly, *Religion, Law and Power: The Making of Protestant Ireland, 1660–1760* (Oxford, 1992). The literature on Scotland is less full: for relevant discussion and further references see Braddick, *State Formation*, ch. 8. The literature on early America, by contrast, is huge. The classic study of these issues is Rhys Isaac, *The Transformation of Virginia, 1740–1790* (Chapel Hill, NC, 1982). For brief introductions and overviews see Ian K. Steele, 'Empire of Migrants and Consumers: Some Current Atlantic Approaches to the History of Colonial Virginia', *Virginia Magazine of History and Biography*, 99 (1991) 489–512; Timothy H. Breen, 'Creative Adaptations: Peoples and Cultures', in Jack Greene and J. R. Pole, eds., *Colonial British America: Essays in the New History of the Early Modern Era* (London, 1984), pp. 195–232; Jack P. Greene, *The Intellectual Construction of America: Exceptionalism and Identity from 1492–1800* (Chapel Hill, NC, 1993); and Greene, *Imperatives, Behaviors and Identities: Essays in Early American Cultural History* (Charlottesville, Va., 1992). David S. Shields discusses the practices that defined polite society in America in *Civil Tongues and Polite Letters in British America* (Chapel Hill, NC, 1997). For some revealing discussions of the relationship between manners, refinement, and power see C. Dallett Hemphill, *Bowing to Necessities: A History of Manners in America, 1620–1860* (Oxford, 1999); Michal J. Rozbicki, *Transformation of the English Cultural Ethos in Colonial America: Maryland, 1634–1720* (Lanham, Md., 1988); and Rozbicki, *The Complete Colonial Gentleman: Cultural Legitimacy in Plantation America* (Charlottesville, Va., 1998). The changing forms of American politeness in the eighteenth century are the subject of Richard L. Bushman's fine study of *The Refinement of America: Persons, Houses, Cities* (New York, 1992). The effect of racial diversity on the expression of social distinction is a central theme of Kathleen M. Brown, *Good Wives, Nasty Wenches and Anxious Patriarchs: Gender, Race and Power in Colonial Virginia* (Chapel Hill, NC, 1996). For broader discussions of such diversity see Bernard Bailyn and Philip D. Morgan, eds., *Strangers Within the Realm: Cultural Margins of the First British*

Empire (Chapel Hill, NC, 1991). For the impact of empire on the expression of social distinction at home see James Walvin, *Fruits of Empire: Exotic Produce and British Taste, 1660–1800* (Basingstoke, 1997).

Many of the suggestions laid out below for further reading on gender, class, and race are also relevant to the themes of this chapter.

Chapter 6: Gender

There is not yet anything like a textbook on the subject of gender and the British Atlantic. Nonetheless, the rich literature on gender and especially women provides many avenues of approach, of which only an extremely limited number can be mentioned here. Valuable historiographical coverage is provided by: Linda K. Kerber, 'Separate Spheres, Female Worlds, Woman's Place: The Rhetoric of Women's History', *JAH*, 75 (1988) 9–39, and the forum by Linda Kerber and others in 'Beyond Roles, Beyond Spheres: Thinking About Gender in the Early Republic', *WMQ*, 3rd ser., 46 (1989) 565–85; Amanda J. Vickery, 'Golden Age to Separate Spheres: A Review of the Categories and Chronology of English Women's History', *HJ*, 36 (1993) 383–414; and Kathleen M. Brown, 'Brave New Worlds: Women's and Gender History', *WMQ*, 3rd ser., 50 (1993) 311–27 and her 'Beyond the Great Debates: Gender and Race', *Reviews in American History*, 26 (1998) 96–123.

General overviews include: Anne Laurence, *Women in England, 1500–1760: A Social History* (London, 1994); Robert B. Shoemaker, *Gender in English Society, 1650–1850: The Emergence of Separate Spheres?* (London, 1998); Hannah Barker and Elaine Chalus, eds., *Gender in Eighteenth-Century England: Roles, Representations, and Responsibilities* (London, 1997); Patricia Crawford and Laura Gowing, eds., *Women's Worlds in Seventeenth-Century England* (London, 2000); and, for the mainland American colonies, Carol Berkin, *First Generations: Women in Colonial America* (New York, 1996); Joan R. Gunderson, *To Be Useful to the World: Women in Revolutionary America, 1740–1790* (New York, 1996); Ronald Hoffman and Peter J. Albert, eds., *Women in the Age of the American Revolution* (Charlottesville, Va., 1989); and Larry D. Eldridge, ed., *Women and Freedom in Early America* (New York, 1997).

The following texts represent classic full-length studies in their respective geographical areas. For the mainland colonies, consult Laurel Thatcher Ulrich, *Good Wives: Image and Reality in the Lives of Women in Northern New England, 1650–1750* (New York, 1980) and her *A Midwife's Tale: The Life of Martha Ballard, Based on Her Diary, 1785–1812* (New York, 1990); Mary Beth Norton, *Liberty's Daughters: The Revolutionary Experience of American Women, 1750–1800* (Boston, Mass., 1980) and her *Founding Mothers and Fathers: Gendered Power and the Forming of American Society* (New York, 1996); Linda K. Kerber, *Women of the Republic: Intellect and Ideology in*

Revolutionary America (New York, 1980); Carol F. Karlsen, *The Devil in the Shape of Woman: Witchcraft in Colonial New England* (New Haven, Conn., 1987); Cornelia Hughes Dayton, *Women before the Bar: Gender, Law, and Society in Connecticut, 1639–1789* (Chapel Hill, NC, 1995); and Kathleen M. Brown, *Good Wives, Nasty Wenches, and Anxious Patriarchs: Gender, Race, and Power in Colonial Virginia* (Chapel Hill, NC, 1996).

For England, see Leonore Davidoff and Catherine Hall, *Family Fortunes: Men and Women of the English Middle Class, 1780–1850* (Chicago, 1987); Susan Dwyer Amussen, *An Ordered Society: Gender and Class in Early Modern England* (Oxford, 1988); Amy Erickson, *Women and Property in Early Modern England* (London, 1993); Anthony Fletcher, *Gender, Sex and Subordination in England, 1500–1800* (New Haven, Conn., 1995); Margaret R. Hunt, *The Middling Sort: Commerce, Gender, and the Family in England, 1680–1780* (Berkeley, Calif., 1996); Laura Gowing, *Domestic Dangers: Women, Words and Sex in Early Modern London* (Oxford, 1996); and Amanda Vickery, *The Gentleman's Daughter: Women's Lives in Georgian England* (New Haven, Conn., 1998). The rest of the British Isles are less well covered, but see Margaret MacCurtain and Mary O'Dowd, eds., *Women in Early Modern Ireland* (Edinburgh, 1991); Elizabeth C. Sanderson, *Women and Work in Eighteenth-Century Edinburgh* (Basingstoke, 1996); and Terry Brotherstone, Deborah Simonton and Oonagh Walsh, eds., *Gendering Scottish History: An International Approach* (The Mackie Occasional Colloquia Series 1, Glasgow, 1999).

Similarly, more treatments of gender in the British Caribbean are needed. The classic study is Barbara Bush, *Slave Women in Caribbean Society, 1650–1838* (London, 1990). There are also helpful articles in the following collections: Verene Shepherd, Bridget Brereton, and Barbara Bailey, eds., *Engendering History: Caribbean Women in Historical Perspective* (London, 1995) and David Barry Gaspar and Darlene Clark Hines, eds., *More Than Chattel: Black Women and Slavery in the Americas* (Bloomington, Ind., 1996).

There are far fewer studies of masculinity, although this situation is rapidly changing. For Britain, see Elizabeth A. Foyster, *Manhood in Early Modern England: Honour, Sex and Marriage* (London, 1999); Tim Hitchcock and Michèle Cohen, eds., *English Masculinities, 1660–1800* (London, 1999); and Philip D. Carter, *Men and the Emergence of Polite Society: Britain, 1660–1800* (Harlow, 2001). For the American colonies see Kenneth A. Lockridge, *On the Sources of Patriarchal Rage: The Commonplace Books of William Byrd and Thomas Jefferson and the Gendering of Power in the Eighteenth Century* (New York, 1992) and Lisa Wilson, *Ye Heart of a Man: The Domestic Life of Men in Colonial New England* (New Haven, Conn., 1999).

Chapter 7: Class

A good introduction to the development of the concept of class is provided in Peter Calvert, *The Concept of Class: An Historical Introduction* (London,

1982). Readings from both theorists of class and the historical literature of
class are usefully collected in Patrick Joyce, ed., *Class* (Oxford, 1995).
Changing perceptions of the social order in the early modern period are
examined in Penelope J. Corfield, ed., *Language, History and Class*
(London, 1991) and M. L. Bush, ed., *Social Orders and Social Classes in
Europe since 1500: Studies in Social Stratification* (London, 1992).

The literature on the social structure and social relations in early
modern England is vast. For introductions to these issues with guides to
further reading, see Keith Wrightson, *English Society, 1580–1680*
(London, 1982) and Keith Wrightson, *Earthly Necessities: Economic Lives in
Early Modern Britain* (New Haven, Conn., 2000). For landed society,
good introductions are M. L. Bush, *The English Aristocracy: A Comparative
Synthesis* (Manchester, 1984) and Felicity Heal and Clive Holmes, *The
Gentry in England and Wales, 1500–1700* (London, 1994). The 'middle
sort' are well served by Jonathan Barry and Christopher Brooks, eds., *The
Middling Sort of People: Culture, Society and Politics in England, 1550–1800*
(London, 1994). Some of the most important of E. P. Thompson's enor-
mously influential essays on laboring people are collected in his *Customs
in Common* (London, 1991).

Social structure and class are less directly addressed in the historiography of
Scotland and Ireland. However, useful starting points are provided for
Scotland by T. M. Devine, *The Transformation of Rural Scotland: Social Change
and the Agrarian Economy* (Edinburgh, 1994) and R. A. Dodgshon, *From
Chiefs to Landlords: Social and Economic Change in the Western Highlands and
Islands, c. 1493–1820* (Edinburgh, 1998). In the case of Ireland, Gaelic
society is anatomized in Mary O'Dowd, 'Gaelic Economy and Society', in
Ciaran Brady and Raymond Gillespie, eds., *Natives and Newcomers: Essays on
the Making of Irish Colonial Society, 1534–1641* (Dublin, 1986), pp. 120–47.
Its passing is the subject of Steven G. Ellis, *Ireland in the Age of theTudors,
1447–1603: English Expansion and the End of Gaelic Rule* (London, 1998).
British colonization and the making of the Protestant 'ascendancy' are
thoroughly examined in Nicholas Canny, *Making Ireland British, 1580–1650*
(Oxford, 2001) and S. J. Connolly, *Religion, Law and Power: The Making of
Protestant Ireland, 1660–1760* (Oxford, 1992).

Class is very little discussed in the historiography of early America. J. T.
Main's *The Social Structure of Revolutionary America* (Princeton, NJ, 1965)
remains indispensable for the situation at the close of the colonial period,
and can be fruitfully compared with the early chapters of Gordon S.
Wood's *The Radicalism of the American Revolution* (New York, 1993) and
Gary B. Nash's *The Urban Crucible: Social Change, Political Consciousness and
the Origins of the American Revolution* (Cambridge, Mass., 1979). For the
development of colonial societies in the seventeenth and earlier eighteenth
centuries, excellent introductions are provided by two valuable collections
of essays: Jack P. Greene and J. R. Pole, eds., *Colonial British America:*

Essays in the New History of the Early Modern Era (Baltimore, 1984) and Stanley L. Engerman and Robert E. Gallman, eds., *The Cambridge Economic History of the United States*, vol. 1, *The Colonial Era* (Cambridge, 1996). Three stimulating interpretative overviews of social change in colonial America are also highly recommended: Edward S. Morgan, *American Slavery, American Freedom: The Ordeal of Colonial Virginia* (New York, 1975); T. H. Breen, *Puritans and Adventurers: Change and Persistence in Early America* (New York, 1980); and Jack P. Greene, *Pursuits of Happiness: The Social Development of Early Modern British Colonies and the Formation of American Culture* (Chapel Hill, NC, 1988).

Chapter 8: Race

For synthetic views of European attitudes toward non-Europeans during the modern era of colonization, see Margaret T. Hodgen, *Early Anthropology in the Sixteenth and Seventeenth Centuries* (Philadelphia, 1964), Winthrop D. Jordan, *White over Black: American Attitudes toward the Negro, 1550–1812* (New York, 1969), the essays in the special issue on 'Constructing Race', *WMQ*, 3rd ser., 44/1 (January 1997), Alden T. Vaughan, 'From White Man to Redskin: Changing Anglo-American Perceptions of the American Indian', *AHR*, 87 (1982) 917–53, Robert E. Berkhofer, Jr, *The White Man's Indian: Images of the American Indian from Columbus to the Present* (New York, 1978), and P. J. Marshall and Glyndwr Williams, *The Great Map of Mankind: Perceptions of New Worlds in the Age of Enlightenment* (Cambridge, Mass., 1982), chs. 1, 2. The origins of a European anti-colonial critique are discussed in William S. Maltby, *The Black Legend in England: The Development of Anti-Spanish Sentiment, 1558–1660* (Durham, NC, 1971).

Additional overviews of the ancient world, xenophobia, and slavery are contained in François Hartog, *The Mirror of Herodotus: The Representation of the Other in the Writing of History*, trans. Janet Lloyd (Berkeley, Calif., 1988), and Peter Garnsey, *Ideas of Slavery from Aristotle to Augustine* (Cambridge, 1996). European focus on lineage (especially scriptural genealogies) is further discussed in Colin Kidd, *British Identities before Nationalism: Ethnicity and Nationhood in the Atlantic World, 1600–1800* (Cambridge, 1999) and William McKee Evans, 'From the Land of Canaan to the Land of Guinea: The Strange Odyssey of the "Sons of Ham"', *AHR*, 85 (1980) 15–43. The eighteenth-century definition of race as a natural category is explored in Phillip Sloan, 'The Gaze of Natural History', in Christopher Fox, Roy Porter, and Robert Wokler, eds., *Inventing Human Science: Eighteenth-Century Domains* (Berkeley, Calif., 1995), pp. 112–51. The significance of epidemic disease to ideas of race is discussed in Joyce E. Chaplin, 'Natural Philosophy and an Early Racial Idiom in North America: Comparing English and Indian Bodies', *WMQ*, 3rd ser., 44 (1997) 229–42.

In addition to Gregory Evans Dowd, *A Spirited Resistance: The North American Indian Struggle for Unity, 1745–1815* (Baltimore, 1992), Theda Perdue, *Slavery and the Evolution of Cherokee Society, 1540–1866* (Knoxville, Tenn., 1979) and Nancy Shoemaker, 'How Indians Got to Be Red', *AHR*, 102 (1997) 625–44 have discussed Indian ideas about the body and identity.

The British colonies' and the United States' exclusion of non-whites from full citizenship is discussed in A. Leon Higginbotham, *In the Matter of Color: Race and the American Legal Process: the Colonial Period* (New York, 1978), Bernard W. Sheehan, *Seeds of Extinction: Jeffersonian Philanthropy and the American Indian Policy, 1783–1812* (Chapel Hill, NC, 1973), and Brian W. Dippie, *The Vanishing American: White Attitudes and United States Indian Policy* (Middletown, Conn., 1982).

Comparative perspectives on racism, European colonization, and understanding native peoples are available in George M. Fredrickson, *White Supremacy: A Comparative Study in American and South African History* (New York, 1981) and Patrick Wolfe, 'Land, Labor, and Difference: Elementary Structures of Race', *AHR*, 106 (2001) 866–905; Edward G. Gray, *New World Babel: Languages and Nations in Early America* (Princeton, NJ, 1999) examines English comprehension of native languages, and Jorge Cañizares Esguerra, 'New Worlds, New Stars: Patriotic Astrology and the Invention of Indians and Creole Bodies in Colonial Spanish America, 1600–1650', *AHR*, 104 (1999) 33–68 look at the construction of race in Spanish America.

Chapter 9: Empire and State

Scholarship on the relationship between empire building and state formation is of such recent vintage that there is not yet a book-length study. A handful of recent studies on states or on empires do address the problem: see James Muldoon, *Empire and Order: The Concept of Empire, 800–1800* (London, 1999); Michael J. Braddick, *State Formation in Early Modern England, c. 1550–1700* (Cambridge, 2000); and David Armitage, *The Ideological Origins of the British Empire* (Cambridge, 2000). Many of the essays in James D. Tracy, ed., *The Political Economy of Merchant Empires: State Power and World Trade, 1350–1750* (Cambridge, 1991) offer important insights into economic relationship between empires and states. Articles by Elizabeth Mancke examine aspects of the role of the British state in the early modern empire: 'Another British America: A Canadian Model for the Early Modern British Empire', *JICH*, 25 (1997) 1–36; and 'Negotiating an Empire: Britain and Its Overseas Peripheries, c.1550–1780', in Christine Daniels and Michael Kennedy, eds., *Negotiated Empires: Centers and Peripheries in the New World, 1500–1820* (New York, 2002). On overseas expansion and international relations, the best narrative study is Max Savelle, *The Origins of American Diplomacy: The International History of Angloamerica, 1492–1763* (New York, 1967). The editorial notes in the first two volumes of Francis Gardner Davenport, ed., *European Treaties Bearing on the History of the United States and its Dependencies*, 4 vols. (Washington, DC, 1917–37) contain invaluable insights into the dynamics of overseas expansion on international relations. A theoretically grounded study of the impact of overseas expansion on international relations, however, remains to be written.

Chapter 10: Revolution and Counter-Revolution

Despite the relative novelty of Atlantic history, the history of the revolutionary Atlantic is the subject of an extensive, well-established literature: see esp. J. G. A. Pocock, *The Machiavellian Moment: Florentine Political Thought and the Atlantic Republican Tradition* (Princeton, NJ, 1975); Angus Calder, *Revolutionary Empire: The Rise of the English-speaking Empires from the Fifteenth Century to the 1780s* (London, 1981); Marcus Rediker and Peter Linebaugh, *The Many-Headed Hydra: Sailors, Slaves, Commoners, and the Hidden History of the Revolutionary Atlantic* (Boston, Mass., 2000). For the European, Hispanic, and Haitian dimensions see R. R. Palmer, *The Age of the Democratic Revolution: A Political History of Europe and America, 1760–1800*, 2 vols. (Princeton, NJ, 1959–64); Lester Langley, *The Americas in the Age of Revolution, 1750–1850* (New Haven, Conn., 1996); Jaime E. Rodríguez, 'The Emancipation of America', *AHR*, 105 (2000) 131–52. Questions of race and slavery are treated with particular insight in David Brion Davis, *The Problem of Slavery in the Age of Revolution, 1770–1823* (Ithaca, NY, 1975); Robin Blackburn, *The Making of New World Slavery: From the Baroque to the Modern, 1492–1800* (London, 1998).

The literature on the British context of the seventeenth-century revolutions is vast and growing, but see J. G. A. Pocock, ed., *Three British Revolutions: 1641, 1688, 1776* (Princeton, NJ, 1980); Brendan Bradshaw and John Morrill, eds., *The British Problem, c. 1534–1707: State Formation in the Atlantic Archipelago* (London, 1996); David Armitage, *The Ideological Origins of the British Empire* (Cambridge, 2000). On Ireland, see Nicholas P. Canny, *Making Ireland British, 1580–1650* (Oxford, 2001); S. J. Connolly, *Religion, Law, and Power: The Making of Protestant Ireland, 1660–1760* (Oxford, 1992). Conrad Russell, *The Causes of the English Civil War* (Oxford, 1990) traces the collapse of Charles I's English authority to events in Scotland and Ireland; Robert Beddard's edited volume, *The Revolutions of 1688* (Oxford, 1996), takes a similarly broad view of the Glorious Revolution. On England's growing military and imperial power see Michael J. Braddick, *State Formation in Early Modern England, c. 1550–1700* (Cambridge, 2000); see also Stephen Saunders Webb, *The Governors-General: The English Army and the Definition of the Empire, 1569–1681* (Chapel Hill, NC, 1979). The colonies are well served by two classics: Richard S. Dunn, *Sugar and Slaves: The Rise of the Planter Class in the*

English West Indies, 1624–1713 (Chapel Hill, NC, 1972) and Edmund S. Morgan, *American Slavery, American Freedom: The Ordeal of Colonial Virginia* (New York, 1975); see also Nicholas Canny, ed., *The Oxford History of the British Empire*, vol. 1, *The Origins of Empire: English Overseas Activity to the Close of the Seventeenth Century* (Oxford, 1998).

For the British and Irish unions see Brian P. Levack, *The Formation of the British State: England, Scotland, and the Union, 1603–1707* (Oxford, 1987); John Robertson, ed., *A Union for Empire: Political Thought and the Union of 1707* (Cambridge, 1995); Alexander Grant and Keith J. Stringer, eds., *Uniting the Kingdom? The Making of British History* (London, 1995). The nature of British identity during the eighteenth century is the subject of two conspicuously divergent studies: Linda Colley, *Britons: Forging the Nation, 1707–1837* (New Haven, Conn., 1992) and J. C. D. Clark, *The Language of Liberty, 1660–1832: Political Discourse and Social Dynamics in the Anglo-American World* (Cambridge, 1994); see also Colin Kidd, *British Identities before Nationalism: Ethnicity and Nationhood in the Atlantic World, 1600–1800* (Cambridge, 1999). On the politics of Britain's eighteenth-century expansion see John Brewer, *The Sinews of Power: War, Money and the English State, 1688–1783* (New York, 1989); Kathleen Wilson, *The Sense of the People: Politics, Culture, and Imperialism in England, 1715–1785* (Cambridge, 1995). Stephen Conway, *The British Isles and the War of American Independence* (Oxford, 2000) examines the British and Irish dimensions of the American war; see also H. T. Dickinson, ed., *Britain and the American Revolution* (London, 1998). For the wider empire see C. A. Bayly, *Imperial Meridian: The British Empire and the World, 1780–1830* (London, 1989); P. J. Marshall, ed., *The Oxford History of the British Empire*, vol. 2, *The Eighteenth Century* (Oxford, 1998).

On the transatlantic origins of the American Revolution, see the different – though complementary – interpretations in Bernard Bailyn, *The Ideological Origins of the American Revolution* (Cambridge, Mass., 1967); Jack P. Greene, *Peripheries and Center: Constitutional Development in the Extended Polities of the British Empire and the United States, 1607–1788* (New York, 1990). The British and imperial context is the subject of Eliga H. Gould, *The Persistence of Empire: British Political Culture in the Age of the American Revolution* (Chapel Hill, NC, 2000); see also T. H. Breen, 'Ideology and Nationalism on the Eve of the American Revolution: Revisions *Once More* in Need of Revising', *JAH*, 84 (1997) 13–39. For the experience of blacks and Indians see Sylvia R. Frey, *Water from the Rock: Black Resistance in a Revolutionary Age* (Princeton, NJ, 1991); Colin G. Galloway, *The American Revolution in Indian Country: Crisis and Diversity in Native American Communities* (Cambridge, 1995); Edward Countryman, 'Indians, the Colonial Order, and the Social Significance of the American Revolution', *WMQ*, 3rd ser., 53 (1996) 342–62. Andrew Jackson O'Shaughnessy, *An Empire Divided: The American Revolution and the British Caribbean* (Philadelphia, 2000) examines why the

West Indies remained loyal; Peter S. Onuf, *Jefferson's Empire: The Language of American Nationhood* (Charlottesville, Va., 2000) explores the continued resonance of 1776 in the new republic.

Chapter 11: The Politics of Slavery

The political history of slavery is best approached first through social and cultural history, especially Ira Berlin, *Many Thousands Gone: The First Two Centuries of Slavery in North America* (Cambridge, Mass., 1998) and Philip D. Morgan, *Slave Counterpoint: Black Culture in the Eighteenth-Century Chesapeake and Lowcountry* (Chapel Hill, NC, 1998). Richard S. Dunn, *Sugar and Slaves: The Rise of the Planter Class in the English West Indies, 1624–1713* (Chapel Hill, NC, 1972) and Elsa Goveia, *Slave Society in the British Leeward Islands at the End of the Eighteenth Century* (New Haven, Conn., 1974) provide parallel surveys of the British Caribbean.

Slave resistance and insurrection in the British West Indies have been examined thoughtfully and extensively in Michael Craton, *Testing the Chains: Resistance to Slavery in the British West Indies* (Ithaca, NY, 1982). The difference gender made in these conflicts is considered in Hilary McD. Beckles, *Natural Rebels: A Social History of Enslaved Black Women in Barbados* (New Brunswick, 1989) and Kathleen M. Brown, *Good Wives, Nasty Wenches, and Anxious Patriarchs: Gender, Race, and Power in Colonial Virginia* (Chapel Hill, NC, 1996).

Richard B. Sheridan, *Sugar and Slavery: An Economic History of the British West Indies, 1623–1775* (Barbados, 1974), Lowell Joseph Ragatz, *The Fall of the Planter Class in the British Caribbean, 1763–1833* (New York, 1928), and Eric Williams, *Capitalism and Slavery* (Chapel Hill, NC, 1944) treat the conflicting economic interests that slavery generated. For a subsequent assessment of Williams's controversial classic see Stanley L. Engerman and Barbara L. Solow, eds., *British Capitalism and Caribbean Slavery: The Legacy of Eric Williams* (Cambridge, 1987). The British slave trade is placed in its political and institutional context by K. G. Davies, *The Royal African Company* (London, 1957) and Roger Anstey, *The Atlantic Slave Trade and British Abolition, 1760–1810* (London, 1975). The impact of war on slavery and slavery on war is measured in Sylvia R. Frey, *Water From the Rock: Black Resistance in a Revolutionary Age* (Princeton, NJ, 1991) and Roger N. Buckley, *Slaves in Red Coats: The British West India Regiments, 1795–1815* (New Haven, Conn., 1979). Planter politics during the revolutionary era has received renewed attention in recent years. See especially Robert Olwell, *Masters, Slaves, and Subjects: The Culture of Power in the South Carolina Low Country* (Ithaca, NY, 1998), Andrew J. O'Shaughnessy, *An Empire Divided: The American Revolution and the British Caribbean* (Philadelphia, 2000), and David Geggus, *Slavery, War, and Revolution: The British Occupation of Saint Domingue* (Oxford, 1982).

The classic studies of the origins of the anti-slavery movement are David Brion Davis, *The Problem of Slavery in Western Culture*, 2nd edn (Oxford, 1988) and Davis, *The Problem of Slavery in the Age of Revolution, 1770–1823* (Ithaca, NY, 1975). The British anti-slavery movement is tracked in greater detail by Seymour Drescher, *Capitalism and Antislavery: British Mobilization in Comparative Perspective* (London, 1986) and Moira Ferguson, *Subject to Others: British Women Writers and Colonial Slavery, 1670–1834* (London, 1992).

Index

m = map; n = endnote (indexed for background information only, not for citations); t = table